DATE DUE

DE 18 07			

DEMCO 38-296

I·N·H·E·R·I·T·O·R·S

O·F T·H·E S·P·I·R·I·T

Mary White Ovington

and the Founding of the NAACP

Carolyn Wedin

John Wiley & Sons, Inc.

New York · Chichester · Weinheim · Brisbane · Singapore · Toronto

To my children,
Monika, Mario, and Brendan

Library of Congress Cataloging-in-Publication Data

Wedin, Carolyn.
    Inheritors of the spirit: Mary White Ovington and the founding of the
      NAACP / Carolyn Wedin
      p. cm.
    Includes index.
    ISBN 0-471-16838-6 (cloth : alk. paper)
    1. Ovington, Mary White, 1865–1951. 2. Civil rights workers—
United States—Biography. 3. Women civil rights workers—United
States—Biography. 4. National Association for the Advancement of
Colored People—History. 5. Afro-Americans—Civil rights—
History—20th century. I. Title.
E185.98.095W44 1997
323.1'96073'092—dc21
[B]   97-1490

Contents

Preface and Acknowledgments

WHEN I BEGAN collecting material by and about Mary White Ovington many years ago, some of the first letters I came across were from the 1940s, when she struggled to come back from strokes, eye problems, shock treatments, and depression to finish the book that was her legacy, figuratively and literally, to the National Association for the Advancement of Colored People, *The Walls Came Tumbling Down*, published by Harcourt, Brace in 1947, when she was eighty-two. I was enormously touched and inspired by this woman's resilience and spirit and wondered what had sustained her over forty years of battling for persecuted blacks and forgotten poor.

Now that my years of searching, writing, rewriting, cutting, and refining are to finally appear in print, I find myself much closer to those years of life when one hopes wisdom outweighs or at least balances the irritating and then seemingly impossible disabilities of aging. And in this transition, I find Ovington just as interesting, just as inspiring to me as she was when I first saw her trembling, aging hand writing, "I haven't much courage."

Mary White Ovington looked clearly, thought bravely, acted creatively, related kindly, shared generously. She balanced motivation by ideals with practical actions. She faced ugly violence without resorting to mean-spiritedness. She was ignored and pushed around and knocked down by expectations for women, by America's race hatred, by devaluation of age. And over and over again she got up gracefully and stood for all the best the human being is capable of, sharing her thoughts and words and deeds. A man she dearly loved, James Weldon Johnson, called her, in *Black Manhattan* in 1930, one of the few remaining "inheritors of the abolition spirit," and that she was seeking always to bring the ideals of the United States into reality.

From her life story we can cull seeds to plant in our own lives as we ponder questions that don't go away, and act on problems that seem to come in cycles through the human community. And as for the need for her life's story in the profusion of information we imbibe daily, if anything, it has increased over these years. Those who are privileged and self-centered in our world seem not to have the joy she continually exuded in giving of herself to those less fortunate. And those who see need around and seek to do something about it, struggle, as she did, with causes competing for one's energy: socialism, feminism, pacifism, civil rights, environmentalism, trade unionism, and world federalism.

Like good essays and books, good lives have themes. After living with her for so long, I believe that the theme of Mary White Ovington's life was integration in all its dictionary definitions. "Removing the legal and social barriers imposing segregation upon racial groups" is one definition. She founded the gutsy, radical NAACP. For almost forty years, she was central to making it work. She put its autobiography before her own.

Her strength came from "organization of various traits or tendencies into one harmonious personality," which is integration in the psychological sense. Her life wove thought with action, goal with means, model with method, realism with hope, practicality with idealism, and fun with work, beginning in childhood and youth.

And she believed the human community benefits from difference, seeking "to make whole or complete by adding or bringing together parts," integration in a third sense. She reached across boundaries of gender, class, geography, age, and race. She tried to liberate the best in others, to make it possible for people to do their best. In her eyes difference was not to be feared or squelched, but used and celebrated.

Ovington was granted a childhood security that allowed her to go beyond the accepted and expected. With a child's sense of justice she wondered why some people never had oysters or chocolate, heard a story read, got out of the city to the mountains or seashore. Some people, she found, had more money than they needed, some had enough, some had too little, even though they worked harder. Why?

The Unitarian church and her early minister encouraged her questioning. But there have been many Unitarians, and only one Mary White Ovington. Church teaching was necessary, but not sufficient to propel her activism. With a Unitarian sense of reason she put together from books, friends, mentors, thought, school, the city, flowers, and stars the ideal of economic equality that fueled her life.

She moved from her general mission of equality to the specific fight for civil rights, appalled by the violent separation of whites and blacks in the United States. The Atlanta riots of 1906, the Springfield riots of 1908, the East St. Louis riots of 1917, the Washington, D.C., and Chicago and Arkansas riots of 1919, the Harlem riots of 1943, and in between, lynchings and maimings and beatings, even of the NAACP secretary. Violence provoked response over and over, like a repeating automatic being used as a starting pistol.

Was there progress? Was there hope for equality someday? In America's messy history of reform race bias springs up among those devoted to justice in other areas—social workers, feminists, Socialists. Abolitionists and New Abolitionists debate when to accept what is possible and when to demand the ideal; when to cooperate and when to fight; *how* to cooperate and *how* to fight. Through a long life, Ovington juggled, thought about, and debated those concerns. There is so much we can all learn from her.

———————

OVER THE MANY years of my working on Ovington's story, I have found help and inspiration from innumerable kind and intelligent and patient people. My hands tremble on the keyboard as I attempt to list just some of them, hoping that the kindness of the many left out will once again be extended to me.

My first stays in Washington, D.C., to work at the Library of Congress were made possible by the wonderful people who housed me: Gayle and Gene Binford, whose son Joel enables me to say, "Some of my best friends are Republicans"; Val and Randall Wedin; Sue Hulsether and Mark Matthias. As my searches extended geographically, many others joined the list of those I wish to thank, not just for bed and board, but for great conversation and questions and ideas: Gloria and Milton Matthews, who have let me live in Ovington's beloved western Massachusetts Riverbank, which they call "Rivendel"; Leslie Haynes, in whose apartment in the Shaker village of New Lebanon, New York, which is Darrow School I stayed on my weekend escapes from New York City in 1989; Joy Bale and Andrea Nye, who nourished my husband and me in Connecticut and Vermont when we returned from a year in Poland in 1992; Mary-Margaret Kellogg in Great Barrington, Massachusetts, who shared not only her beautiful eighteenth-century home, but also her husband's notes and papers for the second volume of the NAACP history, which he was not able to write before his death.

To me, one of the greatest joys of a project like this, which uses almost entirely unpublished materials, is working in archives, which are staffed with especially interesting and interested people. Philip Mason, now retired, at the Archives of Labor and Urban Affairs at Wayne State University in Detroit, where Mary White Ovington's papers are housed, has been sheer joy to know and work with, as have the rest of the staff there. I send them all enormous thanks for their unceasing help. Esme Bhan, whom I first came to know at Moorland-Spingarn Research Center at Howard University, has been deservedly thanked in many, many books; I add my warm gratitude, with fond hopes that she will soon be struggling to write a preface herself.

Modern technology has meant that some archives have come to Wisconsin instead of me going to them. For all those who have helped me obtain microfilm of papers, many thanks: the reference staff at the University of Wisconsin-Milwaukee Golda Meier Library; Jim Danky and others at the State Historical Library in Madison; and especially Betty Haban, retired from the library at the University of Wisconsin-Whitewater.

I have been assisted in doing this biography by many grants, fellowships, and seminars; my great appreciation extends to leaders, participants, and the many who have written letters of recommendation for me. The National Endowment for the Humanities has been of great help through travel grants to archives and through Tom Bender's summer seminar at New York University in 1989. I arrived in New York City that June having experienced the researcher's nightmare: a car break-in and theft of all of my books, notes, computer, computer disks, and manuscript at a motel outside Youngstown, Ohio. The seminar participants saw me through; I thank them all by mentioning one whose kindness continues, Jennifer Bradley.

I have also enjoyed a year-long fellowship at the Institute for the Humanities at UW-Madison and a semester at the Institute of Race and Ethnicity at UW-Milwaukee, where Winston Van Horne and Tom Tonnesen and their staff treated me royally. Many are those who have helped me obtain these grants and enabled me to take leaves from my teaching duties: my department chairs, Ruth Schauer and Mary Pinkerton; and colleagues Becky and Joe Hogan, Susan Thurin, and Mary Quinlivan.

There truly is a fellowship of scholars that supports and motivates a book such as this one, though of course none of them are responsible for my conclusions. I am exceedingly grateful to David Levering Lewis, whose help has made this publication possible, whose conversations are always intriguing, and whose books are a model of great research and great writing. James McPherson and I actually went to Gustavus Adolphus College together. I remember him, a brilliant senior history major, though he does not, of course, remember me, a shy, country freshman. Through his books and correspondence, Jim has continued to represent to me what is possible in scholarship and writing. We are all fortunate that Ralph Luker convinced the Feminist Press to reissue Ovington's "Reminiscences" from 1932 to 1933 as *When Black and White Sat Down Together* in 1995; I have appreciated coming to know Ralph through our work on that book. And William Van DeBurg, another historian of black America, has been my teacher, both literally and figuratively, for twenty years.

There are thank-yous that can never adequately reflect the debt a writer owes to those whose help encompasses the professional and the personal over decades of life, but I must try to put these thanks into words. Mary White Ovington's family, Ted Kingsbury, Betty Friedmann, and Joan Foster, are wonderful people who carry on the lust for life and for meaning that their ancestor represents. Visiting with and corresponding with her niece, Betty, I feel that I am in direct touch with Ovington's activist energy and intellectual curiosity. I am so very grateful for Betty's friendship and help; she should have her own biography.

Some people have read and critiqued and edited and seen so many drafts of this biography that they know it better than I do. Ray Griffith has never failed in his faith and enthusiasm, even after struggling through my quirky, wordy, expansive first drafts, which were helped by the advent of word processing only in that he didn't have to read my terrible handwriting. Donna Lewis can even read my handwriting; her friendship and help over thirty years of teaching and writing are a key to any success I have. Andrea Blair, a more recent convert to this project, gives me competent and comforting assurance that the book can go through its final stages even while I am in Norway as a Fulbright Roving Scholar.

I want to thank Claire Smith at Harold Ober Associates for "taking me on" as a client on David Lewis's recommendation, and Phyllis Westberg for her continuation of Claire's belief that this book should and could reach a wide audience. I have found Hana Lane, editor at John Wiley & Sons, to be insightful, careful, and gentle in her guiding of me and my unwieldy manuscript into its present form, and I thank her as well.

My family will believe this book only when they see it, they have waited so long. My children and dozens of nieces and nephews have grown up hearing about Mary White Ovington. My brother and sisters become more supportive each year we age together. And finally, my husband, Anthony Rolloff, claims he only married me six years ago because he thought the book was finished. Well, it was, Tony, and as you know, it has been finished several times since. My hearty and heartfelt thanks to you all.

Carolyn Wedin
August 1996
Whitewater, Wisconsin

Foreword

CAROLYN WEDIN WRITES that Mary White Ovington's life "wove thought with action, goal with means, model with method, realism with hope, practicality with idealism, and fun with work, beginning with childhood and youth." Born to privilege in the old New York Protestant upper middle class at the end of the Civil War, Ovington embodied the social uplift values of her class superlatively. She loathed cant and hypocrisy and was as resourceful as she was tireless in mobilizing others to join her lifetime crusade against racial oppression. This portrait of a crusader whose pragmatic idealism also combined "fun with work" is a pleasant revelation, however. Until now, most students of the causes to which Ovington dedicated herself have seen her as a latter-day version of those doughty, prim Yankee female teachers who went south after Appomattox to spread light and learning among the newly freed people of the defeated Confederacy. Professor Wedin's engrossing biography speculates, on the basis of strong circumstantial evidence, that Mary Ovington (dutiful spinster daughter to infirm parents) had an affair at age forty with vibrant John Milholland, the wealthy New York industrialist who founded the influential Constitution League, a precursor of the American Civil Liberties Union.

One wants to believe with Professor Wedin that this in fact did happen—not because of some quaint notion that Ovington needed to be romanced by a progressive Galahad but because, at least once in her life, her passionate devotion to high principles and bold actions deserved to be requited in tender intimacy by someone who shared these values in equal measure. I confess to having entertained a fleeting suspicion, in the first stage of research for his biography, that Ovington might have been romantically drawn to W. E. B. Du Bois. Her admiration of him, expressed in correspondence whose Late Victorian prose invites literal and anachronistic misreadings, inclined me to speculate tantalizingly about their early relationship: coy and almost submissive letters to him; his to her, a mixture of imperiousness and sensitivity. Finally meeting the man whose career and counsels had begun to influence her deeply, Ovington's rapture was palpable as she sat by Du Bois in Atlanta University's faculty dining room in the spring of 1905. His noble head was "like Shakespeare's done in bronze," she rhapsodized. Her "cup of happiness" at meeting him "was full." But the bond between Ovington and Du Bois, as I soon realized and as Professor Wedin has now wonderfully fleshed out, was the exclusive and consuming one of social and economic justice. It was the romance of reform.

Had they somehow met when both were students in Cambridge during the early 1890s. it is very likely that Ovington and Du Bois would have instantly recognized their ethical kinship, notwithstanding a temperamental dissonance that would gradually engender considerable discord in their future collaboration. The young woman who persuaded a handsome date to attend a public lecture by Frederick Douglass, despite her companion's strong disapproval of Douglass's second marriage to a white woman, would have relished an encounter with Harvard's most unusual graduate student. She, like Du Bois, criticized the smug economics served up by Harvard instructors during the 1890s—no Henry George for Ovington, no Marx for Du Bois. Only three years after the reversal in family fortunes had compelled Ovington to withdraw from the Harvard Annex, the university underwrote the publication of *The Suppression of the African Slave Trade to the United States* (1896), Du Bois's monumental doctoral dissertation. There is no indication that Ovington read it then, but she would almost certainly have heard it discussed, and when she finally took it up (which as a voracious reader and an author of a Du Bois profile she must have) she would have heartily subscribed to the categorical imperative that governed not only the book's argument but the public life of its author. "From this," Du Bois sternly lectured his readers, "we may conclude that it behooves nations as well as men to do things at the very moment when they ought to be done." Doing things at the very moment they ought to be done was precisely Ovington's motivation in the first weeks of 1909 when she was finally able to bring two like-minded reformers together in Walling's New York apartment in order to find some meaningful response to the terrible Springfield, Illinois, race riot of the previous year.

"It was there, in a little room of a New York apartment, that the National Association for the Advancement of Colored People was born," writes Professor Wedin. The mercurial socialist and gifted journalist William English Walling had written "Race War in the North," a powerful essay in the *Independent* provoking much anguished commentary but also an equal amount of inaction among progressives. Ovington virtually shamed Walling and Charles Edward Russell, another prominent parlor socialist, into action. Several later meetings there, and then at the Liberal Club, brought social worker Henry Moskowitz, African-American educator Dr. William Bulkley, *New York Post* owner Oswald Garrison Villard, and more than fifty others on board to issue a "call" on February 12, 1909, Lincoln's birthday. The rest—the historic meeting at Cooper Union in May of that year and at the Charity Organization Society in May of 1910—is history, as they say, with Ovington demurely but determinedly serving as indispensable mediator among a volatile mix of largely male egos and contentious agendas. As this biography makes clear, it was largely due to Ovington and the support she obtained from Walling, Russell, and Milholland that the wealthy Villard's objections to Du Bois's becoming a salaried member of the new association were overcome. An NAACP without Du Bois would've been like socialism without Eugene Debs or the March on Washington without Martin Luther King Jr.

Having played a crucial role in recruiting Du Bois to the NAACP, Ovington would remain his most loyal (although by no means uncritical) ally in an association most of whose original directors were white and several of whom were, like Villard, opinionated innocents in the field of race relations. She understood far more clearly than many of her fellow board members that the new civil rights organization would commit a fatal error by seeking a close collaboration with Booker T. Washington's Tuskegee Machine and its often well-intentioned white supporters. Ever since hearing him speak in Brooklyn in 1901, Ovington had remained unimpressed by the principal of Tuskegee. Washington's ingratiation of white people and trivialization of racial indignities suffered by black people set her teeth on edge. But if Ovington's idealism had caused her to recoil from the Bookerite ideology of racial accommodation, she would emerge from firsthand encounters with southern white supremacy during 1905 and 1906 as that rarest of northern whites, an ardent opponent of the racial status quo whose worst features she had seen, in the language of the day, red in tooth and claw as special correspondent for Villard's *New York Post*.

The ghastly Atlanta Riot of 1906 and Booker Washington's "Eulogy," a bromide that tended to exculpate white perpetrators, sickened her. Hurrying to the city by train from Alabama, Du Bois had written "A Litany at Atlanta," a thunderous indictment of racist barbarity. On the Pullman taking her north, Ovington's feverish thoughts would lead to "The White Brute," a moving, widely read essay in which she unmasked the sexual abuse by white men of black women as the hidden perennial in the white South's hegemony over its black citizens. Black rape as the cause of white violence Ovington dismissed as a lie, as had the African-American feminists Ida B. Wells-Barnett and Fannie Barrier Williams before her. Ovington's contribution as a white woman was to universalize the tyranny of sexual exploitation. Recalling the fear that young female Irish domestics had felt around the well-bred males of her own college days, she stipulated in her uncannily modern essay that sexual abuse of women was an essential component of all societies in which extremes of power and subordination exist. As *Half a Man*, her 1911 classic study of race and urban poverty evinces, Ovington was always a remarkably perspicacious student of the myriad ways in which power and money function to oppress classes, races, and genders, while invariably blaming the victims themselves.

In its densely researched, sensitively interpreted, and crisply written evocation of her subject's career, Professor Wedin's biography opens a wide window onto much of the inner life of the NAACP as it evolves from a virtual one-person show scripted by the incomparable (and sometimes insufferable) Du Bois through the unflappable stewardship of James Weldon Johnson and the manic operational brilliance of Walter White to become, in classic Weberian progression, a well-honed bureaucracy of lawyers, accountants, field secretaries, and lobbyists—and, overwhelmingly, of African-Americans. Yet, *plus ça change*, the more Carolyn Wedin shows us an Ovington whose essence remains unchanged as she keeps the feet of whites to the civil rights fire, composes what amounted to middlebrow white America's introduction to black America's leadership class (*Portraits in Color* [1927]), writes syndicated book reviews and a history of the NAACP (*The Walls Came Tumbling Down* [1947]), and despite advancing years lectures widely and circuit-rides among the association's far-flung branches. To a degree somewhat difficult to gauge, Ovington seems to have softened the hard-edged elitism of the bureaucratic NAACP by serving in her later years as a kindly, walking institutional memory, a venerable emissary who could be counted on to relay suggestions as well as grievances to remote national headquarters in New York.

Inheritors of the Spirit represents a large step toward a much needed institutional history of the NAACP, even though its discussion of Du Bois's return to the NAACP in 1944 (after a ten-year absence) verges, I think, on unsympathetic caricature in a work otherwise distinguished by interpretive nuance and prudence. It is a welcome addition to a sparse literature, some of whose most valuable titles include Charles Flint Kellogg's *NAACP* (1967), the late Professor B. Joyce Ross's biography of the NAACP's other significant white stalwart, *Joel Spingarn and the Rise of the NAACP* (1972), and the essays by Professors August Meier and the late Elliott Rudwick in *Along the Color Line* (1976). Professor Wedin has rescued Mary White Ovington from the indexes of monographs and given us a vibrant, valuable chronicle of an eighty-year dedication to economic, racial, and gender justice.

David Levering Lewis
March 1997
New Brunswick, New Jersey

1

Finding Her Avenue

MARY WHITE OVINGTON was born on a quiet and unpretentious street in Brooklyn, New York. Three stories and a basement housed her extended family. She grew up with a feeling of space and possibility, from a large bedroom shared with her sister, with its expansive mahogany bed and tall bookcase-bureau, to the brightly lit basement kitchen and dining room where the full family dined each evening amid smells of fresh bread and smoked beef or sardines.[1]

Reminders of the Union's recent war against slavery framed the table. Between two windows hung Abraham Lincoln's portrait and opposite an engraving of the signing of the Emancipation Proclamation. Blond, handsome, Theodore Tweedy Ovington presided over the Family. Shy and principled, he liked listening to anything but housekeeping details or gossip. At the other end sat Grandmother Ketcham, an abolitionist from her youth in Brooklyn, Connecticut.

May's (Mary's) childish spirits overflowed in mild mischief. Night after night she teased her grandmother with chocolate mice hidden under her plate. Or she hid under the big table before anyone else arrived, staying there while the dinner bell rang its second time, listening to her family's amazement that she would miss any chance to eat. Her older siblings often teased her. It seemed to May they were jealous of her having been with her parents to Europe when she was seven. For a few weeks after their return she was allowed to tell of her travels, but later, as she recalled, "if I began with some little remark about the Swiss mountains or the dolls I had seen in Paris," they would cry, "Oh, yes, when I was in Europe," and stop any further remarks.

1

One night she was interrupted many times while talking about the trip and left the room in tears. "They were not deep tears," she recalled, "only drops kept at the surface for slight occasions." Insightful about how response to hurt might injure in return, she remembered that she felt bad herself, but "was anxious that my brother and sister should feel worse." Occasionally there would be guests at mealtime: her mother's cousin, reporting her latest adventures, or the minister and his wife. Then the food was especially wonderful—fried oysters and potato biscuit—but May was pained to have to sit at a side table with her little sister Helen.

In the backyard, Ovington as a child found a world of infinite possibilities. She climbed the arbor to eat Isabella grapes. She circled her velocipede on its path, rested on the large swing made by Grandfather Ketcham, and refreshed herself with a peach from a nearby tree. Most of all, even as a small child, Ovington loved flowers. In her yard and her cousin's next door, masses of color overflowed their beds: deutzia, syringa, lilies of the valley, fragrant little white roses, morning glories on strings against the fence, and portulacas edging the stone curb. In winter Ovington's twenty-five-cent allowance went for cream cakes and butterscotch, valentines and writing pads, but in spring it was spent on blue and yellow pansies and purple violets.

The winter world was full of indoor activities, for the family doctor did not believe children should play in the cold. They romped and tumbled in the kitchen, where the cook told stories of Irish lore. They wrote elaborate "Plans for Plays" and acted out books, willing to be as grotesque as any part demanded.[2] Billiards, cards, word games, and pencil and paper games developed quick wits and rhyming tongues. May took up whist, or bridge, at age nine and played and wrote about it the rest of her long life.

There was much reading aloud. "What made the good times especially happy to me was that my father and mother took part in them. Like many children, I loved the society of grown-ups," Ovington recalled. They read Thomas Nelson Page's stories in the *Century Magazine,* of the faithful black uncle or mammy; Eliza crossing the ice to freedom in *Uncle Tom's Cabin;* Box Brown and Anthony Burns and Frederick Douglass—most dramatic because he wrote his own story. All of these heroes joined her gallery of exiled kings and soldiers and pioneers from Shakespeare and Hawthorne.

Her psychological suffering was sometimes intense, coming from her active imagination or fatigue. She had only one dread, a nightmare of abandonment that began "when I was five years old [and] my nurse left me." The dream began on the dark stairs to that same warm basement dining room:

> There terror seized me. I was cold with it, for instead of finding my old nurse in the familiar seat a great, ugly . . . woman . . . looked up at me. I shook with terror, clenched my hand, and tried to cry out, and then I wakened gasping with fear. This nightmare lasted for years. . . . I would waken with a sob and turn to touch my sister in the bed beside me, needing to feel something that was kind and good to me after this ghoulish figure that sat in the place of someone I had dearly loved.

The dream hinted that her secure world was not the world of all children. Already at this young age Ovington sensed that her comfortable home at 69 Livingston Street was a happy accident that could at any time disappear. And she felt a curiosity and concern for those who were born into a colder, crueler world than her own.

———

HENRY ALEXANDER OVINGTON, Mary White Ovington's paternal grandfather, was born in 1798, two years after his parents arrived in the United States from London. He married Mary Hubbard White of Brooklyn, New York, two years younger than himself, in 1818. He worked steadily until his death in 1886 as assistant chamberlain of New York City.

Restless, Grandfather Ovington moved his wife and eight children between winters in rented houses and summers on a farm in Bay Ridge. In the 1850s, he turned over some china held for a bad debt to sons Theodore and Edward, setting them up in a little shop on Brooklyn's Fulton Street. Soon the twenty-five-year-old Theodore fell hard for Ann Louisa Ketcham, a pretty violet-eyed seventeen-year-old who was a student at Mr. Greenleaf's Seminary for Young Ladies. "I am

Henry Alexander Ovington, Mary White Ovington's paternal grandfather. Painted by a family member. (Courtesy of Joan Callin Foster)

Mary Hubbard White (Mrs. Henry Alexander Ovington), Mary Ovington's paternal grandmother. Painted by a family member. (Courtesy of Joan Callin Foster)

Emeline Franklin (Mrs. Alfred T. Ketcham), Mary White Ovington's maternal grandmother. Photograph probably by J. Renowden. (Courtesy of Joan Callin Foster)

Alfred T. Ketcham, Mary White Ovington's maternal grandfather. Photograph by J. Renowden. (Courtesy of Joan Callin Foster) nothing but a child," she told him. But he filled a year with lovely letters and gave up his ale, cigars, cards, and billiards for her. "I know, Louisa, that I am a strange fellow. . . . I am not the one to gain the affection of any." Louisa's single letter in response to this barrage was modest and reluctant, but finally, encouraged by family and friends, she consented to his marriage proposal.[3]

Upon their wedding in July 1855, Theodore took a drastic step for an Ovington, prominent at Congregational Plymouth Church, and followed Louisa and her family to Second Unitarian. They held outspoken abolitionist sentiments during the Civil War, and in the rush of expansion afterward, Theodore worked at being an ethical businessman, bemoaning to "Dear Loo" their lack of money but repeating that it was better to be honest in serving, rather than exploiting, customers and society.[4]

Their first child, Charles Ketcham Ovington, was born in 1856, Adele in 1861; and Mary on April 11, 1865, just three days before President Lincoln's assassination. Ovington recalled her mother telling her that "my copperhead nurse . . . gave us both a sad shock when she rushed into our bedroom, crying, 'They've shot the president, and I'm glad of it.'" Mary's sister Helen was born in 1870.

Brooklyn was then a community of trees, fresh air, and comfortable folk, the nation's third-largest city and culturally rich. There, while growing up, Ovington saw Julia Marlowe in Shakespeare's *Twelfth Night* and Edwin Booth playing Hamlet. "Economy had to be practiced at home, but money was always found for us to see two or three plays." After school she slipped into rehearsals of the Brooklyn Philharmonic, where conductor Theodore Thomas's favorites—Beethoven's Fifth and *Pastoral* symphonies, Wagner's *Lohengrin* and *Tannhäuser*—became as familiar to her as the hymns sung around the piano on Sunday nights.

Most shopping, too, was done in Brooklyn. Jornay and Burnham sold blankets and sheets, towels, umbrellas, gloves and stockings, men's clothing, and women's underwear. The rest of a woman's attire was made at home by a dressmaker and seamstress. Ovington's father hated this fussy time, and so did his middle daughter, whether she was told to run for paper muslin or spool silk, or had to stand still under the scissors. She rejoiced in later years when dresses grew shorter, simpler, and less voluminous, letting girls and women move their limbs.

She preferred hat shopping, trying them on one after another at Balch Price: "leghorn, chip, rough straw, trimmed with buttercups and

Louise Ketcham Ovington, Mary White Ovington's mother. Photograph by G. Frank E. Pearsall. (Courtesy of Joan Callin Foster)

Theodore Tweedy Ovington, Mary White Ovington's father. Photographer unknown. (Courtesy of Joan Callin Foster)

Louise Ketcham Ovington with baby Mary White Ovington, 1867. Photograph by C. H. Williamson's Photographic Portrait Gallery. (Courtesy of Joan Callin Foster)

Mary White Ovington. Photograph by Fredricks' Knickerbocker Family Portrait Gallery. (Courtesy of Joan Callin Foster) daisies, that with black velvet on a white leghorn—ah!—to tuck an elastic under your chin and look at yourself in the long mirror" and try to decide until your mother chose for you. The delicate-featured child who looked back in that mirror with her shining blond hair and light but intent blue eyes loved being treated to an ermine fur tippet and muff, which she was allowed to wear walking to church beside her grandmother.

Occasionally she went with her mother to Manhattan, which bore little similarity to the city of today. Church spires towered above the highest houses. There were no apartments, no elevators, no pavement; horses' feet struck cobblestone; the lamplighter raised a long pole to light the gas of the streetlamps; city nights were dark; city days were filled with sunshine. Five ferries made their way between Brooklyn and Manhattan. Weighed down in shirt and drawers, flannel and cotton petticoats, May watched the crowds of businessmen pressing forward and rushing to Wall Street, sure they would fall in the water and be crushed by the boat.

They would walk first to Uncle Charles Franklin Ketcham's stationery store at Nassau and Cedar. Dad's and Uncle Edward's china shop was mildly interesting, but this one was fascinating with its pencils, pads, and paper. Here the Ovingtons brought their *St. Nicholas* magazines to be leather-bound for young hands.

Old-fashioned stagecoaches with seats along the sides ran up and down Broadway through the shopping district. As they jounced like jelly over the cobblestones, Louise Ovington would look with concern at May, for children often gave up their breakfasts to these vehicles. Their usual destination was A. T. Stewart's department store at Broadway and Ninth.

The child was dazzled by the fabrics displayed around the white rotunda, dramatized by sunshine streaming in. In the dimmer warm light of the gaslit rooms, she tingled at the heavy silk and satin "shot with silver, rich cream color full of shadows, crimson, lovely cerulean blues."[5]

They lunched outdoors at the Viennese bakery at Ninth and Broadway. May loved the heavy table linen and napkins, the crisp-crusted bread chunks, the rich French chocolate, and her favorite—fried oysters. Then they might browse through new books at Houghton Mifflin or go into Tiffany's on Union Square. There a marble nude impressed the girl with the beauty of the unadorned, undistorted human form.

She said she "walked in a dream" in those youthful days, but Ovington was also aware of monotony and ugliness in the world around her. If she played "relievo" or "box of ribbons" on her front stoop, she saw little girls from lower down her street, where conditions grew increasingly dingy and ill smelling. On one of the rare, memorable occasions when she walked there, she recalled:

> I shrank from the straggly-haired little girls playing on the pavement. They were untidy, their clothes were dirty. . . . I wanted to get past them as soon as I could. . . . Once, I took this walk when returning from a children's party where Santa Claus had thrown great handfuls of candy from his bag. The rude and energetic children had gathered them up by the dozen, the bashful and timid had secured one or two or none at all. Was the world like that?

She preferred walking down the street in the dim late afternoon, fetching a loaf of bread for supper, when she could see tables set for the evening meal, or even families eating, homelike, amid the ugliness.

Even in her own wonderful home, the big world intruded in unpredictable economic cycles. "We were not rich people," Ovington understood, and, in fact, compared to classmates she sensed they "were poor." That she didn't mind, but sensed "the shadow that touched us was the difficulty and worry that attended the securing of such means as we possessed."

The Ovington Brothers, taking sons Edward and Charles into partnership in 1879, kept their heads above water, even coming back from the fiery destruction of their original store in 1883. But looking down the plentiful spread of the supper table to her father's harassed, wrinkled brow, she prayed: "I don't want anything more, God, only can't we have what we've got without my father's having to worry so!"

She was shocked and saddened to see something happening to young men in the fierce competition of the city. Hearing the advice given to a fourteen-year-old going to his first job in New York made a deep impression:

> It was as though he were leaving this pleasant country place with its pure sunlight and sparkling water to enter a dark, tiger-infested jungle, thick with poisonous plants, where he would be destroyed unless, like his antagonists, he used his claws.

As she watched her kind uncle's face grow grim while advising the young man, she thought, "Perhaps most men, when they went to their

Drawing of the ruins of the Ovington Brothers (Theodore and Edward) and Sons (Charles and Edward) china shop on Fulton Street in Brooklyn after a fire on Saturday, January 6, 1883. (*New York Daily Graphic*, January 9, 1883)

Ovington Brothers store at 246–252 Fulton Street and 110 Clark Street, Brooklyn, from the Ovington Brothers catalog of *Blue and White China* from 1888.

work, must assume a hardness which they hated, if their children were to inherit a crumb of the world's riches."

Another irony was obvious even to a child, the land of plentiful forests and fields being despoiled thoughtlessly and pointlessly. In 1880 Adele came back from Florida furious. She had seen passengers standing on the deck of a little steamer moving up the Oklawaha River shooting glittering white herons and tiny warblers. "And no one seemed to mind!" she cried to her sister. "The steamer kept going on and they kept on shooting." Her sister May said that

> one would suppose that during this prodigal use of our magnificent continent no one would suffer want. But even an unobservant child like myself could see poverty. I had only to walk a block from my home to come upon it, smelling of sweat and dirt though in the open air.

She saw poverty, but what could she do about it? No one gave her any ideas, at home or church or school, though she was steeped in fictional and historic heroism. She wept over poor children in her books who were saved by some wealthy benefactor, but there were no settlements then, no boys' and girls' clubs, no outlets for "sentimental emotions concerning the poor." She wrote later:

> I was not consciously snobbish, but I lived in my own world, and knew no more of the life of the world at my street's end than of the life of the deep-seafishes far below the water whose surface I watched when I made the great journey of my childhood across the Atlantic. But the water that hid the sea's treasure was fresh and clear and beautiful, while the barrier that separated me from my brothers and sisters was thick with slime.

Shrinking from ugly sights and smells, Ovington came to believe, was not only natural but right; she never romanticized impoverishment. In the country, perhaps My Lady Poverty had "some slight charm," she said, but in the city street, "she is obnoxious."

Throughout her life Ovington shared with her class a hatred of dirt, odor, ill health, ignorance, uncouth gestures, and vulgar laughter. But she differed drastically from other upper-middle-class genteel family members and friends in her response. Instead of avoiding the ugly, she committed herself to doing something to change that which she hated. As she looked back to her dear childhood home and all its pleasant happenings, she wrote:

> My heart is full of gratitude. But when I leave it in memory I can no longer turn up the street to watch the houses grow bigger and more spacious, and to look upon health and comfort and beauty. Now I must turn down and walk among the little ragged children whose presence fills me with an overwhelming shame.

THE BROOKLYN OF Mary White Ovington's youth was jokingly called "one vast Hennery," both for its growing reputation as a bedroom for Manhattan, and for its most distinguished citizen, Henry Ward Beecher. In November 1872 suffrage crusader Victoria Woodhull charged that the famed orator of Plymouth Congregational was having an affair with the wife of Woodhull's longtime admirer (and Beecher's former protégé) Theodore Tilton.[6]

Woodhull's publicizing of the affair led to a three-year lawsuit and scandal that became the stuff of songs, skits, jokes, burlesques, and newspaper copy, until Beecher was reprieved by a hung jury and exonerated by a church board. He went on writing and drawing crowds until his death in 1887, when forty thousand people passed by his coffin.

The infamous trial divided families and broke up friendships, but there was no division among the Ovingtons; they were all staunch Beecher supporters, even though the Tiltons were neighbors and May went there for dancing class. She was overwhelmingly curious about it all, but each night her parents rushed her and Adele off to bed before reading trial testimony in the *Brooklyn Eagle*.

Uncle Edward and Aunt Maria became prime witnesses in the long trial, their actions, demeanors, and statements receiving multipage summaries and transcript coverage. Plymouth Deacon Edward, with his red hair, mustache, and beard, mounted the witness stand in a packed courtroom looking, as the *New York Times* reported, "constrained and embarrassed." Led by the suave prosecuting attorney "from one absurd position to another . . . until it seemed as if the witness would swear black was white on the slightest provocation," he stepped down to a roar of courtroom laughter. His wife fared better, with "answers . . . given with perfect freedom from embarrassment, . . . remarkable clearness," "and with an evident desire to be strictly accurate."[7]

The Ovington children continued to slip into their grandfather's pew at Plymouth on Sunday nights to hear Beecher. In 1883 May went with her lively, unmarried "Aunt Renie," self-dubbed "the Scalawag sister" to the minister's seventieth birthday party, with the church packed and twelve hundred more people outside. The crowd stood and cheered for every speaker, ladies wildly waving their handkerchiefs. The loudest screams, May Ovington excitedly told her mother, were for Beecher's sister, Harriet Beecher Stowe, author of *Uncle Tom's Cabin*. Mrs. Stowe seemed very small and frail, May thought, but she liked the author's face very much.[8]

For excitement and sheer popularity, Beecher's Plymouth was the church to attend. But at tiny, struggling Second Unitarian, where Theodore and his children had followed his wife's family, a very different leader preached from 1864 until five years into the new century. John White Chadwick came to his first and only parish as a radical. With Unitarian founder William Ellery Channing, he believed reason was humankind's most godlike gift, and he took joy in the words above the church portal: "The truth shall make you free." To Brooklyn's mainline churchgoers, he was a satanic iconoclast.

He permitted no indulgence in what the young Ovington often longed for: the "pleasures of religious sentimentalism." Dreamy beauty and half-believed liturgies had no place at Second Unitarian. Every hymn had to express conviction. No miracles were recited from Chadwick's pulpit. What he did give the young Ovington, however, was inestimable in its influence. "Preacher, poet, man, and friend," she called him in a poem celebrating his twenty-fifth anniversary at the church. Beecher packed Plymouth with his oratory; Chadwick wrote out and read everything word for word. Physician Robert D. Brockway much later remembered the weekly scene:

As if it were yesterday I, a small delicate little lad sitting quietly observant between my parents gaze across the pews watching with delight

John White Chadwick, minister of
Mary White Ovington's church,
Second Unitarian, Brooklyn, for
her first forty years. He was a good
friend and a model of living by
reason. (Courtesy of Ruth Temple,
Chesterfield, Massachusetts Historical Society)

John White Chadwick at his desk
in his summer home in Chesterfield, Massachusetts. (Courtesy of
Ruth Temple, Chesterfield, Massachusetts Historical Society)

the arrival of the Ovington family, handsome father and mother and brother Charles, and three so very beautiful sisters, Adelaide [*sic*], Mary and Helen. . . . What a select, intelligent group of earnest, noble souls were they who each Sunday morning for nine months of the year gathered in the quaint little church (wasn't it designated "The Church of the Holy Turtle"?) to commune quietly together and learn great moral truths from another very humane, comprehending and poetic soul.[9]

John White Chadwick's sermons had just the right amount of poetry, Ovington thought. He read in a monotone, but he wrote with such clarity that she awaited the powerful conclusion of a Chadwick sermon as if it were the climax of a play. "Later when I read [Ralph Waldo] Emerson, he seemed muddled. I had already heard much of it from my own pulpit, much better argued." Chadwick published thirteen volumes of sermons, biographies of Channing and fellow Unitarian clergyman Theodore Parker, three books of poetry, and several theological studies, as well as hundreds of reviews and magazine articles.

Chadwick wrote poetically of a life of reason. Ovington would later think back often to the crimson cushions and simple stained-glass windows, and of the homely, rugged man in the pulpit, and recover the feeling she had then, that there was nothing humans could not do, no difficulty that they might not overcome.

A young Felix Adler, founder of the Society of Ethical Culture ("Deed, not creed"), held forth at Second Unitarian, too, and married one of the Goldmark girls who sat in front of May Ovington. (Her sister, May's school friend, married Louis Brandeis, eventually a justice of the Supreme Court.) Octavius Frothingham, a famous liberal, also exchanged pulpits with Chadwick. Rabbi Gottheil spoke there, as did George William Curtis, who helped Thoreau build his cabin at Walden Pond. "It was a pleasant little society," Ovington remembered, "growing poorer as the conservative element left it, but able to hold its Sunday services and to leave its minister untrammeled."

"Blatant unorthodoxy" in the City of Churches led to some mild persecution of the child who took its teachings seriously. May Ovington was hurt but pleased when a Presbyterian schoolmate, discovering she was walking with a Unitarian, crossed to the other side of the street. The sensation of being different was even more intense on "Anniversary Day," the annual Brooklyn Sunday school procession of children from the Protestant churches, marching in white, carrying banners, wending their way through residential neighborhoods. May and Helen would sit on their front steps and "watch these Christians go by, unpolluted by heretics."

A school friend telling May of her religious creed, said, "This of course, I *have* to believe, but besides that, I believe." There was nothing the young Ovington, steeped in Unitarian teaching, *had* to believe; it all had to be worked out through the labors of her understanding mind.

In thinking back on this experience, Ovington felt that her intellectual snobbishness could be excused, or at least explained, by the strain for a highly emotional young girl of living by reason. Other girls she knew "got religion" and found it beautiful. May could have outshouted any of them at a revival, but she was always held back by her training:

> Some form of social service might have helped me at this time, but nothing was presented. So, a little lonely at heart, I held my head high and carried Herbert Spencer's *First Principles* to school. One of my teachers, Mary Brigham, assistant principal at Professor West's, saw me reading it one day and stopped to talk. She tried to show me that science must not affect our belief in Christianity. She had been interested in evolution, but, finding it attacked that which she loved most in her belief, had put it aside. I clutched Spencer the tighter.

Here was a young person reversing the usual roles of church and school by carrying her commitment to intellectual honesty into the latter to argue with a teacher. No single influence from her teen years was more powerful, she thought, than "this religious call to intellectual sincerity":

> I would leave it, I sometimes think, if I could, but I cannot. . . . I do not know how to get at the truth of anything except by studying it, looking at it from all sides, taking the testimony of its adherents and its antagonists. And if a new, destructive idea presents itself I must grapple with it, no matter how painful it may be.

Unfortunately, no one helped her reconcile the impressions she gained of business, of waste, of pitiful poverty in the midst of prosperity, with the teaching of her church. Unitarians were skeptics in religion, but (in Ovington's words) "on economic questions they were as sure of the righteousness of their present competitive system as any dogmatic Calvinist was sure of heaven and hell." No one spelled out for her the way in which faith unaccompanied by emotion but buttressed by reason and experience could be combined with good works.

Ovington's Unitarian training goes a long way toward explaining her later commitment to socialism. She became a socialist, she explained, not because of emotional appeal, tremendous though that was; nor because someone told her to; nor even because she wanted to become one, but "because the years have brought to me one hard fact after another which I have faced and have striven to remedy. And this effort has led me, through my reason and understanding, into that political movement of the world's laborers, called Socialism." Her own early life was happy and rich with nurture to body and mind and soul. It made all the sense in the world to believe that every child should have that wealth and opportunity. It made all the sense in the world, eventually, to spend one's life working toward that end.

———————

MARY WHITE OVINGTON happily found a mystical substitute for an aspect of religious experience denied Unitarians. "It was not until I was eleven that I found Nature in the valley of the Androscoggin," as she described her epiphany.

Louise Ovington and the children usually spent summers in the country close enough for Theodore to get out on the weekends, in the Berkshires or the Hampshires in the comforting hills around Chesterfield, Massachusetts. But in 1876, it was decided that father, too, needed a vacation, so rooms were rented at Gates Cottage in Shelburne, New Hampshire. The twenty-four-hour trip began with the tiring excitement of the Fall River Boat and continued by train. In Portland, sticky and uncomfortable, on the bumpy Grand Trunk Railroad, cinders flew through the screenless windows, and one hit May in an eye already irritated. Mother brought out sandwiches and a great round country cheese, and May's discomfort grew with bumpy indigestion. Heat increased; the plush train seats scratched. She managed, finally, to sleep a bit, easing the pain in her eye. She woke to the family gathering up luggage and, listless and bedraggled, followed them onto the platform at Shelburne.

In the midst of a family discussion about how to proceed May wandered off down a pathway. Later she recalled what she found:

> The green of the meadow was to my right, and to my left, not a familiar brook but a side river. The sun had just dropped behind a mountain, and the subdued light was restful, like a song heard at a distance after you had gone to bed. The river made a gurgling sound as it went over the rocks. On either side the hills looked down, shutting out the world. It was all so calm, so full of peace. Wave after wave of emotion swept over me, and I was there baptized in the stream of Nature's peace. I have been faithful to her through the years, and have learned, with the poet I love best, that "Nature never did betray the heart that loved her."

"Plenty of writers have tried to make me recant," the mature Ovington later wrote, writers who insisted that friendly stars were "noisy, wild-rushing gobs of matter" and the thrush's love song temporary protoplasm. "How foolish! One might as well tell the young doctor, when he looks at the girl he loves, to deny her beauty of face and form and see only her bones and viscera."

Periodically, the peace of being enveloped by nature sustained her. At age eighteen, she tried to express some of what she knew in a poem sent to her mother.

> O wondrous night. The vast and boundless ocean
> Of all eternity we seem to see
> When thou dost fall. And every star of heaven
> Cometh to shine on thee.
>
> Our earth seems but an atom mid this grandeur.
> Tossed on the boundless and eternal space.
> A little spot in all the heaven's brightness.
> Filling its tiny place.
>
> And what are we in all this solemn vastness?
> A merest speck, a moment here, then gone.

A little drop amid its countless fellows
On the great ocean home

And yet the smallest things are oft most precious
Each tiny gem is filled with beauty rare
And we may have within us something grander
Than any starry sphere

A human soul. It goes we know not whither.
And comes we know not whence. It is as deep
A mystery as any starry splendor
That silent watch doth keep.

And let us keep it there so pure and spotless
So full of tender, deep and holy love
That God may find it greater and more precious
Than any stars above.[10]

Church and school both made Mary White Ovington a strong individualist. "Being a person who took my own way, I studied as I liked," she recalled. Undiagnosed astigmatism abetted the child's erratic approach to education. Her eyes would last only until spring each year, when fatigue and headaches sent her home to be tutored.

Between the ages of ten and fifteen, she attended the Bracketts' school. George, Mary, and Ellen Brackett, enthusiastic, natural teachers, gave no points for effort, and a wrong answer meant staying after school. With their pupil, they shared a passion for history and literature. One of Ovington's unpublished papers, titled "Literature for Young Girls," asks, "Did you, when you were a girl, read books worth remembering?" She goes on to describe what was close to her own experience as a fourteen- to sixteen-year-old: "When the girl is learning to be a woman, when the selfish instincts of childhood come in conflict with the altruism of mature life, impressions are strong and profound, and the benefit of the right word rightly spoken is beyond compute."

She found poetry to be ideal for understanding and for reaching beyond oneself. Studying history through biography and autobiography appealed to her imagination. Adventure books written for boys were better than sentimental novels in counteracting adolescent girls' tendencies to morbidness. Any novels read should be strong in ideals, Ovington concluded. "The good must be triumphant, and the evil must perish. The book need not necessarily be happy, but the sadness must be glorious and full of hope."

As for instruction in "the sexual question," Ovington counseled, "it is a vexed matter how much physiology a girl should know." She would learn something of it whether or not the parents wished it, Ovington knew. It was best for the young woman to talk honestly with an intelligent, sensitive older woman Ovington concluded, and to toss birds and bees stories into the wastebasket.

Finally, she believed, one should "never tell a girl not to read a book. It is sure to make her long to. . . . If you disapprove of a book, don't talk about it."[11]

IN THE 1880s the seesaw of capitalism gave a boost to the Ovington Brothers business, and the family moved to a larger house at 69 Willow, one block from Columbia Heights and the East River. In this neighborhood of elegant Greek revival row houses, the three beautiful Ovington sisters entered society.

The new house hummed with happy times. May joined her siblings and cousins and friends in clearing the wide drawing room, donning pretty gowns, and dancing herself into joyous fatigue with pleasant partners. For three years she threw herself wholeheartedly into having a good time, with whist, progressive euchre, fox and geese, geography games, play reading and acting, and long Sunday walks with men friends.[12] It was expected and it was what her mother wanted.

Summers were less predictable for an attractive and protected young woman. With her brother, Ovington explored. Their travels included early spring train trips up the Harlem road to Copake Falls to wander where snow still lay in the hollows, gathering the white and pink arbutus; or further into the Berkshires to the Shaker settlements at Hancock and New Lebanon, Stockbridge and Lenox—one of May's favorites; month-long wanderings into the wilds of western New Jersey, eastern Pennsylvania, and the foothills of the Catskills by train

Charles Ketcham Ovington, Mary White Ovington's brother. Photographer unknown. (Courtesy of Joan Callin Foster)

Adele Ovington (Mrs. James Haviland Merritt), Mary White Ovington's sister. Photograph by Fredricks' Knickerbocker Family Portrait Gallery. (Courtesy of Joan Callin Foster)

Tintype from "Harriet Falls, July 8, 1878." Second from left, Marty White Ovington; seated on her left, Charles K. Ovington; behind him and to his right, Adele Ovington. (Courtesy of Joan Callin Foster)

Mary White Ovington. Photograph
by "Dampt," The Montague
Studio. (Courtesy of Joan Callin
Foster)

Helen Ovington Kingsbury (Mrs.
Edmund Kingsbury), Mary White
Ovington's younger sister. (Courtesy of
Elizabeth Kingsbury Friedmann)

and ferry, horse and dusty macadamized road; and visits to quaint hotels and boardinghouses with mill ponds to read by, old turnpikes, walks in the mountain woods, and frolics in the brooks.[13]

Three years of "society" meant May Ovington had plenty of chances to choose marriage, but the man who would marry her and the man she would marry were never the same, she laughingly explained. Later comments suggest that the men in her life had little interest in her abolitionist history or appreciation of her questions about the world. Once when Frederick Douglass was speaking at Plymouth Church, she asked her "young man of the moment" to escort her. This conspicuously beautiful blue-eyed blond vehemently defended Douglass's marriage to a white woman while her companion, from Baltimore, retorted: "How could she do it. How could she do it." But as the organ pealed "John Brown's Body" and Douglass mounted the platform, with his powerful build, bronze skin, massive features, and bushy white hair, even May's escort was converted. He turned to whisper, "I don't wonder she married him. He looks like Aesop!"

She said the friendships of those days "just happened; they were not made in mutual high interests and they therefore disappeared with the ease with which they came." The pattern worked reasonably well for other young women: her older sister moved predictably from dances into marriage with James Haviland Merritt at age twenty-three, in an evening wedding in the rose-decorated living room at 69 Willow. Cousins Jeannette and Florence also married there in ceremonies described in the *New York Times* and *Brooklyn Life*.[14]

By the time May was twenty-three, Adele had lost her first child and suffered a nervous breakdown. Younger sister Helen married at twenty-four, but waited twelve years for her first child. The experiences of the older sister clearly had an impact on May and Helen.

Unfortunately, her class's expected alternative to marriage did not appeal to Ovington, either. She dreaded becoming the unmarried daughter staying on to care for her parents. To her friend Corinne Bacon she confessed that "to live on in an eternal round of home duties without any outside fun or any outside work even would just about kill me." Even if married, she would not stay home. "It tires me so much more to put all my strength in one set of things than to have more interests on hand." If she could not find a teaching job, the most obvious path in her world, she would find other activities, she joked:

secretary to the Board of Foreign Missions; habitué at the Boy's Club; leading lady of the drama association; or treasurer of the ladies' literary society.[15]

But the slim choices on the list were not at all funny. Later when she did find challenging work, she claimed, "I think now if I had to go to a dance, and hand out a favor to an expectant man, and, above all, sit up until two in the morning talking to him, I should be exhausted beyond any physical or nervous fatigue my present labors as a radical expose me to."

By 1887 dances and card parties at 69 Willow mellowed into smaller, literary club papers and discussions, such as May's presentation on Venetian history.[16] She grew embarrassed at her uselessness and tried teaching in a private school with nineteen girls. It did not go at all well. Only the slow children interested her; the quick ones could get along without her help, she thought. But without challenge the brighter students lost all ambition to learn. Worse yet, she was sure she knew more than the principal, and disputing him got her fired, humiliated for the first time in her life.

While she drifted, at odds with all expectations for her, Ovington ventured into philanthropy, volunteering in a kindergarten one morning a week. Again she knew nothing about its methods and found the work uncongenial. "This initiation did not happen to make me want to know more," she observed. A Unitarian minister encouraged her to teach in a mission Sunday school. These little girls would be poor—"I should indeed be the Lady Bountiful of the story books that I knew so well," Ovington mused. Dressed in everyday clothes (to the disappointment of the girls), she entered the crowded, ugly mission, sat through what she thought a stupid service and roaring "song," and tried to make herself heard by her six immigrant eleven-year-olds. She endured because she wanted to visit their homes. "I shall call on Emily this week," she responded to their inviting cries, and suddenly "felt that the door had opened upon my philanthropic life."

Emily lived over a saloon. Fearfully climbing from twilight to darkness, feeling for the banisters, jumping when a board creaked, Mary Ovington climbed the first of the tenement stairs that in her subsequent careers would number in the thousands. But from the dark upper hall, the door opened to a sunny kitchen with shiny dishes, steaming kettle, and geraniums and begonias everywhere. A big, shy

Swedish woman put down her knitting, rose, and offered her a chair. Ovington was forever grateful to Emily's family for living so neatly and pleasantly: "They gave me courage to face many other dark stair-ways, confident that at the top I should meet brightness and good cheer." Energetic laborers, she found, passed up the dark, easily accessible lower rooms for sunlight and fresh air above.

That was all Ovington learned from this venture. Her pupils, of northern European parents, were fairly comfortable, and monthly visits revealed little of the real child or family. She did not find either the experience or knowledge she longed for, and it all came to an uneventful end.

When jolly times palled, and teaching and philanthropy proved unworkable, Ovington matriculated at Brooklyn's most prestigious (and least prudish) girls' school, the Packer Institute. In spacious buildings that included a well-stocked library, an art studio, and science laboratories, classes were small. Most students were in the lower grades, but one could also prepare for a four-year women's college like Vassar or Smith.[17]

Ovington intended to make up for her previous unsystematic education by preparing seriously for college entrance exams, but it was not to be. To the Latin syntax she hated, she would have to add Greek and advanced mathematics, and she refused to use her mind on "something that I believed would mean no more than learning the business signs on Broadway from the battery to Harlem." She wanted to follow current thought of her own land, of England, and of the Continent, and her only modern languages were her own and French. So, once again, she studied what she liked.

———

AFTER THE OVINGTON family moved to Willow Street, Louise Ovington decided to take them each summer to Seal Harbor, Maine, on Mount Desert island. There, in 1890, after a happy, flower-filled graduation in June after two years at the Packer Institute,[18] May heard about a college that she might get into. At Seal Harbor, a center of fashionable sport—tennis, sailing, rowing, horseback riding, and mountain climbing—the beautiful Ovington girls found much to do and many young men to play with.

One day Ovington sailed with Harvard graduate James Brown Scott from Seal Harbor to nearby Sorrento to play baseball and dance. Maybe she should try a place called the Harvard Annex, he suggested on their sleepy way home. Harvard professors came to a separate building to teach women.

"I woke up," Ovington said. Within a year, with the Ovington china business doing well, she moved to Cambridge as a special student. "To study favorite subjects under distinguished teachers, to have no financial worry—that I left to my father—what could be more delightful?" she mused.

Cambridge enchanted her. Great figures who echoed her abolitionist roots—Josiah Royce, Charles Eliot Norton, Thomas Wentworth Higginson—walked the tree-shaded streets along the winding Charles River. Here had lived writers whose names she cherished—James Russell Lowell and Henry Wadsworth Longfellow. She roomed with a family named Newell in Fayerweather House on Brattle Street and grew to love colonial structures and the unaffected, cultivated people who lived in them, people whose riches lay in books and art more than money.[19]

She reveled in her first winter away from a large city. From a window seat in the Harvard Library she gazed delightedly at the swirling flakes that collected on the broad common and hid the paths. Deep purple shadows webbed the drifts as she walked briskly through the twilight. She described it as "the winter's heaven of purity," and Mrs. Newell's greeting by her open fire hearth "marked a perfect spiritual ending to a long and happy day."

The freedoms of Cambridge encouraged Ovington's independent bent and moved her toward social and intellectual challenges. Socializing centered on Harvard men and pulled together the fun of her society years with the search for truth she longed for. Sitting by fires or drifting down the Charles, they talked of "the riddles of life." Choices seemed infinite—"anything was possible on this wonderful, inexhaustible earth," Ovington remembered.

With these carefree students she "devoured" poets. The Browning Club had two rules: that there always be a break for food and that no man should escort the same girl twice. They moved among prized old buildings: Stoughton, Hollis, Holworthy. She remembered an embarrassed Robert Morss Lovett, later professor of English at the University of Chicago, piloting a burly ice cream delivery man to his bedroom. Lovett would remember Mary Ovington in his autobiography as "austerely beautiful."

Many wrote poetry, too. Three in her group published volumes of verse during her second year: Algernon Tassin, Philip Savage, and Hugh MacCullough. The undoubted genius among them waited until later to make his writing public—William Vaughn Moody seemed shy and aloof. Ovington "had the feeling that he disliked our prying into poetry."

Mary White Ovington looked back on those animated discussions amazed that she had not realized this was a charmed oasis of green trees and water, and not the real world. Their discussions, she realized later, never encompassed "the encircling desert, its intolerable noonday heat, its shifting sands."

Ovington studied at the Annex (officially the Society for the Collegiate Instruction of Women) before it became Radcliffe College in 1894, and made its admissions and degrees correspond with those at Harvard.[20] Thus she and her two hundred classmates had only one course requirement, three years of English. Of twenty women entering with her, all but six were younger, and most were from the Boston-Cambridge area.[21]

Ovington's lowest grade her first year was in English: a B minus. In this class her independence was not fully appreciated. In a paper on Charles Dickens, she emphasized his social commentary, and her professor commented, "Excellent, though not as literary criticism. It might be entitled Why we read Dickens." In "Heroines of English Novels," she noted that older (male) novelists allowed only wicked women to have great strength and determination. "The beautiful, trustful heroines are rather weak and inane creatures—their feebleness is quite appalling," she observed. George Eliot, on the other hand, was able to thoroughly and truthfully depict her own sex.

Ovington speculated about the writing of her own day. If novelists represented the habits, customs, and people of a time as history never could, "are we willing to leave our time and country to their mercy? Can we feel that a century hence the reader of fiction will find just representations of the American woman of the present in the novel our age bequeaths him?" She then offered qualified praise to Henry James and Nathaniel Hawthorne.[22]

Most professors encouraged ignorance of contemporary events, Ovington found. She was assigned John Stuart Mill (1806–1873) and

Adam Smith (1723–1790), but Henry George's *Progress and Poverty* (1879), even then making history in England and the United States, was slightingly dismissed. Populism was at its height but ignored. "They frequently called our attention to great epochs of the past, but never once were we made even dimly aware that there might be a 'present Crisis.'"

The exception, the gem of Ovington's brief mining of higher education, came to Harvard in 1892 from the University of Toronto and Oxford. Through William J. Ashley she read the past "through the virile study of economic life." Influenced by social reformer Arnold Toynbee, and a friend of Beatrice and Sidney Webb, Ashley was a socialist with a strong belief in trade unionism.

His appointment to the economics faculty at Harvard challenged its orthodoxy, for he lost no time in asserting his historical, antitheoretical approach. In his introductory lecture he announced his two "great principles": "that economic conclusions are relative to given conditions, and that they possess only hypothetical validity."[23]

William Ashley immediately impressed Mary White Ovington, and she him. His little class of five women at the Annex doubled his workload; he thought it was foolish to separate them from the men.[24] Yet it came also as something of a relief, for Harvard men made fun of his British "weres" and "beens" and mannerisms: large eyes fixed too intently; tipping a chair forward as he became excited, putting a foot up as though climbing the chair, and jumping as it clattered down again. All his women students received A's (Ovington and her friend Frances Davenport A pluses) at midyear. Ovington's highest final grades were in Ashley's classes, three out of the seven she took in her two years at the Annex.[25]

Ashley selected Ovington and Davenport as research assistants, with two great benefits for May. She discovered the methodologies by which impartial history could become a tool of social reform, particularly in analyzing class structures and economic conditions, and she was permitted to use the Harvard Library stacks. There Ovington articulated for herself what would in the profession be dubbed "The New Social History" over fifty years later:

> I used to look at the few volumes of original material on my subject, the Peasants' Revolt. . . . There was the Chronicle of Saint Albans that described the peasants' rough handling of the monastery oven, but no line from the peasants as to how they felt on the matter.

In a book read for Silas MacVane's class in modern European history, she noted the many pages devoted to the Reign of Terror during the French Revolution, the tearful descriptions of men and women guillotined under the rule of Danton and Robespierre. Then she turned to read,

> in one paragraph, that more people had been killed in the White Terror following the revolution than in the Red Terror. . . . It told nothing in detail of these murdered men, women, and children. . . . This neglect of the suffering of the worker, this continual presentation of facts by historians from the standpoint of the propertied classes was something not to be forgotten.

Ovington's friend from Brooklyn, Frances Gardiner Davenport, was very much a scholar, and her companionship at the Annex was more enduring than that of either would-be poets or professors. They shared passions for history and argument, but Davenport was more exact. "You use words too often in their poetic sense," she told her friend May.

Ovington and Davenport spent several vacations in England and Norway, but their first was the most intellectually memorable. In the summer of 1892, they went to the old Ovington summering place at Chesterfield, Massachusetts. Each morning they climbed to a meadow above the town and, looking down on a little country churchyard, would sporadically open a volume of Shelley and read and talk. Davenport left before Ovington did. The morning after her leaving, May "felt tired enough to be among the dead. After some moments I opened the volume I had chosen—*Alice in Wonderland.* The ten days had been the most exacting mental exercise I had ever known."

Harvard Annex awarded certificates for the equivalent of a B.A. at Harvard. Ovington received a certificate of attendance as a special student, 1891 to 1893, but was never to have a true college degree. "Women who studied at Radcliffe in the 1880s did so primarily for the love of learning or to prepare themselves for teaching," suggests the official centennial history of the school, adding that the only other available careers were in social work and nursing.[26]

Cambridge and the Harvard Annex influenced Ovington profoundly, particularly the rebel economist Ashley. But many years would pass before she would clearly see a course of action, a way to live her life both usefully and by principle, before she would have both a career and a cause. As she returned to Brooklyn with her father's business now in collapse, one misty matter had clarified, however. At age twenty-eight she had passed the height of pressure to marry and would face the somewhat different expectation that she would stay home and care for her parents. Both the happy fun and the serious fun of her youth were past. It was time to get to work.

2

Taking Root

TWO YEARS LATER, at age thirty, May Ovington still drifted. She anticipated losing another job that did not engage her, as registrar at Pratt Institute in Brooklyn. But her boss, Frederick Pratt, took pity and asked her to try heading a settlement in Greenpoint, in the Astral model tenement built with his father's money.

The gift shop family business had gone from bad to worse after the depression of 1893 and had forced her back to Brooklyn from the Harvard Annex. The third fire in ten years had destroyed their new four-story brick building on Flatbush Avenue in 1894. Now, in 1895, the sheriff of Kings County at high noon had closed the Brooklyn store on attachment for debts, forcing it to reorganize.[1] How selfish it was, she felt, depending on her father and brother for her living—she had to work, and she might as well try a settlement.[2]

Greenpoint lies far north in Brooklyn, near what is now La Guardia Airport. A native of the city through and through, Ovington had yet never been there. From Brooklyn Heights she boarded a trolley that jerked through a familiar mile, and then she gazed at all new territory. She caught glimpses of men in undershirts in a steamy sugar refinery, felt the burst of heat, and snatched a whiff of the sweet sickening odor.

Stepping off at 184 Franklin Street, she stared up at the huge Astral, filling a whole block between Java and India streets for six stories with six separate houses. Patterned brickwork and rock-face brownstone cohered in the arches and lintels. Apartments were rare for any class at

31

the time, and most worker families crowded into firetraps of houses, yet here was ultramodern housing that Charles Pratt had commissioned for his kerosene refinery workers.[3]

Breathless, she knocked at the fifth-floor door of a domestic science teacher from Minneapolis, who told her more about factories, children, tenements, health conditions than Ovington, living six miles away, had even thought to ask. Seeing the vacant apartment across the hall piqued her interest. She looked down on the East River and glimpsed the glowing spires of St. Patrick's Cathedral. There were a fireplace, bookcases, enough corner space for a table and gleaming kerosene lamp, and light buff walls gracing the living room, two bedrooms, kitchen, and scullery.

The women climbed to the roof and walked down into another section where a basement room became a gymnasium at night and a kindergarten in the morning. Nearby were spaces for domestic science and sewing classes. Together with a library already busy with neighborhood children, this made up the tenement's social service work.

Ovington was to serve as first vice president of the Pratt Institute Neighborship Association, which sent volunteers to the Astral. President Margaret Healy believed that the newly instituted extension work needed a full-time resident to coordinate and expand activities. She would need tact, sympathy, resourcefulness, and inventiveness, and must not rouse any suspicion of "reform work." Ideally, the head resident would be considered a teacher.[4]

Ovington had entered a strange land, for class lines in the United States, then as now, were real if subtle. Crossing them to live among the workers had just begun to capture the imaginations of young middle-class women in 1895. Only a few cities had settlements—New York, Chicago, Boston, London—and all of these were in their first decade. So it was with a distinct feeling of daring that she unpacked her trunk that September in her new flat.

Trolley cars crashed down the street below, steamboats whistled on the river, factory whistles shrieked early and late, bugs invaded from upstairs—but it was all hers. With her favorite possessions she enjoyed putting her four "viewsome little rooms" in order.

In her mind, Ovington's ideal settlement differed from Jane Addams's communal living at Hull House in Chicago. "The cluttered companionship of settlements tends at times to confuse rather than to clarify our ideas," she thought. For her first two years at Greenpoint, she was largely alone when she retreated to her own rooms, even though a cousin just out of college stayed with her one winter, and Frances Davenport worked nearby and lived at the Astral.[5] A neighbor woman cleaned once a week; otherwise she did her own housework.

Ovington threw herself into the art of the settlement. She visited Women's University Settlement in London in 1896, and Hull House for the first time in 1899. But primarily she learned firsthand for seven years. "I was a scholar as truly as when mulling over the book stacks in the Harvard Library. . . . I wanted knowledge. . . . I got a little."

OVINGTON QUICKLY FOUND that her first and last concern in seven years at Greenpoint was the street boy. Mothers and fathers, babies and working girls came and went, she found, but "the street boy stays by the settlement forever. He is its Alpha and Omega."

"Say teacher, when yer going to take us to the park again?"

"Say, teacher, that guy living below yer give me a kick when I went by. Naw, I didn't ring his bell, Jimmy done that."

"Say, can't we have a club, too? We ain't got no club."

Nothing rebuffed this lad. Dismissed sternly from a class one day he turned up innocently the next. Quite ingenious, he could prove he didn't steal the knife in woodworking class even if you saw him slip it into his pocket.

Ovington found the street boy a frustration, a delight, and a key to American character. His affection was transient. He would run to walk close at her side, but a wagon, trolley, or fire engine would attract his attention, and he was off. He rushed through basketry, chair caning, weaving jute mats, whittling, and hammock making indifferently.

"His only playground is the street" was the Greenpoint reality, for once out of mother's arms, children had no place else to be. Ovington brought Mrs. Dennis blocks for her toddler, James, and later unthinkingly asked about them. The mother looked embarrassed. "I had to throw them things in the fire. They was always under my feet." Children, too, were always under someone's feet, so the sooner outside the better.

Streets by the Astral, while not wicked, were outrageous places for play, Ovington could see. No game could ever be finished. Her boys threw balls when the policeman's back was turned; footraces were interrupted; a top would be kicked just when spinning its best. Shooting craps and throwing dice, she thought, became so popular because they could be carried on in a retired doorway.

At school they learned some reading and arithmetic that they might use when they went out to work, but mostly it had no relation to their lives. No lessons trained active young hands to create useful things, or to repair broken chairs and machines at home. They knew only how to hang onto a trolley car or awkwardly grasp a pencil. Only those young men the schools defined as incorrigibles and truants received any manual training. Otherwise school meant sitting still, which led to the wildness of young colts at the end of the day.

Street boys loved coming to her rooms to recite their exploits while she tried to read to them. Once with the youngest, she held up alphabet cards to find that they knew only *S*, *C*, and *P*, for cities with baseball teams. Those a bit older read newspapers for drama, a fight, or a robbery, and they read books not at all. There were no moving pictures to arouse their imaginations. Their ethnic backgrounds made no difference. "Scotch, Irish, Jew, German, Swede, Italian, English, they were all daredevil Americans."

What could the settlement do with this energy? They had none of the equipment needed for trade work, and Pratt volunteers taught sewing or millinery or home nursing—girl stuff. Ovington had an idea. Why couldn't desperate mothers find cooking help in their sons as well as their overworked daughters? She picked a half dozen boys and told them of the great chefs of the world, emphasizing wages. Then she left them with a charming volunteer and went to her office. In fifteen minutes, the young woman was at her door in tears.

"I can do nothing with them," she cried. "They eat every bit of food I give them to cook—flour, butter, sugar, salt, potatoes. . . . They've eaten every single thing except the meat." So much for cooking classes for the boys.

The fifteen- and sixteen-year-olds wanted to stage a show and raise money for gym equipment; they would take care of everything, they assured Ovington. She set a time limit for the event, and confidently invited her governing board, expecting to be bored with this thing they called Vaudeville. Instead she was mortified.

The curtain on the makeshift stage opened to a Jew and an Irishman who "greeted each other with all the vulgarity of America," as the shocked Ovington described it. After insults, one knocked off the other's hat, the other punched back, and both sprawled on the floor to loud, delighted applause from the audience. Through slapstick and horseplay, jokes and punches, drunks and boobs, even a girl doing the splits, the cheeks of Miss Ovington burned.

"I sat at the rear,"

long skirt to within two inches of the floor, white shirt waist with a high collar, and looked, first at the stage then at the door, watched for the moment when one of my Board members might come. This was what I was doing! This was the culture that was being brought to Greenpoint! No excuse could be made. I was responsible and I alone.

The clock ticked away the long minutes, but thankfully, no one came from headquarters to see her shame. Suddenly, the boys set up a long table and began to open bottles that looked like beer. She rushed up to be told reprovingly, "Nothing but soft drink, Miss Ovington," as they poured ginger ale and sarsaparilla. It was a long time before she was able to laugh about that night.

Ovington tried all the latest hypotheses. They would open their doors to all the youngsters space allowed. Every Wednesday night the happy mob invaded the gym—and every Thursday morning a line of tenants complained at her office. They tried small groups. "And they came, of course they came, when it was their night and when it wasn't!"

She and her staff never really entered into the life of any boy that she could see except to give him a fairly good time. "His world and ours did not click." In all, these capable, intelligent boys led bleak lives. "Undirected energy, moving without purpose or if with purpose an unsocial one, is dull at heart," she believed.

Summers were better, when swimming in the river lent the luxury of cleanliness. Summer also meant Country Week, which had both the health benefits of being scrubbed to go and the time in the country itself. Sentiment buttoned up under winter jackets, emerged in the open fields. One perpetual rascal shyly handed her a bouquet of daisies, murmuring, "It makes you feel good to be here, doesn't it?"

Ovington and her staff created one of the first playgrounds in the city in a vacant lot facing the river. Carpenters donated time, shops provided nails, and lumberyards gave timber for swings and sandboxes and awnings. She had not realized until then how many friends they had or how eager people are to cooperate in a healthy project.

She loved to sit on a bench near the children's ceaseless activity. Which summer sound was sweetest to tired hearts? she asked in "By the Playground," published in *Outlook*. Her family teased her for her poetic answer. Sweetest was not the sound of the country or the sea. "Childhood's treble of hope" on that East River playground got her vote.

> Hot winds bearing the noise
> Of a city's traffic and cries,
> And from the little square
> The voices of children in song.
> Hundreds of children at play
> Circling and singing their glee;
> . . .
> This is the summer sound
> The sweetest the tired heart knows.[6]

"If you like it it gets you; if you don't it's bedlam," she laughed. "It was the children, their riotous spirits, that kept us alert, courageous, even optimistic in Greenpoint."

Only a few grammar school graduates went to high school in Greenpoint; most went to work. The racing, snitching, daredevil street boy became reasonable overnight and brought his pay home to mother. They learned discipline and sometimes moved into the white-collar class. But Ovington saw painfully that most were cheated out of a good childhood, and gangs inevitably had more appeal than school or settlements. Unfortunately, she found, "the world of crime could seem heroic, but the virtuous world, as we make it, has nothing to offer but a song or pingpong."

Her unadulterated success with youthful energy was in dance, winter or summer, hot weather or cold. Young people needed fun, in her view; perhaps the working class more than most. Millinery, cooking, sewing, gymnasium grew tedious, but dancing, never. She wrote: "My but it's hot," one of the boys would say, mopping his brow, as he led his partner to her seat. "It's too hot for anything but to dance," and he would lead another partner upon the floor.

Girls enjoyed the playground, country week, and dances, too, but they had different needs, expectations, and limitations. Ovington first determined to concentrate on the seemingly forgotten females but soon realized why most agencies did boys' work. Boys needed activity; girls were swamped with responsibilities at home. As soon as they could hold a plate, they were in charge of wiping dishes. Little more than babies themselves, they diapered and wheeled the latest family addition. They seemed to need strenuous physical activity; once freed to let loose, the street boys' sisters could be just as rowdy as the guys.

The head resident found coming to grips with the girls' sexual precocity more difficult. She allowed four thirteen-year-olds to give a raucous mixed Halloween party. Ovington returned from fetching a broom to sweep up tossed cake to find half of the girls "sitting double" in the boys' laps.

After a few days she invited the young hostesses to dinner to talk over the party. "Do you think it is right for girls to sit in boys' laps?" she asked them. One girl blushed and fell silent, but another earnestly stood to their defense. Ovington was making too much of it: "We had to. There were not enough chairs to go round."

"I had all of the romantic conception of sex given me by the Victorian novelist and little knowledge of its ugly aspects," Ovington recalled. One girl stood night after night in the tenement hallway, unwilling to enter the classroom. Soon her family moved away and she disappeared. Another very pretty girl became the mistress of a New Yorker, making her mother both ashamed and pleased with the money.

Young girls talked and walked with men in doorways and poorly lit thoroughfares, surprising and disturbing the head resident. But then Ovington thought of her own courting days and understood the young women's need:

Maggie could not get to know her young man if she only met him by the kitchen stove under the eyes of questioning parents and teasing brothers. What chance did this give for the half rude, half coquettish answers to sly questions that went with the making of a "gentleman friend"? The birds fly thousand of miles for their courtships, and are free from infantile interruptions or parental demands. Maggie was justified in slipping down stairs.

Mary White Ovington, 1893, at age twenty-eight, from a *carte de visite*. Photograph by Notman Studio, Boston. (By permission of the Archives of Labor and Urban Affairs, Wayne State University)

Mary White Ovington, 1902, at age thirty-seven. Photograph by Gardner and Company, Thos. W. Taylor. (By permission of Archives of Labor and Urban Affairs, Wayne State University)

In a short unpublished story Ovington explored her understanding of how living conditions led to promiscuity and prostitution for young women of the poorer classes, and, more important, how privileged men took advantage of and perpetuated these circumstances. In "The Price of a Coat," a hungry, young, working woman has accepted a restaurant meal from a wealthy man. When he subsequently tries to "have his way with her" in an alley, she berates him with his attempt to purchase her self and honor with the price of the cheap coats she sells all day long.[7]

A settlement worker didn't wait for people to come to planned activities; she visited homes. If the children were rude American style, the parents exuded Old World courtesy. But the streets and houses in which they attempted to live decently displayed deepening darkness, disease, and death. Ovington climbed tenement steps to talk with mothers over stoves and washtubs. Annie needed gymnasium work. There was a chance they could find Otto a job. She persuaded Mrs. Mulvaney to go to the hospital and sat by Christina at the dental clinic.

Ovington's visits included the "railroad tenements" in the poorer area neighboring the Astral. Workers crammed the twenty-five-by-one-hundred-foot buildings; air and light disappeared. Between the front parlor and rear kitchen squeezed two or three tiny bedrooms, windowless or opening on a narrow, foul-smelling airshaft in which garbage collected and where vermin squirmed.

Railroad tenements were expensive; cheaper were old houses remodeled for housekeeping on each floor, with more light but execrable sanitation. The last resort was the rear house, where the breath of life became a luxury. On summer evenings mothers rocked babies at the front windows, fathers stood on the sidewalk smoking or left for the saloon, boys and girls raced over the hot pavement until midnight. Exhaustion was a prerequisite for sleep in the suffocating inner rooms.

As she clambered up dark, foul-smelling stairs, Ovington never ceased to contrast these homes and lives with her own. The space and sunshine of her childhood were the right of every child: "the right to health and beautiful surroundings, to companionship and privacy," the right to a bed of one's own, to books and pictures. Each week, month, and year one lesson was indelibly etched:

> That the men who dug the sewers and paved the streets, who laid the tracks and ran the cars, who tended the machinery of the mill and stood at the anvil, who built the houses and pointed the spires of the great

churches, however hard and faithfully they worked could not give their children what my father had given me.

Ovington enormously admired the women who managed households under these conditions, and tried to give them some help. One success was the Penny Provident Bank. On Monday nights the hall filled with youthful depositors sent by their mothers with a quarter or dollar, saved for a winter coat or next month's rent. Bennie, clutching his nickel, told Miss Ovington, "Me brother gave it to me—fer sleeping on the inside of the bed." Into the bank it went with other nickels and dimes in exchange for a stamp to be cashed in later.

All family funds, from the wages of the husband to the smallest earner, went through the wife's hands, and each family member's needs were met. Some "mother administrators," Ovington noted, were ambitious enough to move the family into one of the suburbs beyond Long Island City. When babies stopped coming and young people started earning, then the mother could look ahead. One young settlement resident, chosen to do the group's marketing, conversed with a neighborhood woman over the cabbage. "Prices are going up—I don't know how am I going to fill the mouths of eight children," she lamented. "And I have to shop for ten," said the resident. The older woman patted her reassuringly: "They be a comfort to you when they grow up."

The settlement organized a kindergarten mothers' meeting to study poetry. The leader, Caroline Weeks, told her surprised and pleased boss: "We read Wordsworth—they understand 'the weary weight of this unintelligible world.'" Adult education should discover shared interests and passions, Ovington concluded. "It is our common life that matters, and . . . to stay apart from it is the death of art, of politics, and of religion."

Ovington often took mothers and babies on day trips, particularly in the summer. One year the local streetcar company sent them to the beach in private cars. With "joyful arrogance" they zipped past the pedestrians and out into the open fields. The return was a bit less cheerful, with tired mothers and cross babies, but such events were respites in demanding lives.

On one trip for young people on a crisp November day, to the home and woods of a clergyman friend of Ovington, she felt the frustration of the young women who could see only lives like their mothers' ahead. They scuffled in fallen leaves and gathered hickory nuts, before being entertained by the minister's children singing a vesper hymn. Returning on the train, Ovington sat next to a hardworking German girl from a large family who murmured, her eyes wet: "Please don't think that we wouldn't like a home like that. We know what it means. . . . But we just can't."

In the dirty, low-paying jute mills near the Astral, while the settlement residents turned over for a last little doze, factory whistles ordered the girls of Greenpoint to rope and rug making. For ten hours a day noise of machinery filled their ears, and overheated, dusty, devitalized air filled their lungs. Mills were dangerous, and employees often younger than the law allowed. One day a doctor came to the settlement clinic about an injured girl. Ovington hurried to find the child lying in sickly gray light, one of her fingers cut off and her hand badly bruised. Mamie was eleven.

Ovington sought out the factory superintendent, who knew all about it. The girls had been warned, but the child had stuck her finger into a fascinating little hole. "I am very sorry for Mamie," he went on earnestly, "and I want you to know that we shall always find something for her to do at the mill." The factory doctor took care of her hand free, and soon Mamie was back at work.

Ovington ended up in the same trap as the parents, for the families desperately needed the money. From a friend in the mill, she learned that many children were employed illegally. When inspectors came, the little ones rushed of their own accord to hide. The only labor unions were weak and did nothing. Correcting a small wrong without dealing with the larger economic injustice was no solution. Ovington did nothing, either.

Slowly she learned the way of the world in Greenpoint. In one class a mischievous Clarence Manderson took two bags of candy from the Christmas tree so ingratiatingly that commenting on it seemed to betray a trust. Soon he was in her assistant's club giving the name Chalker. Ovington called on the family and brought up the two names. Clarence's fine-looking father looked her over carefully and decided to confide.

"I'm a trolley driver and was a leader in the strike we had in Philadelphia a while ago. They got me on the blacklist so I came here and used my wife's name, Chalker. But Clarence, he forgets about it."

Clarence, listening intently, grinned. "I told 'em Chalker the last time."

Ovington had considered strikes and strikebreaking from the point of view of the official violence of the breakers. One of her friends from childhood, for example, had been called in to break up a strike as a member of Brooklyn's Thirteenth Regiment. He assured her that you had to fire on the mob and let them know you meant business. Mr. Manderson was her first face-to-face acquaintance with a striker. "I grew to know a little about labor, its hours, its conditions, its power when organized, its helplessness when, like the little girls, it can only run into a closet."

Ovington's friend Helen Marot of the Women's Trade Union League told settlement workers that a girl in organized labor would have nothing to do with a settlement, that she would resist the suggestion of charity. But unions were not strong in Greenpoint, and there were no strikes of any importance during Ovington's seven years there.

Did the settlement and its activities make any difference in the lives of these working girls? The greatest benefit was indirect, Ovington thought, through the marching and club-swinging of the girls' athletic drill team, who performed to filled gymnasiums. The young women were much helped by exercise, Ovington reported to her board: they carried themselves better and grew more muscular. "Indeed," she added, "were it only that the scholars are obliged to wear loose, healthful clothing for one evening a week, great good would have been accomplished"![8]

But as a whole, she felt her work was "next to nothing in those deadly wearisome, monotonous lives. While the factory stood there and drew these girls into its maw we were ridiculous, pulling an occasional girl from this life, but making not the slightest impression on the conditions that debased youth."

No one on her staff was capable of handling a men's club, so she made no attempt to organize them. Their primary social activity— heavy drinking—created havoc in many families, however; she heard the cursing and fighting nightly. Ovington's observations supported later findings that two men out of seven were unable to take alcohol without serious results. The problem drinkers were often good workers and kindly fathers and husbands, but when they fell into the habit encouraged by their friends and by saloon keepers, the family found little help.

One such family broke Ovington's heart. The MacClarens on the first floor in her unit had a toddler, John, whose father drank up his weekly pay. Mrs. MacClaren had a hard time making ends meet and, with the arrival of another baby, took to drink herself. Ovington wanted to adopt little John MacClaren. Throughout her life she befriended and mentored children, but John MacClaren may be the only child she considered making legally her own. She wrote:

> I would go by the window just to see him there and would want him so! But how could I with all the work I had to do take care of a child as well? That they would let me have him I did not doubt. One day I missed him. When the next morning the window sill was again empty I went to the superintendent.
>
> "The MacClarens! Turned 'em out. They didn't pay their rent and were a disgrace. When a woman gets to drinking!"

Drinking meant the same to all classes—"People want a good time and after a hard day's work a stiff drink brings a good time." Yet, as Ovington saw it:

> when you bid good-by to a young soldier he has about the same chance of being killed or disabled as the drinker has. Isn't it justifiable to be anxious even fearful for him? So we who have seen our John Mac-Clarens may be excused for our old fashioned views, our anxiety.

One man of Greenpoint became a special friend. Jack Dennis looked like Kipling's Captain Courageous, a tall, black-eyed former sailor. He had visited ports of the Orient and the Occident and had worked with all races of men. When their talk turned political, she asked him if he had voted for Seth Low, mayoral candidate on the reform ticket.

"No"—he shook his head. "I used to be a democrat, but I believe now it's my duty to join with my class and vote its ticket."

"What ticket is that?" she asked, mystified.

"The Socialist," Dennis responded.

ONLY LATER DID she understand. But for the first time Mary White Ovington had met a person of the party she would promote and follow the rest of her life. She came to socialism through one who voted with his class, not through middle- and upper-class adherents she would meet in the Social Reform Club.

Family ties were strong in the homes of her settlement clients, but living conditions meant real constraints on family activities. The only vision was escape, and every year, the most prudent and thrifty did just that. Every year, the settlement boys and girls with the most ability came to say good-bye:

> And though sad at heart, we rejoiced at their good fortune and watched new boys and girls and fathers and mothers move into the tiny, unattractive quarters that the vision had made vacant. For conditions never improved, larger numbers were always coming to take the places of those who had left.

As Ovington studied working-class families, she formulated her "law of average ability":

> If you take a large group of people in any community and compare it with a large group of people in another community you will find that the average of ability is about the same; and this average will show the bulk of the population at the mean with a few above and a few below.

She illustrated her law from her college experience, where Harvard students (men) were graded with about 20 percent *A*'s or *B*'s; 20 percent *D*'s or *F*'s; and 60 percent, the majority, among the *C*'s, and if you went a little way up into the *B*'s and a little down into the *D*'s, you would have close to 70 percent of this population right in the middle. (This did not apply in the same way to the women at Harvard Annex, she noted, who were a very select, studious group.)

She applied this "law" to Brooklyn Heights and Greenpoint. First, every community had the same distribution of ability, with the majority average, unless immigration had lured the ablest, or popularity brought to a district an exceptional amount of ability. Diversity within groups was thus more significant than differences between communities.

Second, in every neighborhood the *A*'s, unless handicapped by illness, would forge ahead. In Greenpoint they might become union leaders or political bosses, or, more likely, would move away and see their children scramble into the class above. They would avail themselves of settlement help. The *F*'s in Greenpoint would have to be helped at home, or receive organized charity, or would make their sad way to the hospital or almshouse or prison.

She was most interested in the large majority—those 60 to 70 percent who were *C*'s, low *B*'s, and high *D*'s. She watched an *A* boy, Malcolm, weaving a reed basket. He did not enjoy it, but the task was there and he meant to finish. He had a clear mind and persistence. Settlements and the United States offered him much; he would succeed. But next to Malcolm sat four good-natured, ordinary youngsters who worked when they felt like it and quit when it bored them. They were capable and intelligent, but lacked Malcolm's intensity. What was their future?

Here class and community entered with a vengeance, she concluded. In Brooklyn Heights, business and professional opportunities awaited boys like this. With average good work, they would live comfortably. But Greenpoint boys of the same ability and working to the same level, were condemned. She wondered:

> How was it then? Would the great majority of the children of the working class always be poorly clothed and underfed, forced to spend their lives in cramped rooms on ugly streets? Would the summers always find them in their crowded quarters choking, restless, nervous, while a few blocks away the closed blinds of spacious houses showed that the children of the well-to-do class were by the sea, bathing in the refreshing water, or at the mountains, climbing in the clear, bracing air, or dabbling in sundappled brooks? . . . Was the child of the working class always to be shut out from the beauty and health and stimulating surroundings that had made my own childhood so happy and so excellent a preparation for future work?

She had no answer, but the question had been posed.

Greenpoint Settlement (officially The Neighborship Settlement), under Mary White Ovington as head resident between 1895 and 1902, was by any assessment except perhaps her own long-term one, a success. After her first year, she was euphoric at being "young and strong and at work in the world of men." They had served several hundred residents with a kindergarten; classes in sewing, cooking, gymnastics, manual training, millinery, art, commercial arts; a library; and a part-time medical clinic. She had a staff of five residents and thirty-four volunteers.

They needed more space and residents. Ovington recommended settlement work to "anyone who has been lonely in her student life." She took Thomas Carlyle's cry as their watchword:

> It is great and there is no other greatness. To make some nook of God's Creation a little fruitfuler, better, more worthy of God; to make some human hearts a little wiser, manfuller, happier,—more blessed, less accursed! It is work for a God.

Eventually they filled the whole of House F, one-sixth of the block-long building, forty rooms, with a full-time librarian and an assistant, kindergarten and music teachers, a nurse, an assistant to the head resident, and Laura Steel, who would take over as head after Ovington. They hired a cook, and like Jane Addams, Ovington headed the table and carved the roast beef.

Ovington was very clear on the differences between settlement work and charity; in her reports and in speaking to the Brooklyn Ethical Association, she repeated variations of the words *neighbor* and *friend*. "The power is with the people"; the settlement was "to help them help themselves."[9]

But she also recognized the near-impossibility of the privileged entering the lives of working people. To truly aid the poor not just "when the suffering is so extreme we are shocked into a moment's generosity," but for life, would require that we sell all we have. Even more difficult, Ovington saw, we would have to renounce

> our most cherished possession, our attitude of superiority to our fellows. Caste, more than wealth, is our jasper, our stone most precious. . . . We seek by entertaining to gladden poverty. . . . At the summer blossoming we gather flowers . . . together, but we are always Lady Bountifuls, and they are always children of the Poor.

Frequent trips across the East River helped Mary White Ovington weave together observation and theory. The ferry waited four blocks from the Astral, and New York lay closer than her parents in Brooklyn Heights. At the southern tip of Manhattan, every man had his three-cent *New York Evening Post*. Here, everyone had in hand the one-cent New York *Journal*.

Ovington had grown up despising the latter's sensational yellow journalism, and she wondered at its popularity in Greenpoint. For months she read and compared the two, questioning those who were fond of the one-center. She published her conclusions in an article in one of America's most powerful weeklies, the *Outlook*, in 1904.[10] In Brooklyn Heights, reading the newspaper was a way to access "news": matters of city, state, national, and world affairs. Crime and sports stories were not prominent.

The *Journal*, which papered Greenpoint, met different needs. It was the home library in a working-class community, giving readers

fact, dramatically dressed up, fiction in perfectly unimportant stories of people wholly unknown. Crime, featured to take the place of Anna Catherine Green's *Hand and the Ring* or Rider Haggard's *She*. Essays, Arthur Brisbane was a good essayist, and even poetry in Dora Wheeler Wilcox. Why should I expect my girls to take out library books when in a column, or even a paragraph, they could get it all in the *Journal?*

Ovington had no objection to imaginative literature, but she was "enraged" that "news" in either the staid or the sensationalist press was so limited to the unusual. "We learn nothing of the every day life of a people."

The *Journal*'s Labor Section held nothing but notices of union meetings. Ovington observed that, "Here was this community of people ignorant of what was happening about them, never brought together for any common purpose, reading as news, matters that had no bearing upon their lives."

The reporters who came to write up settlement dances did not begin to meet the need for information. They "skimmed over the water like some long-legged monstrosity but knew and cared nothing for what went on beneath." Later, as she learned more about manipulation of and by media, she understood that, even had the reporter "dropped down and pulled up some tightly shut oyster, he would not have been allowed to open it." America's newspapers served the haves and kept the have-nots quiet.

The Social Reform Club (SRC) on Manhattan gave her analyses a boost, though she was first drawn to it by "social good times, which to a young woman means good times with men." The SRC brought together people who did not normally meet in economically class-conscious America: the intelligentsia or business class, and the working class. If possible, there were to be equal numbers of wage earners and others. Members were to have a "deep interest in social reform," especially the "elevation of society by the improvement of the conditions of wage-workers."[11] The intelligentsia came eagerly, and, Ovington quickly observed, did most of the talking. Single-tax advocate Ernest Howard Crosby was a talker, and also a "whole-hearted gentleman," she discovered. W. J. Ghent, who created a stir with an article on "Our Benevolent Feudalism," was "one of our ardent conservative socialists," Ovington remembered—perhaps with a double entendre on "ardent," for Ghent became a close friend. Novelist and "Dean of American Letters," William Dean Howells read from his books. Among the "more practical" male club participants, Ovington particularly remembered Charles Stover, who started America's first playground.

Two women influenced her. The first, Josephine Shaw Lowell, represented the best of the intelligentsia membership. Sister of Robert Gould Shaw, leader of the Black Fifty-fourth Massachusetts, and widow of a man who had also died in the Civil War, Lowell always wore black and had the steadfast appearance of a nun. She believed that the privileged class "should toil as any working girl would have to toil, as their wages just happened to be paid in advance."

Leonora O'Reilly came from the other end of the social scale. "As the membership stands at present I am the only woman wage-earner," O'Reilly told a correspondent, "that is: a woman who works at a common trade, and gets about half of what she is worth." In discussions that needed the working woman's point of view, she noted, "My sister members of the SRC insist on my taking the trouble to torture the rest of the members with my eloquence and my factory made logic."[12]

Ovington knew the basic Marxist argument, that under socialism the economic life of the people would be in the hands of the state, administered for the benefit of all the creators of that wealth. She read "the books that my friends were finding publishers for and sending out into the world": the works of Ghent and British-born author John Spargo and muckraker Charles Edward Russell, and "millionaire socialist" Robert Hunter. These works left no doubt in her mind about "the horrors of the present system but . . . did little to describe the state to come."

But she had ever fuller contexts for her observations. As she said, when you first found out such things as that 10 percent of the people of the country owned 90 percent of the wealth, and were familiar with some of the vile vile conditions of poverty, the dark tenements, the exhausting toil in the factory, the life so far from the beauty and health of the life that had always been yours, your hatred of present day conditions became [the] most intense emotion of your life.

Ovington was already thirty-six years old when a Social Reform Club event changed her life forever. She was chairman of a committee planning a dinner for Booker T. Washington.[13] One of the committee members was Charles Spahr, an editor of *Outlook*, where Washington's autobiography, *Up from Slavery*, had been appearing. Spahr wanted the speech to include mention of conditions in the North, including New York City.

Ovington read the *Atlantic* as well as *Outlook*, so had seen W. E. B. Du Bois's two essays that were soon to be part of *Souls of Black Folk*. Thus she was fully aware of the deepening division between the black leaders themselves, and leaned toward Du Bois, who "stirred complacency," while Washington "made everyone happy." Yet Washington's speech at the dinner in April 1901,[14] shocked Ovington in its revelation that there was a "Negro problem" in her backyard, something she had not considered: "I accepted the Negro as I accepted any other element in the population. That he suffered more from poverty, from segregation, from prejudice than any other race in the city was a new idea to me."

She left the dinner with her head abuzz and her heart ablaze. She climbed the stairs to her rooms at the Astral and took down James Russell Lowell's "The Present Crisis." Her eyes slid over the words she knew by heart.

> Once to every man and nation
>   Comes the moment to decide
> In the strife of truth with falsehood
>   For the good or evil side.

That night she chose the cause against wage slavery. But big choices are easier than the small ones that implement them, and she still did not know what exactly she was going to *do*.

When she left Greenpoint, much there had changed. The public school held classes in settlement subjects—cooking, sewing, handicrafts—and their kindergarten and library had become part of the public systems. Churches did club work they had initiated, and the YMCA had taken over activities for boys. "We were not as needed as we had been," Ovington could see. Their real contribution to social welfare work was in pioneering.

Mary White Ovington resigned in June 1903, tired, unhappy, and unsettled. She returned to the White Mountains of Shelburne, New Hampshire, within three miles of the site of her epiphany in nature at age eleven.

The drought of 1876 was repeated in 1903, and the slowly burning mountains towered close at hand:

> Leaves that at a touch dissolved into ashes floated through the air. The pleasant haze so often over the mountains became a dull grey that each day obscured the landscape a little more until we seemed in a dry fog. And in this growing twilight was always the smell of smoke.

Ovington said later that she *chose* in New Hampshire to come down with the only severe illness of her life, typhoid fever. Undoubtedly she meant that her body and soul, needing closure and renewal, chose for her. Since she "did nothing by rule," her illness, too, was different; extremely intense but also very short—otherwise "I would have burned up like a mountain tree on Baldcap." Her inexorably cruel delirium convinced her "that the idea of heaven and hell undoubtedly came from the effects of a high fever on the human body." She ascended again into the world just as nature, too, recovered from its trial by fire. She recalled:

> It was raining, a quiet steady rain, one of the loveliest things to feel on one's face, a rain that I knew was quenching the fire and soaking the hot, thirsty earth. Next morning I heard purple martins chuckling as they flew home and saw the light in my mother's face.

Recovery from severe illness was "always memorable," she thought, but especially so in "an enchanted room that looks out into the trees and where the air is filled with songs of birds and insects," and where nature's life has newly begun with one's own. Her recovery was a "rare and beautiful experience," accompanied by a prodigious appetite, "as though one had never eaten before and all the luscious tastes that had become commonplace were fresh unknown, like the first taste of ice cream to a thirsty child."

The doctor prescribed fish, and Ovington's mother, who had never fished in her life, threw a line in the brook and caught a half-pound trout. "So everything luscious and tempting was placed on a golden platter before me while the beauty of the world, its love and its gentle peace was given to me as though I were newly born."

Her friend and minister, John White Chadwick, was also very ill that early summer. He wondered affectionately from Chesterfield, which of them came nearer the Fortunate Isles. "Both of us pretty near, I think." Such an experience had a touch of solemnity, he found, but it also dramatically deepened joy. "These hills and streams and skies never seemed as beautiful to me before, nor the books so good, nor the friends so precious,"[15] he wrote.

The need for a long period of no work and no worries, delayed decisions for almost a year for Ovington. She idled through the winter with her parents, and in the spring they all went to Sicily for four weeks. Here she had to face once again the pollution and poverty of the world.

Her mind expected the loveliness of Hawthorne's *Tanglewood Tales*, with Pluto stealing Proserpina from the lush Garden of Europe, but her senses found wispy patches of grain, denuded mountains, and rivers of mud. "Sicily had been raped, not by a God but by man."

What was she going to do? She was close to forty and as undirected as a child. Home with her parents she could have anything she wanted. It was the expected thing that an unmarried woman would "accept as her responsibility the companionship of her parents." But she knew if she did not find continual, challenging work, she would become one of those women on whom she looked with condescension, "who served on committees like the old ladies home and the free kindergarten [and] the Y.W.C.A. and the Improvement of Civic Conditions, a dabbler in philanthropy." She abhorred such a prospect.

Perhaps she could create a settlement where she had learned there was most need in New York: in the black community. Of course there would be much she must learn. Slowly, she outlined a plan of study and action. Once again, nature sent her back to the city, sustaining the heart that loved her.

3

From Social Researcher to Activist

TO ACT ON her new resolve to work toward a settlement for blacks on Manhattan, Mary White Ovington would have to venture into forbidden territory. Black Americans in the first decade of the twentieth century were invisible even to settlement workers, reformers, socialists, and university social scientists.[1]

She turned to the man who by 1903 was Booker T. Washington's foremost opponent in seeking black equal rights: W. E. B. Du Bois, professor of sociology at Atlanta University, author of the critical essay "Of Mr. Booker T. Washington and Others" in his 1903 *Souls of Black Folk*. The two men disagreed on the most effective way to seek full equality. Washington thought that black economic power achieved through basic, essential work supported by vocational education would eventually lead to full rights for black people. Du Bois believed that civil rights and voting rights must be demanded simultaneously to protect property and that education must go beyond the vocational.

Over the following years Mary White Ovington almost invisibly became more than just a barometer of the shift from Washington's gradualist, accommodationist, segregationist, low-pressure position to the high pressure of Du Bois's demands for total equality. Ovington helped create the climatic change both in her influence on Du Bois and in pushing three powerful men toward his side: John Milholland, a wealthy industrialist, and Oswald Garrison Villard and Ray Stannard Baker, influential journalists.

Ovington first wrote Du Bois from her summer study at the School of Philanthropy in New York in 1904, where she was researching the "economic opportunities for young Negro men and women in New York." She had read his work, and thought he would have information and contacts to suggest.[2]

Mutual interests and contacts quickly spurred Ovington and Du Bois into a strong friendship. Three years older, Ovington became the expert Du Bois depended on for news of conditions in New York. His analytical approach to race in the United States resembled the scientific analysis and action promoted by William Ashley at the Harvard Annex.

She told Du Bois immediately that her goal was to open a settlement for blacks in Manhattan—she didn't want just to add a few facts to knowledge of their conditions. She had experience—seven years as head resident in Greenpoint. "I want very much to talk with you," she concluded. "You see, you have talked to me through your writings for many years and have lately made me want to work as I never wanted to work before." She recognized the taboo she faced: "I shall want to recommend the two races working together in a settlement, and that shall seem very radical."

Despite the number of unsolicited letters Du Bois received, he replied quickly. Surprised at this request from a white woman, Du Bois also warned her that she would need to meet with Negroes, and not shy away from them. "Indeed, I think it is you who must shrink from me," Ovington responded warmly. "When I read the . . . nauseating magazine and newspaper writing on the race question I feel ashamed and abashed." It was no time for the Anglo-Saxon "to rejoice in his race's generosity or gentleness of spirit," Ovington believed.[3]

The two continued to write while she attended Hampton Institute's summer conference in 1904, her first plunge into the Negro world. Never had she seen more attractive people or been so pleased by clarity of thought, ably expressed. "These colored speakers could have debated any Southern writer I had read and wiped the floor with him."

Could Du Bois give her suggestions for her reading? Was there anyone besides Du Bois himself who gave facts, not just opinions? She wanted to know what the Negro had done and was doing here and in Africa. By October Ovington found it impossible to write as though they had not met.

If you will imagine yourself in my place go to your bookshelves and pick out one of our modern writers whose work you put among the best. Do you remember how you seized a magazine with that name on it, and read standing, too much interested to think to sit down? Wouldn't it be hard to write to that man or woman as though he were a stranger to you? Such a person is your friend, giving you courage and inspiration, and it is well nigh impossible to remember that while you know him he does not know you.[4]

That month, Du Bois published in the *Independent* his subsequently famous "Credo": "I believe in God, who made of one blood all nations that on earth do dwell." "I believe in Pride of race and lineage and self. . . . " "I believe in Service. . . . " "I believe that War is Murder." "I believe in Liberty for all men. . . ." "I believe in the Training of Children. . . . " "I believe in patience. . . ."

The Credo "makes me ache with anger at . . . my impotence," Ovington wrote him.

> Is it as hard, I wonder, when one is alone, away from the outside world, to be of a despised race as of a race that does such despicable deeds—I believe not.—But thinking of my own problem, it isn't the Negro only who suffers from the greed and the scramble for social precedence here in New York. I'm glad I have done many years of work among the laboring people before taking up a special race problem. I know how fierce the fight is for everyone.[5]

She enclosed a contribution to Du Bois's annual Atlanta publications. She didn't need her fellowship salary right now, she told him, since she was living with her parents.[6] Clearly Ovington tied her "impotence" to her lack of big money, understandable given the size of white contributions to Booker T. Washington and his "Tuskegee Machine." About her "widow's mite" contribution Du Bois jokingly asked if he had been unwittingly entertaining a millionaire, and expressed his happiness that she had read his "Credo." He was sorry she had been pained by it, though, for he believed that there were marvelous compensations.[7]

The "Credo" powerfully expresses Ovington's and Du Bois's focused idealism, phrased from the general ("Liberty") to the specific ("the right to vote, the freedom to choose . . . friends, enjoy the sunshine, and ride on the railroads"). Ovington sent Du Bois a decorated copy of it, and he sent her a separately printed version for framing. Appropriately, it arrived just after the death of her Unitarian mentor and friend, the Reverend John White Chadwick.

"We in Brooklyn have lately met with a deep loss," she wrote to Du Bois. "To those of us who had always known him, to whom he was not only the most inspired of preachers but the dearest of friends, it is like losing one's way in the new year."

In *Unity*, Ovington published a poem in Chadwick's memory in March 1905 which sought inspiration from his "empty seat, / and blackened ash."

> "Oh Lord," I pray, "let not my taper fail
> Now that his guiding fire has ceased to burn!
> Make quick with his my fading flame and pale
> That something of his light I may return."

In Chadwick and Du Bois, Ovington found friendship. In Du Bois she also found idealism combined with practical, interracial activism.[8]

Ovington's New York work began in Greenwich Village. The Greenwich Village Improvement Association was located from 1902 to 1917 at 26 Jones Street, a block crammed with fourteen hundred people from twenty-six countries. Men found drink at five saloons; children made artificial flowers; homeworkers made loaded dice.

Greenwich House and its head resident, Mary Simkhovitch, were associated with groups and individuals Ovington knew well: the Co-operative Social Settlement Society, with Jacob Riis and Felix Adler and Robert Fulton among its incorporators, and the Charity Organization Society (COS) and Josephine Shaw Lowell.[9] Greenwich House committees run by Columbia University professors sponsored research that "grew out of our daily experience," as Simkhovitch said. The committee on social studies published work on local housing, factory conditions, and old age poverty.[10]

Ovington pushed attention to the excluded blacks. "The feeling is so keen against them that it would not do to have them meet here in the House," Simkhovitch said.[11] But Ovington got the support of the COS and told Simkhovitch she wanted to "do some work among the Negroes, that I couldn't go on any longer at other settlement work, because I wanted to do work among that race and no other."[12]

So Simkhovitch told her board that

> it just so happens that . . . Miss Mary Ovington, formerly head worker at
> the Greenpoint Settlement, whose education at Radcliffe and at Pratt

and whose experience and sympathy eminently fit her for the best kind of settlement work is free and is very anxious to do settlement work among colored people. Perhaps if next year she could make a special study of the economic conditions of the negro [*sic*] in New York under our Social Investigation Committee especially as to employment and rent, the way would best be paved for social work of the best sort among colored people.[13]

The Greenwich House Committee on Social Investigations, of which Ovington became a Fellow, was ideal for her research. It maintained independence from the settlement board. Edwin R. A. Seligman chaired, and Vladimir G. Simkhovitch was secretary. Other members were the anthropologist Franz Boas, Edward T. Devine, Livingston Farrand, Franklin H. Giddings, and Henry R. Seager— "an august committee," Ovington said. "If I ever need especial guidance I may knock at any one of those Columbia college doors." Dr. Seligman, especially, was "genuinely sympathetic and anxious that I should find out some means of material and social betterment for the Negroes here in New York."[14] Seligman took advantage of Ovington's work by adding race issues to his College for Social Settlement Workers at Columbia.[15]

Ovington conducted her research as a "participant-observer," working on Cornelia Street one day a week for Greenwich House, forming a home library with the girls and beginning a boys' club in the evening. On Friday nights she helped Jessie Sleet with her girls' club at St. Phillip's Parish House. She told Du Bois that it would help her assess the effectiveness of this typical settlement activity.

She formed a sounding board of Sleet, visiting nurse for COS; Thomas Bell, secretary at the Colored YMCA, "one of two colored men who know most about social work in New York"; and Du Bois's cousin, Mr. Brown. "I tell them what I have found out and they out of their wider experience let me know better the significance of what I see."

For methodology she used Du Bois's impressive *Philadelphia Negro: A Social Study*, published in 1899, though she feared she could not possibly duplicate it. He received her running accounts. With Jeannette Moffett, a tenement inspector they both knew, Ovington climbed thousands of steps, joking that it was "the hardest kind of day labor." She concentrated on the "San Juan Hill" area with its "human hives, honeycombed with little rooms thick with human beings." On Sixty-first Street between Tenth and West End avenues, she found two Negro banks, two restaurants, a painter, two dealers in coal, a tailor, two grocers, and a shoemaker—"pretty good for one block," right? She devised schedules for calling on families, and directories of "every municipal building, church, saloon, etc. etc. so that one may see what the Negro quarters are like."

She spoke to workers at an Epworth League meeting at Dr. Brooks's A.M.E. church, and made use of a Mr. Mitchell's offer to help.

> I had thought of getting him to find out for me the pool rooms, policy shops and such like places in the region from 54th Street up to 64th. It would be rather jolly to put a Methodist investigating such things as that! and somebody must investigate them and I'm sure I can't.[16]

In her long letters to Du Bois, one sees Ovington's growing sense of the intermediary role she could play with her settlement, Social Reform Club, and liberal religious contacts. "I feel one thing strongly now," she explained, "and that is that the [Negro] leaders are not enough in touch with the municipal and philanthropic enterprises of the city."

Du Bois wanted her to come to Atlanta, but "I am the only one to push anything in regard to my work," she wrote him, "and every now and then there looks as though there were a chance of getting something of the money that is moving about very freely in New York." She had her eye on Henry Phipps's model tenement money.

Her plan would be controversial, but she wanted an interracial settlement in the proposed new building. A kindergarten managed by a board of Negro and white women needed better housing, and she wanted rooms for clubs and classes, and apartments for residents. "My thought was that if there were two white women who wanted to work in the settlement, they could have there [*sic*] own little flat and keep house, the same would be true of two colored workers." The rest of the building would be regular housing.

She knew objections would come from Negroes as well as whites. She had been told "if there is a settlement it should be entirely managed by colored people that whatever glory there is may be theirs." But, she asked, wouldn't there "be more glory if the Negro here in

New York has the white man to push him forward than if he tries to get an audience alone?"[17]

Mary White Ovington ambitiously embraced her new cause in 1904 and 1905. Here was challenging work that fit her concerns for justice and her growing skills in speaking and writing. In W. E. B. Du Bois she had found a colleague and a friend with whom help and inspiration would be reciprocal. Though the foundations of their friendship would crack and chip under personal and societal change, they would hold battered but firm to the end of their long lives.

———

OVINGTON SOON BEGAN to veer off the settlement path onto the larger route of sociological speaking and writing, beginning with a presentation at W. E. B. Du Bois's Tenth Atlanta Conference in May 1905. She had repeatedly postponed travel to Atlanta pending the Phipps project, so Du Bois finally just put her on the program for Tuesday, May 30, and insisted that she come. "Would I come? Of course I would!" Ovington said.

He wanted Ovington and Frances Kellor to address the mothers' meeting on "Child Study and the Kindergarten." "It has always seemed to me one of the humorous situations of mothers' meetings that they are usually addressed by unmarried women," Ovington laughingly responded, but she agreed to "make a try at talking." At least she would learn something from the mothers. Du Bois billed her as a "Fellow of Columbia University" and later featured her in his report to university president Horace Bumstead.[18] Ovington was pleased to speak to a Negro audience, for the white women at New York's Alcott Club, the Women's Club at Hartley House, and the Endeavor Club on Morton Street discouraged her in their objections to working with black women.[19]

On the first of many trips south, Ovington reached Atlanta in time for the baccalaureate on May 28, and stayed through commencement on June 1. At first sight the college was a disappointment—as with all schools built during the Victorian period, too high-windowed for their breadth and her taste; too many long staircases.

But Du Bois's warm welcome more than made up for it. She sat next to him in the large dining hall where black students and white teachers broke bread together. The professor looked like Shakespeare done in bronze, and "my cup of happiness was full," she wrote. He laughed at her initial seriousness. Du Bois commented to a teacher across the table that Miss Ovington seemed to think he was always weeping, and then delighted his northern visitor by talking nonsense through the rest of the meal.

Ovington was impressed with Atlanta University students and teachers. The graduating class, she said, "showed a fine set of young men and women," who would need "a Puritan ability to endure hardness." The rest of Atlanta showed her what they faced. The city was "just a little worse than anyone would be able to imagine."[20]

Back in New York City she put some of her thoughts into "Atlanta: A City Nursing Dead Ideals," published in *Colored American* in July. The Negro had no streetcar seat to call his own; the new library banned Negroes; their few public schools showed vast inequity— "where a white teacher receives $575, a Negro teacher for the same grade receives $75"; Negro men received "brutal" chain-gang punishment for minor crimes.

Against Atlanta's bias she put Atlanta University graduates and "the homes of the intelligent, cultivated colored people of the city." Their thoughtfulness, intelligent understanding, hospitality, and kindliness inspired, even when overshadowed by "the sorrowful remembrance of the indignities which I saw heaped upon them by the men and women of my own race."[21]

The piece started a flurry of writing from her travels and research. Repeatedly, she checked plans with Du Bois. She wanted to reach a wide white audience to "awaken interest" in work for the Negro poor. "As long as I was sure of my facts I would do well to give [an] encouraging picture as there are plenty to paint the other side."

She planned to emphasize "their willingness to take care of themselves"; "the lack of criminality among the children as shown by the juvenile court records"; the way the poorest Negro families made their tenements look like homes and made an "attempt at family life"; the "training of the children," better than most city poor; and their religious faith.[22]

Her article, "The Negro Home in New York," appeared in a specialized journal, *Charities*, edited by Paul Kellogg. Even he thought it too positive, and wrote Du Bois to check before publishing it. Kellogg included with the proofs he sent Ovington Du Bois's response, which was that he had no criticism at all of her excellent article.[23]

She published other specialized articles in 1905. "The Colored Woman in Domestic Service in New York City" in the May *Household Research Bulletin* is a rare look at the working woman. "The Settlement in America," in *Colored American,* sought to educate a black audience about this innovative institution. Her definition is noteworthy: "Very crudely stated a settlement is a home in a poor part of a town or city which draws its residents and its support from a group of educated and well-to-do folk of another part of the city, and which aims to be a cen tre for neighborhood life."

The settlement to Ovington was a "home," with all the connotations that suggests, not an "institution" or "agency." The residents are "educated"; "support" is tied to the "well-to-do," implying, as in her own experience, that those who go to make their homes in settlements are not synonymous with the wealthy supporters.

"The training of the resident who has gone into it," she said, is "the best result" of the settlement movement.

> If he be of open mind he learns as time goes on to see the world from a bigger point of view than he used to see it. Old barriers are knocked down, he gets to know the laboring people. . . . He sees the meaning of factory life and of the sweat shop. Such a resident is changed, not in a night, but slowly and through many years.[24]

In "Fresh Air Work Among Colored Children in New York," in *Charities and the Commons,* Ovington emphasized again the barriers to Negro use of social services. It was more difficult to persuade "colored mothers to allow their children to leave them and go into the country" than it had been with mothers she had known in Greenpoint. These mothers "are proud . . . and do not like to accept charity," which "is often a cruelty to their boys and girls who need the help of others."

Racial segregation hurt black and white children. But she did locate one New York City public school that was a model of unsegregated education "where an equal number of white and colored children work and play together, and where, because of love and justice on the part of teachers and principal, much has been done to do away with the race problem—more than can be done in any other way."[25]

Related in theme was a 1906 Ovington article in *Northeastern* on "Working Girls' Clubs." Addressing women's clubs, she sought to bring together wage earners and the "women of means who give of their experience and energy": "Hard working young people need something of excitement, of joyous motion and of gay light and laughter when their day's task is done, and they must be given these under proper surroundings or they will seek them where they may lead to harm, perhaps irreparable injury."[26]

Ovington's first article in the *Voice of the Negro*, where Du Bois published, in February of 1906, was scholarly and technical, providing a clear view of housing conditions for Negroes in New York City, with illustrative photographs, floor plans, and statistics.[27] "The Negro and the New York Tenement" depicts housing in the San Juan Hill area, information much needed by Negroes from the South.

In many ways the most interesting of Ovington's publications before her journalistic work for the *New York Evening Post* was on what she called a "treacherous" topic. In the *Annals of the American Academy* in May 1906, "The Negro in the Trades Unions in New York" again broke new ground. Only 5 percent of working Negro males belonged to unions, but the percentage had doubled in five years. Ovington criticized Booker T. Washington's positions without naming him. "Would the Negro as a workman be better off . . . if there were no labor unions?" "I have heard colored men prominent in industrial school work say that they would be."

But all workers gained from collective bargaining and protective legislation achieved by unions, she argued. Organized labor did not create race discrimination, but there "is a sufficient amount of it in America to make the Negro often occupy the position of a strikebreaker" (she named several instances). Unfortunately, strikebreakers were "indiscriminatingly praised by the Negro world," a stand the leaders "should seriously consider, since they separate themselves from the ethics of the greater part of the labor world."

As with her settlement article, Ovington ended this scholarly piece with a strong integrationist statement: "Caste lines disappear when men are held together by a common interest, and as they feel their dependence one upon another they gain in sympathy and fraternal spirit." Then she told the story of an Irish friend who reported with initial horror that she "ate wid a nayger" from her husband's union.

" 'Well,' I said, 'how did he seem?' 'To tell you the truth,' she said, 'he seemed just like anybody else.' "[28]

Ovington was encouraged by her research more than she expected. "That's where hope lies, don't you think?" she asked Du Bois—"with the laboring people": "When the colored worker is sufficiently valuable to be a factor in the labor world he is bound to be received and that means a good deal of democracy; for the labor men are fine fellows, I think."

In September 1905 Du Bois asked if she had heard of his July gathering of twenty-nine anti-Washington men, called the Niagara Movement, after its meeting place. She replied vehemently:

> Of course I have heard of the Niagara movement. I don't live in the desert! I read of it in the Post and the Christian Register which had a sympathetic account of the matter. Then I subscribed to the Guardian and have grown more fond of Mr. Washington evry [*sic*] day![29]

In Boston, Monroe Trotter was rapidly becoming the most vocal of Washington's opponents. Du Bois called Trotter's *Guardian* wonderful, the best Negro paper in the country.[30] These men would also have their falling out, but at this point, the alliance was firm, and Ovington knew its intricacies amazingly well.

———

MARY WHITE OVINGTON's developing alliances and activities did not occur in a family vacuum, even though she was single and childless. In October 1905, her aunt Irene Ovington died. Lively, unmarried Aunt Renie was likely the person Ovington had in mind to work and live with her at the Tuskegee Model Tenement. As Ovington would do for her own mother, Aunt Renie had provided a home for Ovington's paternal grandmother, Mary H. Ovington, until her death in 1889, had also raised her cousin Florence, and worked at a Brooklyn training school for nurses.

This sudden death came quickly after John White Chadwick's—two role models lost in a year. Ovington was "inexpressibly touched" that her aunt had remembered her in her will. "If she admired me, it could not possibly have been more than I admired her." She received from her Aunt Sarah the little book of her grandmother's that Aunt Renie had always carried, and opened it to find one of her own poems copied in her dead aunt's script. It was almost more than Ovington could bear: "I cannot look ahead."

Her father, too, grew frail with illness that would take his life. After 1902 Mary had been the only unmarried child, and much of the responsibility for their parents fell to her. "It is hard to go away at just this time when there is an indefinite amount to do, but my father and mother are both ill and I must give some time to them," she wrote Du Bois in 1907.

Her life was a game of puss-in-the-corner, dashing from one place to another: "I had elected to do a piece of work on the Negro, but my book was not yet written though my fellowship had expired some time before. I was receiving no remuneration, so at any minute, I might be tagged by my family."

She was amazed at women who juggled child-raising and outside jobs. "A man . . . does not have to assume new responsibility when he puts his key in the door. He's made much of, given the best chair and just what he likes to eat. But when a woman with a family who goes out to work puts in her key, she simply assumes another responsibility."

There were compensations, of course. In Elizabeth Graham, Charles's wife since 1902, and nicknamed "Buster" by him for her china-doll appearance, Ovington gained a lively new sister, trained as a nurse, with whom Ovington would live for eighteen years after her mother's and brother's deaths; and her younger sister Helen, married since 1894, began the family who would be close to their Aunt May throughout her life—Theodore Ovington Kingsbury born in November 1906, and Elizabeth Winchester Kingsbury born in July 1908.

Ovington juggled work and family, choice and duty, and went further, converting family and friends to support her controversial cause. A white woman working and living with black people? Shameful! Dangerous! Ovington used her family's abolitionist history to get the worried Louise Ovington's support for what the adult daughter fully intended to do anyway.

First she hinted to her mother:

You see, I've got a work now that is just as absorbing and I believe just as important as the work the abolitionists did before the war. I'm studying conditions hard, I mean to write or say very little for some time, but conditions are far from being what a democratic country should show towards its people.

Then Ovington laid it all out:

DEAR MOTHER,

It is some time since I have written you after my almost daily letters. Perhaps it is because of a guilty conscience for I have been doing what I know you don't want me to do. But if I am ever to have another settlement I must pull strings for it now, and my heart is just as much set upon work among the Negroes as ever. I am trying to get a New York settlement among them. I may possibly succeed (not to go to work there of course until fall.)

I suppose you have been dreading this last. I really think the possible danger is no greater than among Italians or Bohemians and the Negro neighborhoods are all so delightfully accessible—on the West Side from the Thirties to the Sixties—that I should for ever be near people and you could drop in every time you went shopping.

Do stand by me if you can. It is horrible to feel that I am working against you. Yet I know that unless I take up some task that will absorb me, intellectually and emotionally, I shall break down as Adele has. I can't explain how I feel to you, save that it is as though I must use up the power and enthusiasm in me or burn to pieces. And this Negro work absorbs me—every story I ever used to hear of the Abolitionists calls me to it. You don't guess how I feel about it because I train myself not to show my emotion. Do care about it if you can. I do not believe it will be any harder than the Greenpoint work—no Board would put a settlement in a dangerous neighborhood. Volunteers would not go to it if residents could be persuaded to live there. If you will only try to care about it with me I will promise never to be cross about bundling up or putting on rubbers when I go out again! I wouldn't feel so cross if I only knew you cared about the other things. And this Negro who must mean so much when you think of Grandma and of all you used to feel before the War.[31]

Ovington's abolitionist heritage makes a good story for a fearful mother or a curious reader; Ovington used it in her autobiographical book *The Walls Came Tumbling Down*, too. But a grandmother who fought slavery does not sufficiently untangle the threads that enabled a shy, protected white woman to create and work forty years to perfect the "*new* emancipation." With her mother's acquiescence, we unravel and reweave those strands of innovation, commitment, and sustenance.

———————

WHILE OVINGTON's life cause was coming more clearly into focus as she turned forty, a man who would become a close friend and colleague was undergoing a similar transformation. Blond, blue-eyed, ruddy-faced, and born of Irish immigrants, John Milholland came to the city as a reporter for the New York *Tribune*. He invented the pneumatic mail-delivery system and grew wealthy, with company offices by 1905 in New York, Philadelphia, London, Paris, and Berlin. His diaries reveal strong Christian beliefs and enormous love for his childhood home on Lake Champlain, north of Ticonderoga.[32]

He returned to the "blessed old farm," which he expanded to thousands of acres and named "Meadowmount"; he would travel from Liverpool or London, sometimes with wife and children, sometimes alone. His diaries are replete with self-searching attempts to live a Christian life as a businessman—a characteristic that must have reminded Ovington of her father—and, later, to reconcile "sin" with his Christian beliefs. He recognized others' suffering, as when he noted on Christmas Day 1903, that the "Market place has brought long shadows on many homes."

Milholland's altruistic progression was similar to Ovington's, beginning with concern for the poor, followed by reading Booker T. Washington's *Up from Slavery*. Ovington and Milholland both needed to *do* something about problems, and neither shrank from social association with Negroes. Milholland sought profit for the express purpose of funding an equal rights campaign. He was tired of "spasmodic" efforts. "We must organize in a thorough manner," he told Washington:

We must unite, so far as possible, the various elements of strength, and place the whole thing under the direction of a strong resolute, intelligent committee, whose members care nothing whatever for individual positions or personal aggrandizement, but seek only solid accomplishment.[33]

It is clear why Milholland would gravitate toward Du Bois after the latter published his critiques of Washington, from 1901 onward. Already in 1900, Milholland promoted the franchise as the most necessary, practical means to equality and justice. By the time Ovington met him, the businessman was anxious to move out of Washington's pocket—and to get the latter out of his.[34]

Washington didn't let him go easily, but attempts to control and direct Milholland's energies and money failed drastically. Not vulnerable to media ambush, not dependent on Washington's largesse with other people's money, and not distracted by glory, Milholland cut a clear path through the tangle of Washington–Du Bois disputes.

Ovington and Milholland met at a thirty-cent Sunday-night supper at Greenwich House in early 1905. She had heard that he knew Henry Phipps and might convince him to build one of his model tenements for Negroes.[35] Here was the first white she had come across who put his wealth and energy into race relations and who leaned toward Du Bois. Immediately, Milholland conveyed her ideas to Phipps, who was amenable to Ovington as matron for a settlement in the Negro community if he built it, "and I think he will," Milholland wrote in his diary. "I told Madame S[imkhovitch] on the phone and she was very glad."

Ovington, often with the Simkhovitches, became a regular visitor for tea or dinner at Milholland's New York office and apartment in the Manhattan Hotel. Washington also stayed at the Manhattan when he was in the city, and Ovington would talk with him as well while she visited Milholland. The Alabaman became only a "casual acquaintance," however. "He was far too busy a man to give his time to a woman of very moderate means who, if she subscribed at all to his school, would not be able to go beyond the ten dollar bill," Ovington found.[36]

The Phipps project moved quickly with Milholland's help. By January 20, 1905, the monthly report of the directors of Greenwich House confirmed that Ovington's work was "progressing beautifully." On

February 22, she dashed off a note to Du Bois: "We have the Phipps tenement, and I feel confident that in it I can start the beginnings, at least, of a settlement. Aren't you glad?" In March, the Greenwich House board minutes record that Phipps had decided to build "his first tenement for negroes [*sic*]." The director's report went on: "Miss Ovington now expects that a section of this tenement will be used for social purposes, and that she herself will have an apartment in the tenement where she will live next year."[37]

And what of Milholland and Ovington? Indirect evidence suggests that this conscientious, moral, passionate man fell fast and hard for the striking woman who shared his cause, and that he struggled mightily with his conscience. Milholland's family was in London when he and Ovington first met; when Milholland listed people who took tea with him he referred to her at first as "Mary White Ovington of Negro fame." He sailed for Europe on his twenty-first wedding anniversary, castigating himself for talking too much, "as usual." He spent April in Holland and Berlin, Belgium and France, and the first part of May in London. Then he was back on the Atlantic Ocean, and by May 20 was once again in his New York rooms in the Manhattan Hotel, entertaining the Simkhovitches and Ovington for Saturday evening tea.

It was Ovington's turn to be out of town the following week, leaving for the Atlanta University conference and her first meeting with Du Bois. While she was in Atlanta, Milholland celebrated his forty-fifth birthday on May 29 by taking stock. He was in good health, his weight about 175 to 180. His hair was growing gray, but otherwise he could pass for twenty-two. His energies were at high tide; he was ready to do God's work.

On June 18 he was on a break from business at Delaware Water Gap, getting up in the wee hours of the morning for prayer. He wanted to be found "C-L-E-A-N." On the twenty-ninth and thirtieth of June he was at Meadowmount. In his diary, what looks like the word *Sinful* is scrawled by the first date. This is followed by a long, abstract passage about fire in the brain and the heart that burns more intensely as the summer advances, and by biblical quotes about "iniquities." At the end of the month, he looked forward to "a month of July." "I'm fine," he wrote, "but what a wretched mess I've made of most of it. Out of time; out of time with God's will and ways. Oh the shame of it all: how my old sins, the sins that so easily beset me grip and hold me!

How easily I lapse into the [illegible] I hate; the habit." On July 6, Milholland wrote: "I realize at last how one must never expect to live anything of a social life and do any serious liberal or political work in the world." He wrote to his wife, the following day, thinking about "last night's dream, with the blood of Christ" on his hands.

Back at work in New York City and Philadelphia by July 15, Milholland, among other things, met with Booker T. Washington. "I urged him to stick John Rockefeller for $5000000 and make Tuskegee the Cornell of the Black South," he wrote after the July 21 meeting.

And then he was on his way back to Albany and north to Meadowmount, commenting en route about his lack of sleep and about the rapidity of the fall from right to wrong. His records of the following week are uncharacteristically written from later to earlier, in larger handwriting, and horizontally rather than vertically. Guilt has flown; he is elated. "I am writing backwards; it is Sunday morning and I am at the 'Green cottage.' . . . A whole week of 'Meadowmount', a week of sun and showers, of gorgeous sunsets and dawns, one especially of fresh splendor as [I cant ever forget]." At the top of Wednesday's entry, in comparatively small script, is the note "Family sailed."

Milholland headed back down to New York City with two business friends, evidently, chatting of business schemes. "The Negro cause in the background," he wrote on July 31, Monday, and then added: "A life of action now marked out—Justice for all, Black and white."

On the fourth of August, he met his family at the dock, including "the love of my life and arms," his wife, Jean. On Sunday the sixth, after family worship, he wrote: "Poor Jean! I am so sorry for her but I do not hold Jean blameless yet I think I'm driven." On the farm, without his family, he goes back to large, happy writing. In the city, he feels a failure.[38]

Surely, John Milholland was having an affair with characteristics that assuaged his guilt over breaking the Sixth Commandment and betraying his wife. Was it with Mary White Ovington? This is a possibility. Ovington was in the Adirondacks for three weeks in July of 1905, and again in September. During a 1908 visit she was definitely at Meadowmount; reticence about her two 1905 visits could suggest that she was there then, too.

Does it make a difference whether this was an affair or a close friendship? Probably not, as far as understanding these two people in their public actions. But they were strikingly compatible, with similar personalities, purposes, and sustenance from the natural world. Their differences, too, could attract—for example, Ovington's rational religion and Milholland's "born again" sincerity.

Ovington and Milholland worked together on projects besides the Phipps tenement: the Constitution League of the United States, as well as writing and publishing. The tenement took shape slowly; ground was broken in the spring of 1906, but by the end of May, it was still only a hole, making Ovington very impatient—she could do so much more if she had a place where she could meet people, black and white.[39]

The Constitution League progressed more dramatically, with strong statements against lynching and peonage, and vehement support of the Fourteenth and Fifteenth amendments to the Constitution, guaranteeing citizens due process and equal protection of the law regardless of their color, race, or previous condition of servitude. Washington and his crew, meanwhile, scrambled to make sure that Milholland's money did not find its way to Trotter's Boston *Guardian* and Du Bois's fledgling Niagara Movement. Even if that were to occur, however, Washington was confident that he could put a stranglehold on Milholland's mail-tube income through his contacts with the U. S. Post Office.[40]

The Constitution League's principles and activities foreshadowed the formation of the NAACP in 1909. Ovington served as a link between the Niagara Movement and the League in 1905–1906, as she did later when their activities and memberships melded into the NAACP. In December of 1905, she attended the meeting in New York where Du Bois's organization celebrated the "New Abolitionism" and honored William Lloyd Garrison, and the following month she was active in promoting the Constitution League's big meeting.[41]

The league issued free tickets for the February 1 Cooper Union meeting on "Suffrage Conditions in the South." Ovington dropped by Milholland's rooms at Hotel Manhattan to pick up twenty-five platform tickets and two hundred reserved, "for her white friends," Milholland told Du Bois. "I don't want to have it too one sided," he said about racial balance. Milholland's aim was to "*present a united front*," including publishing the proceedings in full. "It looks now as if we are going to have a tremendous demonstration," he believed.[42]

The *New York Times* headlined "Negroes Have an Inning at the Cooper Union." It emphasized the crowd's racial composition (at least four-fifths Negro) and summarized speeches by Kelly Miller and Mary Church Terrell of Washington, D.C., and Du Bois.[43]

Successful meetings of the league followed in Philadelphia and Washington, D.C., leading Milholland to become more outspoken, and leading Charles Anderson and Washington to worry about "the enemy," Milholland and "his brood." Mrs. Terrell's husband, Judge Robert Terrell, had been Booker T. Washington's inside source of information about the first Niagara Movement meetings in 1905. "One never knows how to deal with families when one member poses as a friend, and another member trains with the opposition," Anderson opined, but soon concluded that "it seems to me, Doctor, that it is high time that this woman should be called down a little."[44]

Simply deciding who was "friend" and who was "enemy," became an unwieldy, constantly shifting data base for Booker T. Washington and his supporters by the summer and fall of 1906. Washington's papers show his predilection for secret agent and double-agent tactics. His men spied and reported second- and third-hand. They supplied material to the press and covered up its source. Washington attempted to control funding at one end of the print media, and distribution at the other. Through his informers, he kept track of who was saying what not only in print or in public, but in private, and noted who was meeting with whom. Stopping leaks was a constant task ("you never know just which one of our folks is over-talking himself," Anderson wrote to Washington on March 23, 1906).

Ovington knew the intricate webs well, and stayed clear. She operated differently, doing much of what she was increasingly skilled at: raising and handling money, as, for example, treasurer of the Association of Neighborhood Workers.[45] Most important, she used her pen to tilt the scales ever more toward the hero she and John Milholland wished to empower: W. E. B. Du Bois.

ONE COULD NOT INVENT a more dramatic series of events than those by which Mary White Ovington helped move the center of gravity of the nation's concern for the "Negro Problem" away from the solutions of Booker T. Washington and toward those promoted by Du Bois.

First, she traveled to the site of John Brown's rebellion against slavery at Harpers Ferry, West Virginia, to Du Bois's second annual Niagara Movement meetings in August 1906. Touched, impressed, and inspired, she wrote powerful articles for the *New York Evening Post*. Then she hopped the train to Atlanta and covered the meetings of Washington's Negro Business League for the same newspaper. Like a good journalist, she maintained "objectivity" but subtly weighed in on Du Bois's side.

Oswald Garrison Villard's *Post* was an ideal outlet for her first straightforward journalism. His name echoed that of his maternal grandfather, William Lloyd Garrison, founder of the Anti-Slavery Society and editor of *The Liberator*, 1831 to 1865. From his father, Henry Villard, he inherited Northern Pacific Railroad shares, Edison General Electric Company (later General Electric Company), the *Post*, and its weekly supplement, the *Nation*.

Oswald added to the wealth: the Fort Montgomery Iron Company, Garrison Realty Company, and City Club Realty. He was a director of several banks. He owned the *Nautical Gazette* and founded *Yachting* magazine. Oswald Garrison Villard was a member and officer of the New York City Club, the Philharmonic Society, the Harvard, Century, and University clubs and the Cosmos Club in Washington, D.C. He wrote and published extensively with amazing speed, not only in his newspaper outlets, but in eleven books reflecting his interest in Negro rights (for example, *John Brown: A Biography Fifty Years After*, 1910) as well as in economics, history, and international affairs.[46]

Until 1906 Villard had concentrated his contacts, support, and publicity on race issues in Booker T. Washington's camp. Such media, money, and sympathy to Negro Americans was irresistible to the Wizard of Tuskegee and necessary to anyone hoping to challenge him. Du Bois had not done well with shifting Villard's sympathies. Ovington did better, placing material leaning toward Du Bois in Villard's influential publication and nudging Villard himself.

She had offered to cover the Niagara Movement meetings at Harpers Ferry in the summer of 1906. Villard probably then suggested that she do the Negro Business League meetings as well. Washington regularly paid for reporters to cover his meetings. Villard wrote Washington that Ovington would represent the *Post* in Atlanta, and that she "would prefer to have you set a certain sum, whatever seems right to you, in order that she may be free as to her own travelling plans."[47]

At the end of July, Ovington asked Du Bois if there would be any *women* at Harpers Ferry (not whites). "Would you like me there as a reporter for the N. Y. Evening Post if it should work out that I could go?" She would arrive sometime the first day, and "shall trust that you will be looking out for me, and will see that I have where [*sic*] to lay my head." Since this was to be her first reporter's work, "I shall expect you to furnish me, as all lazy reporters do expect, with most of the matter you want put in the paper," she joked. More seriously, would Du Bois "let me in as a reporter to the members' meetings?" Those would be the "only things of much importance," she was sure. "Open meetings I know very well the value of!"

Du Bois responded quickly that he would look out for her, adding that, though he couldn't smuggle her into the members' meetings, he would slip all important material out to her. Public meetings ran afternoons and evenings, August 15 through 18; Members' meetings, with reports by the movement's fourteen standing committees, were scheduled in the mornings, simultaneous with Women's Meetings.[48]

She opened the second of her signed articles with a communal experience, which the headline picked up:

The Spirit of John Brown Exhibited in Convention at Harpers Ferry. Delegates of the Niagara Movement Make Pilgrimages to the Historic Old Building, His Fort, Where they Hold Exercises, and Sing "John Brown's Body"—Demand for Equal Rights and Suffrage the Keynote of Speeches and of the Address to the Country Adopted by the Convention.

Most of Ovington's article outlined the demands of the movement in Du Bois's speech: "full manhood suffrage," an end to "discrimination in public accommodations," impartial enforcement of laws and the Constitution, education and (with a swipe at Washington), "when we call for education, we mean real education . . . and we will fight for all time against any proposal to educate black boys and girls as servants and underlings."[49]

The Harpers Ferry meetings were "remarkable," not only for the "able and eloquent" speeches, but for the "power and earnestness" of the 150 men and women, Ovington reported. Looking back much later, she saw that "the work was crippled by lack of adequate funds, but it was a beginning." She doubted "if a more resolute, intelligent set of men and women were assembling anywhere that summer."[50] The other assembly to which Ovington went directly was that of the Negro Business League. Atlanta steamed under a late summer sun; the meetings were stuffed into churches; Ovington had "to get out copy every night while suffering from genuine sickness."

This did not prevent her from writing perceptive articles going beyond Washington's organization. In "The Negro's Position: His Comparative Helplessness in the South," Ovington convincingly outlined the problems of the color line. In Atlanta in 1906, that uncrossable line prevented equal representation; it led to discrimination in education and punishment for crimes; it forced unreported criminal assaults on Negroes (and exaggerated or fictitious reports of assaults *by* Negroes); it allowed the use of vagrancy laws to, in effect, re-enslave Negro men. ("To some of us it is an open question whether the poor idler is a greater danger to society than the rich one," she wrote.) Du Bois complimented her good work and proposed to distribute it widely as a pamphlet.

Ovington was also being paid by Booker T. Washington to cover those Negro Business League meetings, and of course she did her job—with shrewd deemphasis of Washington by foregrounding the farmers and businesspeople, "the men who succeed."[51]

Humor and danger and drama she could only report much later. One way in which the meetings of the Niagara Movement were more conservative than those of the Negro Business League, she joked, was that meals were regular and on time. "We anemic whites are not so stoic. . . . We like a luncheon."

More seriously, Ovington recognized the necessity for caution as a white woman interacting with black men. As she walked down the aisle one day to talk with a New Yorker she knew, Philip Payton, she felt his unease even in a black church. "Lynchings were going on at that time in the city and perhaps he was right in thinking that my cordial greeting might endanger him," she concluded.

Richard T. Greener, just back from Vladivostok, Russia, where he was American consul, spoke at Harpers Ferry of John Brown and antislavery days, ending his eulogy: "Who would be free himself must strike the blow."

In sweltering Atlanta, Ovington saw the same man mount to the podium to call for compromise and adjustment. He ended his southern speech: "It is better to bend than to break." As Greener left the platform and walked down the aisle he did a double take as he saw the blond, blue-eyed woman he had met at Harpers Ferry also here in Georgia busily taking notes. He nodded and hurried past.

Ovington was kind. There was truth to both pieces of advice, and an old man should be permitted to utter both with conviction—he had done his work and had outgrown the time for taking sides. "But the leaders and many of their followers were young and could not believe that both sides were right," she added. "Fortunately for the race, they were able to choose where they should stand. Solidarity is good, but independence of thought is better."[52]

Ovington was back in New York City by the tenth of September, joyfully writing to Du Bois that the *Post* had published her reports, although the *Independent*, to which she had also sent them, did not. "I made it too clear as to just where the point of division between the two Negro camps lies," she thought. "Dr. Washington wants to keep this fuddled, and what Dr. Washington wants still goes—'But not for long, oh, not for long.'" She had tried to report "with all fairness, and I praised *through other people's mouths*."

Washington himself was less perceptive of the slant she had given, complimenting Ovington on her "very excellent and helpful reports," and promising to meet with her personally sometime in New York. Ovington thanked him for his "approval" of her report (singular) on the Business League, and added slyly, "I am very glad to know that it seemed helpful to you."[53]

Booker T. Washington's blindness to Ovington's tilt toward Du Bois and to her power not of money but of pen even led the Tuskegean to try briefly to pull her into his informers' network in New York City, writing her for information about one of his own people, Fred Moore. Ovington would have none of it, responding politely that "I have nothing confidential to say."[54]

Booker T. Washington went back to Tuskegee that fall believing he had defused racial tensions in Atlanta. To Villard, he wrote of his handling of "several outrages" which "had recently been committed by colored people on white women": "One of the afternoon papers was advocating openly the formation of a Klu [*sic*] Klux Klan, another had offered a thousand dollars for the lynching of a colored man guilty of one of these crimes." Washington thought he improved things by going to the four Atlanta papers with a statement, which they printed.[55]

Ovington saw the papers and concluded he had made matters worse. "You must feel very happy indeed if you believe that you have been able to change conditions," she told him. Her own impression was quite different: white people to whom she had talked were completely indifferent to his Negro Business League; there was no such "encouraging talk in my hotel corridor as Mr. Fortune tells of in the *Age*, and I did hear much of the 'nigger' diatribe."[56]

To Du Bois she went further. She had not understood the situation in the Georgia city until she read in the *Atlanta News* in one column "Mr. Washington's eulogy," and in the next "a wicked call for a thousand men to hunt the Negro criminal." Washington's approach only submerged conscientious white reaction: "That sort of truckling only makes those Atlanta people who might brace up and get a little courage to stand out against their city's iniquity lean back and say, 'The Negro is a brute anyway, Washington admits it.'"[57] Unfortunately, events soon proved her perception to be accurate.

———————

DURING THE LAST WEEK of September 1906, the biggest southern race riot between 1900 and 1910 erupted in the Atlanta described only three weeks before by both Washington and Ovington. The press that Washington claimed to have used to quiet things kindled the flames by reporting assaults on white women by Negroes. Panicked Negroes, hearing their people were being slaughtered, rushed for protection to Clark University and Gammon Theological Seminary. Others collected arms. Police arrested Negroes for possessing guns and fired into a crowd. Return fire killed one officer and wounded another.

White Atlantans rampaged to destroy Negro life and property, killing four, injuring many, looting and burning. The city was paralyzed: factories closed, transportation stopped.[58] In New York City, Oswald Garrison Villard wrote that "the Atlanta Pogrom" disgraced the entire country.

Ovington feared the real stories were not getting out. "It is more terrible there than the papers have represented," she told the editor. "I keep getting letters from friends. . . . Since I have come to know one subject with some thoroughness, I wonder whether the Associated Press Ass'n exists for the dicemination [*sic*] of fancy rather than of fact."[59]

She thanked Villard for a check: "I assume it is to be an anonymous gift,—so I shall not tell the Treasurer to acknowledge it." Had he decided to support W. E. B. Du Bois's Niagara Movement? If so, he was not the only one shifting from Washington after the riots: in Macon, for example, several hundred Negroes formed a statewide Equal Rights Association.[60]

As the reality of the riot settled in, Du Bois and Ovington wrote with new urgency. He called his "Litany of Atlanta" somewhat hysterical,[61] dashed off as he raced back to the riot-torn city from Calhoun, Alabama. "Done at Atlanta, in the Day of Death, 1906," it opens, and continues in recitation and response, terrified, angry, frustrated.[62]

Ovington responded negatively to its extended, loose form, and then retracted her comments, leading Du Bois to say that she should not withdraw her criticism since he felt the same way. Crisp, staccato language was called for by the event, not phrasemaking, he knew, but he had found the first impossible, so had resorted to the latter.[63]

Ovington's postriot writing began with a letter to *The Outlook,* a white weekly that supported Washington's "pacific" approach over Du Bois's "assertive" one.[64] She disputed that black men's assaults on white women caused "the Atlanta Riots." Cleverly, she said that "as a woman, I would ask to be permitted to say a word upon the matter from a somewhat different standpoint." Southern white males expressed no horror at assaults on black women, especially those by white men. "If assault is a crime, especially assault upon women, then the negro [*sic*] is not the only criminal class."

Ovington drew an analogy that nicely pulled together her insights about class, caste, race, and gender:

Now change the words "white" to aristocrat and "colored" to proletariat, and you have a condition that is not uncommon over all this Christian world. The chivalry of men is often extended only to women of their own class. It would be well if more of us should hear the story that many an Irish girl could tell us of her experience in domestic service. . . . I remember, after a winter of unusually happy times in a college town, hearing an older girl say to a younger one in a working-girls' club, "Don't have anything to do with the college fellows. A decent girl keeps away from them." My own class, that brought me companionship and safety, was known to her as a danger.

Finally, Ovington pointed out that the class (or race or caste) of a guilty man made a huge difference, too.

The citizen who has been well born, who has had education and opportunity, may assault a helpless, unprotected woman and never be brought to justice; he does not belong to the criminal class; but the untrained, unlettered man, whose school has been the dirty alley or the chain-gang, is fortunate if his foul deed leads him to the gallows, not to the stake.[65]

The *Outlook* editors shrewdly noted: "Miss Ovington writes out of a practical acquaintance with the colored population of New York." She received appreciative responses, including from Lyman Ward, principal of the Southern Industrial Institute in Camp Hill, Alabama ("For the Training of White Youth"). "I have been in the South nearly nine years. What you say is so true."[66]

Responses came belatedly to her *Evening Post* articles, which the riots validated. Du Bois thanked her for her great service to the Niagara Movement and the Business League and for her Atlanta piece, which he wanted to publish in leaflet form.[67]

More important to her immediate future was John Milholland's reaction. He liked her *Evening Post* piece on the Atlanta courts "so much that he offered to pay my expenses if I would go again and write more of the same kind," Ovington said later.[68] Actually she was more behind the plans than she indicated; she went to lunch with Milholland in New York on September 20 "to talk up some southern investigation," she told Du Bois. The riots just a few days later intensified and speeded up the plans the two agreed upon.[69]

Du Bois encouraged her. Vagrancy and contract laws would make a very interesting study; he thought she should take Milholland up on his offer immediately. Du Bois also said he wanted from her "lips or pen," a frank comparison of the Niagara Movement and the Negro Business League. He would see her in Atlanta.[70]

4

White Woman in a Colored World

IN THE FALL of 1906 Mary White Ovington sought to advance her chosen work with the John Milholland–financed research trip, with a plan to go to Georgia and Alabama. The black settlement house goal eluded her. Her Greenwich House Fellowship had run out. Journalism—writing—could do some good, perhaps, she felt, and give her some income. Harpers Ferry and Atlanta had loosed her pen.

Much later Ovington said she should have followed Milholland's "instructions," for her research but she "enjoyed dawdling," seeing a lot but writing little.[1] But she was too modest in so describing what she did write, for she published perceptive reports at the time, she wrote much that found print later, and she recorded observations that remained in her manuscripts. She also, as we shall see, influenced a writer with access to the national ear: muckraker Ray Stannard Baker.

"The Atlanta Situation" appeared, she told her readers, just after Christmas in 1906. The riots three months earlier had been much worse than others had reported from the scene. A Negro on his porch riddled with thirty-six bullets, a crippled boy killed while blacking shoes in a city barbershop, a mutilated body dumped at a downtown statue—these images open her lengthy article. Had Atlanta courts improved since the riots? No. Negroes had been convicted, but no white man had gone to jail for killing a Negro. Whites were charged with misdemeanors and received light punishments. Had the press adequately reflected the postriot situation? No, again. The quiet village of Brownsville, for example, was repeatedly called rowdy.

Lessons of the riot were indelible. Most important, whites found and freely purchased firearms, so that "even young [white] boys were on the streets with Winchesters in their hands ready in a second to take a shot at a black face, while colored fathers, in their homes, were forced by the militia to give up their means of defence." Later Ovington wished she had stressed even more "the disarming of the Negroes, the arming of the whites, the aggressors," since that had "made the Negro apprehensive in all these southern cities." Nevertheless, the point was made more firmly in her article than in other analyses of the Atlanta riots.[2]

From Atlanta, Ovington hopped the train for the two hundred miles to Calhoun, Alabama, and bounced to Calhoun Colored School in a quaint open carriage. Here was her rural headquarters for six weeks, from whence she traveled to Montgomery, Tuskegee, Alexander City, Selma, Camp Hill, Birmingham, and Talladega.

Du Bois recommended Calhoun as the site of his research on labor in Lowndes County.[3] Ovington described the school, its history and surroundings, and Charlotte Thorn, its principal, in several later publications. Excited by Booker T. Washington's founding of Tuskegee in an obscure, rural area, Thorn and another teacher from Connecticut had created the place from nothing.[4]

Calhoun fit an Ovington goal: to show that the white South was not monolithic on the race issue, and to encourage whites who departed from the violently enforced norm for their race. An example was Edward Chesnutt, the populist plantation owner who had sold land to the school and become its manager. Kind, sympathetic, and willing to learn, Chesnutt was an Ovington favorite. The land made possible "an experiment in a model community," with homes, fields, and a boarding school. Calhoun came to be called "the first settlement in the South."[5]

Ovington found a beautiful bit of New England in the red clay, dark pines, and shabby houses: white school buildings, walkways edged with flowers, a rose-entwined cottage with an open fireplace, books, and antiques. Black and white teachers staffed the school. Through Emily Hallowell, Ovington heard Negro spirituals as they were originally sung, with unexpected harmonies like those she had heard sometimes in Manhattan's San Juan Hill.

Leslie Pinckney Hill, then at Tuskegee, spent the Christmas holidays at Calhoun and rambled with Ovington round and round the campus. The black man and white woman, soon supportive colleagues, longed for a good run over the neighboring slopes, but they risked lynching if they left the campus together. "Only those who are honestly striving to contribute some little mite to the furtherance of the good cause," Hill told her, "know how deeply encouraging a single word of appreciation is—especially when it comes from another one of the [strivers]."[6] Hill signed the NAACP "Call" in 1909, and remained a lifelong friend.

Ovington was touched by the moral discipline she saw. Christmas was frigid; students kept log fires burning as they prepared the community meal. At dawn, young men set out with baskets for the poor. One seventeen-year-old was gone until late afternoon, for the old woman to whom he was bringing the basket had moved. He was glad he had found her, he said simply; she was "right pleased." Such undramatic unselfishness (he had missed the turkey dinner) impressed the northern visitor. The young man had been sent out to do a job and he had done it.

On January 1, Emancipation Day, old people trudged the muddy roads to sit near the open windows filled with honeysuckle and birdsong. After slow harmonies and drumlike refrains, the reading of the Emancipation Proclamation, the joyful singing of "Oh Freedom over me!" they told their stories of slavery. Most began: "I were sold down in Alabama," or "I was sol' away f'om my chillen," powerful reminders of a system that had treated human beings like cattle. Ovington published several of their stories in the *Post* and the *Independent*. "The old-time field-hands had grown up without parental care, hard-worked, ill-fed," but wouldn't, couldn't, time touch the younger generation more gently? Couldn't opportunity make Emancipation Day "yearly grow more beautiful and real"?[7]

On January 4, Ovington set out for a week with the Joseph Mannings in Alexander City, sixty miles northeast of Montgomery. Manning, a Milholland contact, was an intelligent, educated, white man with six children to feed. He had been harassed and beaten unconscious for his published liberal views. "They mean to kill him," Mrs. Manning told their northern guest. Manning was small, ill-nourished, and jittery, and looked incapable of fighting off attacks, Ovington thought.

Manning recommended for safety that she spend her first week entirely in the white community and then move to the Negro section. He accompanied her to the white church, where she spoke on settlements, and to the white school, where she told about the North and its ice and snow and sleds. Men stopped by the house to talk about the outside world, but women were standoffish. The Methodist minister liked Ovington and wanted his wife to have her to dinner. Three times the invitation was made and then withdrawn. "She knew that I was a 'nigger lover,' as the South gracefully puts it, and she did not mean that I should darken her home," Ovington saw.

That minister provided an inspiring tale, however. He went with Manning and Ovington to a Negro church and school where all three spoke. His outraged congregation threatened to cut his salary, but he stood his ground. He had met with the God-fearing minister of the Negro church, and he had talked to little children whom Christ loved, and he was proud to have met Miss Ovington. The congregation voted him a raise instead. "Men like courage," Manning commented when he told Ovington what had happened.

Nearby, Ovington visited a second principled white man, Lyman Ward, who had written her in response to her *Outlook* piece on the Atlanta riots. Ward believed that industrial training for both races would reduce hatred and violence. The Southern Industrial Institute in Camp Hill was his white version of Washington's nearby Tuskegee.[8]

Ovington's southern travels in 1907 included one other stay in a white area: Winston County, northwest of Birmingham.[9] She heard about it while visiting the legislature in Montgomery. Other legislators spoke of the glorious cause of white supremacy and waved Confederate flags, but not Mr. Barton, the Republican representative from the county that had not seceded from the Union. At his invitation, she spent time in Lynn and Double Springs, visiting, speaking, listening, observing, thinking, and writing.

Winston County had ample grievance against the state for the way school aid was distributed. Money was allocated by total numbers of people, but spent at local discretion. Thus a county like Lowndes, nine-tenths Negro, received a lot of money it could then spend on the one-tenth white population. Winston, however, had almost no Negroes "to count and steal from," as Ovington put it, and thus suffered in its education.

Northern liberals unfairly dismissed these hill people as "poor whites," she thought. There was dire poverty and "monstrous exploitation of labor," but the people were not inherently weak or degenerate. Oddly enough, she observed that in areas where there was a large Negro population, "there creeps in among the white children, at an early age, an attitude of superiority that tends to make them unattractive and stupid," but in the white rural hill country youngsters remained bright and self-reliant without being "bumptious." She wrote: "The descendants of the men who never owned slaves, whose fathers hated slavery, must tell their tale as well; and when it is given to us we shall better understand the whole of the white south."

Ovington visited Booker T. Washington's Tuskegee Institute more than once, including a trip for the Workers' Conference. She was most impressed by the industry and self-sufficiency of the farmers. Most homes had looms, and one man wore a suit his wife had made, beginning with weaving the material. She reveled in artistic displays of winter beets, onions, lettuce, cabbage, carrots, turnips; geese and hens and incubator chickens; cows, bulls, horses, and mule colts; the "Jesup agricultural wagon" used to demonstrate farming techniques in the field.

But she didn't think much of the unrelieved demands of Washington's sermons. The farmers must not borrow, they must paint their houses; they must wipe out gambling and keep women from hanging out on street corners or entering the courthouse. They must support churches and not buy liquor. The man in the homemade suit must not have any pride, but should be about bringing the standards of his church and school up to that of his clothes.

"A very great deal was expected of them," Ovington thought, without so much as a pinch of joy in what they had already accomplished. And it all seemed to be tied in with the image Washington needed to convey. At the end he made what she described as a "wistful" appeal: "Those Negroes up North are hammering at me. . . . You'll stand by me?"

Mary White Ovington's first trip into the rural Deep South gave her insights that would stand her in good stead in trying to change its often brutal race relations. Instead of demanding more success and propriety, more hard work of the oppressed black population, she tried to change the dynamics of the debate. She called the South's racial challenge "a white problem."

That problem, as she saw it, came from prejudice, certainly, but also from a fatty and inadequate diet; from impassable roads and streets with a "plenitude of pigs who strolled about with the easy assurance of old and respected residents"; from poorly funded or nonexistent schooling; from marginal hygiene—one child thought Ovington a millionaire because she had her own comb. Couldn't a group like the Socialist Party arouse these "poorly-fed, weary-hearted white folk" to rebel not as the demagogue directed, against black people, but against "the real enemy—the system that deprives the workman of the best fruits of his labor"? As she rode "the rough, dreary roads," she saw, tangibly, "the folly of allowing a few individuals to gain economic control in a country." "Everything that nature gave was being exhausted, the soil, the noble supply of timber, the hearts of the men and women and little children."[10]

The white problem came, too, from the North, from lumping all southern whites together, past and present, from not helping and encouraging progressive elements. "You people in the north feel that you sacrificed much when you sent your men to battle," said one of the Republicans of free Winston County about the Civil War, but your soldiers were cheered on, they carried the support and pride of the community. But, he went on,

> we in these hills, had to creep past the confederate officers looking for conscripts; we left our women and children knowing they would be in danger from enemies at home. Our lands were ravaged first by one army and then by another. And so they write history and say we did it only to obstruct? We acted from the highest conviction, from the deepest love of the union.

And in the present, she found, not all white southerners sought to deny the ballot to Negroes. From a Republican legislator in central Alabama she heard: "The South should have outgrown the conception that voting is a social matter." There were plenty of white people as well as Negro whom he would not think of inviting into his home. But that didn't mean he would deprive them of their citizenship.

Mary White Ovington, the seeker after facts and understandings, after "sweet reasonableness" and clear debate, was also the creative settlement worker who saw that as people's lives were of a piece, and their health holistic, so must change be organic and comprehensive.

In March 1907, Ovington left Alabama to accompany her parents on a health-seeking trip to Germany, Italy, and Switzerland. On her last days in the South, accumulated dangers overwhelmed her.

The trip from Winston County was disconcerting. Female, un-escorted, she felt as dreary as the damp clouds that hung over the open carriage. An elderly white man, staring rudely at her and her baggage, finally asked "What are you selling?" The driver, lighting a cigarette, followed with "Do you dip snuff?"

The old man followed her aboard the train and trapped her in her seat until Birmingham, where she ran to a taxi to escape. In one man-uscript, Ovington says this man was an ex-governor of a southern state, and in another she describes him as "once high in the state's service, [but] now a lewd old man."

She had invited the secretary of the Socialist Party in Alabama to her hotel. They sat in the balcony, looking out over well-dressed peo-ple following smartly uniformed bellboys. But her one-eyed compan-ion was sickly, his clothes cheap and frayed. To ease his embarrass-ment, she raved about a Jack London speech with its picture of workers of the world uniting.

Then he began to speak. She couldn't possibly understand how other whites hated him for meeting with Negro coal miners who had joined the Socialist Party. "They got hold of us, threw us together, made us kiss one another. They . . . "

He stopped and began again. "I lost my job, of course. I had a good trade, but . . . they blacklisted me. Now I print a little paper for the party. . . . My wife left me. I don't blame her; I couldn't support her like I used to."

Suddenly self-conscious again he blurted out, "I hope you'll excuse me if I've been rude. It's a long time since I've talked with a good woman, as much as six months." She reassured him and expressed her appreciation, they shook hands, and he disappeared into the crowd. Her heart sank. What did she and her socialist friends in New York know of party loyalty? "Our locals talked revolution. This man lived it."

Ovington got to her hotel room shaking and locked the door, and wrote: "This was a strange land to me—my only friends in Birming-ham were persecuted Negroes and a despised Socialist. How thankful I would be tomorrow when I had boarded the express that would take me to New York. I lay awake, lonely and depressed."

Comfortable in her Pullman coach on another cloudy and dark day, she stared at cotton and straggling pines, the squalid cabins and the ragged watchers, the WHITE and COLORED signs over the station doors. "It might have happened here," she thought, and created the sensational story "The White Brute."[11] The fear and helplessness of a woman "nigger lover" traveling alone in the American South of 1907 enabled her briefly to enter the lives of those who were trapped there.

She placed the story in Mississippi, put her protagonists on a Jim Crow car, changing trains at a station like those creeping by her window. Large, strong Sam, a cotton field worker, glows with protective pride for his petite, bright-eyed bride. "You make me feel safe," Melinda murmurs.

But physical strength is nothing against the southern code, which protects white women only. The train they must catch is late, so they walk down the track. Melinda wants to cross to the straggling town and find a drink of sarsaparilla, but Sam cautions her: Negroes left this town after a lynching.

Melinda wants to hear about the shiny cookstove, about the house he has ready for her. But two young white men come, and despite all Sam can do with his wits, they take Melinda to the shanties across the tracks while Sam waits. An old white man sympathizes, but no one can control these guys—one is the sheriff's son, and they have killed more than once.

A different Melinda is returned to him. Blooming roses and violets and honeysuckle and bird calls and a crimson sunset welcome them to their first home. Sam serves her on special blue china. She will not eat. He tries talking—wouldn't she rather have him alive than dead? He cannot hold her. Lying separate, he hears the soft vines rustling, the insects' drowsy chirps, and distantly, a dog's howl.

"A dead man or a live cur," Sam says to himself, and turns on his face with a sob.

The story effectively and accurately reverses stereotypes. Dialogue, description, psychology of female and male, the violently enforced codes of behavior that silenced good white people as well as black are strongly depicted. A middle-aged single white woman has created the claustrophobic, deadly intertwining of sex, race, and power in the South in a way that anticipates Jean Toomer's "Blood Burning Moon" from 1922, or James Baldwin's "Going to Meet the Man" from 1965. The strong black man is her tragic character, Prometheus bound inwardly by chivalry and love, outwardly by the uncontrolled power, lust, and cruelty of his fellowman.

The South in 1906 and 1907, urban and rural, black and white, male and female, was, in Ovington's summation, a place of enormous contrasts in what the human could achieve—for good, or for evil. Might there not be hidden reservoirs to be tapped and directed for a thirsty people, a thirsty land? She had to believe something could be done, and she had to be doing something.

JUST AFTER HER Atlanta articles in the *New York Evening Post* in September of 1906, Mary White Ovington had caught wind of a Ray Stannard Baker writing project on the Negro. With Ida Tarbell, Lincoln Steffens, and John Phillips, the muckraking journalist had initiated the *American Magazine* and was in need of a sensational series to sell it. Ovington scrambled to nudge Baker toward the Niagara Movement radicals, lest a big new national media outlet fall into Booker T. Washington's conservative net.

Ovington was not Baker's only correspondent as he developed the articles that became *Following the Color Line: American Negro Citizenship in the Progressive Era* (1908), but she was the most persistent and militant. She recommended people and places and a methodology of research, including protecting sources, all designed to move Baker toward W. E. B. Du Bois.

Ovington began by telling Ida Tarbell that she knew hundreds of Negroes all over the country, and "some of them I really do know, and they are hard to get acquainted with." (Baker knew none.) Ovington hoped the *American Magazine* "won't straddle, but will give facts as they are" in the South. It would be difficult, she wrote, "for the colored men who know most do not dare or do not think it expedient to tell what they know, and there are numbers of colored people who like to be interviewed who will give only such facts as will help them to get further money from the north."[12]

Ovington followed her introduction to Baker with a bombardment of suggestions. The real story of the Atlanta riots needed telling—the Associated Press had not come near the truth. "You'll keep back in your brain, won't you, the ghastly truth that any unscrupulous white woman has the life of any Negro, no matter how virtuous he may be, in her hand." In the courts, "there is no justice for the colored man if a white man brings a case against him." Baker, she told him, had to meet Du Bois. "He can tell you much more than any other colored man in the South."

Her own interest was in labor conditions. Baker should meet the socialists, since "that is the only party that has any Democracy about it," and the white man hated it. "You may remember that [Ben] Tilman [*sic*] said, 'What shall we do with the socialists? Shoot 'em like we do the "niggers." ' " "The encouragement of race feeling separates the laborers," Ovington went on in a comment of enduring relevance, "and I believe many capitalists are consciously taking advantage of this to keep the laboring class from asserting itself."

The best way to hear the truth and protect his sources, she urged Baker, was to first be with white people altogether, and then "get up and leave your hotel, go to some quiet place, and spend all the time among the colored people." "You see," she went on, "those men whose names I give you are personal friends; I know their families, especially the children, and since the riot, perhaps I am over apprehensive regarding their safety."[13]

At Ovington's insistence, Baker spent a night at Calhoun Colored School while she was there in the winter of 1906–1907. Here he could see the best and the worst: the independent farmers and the share-croppers whose conditions were worse than those of slaves. Calhoun would give him the "best glimpse of the rural Negro that I know of anywhere."[14]

Was Ray Stannard Baker influenced by Ovington's campaign? Certainly her input made him more open to Du Bois's views. He met with people she recommended, such as Dr. Crogman and Dr. W. F. Penn in Atlanta, and even featured them. But she could move him only so far. His article on the Atlanta riots differed in slant from hers in the December 1906 *New York Evening Post*. She made it clear, for example, that problems had not been resolved, and that the best Negroes of the city were heading north. Baker referred to that exodus only briefly, and with no figures to back it up, even though she encouraged him to use her data. Instead, Baker concluded with confidence that "the riot and the revulsion which followed it will combine to make a recurrence of such a disturbance next to impossible."

As for Negro crime as a cause of the riot, Baker equivocated. He early described the gruesome details of two black male attacks on white women, neither of which resulted in lynching, and only later exposed the alleged attacks of the week of the riot as falsely reported and greatly exaggerated. He seemed to excuse the false reports by white women as due to fear. Nowhere did he make Ovington's strong point that Atlanta had given guns to a rampaging white mob, and had taken guns away from respectable black residents defending their homes and families.[15]

As Baker finished his series in late summer 1908, Mary White Ovington shared her sometimes blunt assessment with him. He summarized the two parties into which Negroes were divided: the "greater," Washington's, was "constructive, practical, cheerful," and the "lesser," Du Bois's, was "idealistic and pessimistic; a party of agitation, emphasizing rights rather than duties." He put his hope for the future in "The New Southern Statesmanship"—the whites who sided with Washington.[16]

"It's hard for me to believe that you really think the movement you describe in the August number to be the saving good for the Negro and the South," Ovington protested. She wrote to him: "What aristocracy ever saved an impoverished class? One strong trade union, with colored and white working together, is worth more than . . . all the . . . rich men's schemes for making 'independent' workmen that you can find."[17]

By the time of the book publication of his articles in late 1908, Ovington thought she saw a shift in the muckraker's thinking regarding Negro rights; his final piece, "What to Do About the Negro," seemed to show a more favorable attitude toward agitation. For this she was grateful. Two northern whites who wrote of a cause of which they were not really a part, needed to constantly remind themselves that they did not half know what the life struggle of the Negro American meant.[18]

In pushing and nudging Baker toward a more radical stance, Ovington implicitly recognized how important it was to get Du Bois's principles into national print. "Some Publications Regarding the American Negro," in *Library Journal* in March 1907 was Ovington's small start in making explicit the topic of media, its influence, and its control.

For her list of recommended reading and library acquisition, she first eliminated white-authored material (including AP news) as biased and selective. Next she chopped material by Negroes in white-controlled magazines, stuff that was published only if the tone was conciliatory or facts suppressed. For truth one had to go to the Negroes themselves, especially to their pamphlet publications, which were not controlled by the mass market. The material Ovington then promoted was dominated by Du Bois: his Atlanta University *Bulletin*s and leaflets; the publications of the Niagara Movement; the publications of the American Negro Academy, including a Du Bois article. Among the only books Ovington praised were Charles Chesnutt's novels, especially *The Marrow of Tradition*, and Du Bois's *Souls of Black Folk*.[19]

Ovington and Du Bois knew they had to get their side of the Negro's story out, but money was a perpetual problem, for Washington's Tuskegee funnel sucked up philanthropic funds and distributed them to the media that promoted him uncritically. John Milholland's money helped Ovington travel and write, and Ovington did her best to push Baker to their side, since *American Magazine* did not depend on Washington's largesse.

But both knew that "outsiders" could not be depended on, and that popular outlets would not remain open. The radical side needed its own press outlet. Such an attempt was *The Horizon: A Journal of the Color Line*, the first issue of which came out in January 1907, edited by W. E. B. Du Bois, Freeman H. M. Murray, and L. M. Hershaw. It was published somewhat irregularly until July 1910, when its paid subscribers were transferred to the new NAACP publication under Du Bois, the *Crisis*. Full of short, satiric pieces, editorials, quotations from the Bible, Shakespeare, Wordsworth, and ads for publications not in Washington's camp, the magazine became the brief fragile mouthpiece of Du Bois and the Niagara Movement. "Is it mustard color because it bites?" Ovington asked Du Bois when she saw the bright gold of the first issue.[20]

But Booker T. Washington saw to it that the *Horizon* became no threat. At one point during a publishing hiatus, he noted sarcastically that its backers were college graduates whose "concentrated energy and brains" should at least be able to get a magazine out on time.[21] Du Bois's and Ovington's cause needed numbers of people, money, and some way to stay clear of Washington's manipulation. It would come, but only after time, thought, and trauma.

FOR SEVERAL MONTHS after April 20, 1907, Ovington helped her ailing parents through Europe. In her absence, John Milholland and

Du Bois worked for the compatible goals of the Constitution League and the Niagara Movement, their cooperation enhanced by Ovington's friendship. "Miss Ovington" was in Germany, Milholland informed Du Bois; would he like her address? "I have Miss Ovington's address," the Atlantan responded succinctly. Ovington praised Milholland to Du Bois continually: he is "all right," isn't he? He is certainly in this for all time, she said; he "understands conditions remarkably well."[22]

From the Swiss Alps, Ovington calculated covering the annual Niagara Movement meetings. They would dock on August 27; she could take the midnight train to Boston and be there for the final sessions. This time, she was determined to get something into the *Independent* as well as the *Post*. Probably editor Hamilton Holt had treated the movement carelessly because he hadn't understood it, she mused.[23]

She arrived in time for fireworks between William Monroe Trotter and Du Bois, but left the controversy out of her article. The Third Annual Meeting, she wrote, showed a "marked increase in attendance and enthusiasm," though she gave no numbers. (Twenty-nine people had met at Fort Erie in July of 1905; the maximum membership is estimated at four hundred, reached in 1907.[24])

She highlighted legal challenges to Jim Crow. The final, public meeting at Faneuil Hall was "largely attended by both races," and had the spirit of antislavery days. Ovington emphasized Du Bois's statement that "peonage, the convict system, the holding of men to the soil like serfs, is practised [*sic*] on both races alike, and will be while one man is able to control the labor of another man."

Her laudatory coverage was a press exception. "The Tuskegee Machine sensed the Niagara Movement's deterioration" at this point, says historian Manning Marable, "and moved rapidly to push it into extinction." In typical coverage, the Indianapolis *Freeman* called Du Bois's "Address to the World" a "final shriek of despair."[25]

Privately Ovington's morale sank with everyone else's, and from New York City she queried Du Bois. She had heard terrible criticism of him, including from "the slick ones," who believed that he was "caught at last." She had complete confidence in him, but she could defend him better if she had the facts. This division could fatally split the anti–Booker T. Washington forces. She could see the Tuskegean "rubbing his hands with glee, and calling on the good work to go on."[26]

Booker T. Washington jerked a lot of strings behind the scenes, planting a spy here, causing someone to lose a job there, promising and delivering goodies to someone who would betray Du Bois, telling newspapers what to say and what not to say (by the time of the 1908 meetings, Washington would give orders for papers not to cover the meetings at all). It is no wonder this stage for Du Bois's voice crumbled.[27]

Washington's information network even caught up with Mary White Ovington that fall. Major R. R. Moton sent Washington copies of letters showing Ovington's and Du Bois's close association with Charlotte Thorn at Calhoun. In a long *"Personal and Confidential"* reply, Washington wrote that "it is evident from Miss Ovington's manner of addressing and writing Miss Thorn that she, Du Bois and Miss Ovington have a pretty thorough understanding." Ovington's Alabama information came, Washington concluded, from either Milholland or Andrew Humphrey of the Constitution League, or "a discredited politician in Alabama by the name of Manning." With these people, "Miss Ovington has in some way become enraptured."

But Washington still dismissed Ovington's real and potential power. Neither Thorn nor Ovington, he concluded, "has a bit of influence among white people of any standing either in the political or business world." It is "pitiable" that "persons who are able to accomplish good in directions that Miss Ovington is . . . should yield to the temptation of giving time and strength to mean, little, petty gossip in directions that will do good for no one."[28]

Ovington tried to pull something positive out of the Niagara wreckage. She sent an article on the movement to the British *Review of Reviews;* as she said to Du Bois, she would keep trying "to get a clear statement of the position of the radical Negroes in print somewhere." She expanded her speaking engagements. When she spoke at the winter movement meeting in Boston, she also talked to Negro students at Harvard about graduate scholarships and the need for research in history, ethnology, and sociology. In New York City, she lectured to a public school–sponsored forum on the rural South, and pleaded with Du Bois to publish his Lowndes County research.[29]

The American economy slumped seriously in 1907. The downturn hit business, including the Ovington Gift Shops, her father's and brother's business, and affecting Ovington's own status as a dependent. It also hit contributions to schools and causes. Atlanta University invited Ovington to the inauguration of E. T. Ware, but she couldn't afford to go—even if she could, she would rather give her traveling expenses to the university. To Du Bois's urgent invitation to his conference the following spring, she also had to say no; it simply cost too much. But "you certainly don't need any little candle light like myself" since Jane Addams was to be there.[30] Belt-tightening made her much-delayed plans for a settlement in the Tuskegee urgent; she needed an income and hoped simultaneously to advance the cause.

————————

MARY WHITE OVINGTON moved into the Tuskegee at 233 West Sixty-third Street, in the all-Negro San Juan Hill area of Manhattan, in February 1908, the only white in the building and neighborhood. Modernity meant steam heat and bathrooms with unlimited hot water. For her second-floor, three-room apartment, reserved from the beginning, she asked that the partition be left out between the front rooms, giving her more space for people in the midst of her books and desk. Her bedroom was a mere cubicle, but with plenty of air and light—and noise.

Suddenly Henry Phipps, a prominent Washington supporter, grew adamant that there be no settlement in the Tuskegee.[31] Frustrated but determined, Ovington stayed as long as she could without an income, giving her rooms over to children and mothers in the daytime, Negro and white men and women eager to discuss "the race problem" at night. One reason she wanted to live there was to entertain racially mixed groups; even into the 1930s in white areas of the city, Ovington would run into problems with landlords and neighbors.

Her white friends and family worried about her safety, especially her mother. But Ovington did not find it a dangerous building or neighborhood, even though increasing numbers of the better-off families were leaving for Harlem. Her closest neighbors were hardworking men and women rarely in trouble. In the area she saw a lot of "loose living," men who lived on their "girls' earnings," evidence of "lusty sex life," and much gambling. Men's infidelity was common; heartbroken wives told her about it. But what went on after her eleven o'clock bedtime was not her affair, and no one ever bothered her, molested her, or even questioned her right to be there.

The Astral Model Tenement, where
Mary White Ovington conducted the
Greenpoint Settlement, from 1897 to
1904, as it looks today in the Polish
section of Brooklyn.

The Tuskegee Model Tenement as it
looks today, where Ovington lived in
the all-black San Juan Hill section of
Manhattan in 1908.

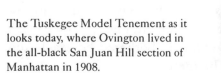

After the collapse of her settlement plans, Ovington found other organizational outlets. A good friend from the black middle class, Dr. Verina Morton Jones, suggested that she do something for her native town. Ovington was shocked at the deplorable conditions in Brooklyn and ashamed of her ignorance of conditions in her own backyard.

Dr. Jones pleaded with her to establish a settlement there. "Impetuosity had its disadvantages," Ovington said later. She liked the idea even though she would not be there as head resident, but she really did not know what a big task it was. She said yes; the two women gathered a board together with Ovington as president, rented a house, and began Lincoln Settlement. For two decades Ovington raised the money for Lincoln so the residents could concentrate on their work.[32]

Lincoln Settlement was more a community center than a full-blown residence for workers. It went through three head workers before 1911, when Dr. Morton Jones sacrificed much of her medical practice to take on the job. The work grew, with many volunteers, clubs, and classes added to the original kindergarten and day nursery. The board eventually bought the house and an adjoining playground. When Ovington moved to New York in 1923, the Urban League took over the finances of Lincoln Settlement.[33]

Ovington was a founder and board member/officer of several groups that merged to form the Urban League in 1911. In May 1906, sixty Negroes and whites (seven women), met in William Jay Schieffelin's home to form the Committee for Improving the Industrial Condition of the Negroes in New York, a kind of umbrella organization of forty, with subcommittees doing the work.[34] Ovington was on the Executive, Tradesmen, and Employment committees, and chaired the Neighborhood Work Committee.[35] This group, the Committee for the Protection of Colored Women (for which Ovington raised money),[36] and the Manhattan Trade School for Girls, in which she was also active, eventually were subsumed into the Urban League.

Ovington's work moved ever closer to that of the two men who would be so important in the founding of the NAACP, one black, one white. In W. E. B. Du Bois she found an intellectual activism of fighting for rights that thrilled and spurred her. In John Milholland she found the altruistic passion for the underdog, for black America, a passion that vibrated with increasing vehemence in her own heart. And increasingly, as the sole white member of the Niagara Movement, and as the only white resident on San Juan Hill, Mary White Ovington saw that any successful change in the race situation in the United States would have to combine the resources of concerned and courageous blacks and whites. Together, their power would be greater, their options larger, and their support fuller.

ON SAN JUAN HILL, Mary White Ovington had come to know the poor, the working poor, and the newly arrived southern immigrant. She also knew many well-established Negro middle-class families, most of whom lived in Brooklyn. Spontaneously, a little club had grown up out of the latter group in the spring of 1906, calling itself the Cosmopolitan Club, and meeting in various homes to discuss race issues. It was New York's only club with equal numbers of whites and Negroes and both sexes.

All Negro or interracial groups had one thing in common, she observed: no decent, attractive place to meet. They needed a sort of clubhouse, "a Clinton Hall on the West side designed especially for Negroes." If interracial groups could meet in the crowded neighborhood they were working for, they would do more energetic work, she thought. A large hall would, she wrote:

> encourage the discussion between white and black of important local and national issues that affect the Negro. We have some fine, intelligent colored men and women in our city, but if they are kept segregated much longer, taking no part in matters of public moment, they will grow to think that they have no part in the affairs of the state in the North as they know they have none in the South.

How could they go about building such a place? she asked Oswald Garrison Villard.[37]

By 1908 the Cosmopolitan Club still met in members' homes, however. For their spring meeting with guests they had to find a larger place. Ovington had just been to a socialist dinner at Peck's Restaurant on lower Fulton Street, a favorite for groups "with more ideas than money," and suggested that the Cosmopolitan Club also have a dinner there.[38]

It would be "unique," she told W. E. B. Du Bois; she wished he could be there.[39] Tickets sold well because of the prominent speakers: Villard; Hamilton Holt; John Spargo, a prominent socialist; Reverend Fraser Miller of St. Augustine's Church, Brooklyn; and William Ferris, who would later work for Marcus Garvey and his United Negro Improvement Association. Dr. Owen Waller, Negro physician and secretary of the group, was to preside.

When she entered the restaurant, she happily noted that diners were about equally divided, white and black, including doctors and ministers and social service workers she knew from Greenpoint or Greenwich House, all but one of whom were over thirty. (The *New York Times* later pointed out that most of the men were white, and most of the women black.) The event was sedate and "overserious" in Ovington's estimation. It could have been a group discussing education in a church parlor, she would joke later.

But halfway through the speeches, reporters slid into the room. Villard, a newspaperman, saw immediately what was happening, but Ovington did not, though at least she had the sense to refuse to have pictures taken.

The next day, a storm broke in the New York papers, waxing virulent as it moved south. For once, whites bore the brunt of the condemnation (the Negroes were only their tools), especially Villard and Ovington. The first front-page article in the *New York Times* was modest enough, headlined "Dinner minus Color Line: White Men of a Club Dine with Negro Women and Decry Caste." But the following day, the lead editorial in that paper sounded "An Admonition" in several hundred words:

> This particular banquet, we think, provoking as it must the public disgust and indignation, will serve to call the attention of the community to certain forces of evil that have been rather actively at work of late, and will, if we mistake not, tend in a marked degree to check and destroy them through the odious exhibition now made of what they really mean.

"Brotherhood" was the note of the banquet, socialism its "moving spirit and intent," and "equality" the basis for "settlement workers" discussing racial mixing by intermarriage, an act forbidden "by an instinctive, prevailing, and unconquerable resolve and condition of mind." There was, of course, no "negro [*sic*] question" in the North, but "flabby-minded persons" at this banquet had injured Negroes of the South.

South of the Mason-Dixon Line, the sober dinner became an orgy with drinking and lovemaking between voluptuous white women and smirking black men. In the *Chattanooga Times* it was "An Equality Love Feast"; the *Richmond New-Leader* headlined it as a "Miscegenation Banquet"; the *Houston Post* opined that while both the men and women were obviously "unbalanced," it was the white women who "ought to be locked up"; the *Norfolk Pilot* quoted the governor of Virginia as saying it was "disgraceful." The *St. Louis Post-Dispatch* sought to "consign the whole fraternity of perverts who participated in it to undying infamy." One woman (who was about seventy years old, Ovington noted) was described leaning amorously against a very black West Indian. Young girls in décolleté dress supposedly draped themselves on black men's shoulders. In the *Savannah News*, Judge Thomas N. Norwood described as worst of all,

> the high priestess, Miss Ovington, whose father is rich and who affiliates five days in every week with Negro men and dines with them at her home in Brooklyn, Sundays. She could have had a hundred thousand Negroes at the Bacchanal feast had she waved the bread tray. But the horror of it is she could take young white girls into that den. This is the feature that should alarm and arouse Northern society.

The dinner was even condemned on the floor of the United States Congress.

Ovington saw more reporters the next week than she did the rest of her life. Luckily the papers had given her parents' address at the Hotel St. George in Brooklyn. When she went there the weekend following the infamous event, the mail clerk, Mr. Taylor, kindly had her mail ready to hand her, so that she could get out of the lobby as quickly as possible.

Letters were so unspeakable that she went to her sister's house for a few days to let it all blow over; "We expected you to land in jail," her brother-in-law said. Most were from the South and were truly shocking, illiterate, and "nauseatingly obscene." "I was smothered in mud,"

Ovington said later, a jolt for her, since "like so many women of my class I had led a sheltered life." Some letters made threats, but that was, she thought, "rather jolly": "One is complimented to feel that one may have endangered one's life for a cause." Some letters were severe but dignified, and a few were congratulatory and sympathetic. She received one short, scraggly letter from Maryland that compensated somewhat for the rest: "I am a white man, but I glory in your spunk in standing up for what you believe to be right."[40]

Ovington's sudden notoriety almost destroyed Lincoln Settlement. She and the board had to issue a denial that their Brooklyn building would be used in any way for an interracial dinner club. "Let's work for federal aid for education—and settlements!" she suggested to Villard.[41]

Was Booker T. Washington behind the Cosmopolitan Club Dinner sensationalism? Ovington speculated that it was mischief-making from within the group itself, particularly by a "delightful pagan," Frenchman André Tridon. At least such an event would never be big news in New York City again.[42] Circumstantial evidence suggests, however, that the whole thing had been set up by Washington and his principal New York agent, Charles Anderson, who had arranged for the racially biased *New York American* to cover the event in order to discredit Washington's New York opponents.[43]

Oswald Garrison Villard was "very, very sorry" for what had happened because it probably ended the work of the club—whites would not want to be subjected to such misrepresentation. Personally, he did not regret it, however, and delighted in waging a long information campaign with Cluster Springs Academy in Virginia and Washington and Lee University about a demand that his honorary degree be withdrawn.[44]

But as a male, Villard did not bear the brunt of the criticism or have his personhood slandered in the same way Ovington did. She pointed out that reporters had not zeroed in on white men sitting by Negro women, but on white women sitting by black men, particularly herself. Already she had been cautious about the safety of a black man seen with her alone, particularly in the South. Now she recognized the need for caution about appearances in the North as well, and saw the nasty propaganda potential of any event with white women and black men.

Although Ovington grew wary about giving reporters ammunition, she did not let up on her interracial activities. Just the opposite, in fact.

Unwarranted persecution strengthened her in the cause. Du Bois stated well the credit deserved by someone who could simply walk away from the problem: "You unfortunate folks who are not compelled to stand our campaign of lies, but who are suffering from sheer interest in the cause will deserve undoubtedly a very large and well-fitting crown in the next world."[45]

To Mary Church Terrell, who had also written to express sympathy, Ovington said, "I think that persecution is good for some of us, I am sure it is for me, and my glimpse into the nastiness of thought and expression of both South and North that I have had in the past few weeks will only make me work the harder for those who must suffer most from it."[46]

In *Writing a Woman's Life*, Carolyn Heilbrun says that it is difficult today to grasp "how absolutely women of an earlier age could expel themselves from conventional society . . . by committing a social, usually a sexual, sin."[47] How much more difficult to grasp today how little it took to cause expulsion when race was involved, even without an actual sexual sin. Mary White Ovington committed the social sin of planning and enjoying an interracial dinner with men and women in a New York City restaurant in 1908 and became nationally notorious. But the wonderful irony, of course, in being expelled from conventional society is that there is a lot more freedom outside of conventions than within them. As Ovington would demonstrate, that freedom can be used to invent ways of trying to do good just as much as for personal indulgence.

THE NIAGARA MOVEMENT met the following summer of 1908 at Oberlin College in Ohio. Ovington had planned to be there, writing to Du Bois just before the Cosmopolitan Club Dinner that she would certainly come if he would let her speak on the "Relation of the Negro to the Labor Problem." She wanted to "hammer that side of things into some of the aristocrats who are in the membership." She did not get there after all, although she didn't mind so much after hearing that the delegates would be boarding around in different places. After all, "half the fun of those affairs is when the meetings aren't on, and one can have long talks," she told him.[48]

She sang "John Brown" at a Federation of Colored Women's Clubs meeting in Manhattan in late August, and thought, as always, of the meetings at Harpers Ferry in 1906. "That was a wonderful time," she told the Niagara Movement leader, "and the inspiration from it has helped me often." But where do we go from here? "Go on with your constructive work, with the effort to win the rights of manhood for every Negro in the country," she told Du Bois. "And work with those who are fighting the same fight. You ought to be done with bickering with Republicans or Democrats. There is a working man's party in the country. How can the Negro belong with any other?"[49]

Ovington was elsewhere in the late summer of 1908, having long talks and writing in a socialistic vein while Du Bois's Niagara Movement met at Oberlin. She was at Meadowmount, John Milholland's farm in upstate New York. The following year saw the publication of an Ovington poem in the *Elizabethtown Post,* prefaced by this note:

> The enclosed lines, written on Mount Discovery by the wellknown Settlement Worker and philanthropic reformer, Miss Mary White Ovington, of Brooklyn, while she was a guest at "Meadowmount" last summer will be appreciated by our readers, the closing verse, particularly, even by those who may not share all the ardent Socialistic views held by the gifted writer.

The poem itself, "A Mount Discovery Musing," is dated August 1908. Ovington's handwritten note on the clipping from the paper adds that "the summer of 190[7?] showed a large amount of unemployment among the laborers."

The poem begins describing the "line of blue where the long Lake lies," and girding, watching mountains—the peace of the hills and forests. A small, hungry bird cries from a hemlock tree and is quickly fed by a flashing, grey-blue and gold parent, which picks of the best berries on the hillside to feed its young. The final, "Socialistic," stanza of the four-stanza poem reads as follows:

> Oh, God! There is food when the nestling calls
> And sheltering leaves o'erhead.
> But down, far down, amid stifling walls,

A baby sobs for bread.
While he who would toil till the thick sweat falls,
Stands helpless by the bed.

Ovington had been working for John Milholland's Constitution League throughout 1908, including arranging for Du Bois to speak in New York in February. She and Milholland had joined forces, she told the Atlanta professor: "We are trying to get southern conditions before northern audiences, and to impress the North with its responsibility for outrages against the Constitution."[50]

Ovington was back on the West Side of Manhattan by late in August, reveling in the life of Sixty-third Street on hot summer evenings. She invited Ray Stannard Baker over to her apartment to see the liveliness, which was quite as interesting as the immigrant neighborhood on the Lower East Side, and very different. But, she told him, he should be sure to come on a night that was very warm.[51]

Sadly, she would have to leave San Juan Hill and her apartment, not just her settlement plans for the building. "I would have to give up my dream, go home, and finish my book." Her father was increasingly weak and ailing, and her mother not well, either. She had no job and her savings were depleted; she could not let them support her "while giving nothing in return."[52]

During her last days as the only white person among blacks, everything came together for Ovington in a sustaining sense of community. People of San Juan Hill poured out into the streets those last mild evenings. Graceful, engaging children sang their songs, some learned in kindergarten, some brought with them from the South, like "Sound dem Wedding Bells." The place was a "veritable Hyde Park for propaganda"—she could hear and see a West Indian preacher with an English accent playing a gospel hymn on a violin, men and women marching behind him singing. "Salvation is so convenient, Brother, it is so convenient." Through the door at Union Baptist she heard "salvation for this world"—women being told that they needed to lead moral lives and wear heavy flannels in winter if they wanted to avoid tuberculosis. And on the corner, "dandified-looking men, without words, preached their doctrine of an easy life with a hard-working girl to make life happy."

Three shy little girls called on her in freshly laundered dresses. Ovington accepted a half peanut from the littlest and read *Peter Rabbit* as they sat on her long sofa without fidgeting, a row of bright, shiny eyes. Visiting a family the Charity Organization Society had saved from eviction, Ovington was followed out by daughter Annabel, skipping and jumping down the stairway. "I know what I'm going to be when I grow up," she cried as she twirled engagingly at the bottom of the stairs. "I'm going to be a dancer! . . . I'm going to make *money*. Look at my mother, she works and works and she hasn't got a thing. They took her best chair and my bed."

Ovington peeked at the small, dirty courtyard behind the building to see handwriting on the wall. Expecting obscenity, she was amazed instead to see, in a well-formed hand: "Unless above himself he can erect himself, how poor a thing is man," and below that "No conflict is so severe as his who labors to subdue himself; but in this we must be continually engaged if we would be strengthened in the inner man." "Shakespeare and Thomas à Kempis on San Juan Hill!" she exclaimed.[53]

Mary White Ovington was extremely sad leaving her apartment and her dream of a settlement. The Cosmopolitan Club Dinner had shown her that the work she had planned was important. Her months living in this Negro community had given her joy, a sense of intense living, of belonging, of purpose. What could she do now?

She went to another dinner, this one given by the Intercollegiate Socialist Society. The leading speaker was Lucien Sanial, an old man with a white beard and piercing black eyes who had stood with the workers in the Paris Commune of 1871. Listening to him, Ovington experienced an epiphany of self-recognition and focusing.

> We had eaten well and had opened our program by singing William Morris's "March of the Workers." It is sung to the tune of "John Brown's Body." Well-fed, well-dressed, we stood at our tables and shouted Morris's stirring chorus:
>
> > Hark, the rolling of the thunder!
> > Lo, the sun! and low thereunder
> > Riseth wrath and hope and wonder
> > 'Tis the people marching on.
>
> We were mostly middle-aged folk, for the students held their meetings in their colleges. Sanial must have thought of this song when he

stopped in the middle of his talk, and looking down, not at us but through us, said, "Remember, you can be of no use to the workers, no least use, unless you repudiate your class, absolutely repudiate it; and even then," he stopped to look at us again, "even then, most of you would be useless."

I went home profoundly disturbed. I believed then as I do now that the economic problem is civilization's first problem, and that the workers' continued rebellion against their lot is the most profound fact of history, but I knew that I was not one of them. I was only cheering and throwing a few pennies. Very well then, I would cease to work for socialism and give what strength and ability I had to the problem of securing for the Negro American those rights and privileges into which every white American was born. Thus the Negro, if he willed it, should be able to march with the working class. This resolution seemed important to me at the time, and so I put it down here.[54]

Intimidation can have a galvanizing effect, turning intended casualties into determined activists. What had been meant to silence instead empowers. The Cosmopolitan Club Dinner of April 1908 empowered Mary White Ovington. She learned to avoid what could discredit the cause and its adherents, but she was confirmed in her life's course. That the challenge had more dimensions than she had recognized made it even more important that she rise to meet it.

Mary White Ovington believed in food and justice and hope for all human beings. Though she was not wealthy, she had never wanted for these things herself. For four years she had seen a portion of children in the United States denied all three with a frightening vehemence. As she focused her goals and her attention in late 1908 on equal rights for black Americans, she had had just a taste of the enormity of a problem that would consume the rest of her life. But she had also had a morsel of the savor and sustenance of community and of working for a cause with like-minded people. For the next forty years, never would the bitterness of the problem outweigh her joy in the communal struggle against it.

5

The NAACP Is Born

THE NATIONAL ASSOCIATION for the Advancement of Colored People was born into an ugly world. As Mary White Ovington prepared to leave her home in the black San Juan Hill section of Manhattan, race riots raged in Springfield, Illinois. Springfield was the hometown of Abraham Lincoln, and the country was rapidly approaching the centennial of the Great Emancipator's birth.

Those who had become inured to southern news like the Atlanta riots in 1906 took notice of death in the North. For two days, Springfield's "best citizens" raged through the black community after the kind of event Ovington had warned of—an unscrupulous white woman accusing a Negro man of rape. Two Negroes were lynched, six Negroes and whites killed, over seventy Negroes and whites wounded, and thousands driven from the city before four thousand state militia took over the streets.[1]

Ovington saw the news after the August 14 and 15 riots and just as she was in need of a new venture. After the collapse of her settlement plans for the Tuskegee model tenement where she lived, her writing, travel, and social service work did not fully satisfy her. "Socialism had taught me to look below the surface of a problem to the cause. Was I doing anything for the fundamental cause of the race's condition?"[2]

Then she saw the article by William English Walling in the *Independent* in September 1908, "Race War in the North." "Who realizes the seriousness of the situation, and what large and powerful body of citizens is ready to come to [the Negro's] aid?" he asked.

105

"Here was the first person who had sent a challenge to white and colored to battle, as the abolitionists had battled, for the full rights of the Negro," Ovington thought. Du Bois and his Niagara Movement were stymied by small numbers and little money. Here was a white man calling on black *and* white to right the nation's wrongs; it was the only way. "Drums beat in my heart," Ovington declared. Within the hour she sat down and wrote Walling.[3]

Months went by and she heard nothing. Again, after one of his lectures at Cooper Union, she proposed that they form an organization.[4] Still nothing happened until she wrote again, when finally Walling suggested they get together with Charles Edward Russell. Ovington kept the appointment the first week of January 1909 at Walling's apartment. Russell couldn't make it; social worker Henry Moskowitz took his place.

It was there, in a little room of a New York apartment, that the NAACP was born. Walling, a southerner, thought treatment of the American Negro was worse than that of the Jew in Russia. Ovington, the radical Unitarian, shared her firsthand knowledge of discrimination in employment and in public facilities. Moskowitz, with expertise on immigrant conditions, helped them interpret their observations. Their differences generated the birth and symbolized "the help that was at once to come to our aid."[5]

The three immediately drafted a "Call" for a meeting of the "large and powerful body of citizens," to be issued on Lincoln's one hundredth birthday, February 12, 1909, and sent it to several people for comments.

Hamilton Holt, editor of the *Independent*, disagreed with much of it. Testily, Walling responded that it had been sent out to get criticism and Holt had been "more generous to us than everybody else put together in this respect." Villard, wealthy owner and editor of the *New York Evening Post*, thought the statement too long. "In view of his importance to us and the position he took, I asked him if he would be good enough to re-cast it altogether," Walling reported.[6]

Here loomed two problems: possible supporters such as Holt, who were more in the Booker T. Washington camp than in Du Bois's; and Villard's power and need to control. Ovington fed the editor's strong ego by telling the story of the origin of the NAACP, which she wrote in 1914 with Villard as the fifth founder and invited immediately to write the Call.

Ovington made the early group interracial. Though Walling shared with her social work contacts such as Lillian Wald and Florence Kelley, Ovington was the only one with a network of blacks. She brought in Bishop Alexander Walters of the African Methodist Episcopal Zion Church, Reverend William Henry Brooks, minister of St. Mark's Methodist Episcopal Church in New York, and Dr. W. H. Bulkley, black principal of a white New York public school.[7]

Ovington described the Call as powerful and impressive, and quoted it in full in her 1914 pamphlet. What would the Great Emancipator find returning on his hundredth birthday? Villard asked. Disfranchisement reinstated in the South. The Supreme Court of the land putting its stamp of approval on the discriminatory separation of the races. Lawless attacks on the Negro, in the North and the South.

Under such conditions, silence meant approval, he continued. "This government cannot exist half-slave and half-free any better today than it could in 1861." Then: "We call upon all the believers in democracy to join in a national conference for the discussion of present evils, the voicing of protests, and the renewal of the struggle for civil and political liberty." This Call was signed by fifty-three people in Ovington's version, sixty in the copy in Villard's papers.[8]

The signers of the Call did not yet know one another, but they knew Mary White Ovington. Leonora O'Reilly and William Dean Howells were old Social Reform Club contacts. The Reverend John Haynes Holmes and others were Unitarians as she was. John Dewey and other Columbia University personnel she knew from her Fellowship at Greenwich House. Many were contacts she had made among blacks in New York and Washington, D.C., and elsewhere: Du Bois, of course, and Bulkley, Walters, and Brooks; and also J. Milton Waldron, Reverend Francis Grimke, Mary Church Terrell, and Ida Wells-Barnett. Ovington had visited often with signers Jane Addams and Mary E. McDowell in Chicago. Some people she knew through the Socialist Party or publishing networks—Charles Edward Russell, Lincoln Steffens, Ray Stannard Baker. Because Ovington's role has been so incompletely described, no one has yet noted that what unites the signers is the person whose contacts bridged race and class and gender lines: Mary White Ovington.

Though historians have not noted Ovington's networking role, they have frequently used signatures on the Call as indicators of concern about discrimination among social reformers in the Progressive period, who were otherwise noticeably blind to race issues. Allen F. Davis points out that one-third of the signers were involved in settlements. Charles Flint Kellogg says that suffragists are often thought to have been hostile to the Negro cause, but fully one-third of the signers were women. Wilson Record points out that the "instigators" of the NAACP were primarily white and Negro intellectuals, mostly from the North, from the larger urban centers, relatively youthful, largely uninvolved previously with race movements, and included a large number of women. Biographies of well-known Progressives such as Jane Addams frequently cite their involvement in the NAACP as evidence of their not having ignored the race issue.[9]

There are conspicuous absences among the signers. The people Ovington worked with on the Committee for Improving the Industrial Condition of Negroes in New York are absent, both white and Negro—this group would evolve into the more conservative Urban League. Many of her socialist friends are missing, including W. J. Ghent. To her disappointment, the party she loved failed after 1901 to make any platform statement concerning the race problem in America.[10] The militant black Bostonian William Monroe Trotter is not among the signers of the Call, nor is Moorfield Storey, the constitutional lawyer who would become the NAACP's first president.[11]

So discouraged was Villard with the Call's reception that he hesitated about holding the conference it called for.[12] But the other adventurers plunged ahead. Once started, the tall, aristocratic Walling was a dynamo, according to Ovington. The group continued to meet in his centrally located apartment on West Thirty-eighth Street until there were too many people, and they moved to the Liberal Club on East Nineteenth Street.

The first extant minutes, by Ovington, are from a meeting at the club on an unspecified date in March 1909. Charles Russell was in the chair. Most of the sixteen people there had been signers of the Call, but at least one was new: Alexander Irvine, a socialist friend of Ovington and a member of the Liberal Club.[13]

On the Committee of Arrangements, Ovington was a central part of the planning for the National Negro Committee's first convention, despite the death of her father less than two weeks before the event. Meetings began on Sunday, May 30, with a reception at Lillian Wald's Henry Street Settlement, with Fanny Garrison Villard (William Lloyd Garrison's daughter, and Oswald's mother), receiving.

For the next two days, an invited interracial group of three hundred met in the Charity Organization Building. His New York informer telegraphed Booker T. Washington that

> Du Bois, Waldron, Walters, Sinclair, Max, Barber, Wibecan, Dr Moselle, Bulkley, Milholland, Ida Wells, and entire cosmopolitan dinner crowd in Secret conference to-day. Public meeting to-night have had newspapers cover it another secret session to-morrow. Think Villard is with them.[14]

An evening public meeting at Cooper Union drew fifteen hundred people.[15] Ovington cheered the *New York Times* headline: "Whites and Blacks Confer as Equals." The article emphasized the prominent people and women there, before a section titled "Booker Washington Criticized." Du Bois was mentioned as a speaker only in the last paragraph.[16]

Ovington worked for a conference of facts, not opinions, with short presentations by twenty-four scholars. Livingston Farrand (of her Greenwich House Committee and later president of Cornell University) and Burt Wilder of Cornell led a morning's session on ethnology. Du Bois covered labor and prejudice; John Dewey spoke on education. E. R. A. Seligman of Columbia reminded the group that mankind moved very slowly.[17] It was a good plan. Ovington was amazed at how little whites understood "the Negro problem," even though they were interested and sympathetic. Late one night Charles Russell said he had had more education on the issue since ten o'clock that morning than all the rest of his life.

Ovington always found understanding enhanced by informal interactions. Taking her lead from Du Bois's Niagara meetings, she secured a dining room on Union Square, where debates spilled over into soup and coffee breaks. (Ovington went with John Milholland to lunch at least once; his family was not in town.) The combination of formal presentations and informal social time was very effective.[18]

The final session, at which something permanent was to be formed, was stormy for reasons that could not be broadcast at the time, nor fully exposed in Ovington's 1914 pamphlet. In 1932 she wrote that "I think it's legitimate now to raise the curtain a little." The "inevitable" controversy, "part of the time in which we lived," centered on Booker T. Washington. She wrote: "Was it possible to build up any organization, to get support for what we knew would become expensive work, without his sanction? . . . Could we ignore the man who was unquestionably the most influential and the most famous Negro living?"

Ovington thought including Washington would immediately condemn the group, since they would lose Du Bois and "we would start out under suspicion."[19] Unbeknownst to her, Villard had invited the Tuskegee leader and assured him "there is not the slightest intention of tying up this movement with either of the two factions in the negro [*sic*] race." Washington refused the invitation, as Ovington guessed he would if asked. He eschewed "agitation."[20] The Resolution Committee debated the issue of including Washington until the radicals (including Du Bois and Ovington) agreed to include conservatives on the proposed permanent Committee of Forty, and not to name Washington's bitterest enemies.

When the full proposal came to the floor, three hours of debate covered the resolutions phrase by phrase. Negroes wondered if whites were going to be "namby-pamby at the last as so many whites before them had been and counsel halfway measures," Ovington said. "In their experience, the boasted bond of brotherly love had always a loose strand, and a good pull broke the white from the black."

But at last, in Du Bois's words, there was "a visible bursting into action of long gathering thought and brooding." Resolutions sounded much like Milholland's Constitution League and Du Bois's Niagara Movement. They demanded the ballot, the same education for colored and white, and the enforcement of the Fourteenth and Fifteenth amendments to the Constitution. The "Platform Adopted by the National Negro Committee, 1909" denounced disfranchisement, lynching, "wage slavery," and manipulation of workers by appeal to racism.[21]

Some of the debate was valuable, Ovington thought, and some not ("there are always cranks who get into such a meeting"), but chair Charles Edward Russell was "the personification of courtesy." He let everyone talk, but guided them to conclusion by midnight. "Without him we should have been a howling mob," she laughed.[22]

The majority was satisfied, but a minority grumbled in the aisles about the "Committee of Forty." Ovington was relieved to get out into the cool early morning air on June 2. Friends pulled up in a touring car and begged her to join them, but she refused. She needed to be alone, to sort through all that had happened in her personal and public life. She had not had time to confront it before, and now her father's death hit her hard, together with the impact of the meetings. Sometimes she forgot, she told Villard the next day, that "the Negroes aren't poor people for whom I must kindly do something," but "men with most force-ful opinions of their own." She felt that the conference was, all in all, "an important piece of work."

She spent the next two weeks in the country with her mother, recu-perating. There she heard of the "thunderous recriminations" that fell on Walling and Russell, especially from Ida Wells-Barnett, whose name had been left off the Committee of Forty. Her name was reinstated, "and there it stands, where it ought to be," Ovington wrote later.[23]

Compromise might be the only way to move ahead, but compro-misers win no praise. Ovington undertook the difficult diplomacy needed to keep strong individuals working together. She had brought Villard in, and now she had to keep him happy, especially since Mil-holland was totally disillusioned with the *Post* editor, calling him a downright "dangerous leader" with small feet trying to fill big boots who "talks of raising big money."[24]

The first conference of the National Negro Committee left an in-fant organization, alive and kicking, but needing massive nourishment to ever be heard beyond its tiny New York City bassinet. Its platform would, as Ovington described it, "not seem so very radical" fifteen years later, but in 1909 it was "denounced by nearly every white man who gave to Negro institutions," and "a large number of colored peo-ple thought it unwise." The group "was continually urged to side-step the main issue, to unite with the conservatives, to relax a little its un-compromising tone. Had it done this, however, it would have slipped into oblivion."[25] The tightrope between inception and establishment demanded the uncompromising flexibility of a balancing genius. Ov-ington was there throughout this critical period.

PROBLEMS ABOUNDED for the Committee of Forty established that night in 1909. Ovington, the only woman with a continuous, active role, negotiated between the rocky male egos. She had to keep Villard's money and media access on board, but he was in constant contact with Booker T. Washington, who intensified his highly honed control-or-destroy tactics. Chairman William English Walling was anxious that the committee not become "the tool of any faction," but

Villard found Walling erratic and impossible to work with. Ovington had to keep conflicts from messing up her and John Milholland's goal: an outlet for the powerful alternative voice of W. E. B. Du Bois.

Their first office, shared with the Constitution League at 500 Fifth Avenue, was poorly lit and small, with a few chairs and a table. But according to John Haynes Holmes, through all the dinginess shone a woman "who had called the conference on her own responsibility." Ovington "herself assumed the sole direction of this new Association," he recalled, taking on duties with "superb devotion and ability" until paid staff could take over, when "with infinite grace" she stepped aside.

Frances Blascoer, hired as secretary in January 1910, tells of a hair-tearing, devil-possessed place. Villard raged at Walling and repeatedly threatened to resign. Walling had a "damnably acute intelligence" but acted like a baby. Walling's wife, sentimental and tiresome, was in and out. Who could live with Walling anyway? Milholland wanted the Constitution League to "swallow" the National Committee, but Du Bois sent a "fine scheme" for organization. Villard wouldn't stir on the next conference without Ovington. Ida Wells-Barnett had calmed down and might speak if her expenses were paid.[26]

Walling was forced to resign for a time, allegedly for health, but more likely because of a breach of promise suit publicized by the Tuskegee Machine. Ovington (whom the new chairman, Villard, called "a trump") took on everything, beginning with her customary fund-raising. Villard eventually provided office space in the *Evening Post* building and six months' salary ($150) for secretary Blascoer. His mother gave $50, Walling $41.50, and Ovington and Mr. Mack $25 each. Between March and April, she pulled in another $200.

Booker T. Washington squeezed money supply lines from supporters such as John Hope, president of Atlanta Baptist College, later president of Atlanta University. Be careful, Du Bois told Hope. Washington stood for submission. Some had to accept the Tuskegean's money or starve, but acceptance made it impossible to speak out. He might himself end up eventually in that position, Du Bois continued, but he swore he would fight to avoid it.

Washington feared a union of Milholland's and Villard's money and media with Du Bois's sharp pen. He worked on Villard, whom he considered the soft spot in the new alliance; Washington believed the powerful newspaperman would eventually "come around" to his side.[27]

While the men feuded and schemed, Ovington worked harder. She reviewed books to get the radical side of race issues into print.[28] She attended, and sometimes led, meetings of the Committee of Forty, being one of seven who sloshed through a bad storm in December 1909, and one of five on February 14, 1910. She made all the motions then, including postponing the annual meeting from April until May, for she had once again been called on by family to accompany her mother and brother-in-law abroad.[29]

The group voted that "the entire work of the Committee on invitations and arrangements go over until Miss Ovington's return." From sun-filled Jamaica she returned in an April blizzard to find all work on the conference undone. At first she was provoked, but then realized that "I was the only one among the white and colored board of the Association who had plenty of leisure and at the same time a conviction that this was the most important work that she could do."[30]

Her Committee on Invitations and Arrangements was charged with responsibility for raising money. She appealed to Negro clergymen, to businessmen and lawyers, and to John Milholland, and she set up a sale table of disfranchisement literature at the conference. She also chaired the Conference Program Committee, with the topic "Disenfranchisement and Its Effect upon the Negro." She collected documented anecdotes of unsuccessful efforts to register or to vote, endangerments to property rights because of disfranchisement, murderers of Negroes who had not been brought to justice, and deterioration in protection of prisoners.[31]

Those were the short-term tasks. But Ovington, Milholland, and Walling had a larger long-term goal in mind. Bringing Du Bois from Atlanta to begin a publication meant they needed $2,500 a year for his salary alone. Milholland pledged the first $200 and last $500 of their $10,000 goal. Henry Phipps turned them down just as he had nixed Ovington's settlement plans for the Tuskegee in 1908, but Jacob Schiff gave $500 and Mrs. Henry Villard $300. For the rest they increased the committee to 100, and required that each member raise $100.[32]

The Second Annual Conference of the National Negro Committee opened on May 12, 1910, taking the new name "The National Association for the Advancement of Colored People." Its objective was "equal rights and opportunities for all." It would have a National Committee of one hundred, and an Executive Committee of thirty. Half of the latter were to be from New York City, site (thanks to Ovington) of the national office. Legal aid, mass meetings, investigation, and publicity were to be its activities. The Executive Committee elected Walling as chairman, Milholland as treasurer, and Villard as assistant, or disbursing treasurer.[33]

Muckraker Ray Stannard Baker spoke at the Public Meeting at Cooper Union. He had signed the Call and come to some meetings the first year, but still sat painfully astride the fence between Du Bois and Washington. Ovington was not able to win Baker to her cause, but her sales tactics differed from Walling's flattery and Du Bois's lecturing.[34] She wrote Baker about non-NAACP matters, invited him to speak at Lincoln Settlement, and shared ideas for writing and reviews. "It seems to me you are coming very much our way," she told him just before the conference. "If you are not a Socialist you certainly are not anything that is trying to do half-way work."[35] But Baker wrote Washington that his speech "did not meet with the approval of the radicals," and subsequently refused a slot on the Executive Committee.[36]

Competing with the return of Halley's comet and the death of King Edward in England, the final sessions of the NAACP's 1910 meetings made it to only the second page of the *New York Times*.[37] Ovington wrote a full account, "Closing the Little Black Schoolhouse," in *Survey*, emphasizing disfranchisement, the courts, and education.

The NAACP "stands for a full and frank discussion of conditions among Negroes in the United States," she began, illustrated by the range of speakers: Charles Chesnutt, the novelist, who had refused to be involved with the 1909 meetings; Du Bois; Kelly Miller of Howard University; Ida Wells-Barnett; Mary Church Terrell; Oscar Crosby, "a conservative Virginian"; and "labor champion" Clarence Darrow. So good were these presentations and discussions that henceforth they would be open to the public.

In conclusion, Ovington announced the establishment of the permanent NAACP and saved the best for last:

> If sufficient financial support can be secured it is proposed to engage Dr. Du Bois as the head of a committee of publicity and research. The enthusiasm with which this proposition was received at the Saturday night meeting speaks well for its fulfillment.[38]

On June 28, without Villard, six members of the Executive Committee met. Enormously satisfied, John Milholland moved, and Mary White Ovington seconded, that

> Professor W. E. Burghardt Du Bois be engaged as Director of the Department of Publicity and Research of the National Association for the Advancement of Colored People, commencing October 1st at a salary of $2,500 per year, payable monthly.

The minutes of the meeting added that Walling would rent an office for Du Bois with "the name of the Constitution League to be placed on the door."

Ovington later wrote in a private letter that Villard "had always been opposed" to bringing in Du Bois, that "he had not wanted him in the beginning and he had never been convinced that our choice of a Director of Publicity and Research had been wise."[39] But in the summer of 1910, Villard let the radicals work to get their man.

Du Bois saw Ovington as the key link between his previous venture and his moving to New York with the NAACP. In later years, he remembered Ovington at the Niagara Movement meeting in 1906 at Harpers Ferry, and named Ovington, Walling, and Villard as the three who founded the NAACP and then invited Du Bois to join them.

By 1909, Du Bois continued, he saw that an all-Negro organization could not be effective fighting for rights. How could it influence white public opinion or gain coverage in newspapers and magazines or be granted opportunities to lecture? It was vital, he concluded, to have whites involved as well, and it made sense to all be in one organization. So Du Bois recalled the Niagara Movement as melting into the NAACP, with most members switching over to the new group, and his becoming one of its first officials.[40]

Du Bois began planning a magazine immediately in July of 1910, and by mid-August had resigned from Atlanta University, hired Frank Turner as bookkeeper, set up an office with furniture from the Constitution League, and adopted a name for the new publication. In the informal way things were decided at the NAACP offices in those days, several regulars sat talking about poetry, and Ovington piped up that her favorite poem was James Russell Lowell's "The Present Crisis." Walling looked up. "There's the name for your magazine," he said. "The Crisis."[41]

The magazine succeeded immediately. Its first issue appeared in November 1910, sixteen pages long. Published monthly, it sold for a dollar a year or ten cents a copy. On its first cover, in line pencil drawing, stood a long-garbed child preparing to roll with stick in one hand, hoop in the other.

Du Bois adopted features from his earlier *Horizon:* "Along the Color Line" (news items); "Opinion" (reprints of editorial comment from elsewhere); "Editorial" (Du Bois's primary regular writing outlet, with editorials on several issues); "The NAACP" (updates and information about the organization); "The Burden" (factual information, like lynching totals); "What to Read" (book and article summaries and information); and "Crisis Advertiser" (paid ads as well as ads for publications by NAACP personnel). There were also reprints of speeches, feature articles, and poetry.

One thousand copies sold out and the Executive Committee authorized expanding it to thirty-two pages. By the end of its first year the periodical boasted ten thousand readers, and in ten years, one hundred thousand.[42]

The *Crisis* filled a virtual vacuum in reliable materials by and about American blacks. Booker T. Washington controlled most of what was printed in the black press. White magazines perpetuated the plantation tradition with derisive terms, caricatures, ludicrous titles, and derogatory stereotypes.

But in the *Crisis*, the clear challenger to Washington could have full play, with money worries removed. (Ovington and Owen Waller were designated as the Finance Committee in October 1910.) With a new organizational base, increasing financial support, a media outlet, and unity of thought and goal, Mary White Ovington, John Milholland, and W. E. B. Du Bois reached the target of their five-year plan. In hiring Du Bois, Ovington asserted, "We said more plainly than by any number of addresses and pamphlets that we were against the doctrine of conciliation and education confined to industrial subjects, and in favor of the full rights of the Negro in the United States."[43]

WHILE THE WORLD LURCHED toward World War I, Mary White Ovington traveled to four countries on three continents, crafting an international context for her experiences in the United States with race and labor. She spent five weeks in Jamaica with her mother and brother-in-law Edmund Kingsbury. It was "good to see the Negro treated like a man," and to revel in the lush tropical abundance—she carried Gosse's *Birds of Jamaica* and sighted Hopping Dicks and Banana Quits and Green Todys.[44]

Ovington's main introduction was to Sidney Olivier, governor general of the colony, a Fabian Socialist and author of *White Capital and*

Colored Labor. What she admired, she soon found that the English Colonials despised, including Olivier's lack of pomp and whiskers. He even walked Ovington to her carriage after their interview, embarrassing the old driver so that he nearly dumped her out.

From Olivier, she learned much about conditions for the 98 percent of the population that was nonwhite. England has been "so successful in keeping her colonies because she thoroughly understands the principal of divide and rule," she concluded, for "a line as deep and wide as the ocean between themselves and Great Britain was drawn between black and colored [or racially mixed]."

As in her travels in the American South, Ovington left the English and colored communities entirely to immerse herself in the world of "the black Negro." She spoke to black men in a small, dimly lit hall. She found the women of the hills especially attractive:

> I doubt if any queen has so regal a carriage as the girl of sixteen who goes by carrying a tray heaped with potatoes and yams. . . . And she is only one of a long line of women, young and old, moving toward you down the road, splendid figures, with dark bronze faces, and a touch of bright color somewhere, about their dress or in the golden oranges or the crimson ackie of their load.

"What figures those women have. You're attacking this matter of Negro equality the wrong way," laughed her brother-in-law, Kingsbury. "Just get a law passed that everyone must go nude! Then you'd get not equality but Negro superiority."

At the Baptist church they were ushered to the white folks' seats in front. The natural and impressive minister looked down on two dark young men in uniform and said, "Some of you have done some good, and you have been made constables. I believe it has been because you have had peace in your heart." "A policeman with peace in his heart!" Ovington exclaimed. "It is surely many leagues from New York to Mandeville. Yet this fairly represents the spirit of these people."

The poverty that Olivier had spelled out for her was revealed in what she described as "one and two-roomed cabins crowded with children; sickness, often tuberculosis, in the close chamber from which the peasant excludes every breath of night air." She tried to tell those who cried, "Won't you take me to America?" that they would find a rough and ugly social position, but they saw only food and clothing in abundance, and "a bed of one's own." Based on her visit, Ovington would understand something about two famous Jamaicans who came to America—black nationalist Marcus Garvey and poet and radical Claude McKay. She observed, "With both these men the law and order of the English colony made revolt impossible and they came to the more democratic United States."

In the summer of 1911, Ovington met Olivier again at the International Races Congress in London, which had as its object cooperation between white and colored peoples. It was the brainchild of John Milholland, Felix Adler of the New York Ethical Culture Society, and Gustave Spiller of the London Ethical Culture Society. A contribution of $650 from Milholland enabled the NAACP to send Ovington, W. E. B. Du Bois, and Dr. W. A. Sinclair.[45]

The July 26 opening at the University of London included 30 presidents of parliaments; 20 British governors and premiers; over 40 colonial bishops; 130 professors of international law, anthropology, and sociology; and officers of the Council of the Interparliamentary Union. Peace Movement leader Lord Weardale, opening the sessions, looked out on a thousand people representing fifty different "races."[46]

Ovington was one of few women, most from the United States. Repeatedly she acted as a facilitator, particularly at the many social events. The opening reception was at Fishmongers' Hall, a name the Americans found delightful. People sat silent against the walls. "No old-time settlement worker could endure such a situation," Ovington laughed, and began circling the hall, talking to strangers, helping them to talk with one another. Soon she appeared to be the hostess. Author Jean Finot asked: "You seem to know everyone here, will you kindly introduce me to M. Legitime, president of Haiti?" She had not yet met the gentleman, but that did not stop her, and she found him a wonderful, courtly Frenchman.

Another day, when the Countess of Warwick entertained at her castle, Ovington saw his daughter, Mlle. Legitime, a beautiful, dark, graceful woman. Walking across the perfect English lawn, the young Haitian picked up a peacock feather and held it aloft like the scepter of a young queen honoring England with her presence.

Ovington delighted in the beauty and the variety of multicolored humanity. Beneath the great cedars of Lebanon, she sat with Dr. Charles Eastman, the Sioux physician, lecturer, and author on multiculturalism, one of the Congress speakers. While he talked of the worship of trees, representatives from Turkey and Persia, China and

Liberia, Europe and America, "representatives of modern races and of antiquity," she said, moved over the grass before them.

Representatives presented papers in the great glass-roofed hall of the University of London. Despite what the official report called "unprecedented tropical heat" and imperfect acoustics, the crowd came back day after day, hearing Du Bois twice, Olivier three times, and a dynamic Annie Besant, who would, in 1917 at age seventy, become the first woman and last European president of the Indian National Congress. As Ovington described her, she tossed back her gray hair, paced up and down the platform, and shouted her criticism of British rule. The presiding officer rose, and she raised her voice. He rang his bell and she went on. Finally she sat down to wild applause.

Ovington had a very good time, but appreciated Milholland's serious purpose: a permanent world organization that would meet every four years on the world's continents in turn. But her friend, as she described it, "felt a hostile influence" as soon as imperialism was criticized. All provocative papers stopped, and speeches were limited to seven minutes. (The French, she noted parenthetically, could say less in seven minutes than any other nationality.)

The Resolutions of the International Races Congress of 1911 reflect a forward-looking multiculturalism: elimination of race prejudice, study and appreciation of all civilizations and customs, sensitivity training for teachers and colonial administrators and diplomats. Unfortunately, these issues were squelched by two world wars.[47]

Ovington did not sail back with other delegates, but traveled to Scandinavia with her friend Frances Davenport, introducing herself, as in the United States, with her "old socialist ticket." A week's cruise through the Norwegian fjords to Trondheim preceded visits to Stockholm and Copenhagen.

On a park bench overlooking the North Sea, Davenport said she believed war was near—that when the people in power wanted it, it would come. Since college, Davenport had challenged Ovington intellectually, and she did the same in 1911. High on the meetings in London, on the humane ideas, the good work, and the hope of organizations like Baha'i, the NAACP, and the Intercollegiate Socialist Society, Ovington argued that there could not be another great European war, that the working class too consistently demanded peace.

But "when the German troops marched into Belgium" in 1914, "every third man a socialist and an internationalist, I remembered our talk," Ovington said. War once again made workers the tools of imperialism. "I could quote Catherine of Russia who frankly said, 'The only way to save our empires from the encroachment of the people is to engage in war *and thus substitute national passions for social aspirations.*'"[48]

In 1913 Ovington published a long poem that reflects her faith before the war. The first stanza of "Revolution" describes it as a tempest that "flung the loom o'er which the wretched mother hung . . . into the gulf of unremembered things" and "broke dull labor's rack." "And its swift lightning, flash by flash, betrayed / The scarred and ugly homes that ignorance had made."

The second stanza describes the morning after the storm. The sun climbs into a "sapphire sky / To view a nation freed from anarchy." No chains of "hoarded gold" now hold one man to another. Beauty and springtime reign, in playing, dimpled babies, kneeling mothers, clear-eyed children, and aged men "aglow at three-score years and ten." The poem continues, "Unto each came life's most precious thing: / The chance for free, entire, harmonious, blossoming."

The final stanza asked: "What will the comfortable do when this happens?" God is on the side of the workers. If our meat is taken, let us remember that "thy bread of life is sweet." If our homes are dashed to earth, "Brave hearts may learn in joy to roam." If our children are taken, "let brave youth / Rush with the tempest on to battle for the truth."[49]

She traveled abroad again with her mother before World War I had broken out, in early 1914.[50] In rural El Kantara, Algeria, gateway to the desert, she saw the separation of the ruler and the ruled. Walking into the Arab Village Rouge, she could not distinguish the mud houses from the mud streets.

In one of the low doorways she saw the supple figure of a young man in a clinging white woolen burnoose, "doing nothing with admirable grace." Under his white fez, alert brown eyes shone and his mischievous mouth reminded her of the hundreds of boys she had known on New York playgrounds, and she felt immediately at home.

Bemar became her guide, his French accent, she found, "in its departure from Parisian match[ing] mine from America." With him, she entered upon a courtyard of women and children. One of the women let them into her house, a single room with no chairs, one bed, a stove, and beautiful handworked polished brass utensils. What did the woman do? Ovington asked. She cooks and washes for her husband and nurses the baby, Bemar replied. Doesn't it sound dull? wondered the New York visitor. She can go out to the cemetery on Friday to mourn her dead, the young man replied. Would you like to live like that? Ovington asked him, and he laughed. She slipped a piece of silver into the woman's palm and they made their way among dirty children back onto the street.

In an antiwar article Ovington published based on her experiences, she noted that Arab women at home without their veils lost their attractiveness with their mystery. The women she saw in their homes looked fat and unhealthy from oppressive living conditions rarely seen by an outsider.

Ovington kept in communication with Bemar, she reported. She had pleaded with him as they sat together on a curb talking of education and life, as she described:

> "Don't be a soldier," I cried involuntarily.
> "Why not?" he asked.
> "Because a soldier must go out and kill men."
> "Ah, no, madam," the boy said with much earnestness. "A soldier does not kill. It is he who prevents men from warring one upon another. He guards the country. He keeps the peace.". . .
> I did not answer, but I saw clearly that Bemar was no longer of the Orient. He had become a child of France.

From his letters, she learned he had entered the army. In the summer of 1914, she received his last postcard, from the French front. "Bemar has become a number, one of the millions that have stood in the trenches battling for the integrity of the Republic. Was he with the Arabs or the French?"[51]

Ovington also published a poem in late 1914 that expressed the horror war brought to the innocent. "On Christmas Eve" sets the scene of a cozy, anticipatory evening, with fire and candlelight, children unable to sleep, waiting to hear the reindeer and Santa.

> Without, the glistening stars again
> Speak Peace on earth, good-will to men
>   On Christmas Eve.

And then, predictably we might think now, but perhaps as a shock to her readers in 1914 in a family newspaper, came the following:

Crash, deafening crash, the cannon's breath.
Red blood upon the sheet.
The scream of fear, the moan of death
A baby's stumbling feet

. . .

Upon the steppe and plain
Cold children wander desolate
While roars the battle's song of hate
On Christmas Eve.[52]

Yes, we were "over-sanguine" in those years before World War I, Ovington remembered, "but surely we were not such fools as the ruling class that started the war." If they could bring back that summer she had to believe they would act differently; "they would make it up among themselves rather than start a world cataclysm."[53] In a world that could hold a Races Congress and in three years go to war, where was sanity to be found? Perhaps only in the small voice, the small act, the faithfulness to a cause.

———

THE THIRD ANNUAL NAACP Conference was held in Boston on March 30 and 31, 1911. According to the *Crisis*, it was the best yet, showing "the Association in excellent condition, with a host of new friends." Seven hundred of "the best people of Boston" were welcomed by Mayor Fitzgerald in the afternoon and heard speeches by Villard, Du Bois, Rabbi Charles Fleisher, and Adelene Moffat. A thousand people that evening, the *Crisis* report continued, heard Florence Kelley link "the labor problem, the sex problem and the Negro problem" as "the oppression of those who 'do not count.'" John Milholland promoted national aid to education, and L. M. Hershaw and Mary Church Terrell continued exposés of peonage. Friday's business meeting reelected Villard chairman and Moorfield Storey president. It was followed by a reception for 250 at the Twentieth Century Club. The final session that evening drew 800 who heard Reverend G. R. Waller, Mr. Samuel Elder, and Rabbi Stephen S. Wise.[54]

Changes that intimately affected Ovington quickly followed. Frances Blascoer resigned as secretary after sparring with Du Bois and Villard and suffering a mental breakdown. Ovington took on the job, unpaid, for a year, until librarian May Childs Nerney was hired in May of 1912. Villard found Ovington a perfect, always unruffled official, a "ladylike, refined and cultivated person."[55]

On May 25, 1911, Ovington, Villard, and treasurer Walter Sachs executed formal incorporation under New York state law. Ovington carried the proxies of John Haynes Holmes and Du Bois. At the first meeting of the stockholders on June 20, Ovington also held the proxies of Du Bois and Holmes. Villard chaired, Ovington acted as secretary, and Sachs was again the third person present.[56]

The following year, in 1912, the NAACP's conference was in Chicago, necessitating trips by Villard and Ovington to Jane Addams's Hull House in January. Planning was combined with wining and dining by Sears Roebuck magnate Julius Rosenwald at the swank Blackstone Hotel, and soon after, Rosenwald gave the first of many annual gifts to the NAACP that were comparable to what he gave Booker T. Washington; Villard and Ovington had snagged a benefactor whose subsidies proved highly important.[57]

The Chicago conference, April 28 to 30, was a success. A horrendous rain and wind storm pelted the city off Lake Michigan and made the opening session at New Sinai Temple memorable for the thousand people in attendance. Addams presided; Villard finally spoke clearly, as Ovington reported, about "the two schools of thought with reference to the Negro question which are current among intelligent Americans today," before going on to review the legal work of the association.

The last session at Handel Hall in downtown Chicago turned away a thousand people while seven hundred overfilled the auditorium. Ovington was most impressed by Du Bois's lantern slide speech:

> Pictures of beautiful library buildings into which no Negro may enter were thrown on the screen; opera houses, where the Negro may never listen to music; and playgrounds, close to colored quarters, where black children may only peep through the gates, watching the white children at their games. The lecture ended with the black man's and white man's burial places—far apart, in death as in life.

Old and new faces graced the speakers' platform: Charles Edward Russell, Ida Wells-Barnett, and Moorfield Storey, on the one hand;

Julius Rosenwald, Mrs. Emmons Blaine, her mother, Mrs. Cyrus McCormick, Julia Lathrop, William Pickens, and Abdul Baha, head of the Baha'i movement, on the other. The latter had a lasting impact on Ovington.

She described him in the Hull House courtyard. His brown robe and turban, soft white hair and beard, face "ennobled by suffering," and "deep, burning eyes," complemented his wise, noble message. "The colors of . . . race were like the colors of the flowers in a garden. Who would wish to have white flowers only?" As he talked, tension and hurry evaporated, and she felt harmony.[58]

The NAACP's first big legal defense was of Pink Franklin, condemned to death in South Carolina for a killing a constable who had broken into his house at 3 A.M. Franklin was an illiterate sharecropper who had committed the "crime" of leaving his employer after having received an advance on his wages. The NAACP eventually got Franklin's sentence reduced to life imprisonment, but lost their Supreme Court challenge to peonage. A second early sharecropper case, that of Steve Greene, won over to the NAACP the wealthy brothers Joel and Arthur Spingarn.[59]

The NAACP's first big legal success was *Guinn v. United States*, in 1915, when Moorfield Storey successfully argued a challenge to Oklahoma's "Grandfather Clause" before the U.S. Supreme Court. (Such clauses were used to disenfranchise black voters in southern states: voting registration required literacy, *unless* one's lineal ancestor had been eligible to vote prior to January 1, 1866.) In 1917, Storey convinced the U.S. Supreme Court to throw out a Kentucky housing segregation ordinance (*Buchanan v. Warley*).

The national cases had to do more than relieve individuals; they had to challenge and/or set a precedent significant to a large number. Local branches operated with more freedom and quickly aroused Ovington's interest. (New York had formed a branch called the New York Vigilance Committee in 1911, chaired by Joel Spingarn with Ovington as secretary, and with an office on 135th Street in Harlem.[60])

A Negro accused of murder was freed for lack of evidence with the assistance of an attorney sent by the New York Committee—"our first practical job," she said. Soon thereafter, a similar case arose in Lakewood, New Jersey, and the NAACP discovered that it had been "rather expected" when it got there. "Our fame had crossed the North River!" she rejoiced.[61]

The most urgent NAACP work was the most horrifying: publicizing lynchings that were occurring nearly every six days. Newspapers busily showed the Negro as a criminal, so the association exposed the criminality of whites, just as Ovington did in "The White Brute." It marked the spot of each lynching with a pin on a wall map of the United States and soon the lower part was black with pinheads.

The NAACP was quickly known and vilified for its antilynching work. For a November 1911 meeting at New York's Ethical Culture Hall, only the young Reverend John Haynes Holmes and Rabbi Stephen S. Wise dared speak. Publicity quickly traveled south, and soon Holmes brought to the office a postcard that became "our primer" on lynching, as Ovington described it. In the foreground was pictured the dead Negro, and behind him were clear-cut photographic images of the lynchers. Lynching was common and committed with impunity, with the evidence transmitted through the U.S. mail.

Ovington and Mary Maclean gathered such material for antilynching publicity in the winter of 1911–1912. Ovington never forgot the day they readied the dummy for printing.

> It was Sunday. . . . Through the open window we heard the singing at the Church of St. John. . . . While we read, "They cut off his fingers for souvenirs," and pasted it at the top of the second page, the voice of the choir sang, "We praise Thee, Oh Lord. We acknowledge Thee to be our God." Were those men who had committed murder in some church singing from the hymnbook?[62]

Perhaps for her own sanity, Ovington also promoted the positive— for example, her support for the young painter Richard Lonsdale Brown. George de Forrest Brush offered to instruct the eighteen-year-old watercolorist if the association raised the money to support him. Ovington arranged for Brown to exhibit his work at Ovington's Gift Shop on Fifth Avenue, now run by her brother Charles. Brown sold twelve hundred dollars worth of pictures in a week, some painted on the spot, in Ovington's words "little vignettes of sky, with soft clouds passing over." He gave her one of his first, a bare tree against a paling sunset, a painting she later gave to Howard University. "Sometimes I think I never missed a possession so much, and then I know that it is a part of me and can be recalled at any time, even amid devastating ugliness," she wrote in her old age.

Brown's story ended sadly. He gave his earnings to a fatally ill sister. Not long before his own death, he visited Ovington in her Brooklyn studio, with late afternoon lights coming on "like flashing stars" in the office buildings across the East River. She described him saying:

> "You see I never noticed people much in the old days. I wanted to get away and look at the hills about my home. . . . But now, you see, now I've become interested in people . . . in my own people, they're so real and so sad. . . . They're so bright when they start off. . . . "
>
> As he went away he stopped in the doorway and said, "You won't lose faith in me, will you? I can paint before long."

She never lost faith in him, but she never saw him again.[63]

Much to Ovington's sorrow, Mary Maclean also died, in surgery in July 1912. A skilled journalist, she had offered her services after the first meetings of the National Negro Committee and had become managing editor at the *Crisis*. Like Ovington, she believed in Du Bois's genius and knew no color line. Her childhood nickname in Nassau was "Sunbeam," and so she seemed to Ovington from 1909 to 1912:

> As I sit here at her desk, striving clumsily to do the work she did so well, . . . I ask myself what would she wish me to write could she stand beside me and, laying her hand on mine, guide my pen? Her bright spirit sees not dimly now, but face to face. Would her word be like this?
>
> The dear earth is very foolish. It is making such a pother about color and race and forgetting the spirit in man. As though for one moment of the eternal moments it matters whether a man's skin is black or white or red or yellow, whether he lives in a palace or a cabin. These things are not life. They are only shadows. Forget them and stand in the sunlight of gentleness and brotherhood—the light most precious.

Ovington took on more duties at the *Crisis* after Maclean's death, and her name first appeared on its masthead in November that year. She wrote "fillers" of interest, including "Protection." An old black woman being forced out of her one-room cabin is told by her sailor son that he has to leave for Cuba, as Ovington wrote, "to protect American interests. . . . It's a great thing to be an American. Wherever you go the flag follows you and protects you in your rights." Ovington continued:

> The old woman turned to the mantelpiece, and taking the flag from its place, dropped it into the flames.

"You go about yer duty, an' serve yer country," she said, "but that flag ain't fo' me. They can steal from my kin', an' there ain't a jedge down here, or a man up in Washington, or one ob dem deligates dat goes screamin' up an' down de country about human rights, as ud gib a moment ter pertectin' me. Me an' my kin' ain't wanted, unless it's fo' slaves."

She turned back to mantel and laid her hand tenderly upon the picture of the great emancipator.

"Thank der Lord you ain't live ter see it," she said.

She also did editing and layout work when Du Bois was gone on his frequent lecture trips and formed and chaired a committee that raised funds in Maclean's memory for the publication of brochures.[64]

Within horrific contexts Ovington sought spare, sustaining beauty. A page called "The Burden" in the *Crisis* of December 1911 illustrates: numbers of "Colored Men Lynched Without Trial" from 1885 to 1910 are listed with "Total: 2,458," and centered at the bottom of the page lies Ovington's four-line Christmas Poem, "Nativity":

Unto the pure of heart it matters not
  Though they be born to great estate or small.
Within a palace stood Lord Buddha's cot
  While Jesus suckled in an ox's stall.[65]

The back page of the June 1911 *Crisis* announced the publication of Mary White Ovington's first book, *Half a Man: The Status of the Negro in New York*, published by Longmans, Green and Company of New York. This slim, elegant sociological study and her 1913 juvenile novel, *Hazel*, published by the Crisis Publishing Company, demonstrated holistic concerns and skills seen earlier in her shorter publications and anticipated her later work.

Ovington's title, *Half a Man*, came from a young Negro whose father sent him north where he could be a man—"no, half a man. A Negro is wholly a man only in Europe."[66] Perhaps she also had in mind the whole man to whom she dedicated the book: her father, Theodore Tweedy Ovington. Her title is misleading, however, for this book also significantly asks, "Does the woman, too, come to be but half a woman? What is her status in the city to which she turns for opportunity and larger freedom?"

Ovington's chapter "The Colored Woman as a Bread Winner" is remarkable for its thorough and sympathetic portrayal of an invisible group and its revelation of the slant of her feminism. She begins with a cautious generalization: that opportunities differ for black and white working women, both married and unmarried.

For the white "control group," Ovington used her Greenpoint observations: the wife of a laboring man rarely worked outside the home or journeyed far from it, and was a conscientious homemaker and mother. Should unemployment touch her husband, she would take in washing or do day cleaning jobs until he was once again employed; then she would return to "her narrow round of domestic duties." After many years, her life would improve as her children went out to work and brought their wages for her to administer. She might be able to buy new furniture, rent a piano, even move into a better neighborhood. But soon that period would end—children would marry and start households, employed husbands would age or die. Her old age would be "hard and comfortless."

For the Negro woman, the pattern was much different. Self-sustaining work began at about age fifteen and did not cease with marriage, for rarely would a husband's wage be sufficient for a family. She might take in washing at home; she was more likely to work for a well-to-do white family. This had advantages and drawbacks—more diversity and experience in the ways of the well-to-do, but little time with her children. In contrast to her white neighbor, should her husband turn out to be a "bad bargain," she would have "no fear of leaving him, since her marital relations are not welded by economic dependence."

In the next period, her condition improves less than the white woman's. Her children are not trained to bring home their earnings, nor likely to live at home once they start working in their service jobs. She will have to continue her washing and scrubbing. But in her old age, her condition is more likely than the white woman's to improve. For when mothers go out to work, grandmothers become important; in her children's households she will be respected.

Are the lives of the unmarried woman, too, very different between white and black? Yes. The young Negro girl will find many a factory and store job closed to her; she, too, will end up doing housework outside or in the home. Her hours are long and irregular. She does not bring home a pay envelope to her mother, but takes whatever she has earned at the end of the month and decides how to spend it. Very likely, she lives somewhere far away from her parental home.

Ovington used census figures and her own visits to establish her facts on black women's employment. She visited eight hundred married and widowed Negro women, for example, and found only 19 percent who were not engaged in "gainful occupations." The statistics corroborated her work: the figures for white women and Negro women between ages sixteen and twenty, usually an unmarried age, were close: 59 percent of the whites and 66 percent of the blacks were gainfully employed. But in the period of marriage, the percentage of workers outside the home among the whites dropped rapidly—13.5 percent for women age forty-five and over—but among Negro women, it remained high: 53 percent. As for living at home, the figures showed 59 percent of the white unmarried young women living at home, but only 25 percent of the unmarried Negro women. Fully 90 percent of the Negro women were employed in "personal and domestic service," while 40 percent of the white women were so employed.

The high employment rate of black women had a huge impact on their children. Babies were weakened and died from summer heat, from noise and light pollution, but those unhealthy conditions could be somewhat compensated for by breast-feeding. By 1900, 31.4 in every 100 Negro mothers worked outside the home; only 4.2 white mothers did. As a result, Negro babies suffered dramatically more improper feeding than did white, and their mortality rate was double. The irony was painful: "The Negro mother, seeking self-support by keeping clean another's house or caring for another's children, finds her own offspring swiftly taken from her by a disease that only her nourishing care could forestall."

And the five out of seven children who grew up suffered, too, from the mother's absence and from improper care. Negro children did not do as well in school, teachers told her, but not because they lacked innate ability. Nutrition was often poor, good sleep difficult, and no one oversaw their study. In three years of Children's Court, 30.8 percent of the arraignments of Negro children were for improper guardianship, while only 15 percent of Russian immigrant children were arraigned for this complaint—twice as many children without parental care in the Negro community.

At the time Ovington was writing there was a "preponderance in the city of Negro women over Negro men." (The same was true in Washington, D.C., New Orleans, and Atlanta.) By combining this fact with the large numbers of unmarried Negro women not living with parents, Ovington explained the perceived low moral character of black women. (This assumption was given by women's groups as their reason for excluding black women, causing Mary Church Terrell and other black women to found the National Association of Colored Women in 1896.) She wrote:

> In their hours of leisure the surplus women are known to play havoc with their neighbors' sons, even with their neighbors' husbands, for since lack of men makes marriage impossible for about a fifth of New York's colored girls, social disorder results. Surplus Negro women, able to secure work, support idle, able-bodied Negro men.

Ovington explained prostitution among Negro women in New York as a predictable result of limited occupational opportunities. Many chafed under the limitations of housework; others were not capable of doing it well—for it demanded more "mental capacity" than factory labor. "In short," Ovington concluded, "a great many colored girls in New York are round pegs in square holes, and the community is the loser by it." As for the moral standard that permitted a woman to become a prostitute, Ovington blamed white male use of black women going back to slavery:

> Untrained herself, bereft of home influence, with an ancestry that sometimes cries out her parent's weakness in the contour and color of her face, the Negro girl in New York, more even than the foreign immigrant, is subject to degrading temptation. The good people, who are often so exacting, want her for her willingness to work long hours at a lower wage than the white; and the bad people, who are often so carelessly kind, offer her light labor and generous pay. It is small wonder that she sometimes chooses the latter.[67]

In total, there was no doubt in Ovington's mind, that "the colored girl in New York meets with severer race prejudice than the colored man, and is more persistently kept from attractive work." She did not believe the prejudice came from the workers—she had talked with hundreds of white women workers and found them ready to accept Negro women; Jewish girls she found to be especially tolerant. The common spirit engendered among differing nationalities in the Shirtwaist Makers' Strike of 1910, she thought, should benefit the Negro girl as well.

Finally, in answering her own question "Does the woman, too, come to be but half a woman?" Ovington told two stories to illustrate the unpredictable "double jeopardy" of race and gender discrimination faced by the black woman. One was from a Canadian descendant of fugitive slaves. On her first trip to the United States, she was chased off the Jersey boardwalk: "Get out of here! We don't allow niggers." She resolved never to speak to a white person again. "I can never forget that the white people in the North stand for the insult which was cast upon me." The other was told by a white college man who rose to give a train seat to the sister of a Negro classmate. "Never again shall I see such a look of gratitude. . . . It revealed the race question to me, and yet I had performed only the simplest act of a gentleman." Ovington concluded: "In these two incidents we see the undecided, perplexing position of the Negro woman in New York. Today she may be turned out of a public resort as a 'nigger,' tomorrow she may receive the dues of a gentlewoman." Finally, the black woman, Ovington wrote, "beyond any people in the city," needed all that philanthropy, courtesy, respect, and the fellowship of workers could give her. Deprived of family life by slavery and struggling to maintain integrity and purity in the home against degrading environmental odds, she, above all, "needs her full status as a woman."

Ovington had only marginal interest in New York's "four hundred" Negro rich, in their conventional manners, ceremonial church events, social balls, political involvements. They had lost African traditions and folklore, and in trying to forget slavery had also lost its striking music. Her prose brightened somewhat when she wrote of the "conservative" and "radical" ideals of the supporters of Booker T. Washington and W. E. B. Du Bois. Her distinction between the two camps was crisp and simple and delineated a permanent tension in black communities: "they accept or reject segregation."

As Ovington saw it, the conservative group, led by Washington, argued that since the Negro had already been set apart, he had to grow in self-sufficiency, directing education toward Negro-owned and -marketed business and industry, patronizing only Negro stores. If working for a white became necessary, he must not join or strike with a union; in fact, he would be justified "in filling the place of the striking workman, for he has to look after his own concerns." (Ovington does not use the word *scab* here, though she does in later writing.)

The "radical" Du Bois ideal, on the other hand, resisted segregation. It demanded full privileges of a citizen. For workers, it demanded equal training. In business and professions, it meant that one should strive to serve white as well as black. Discrimination should be vigorously protested.

Ovington was subtle indeed, as she went on to say first, that the ideal of "acquiescence to present conditions" was "naturally" popular to whites, "who are themselves responsible for discrimination," but also, among Negroes, "material success sometimes means a departure from the aggressive to the submissive attitude." Yet "the whole question of the Negro as a wage earner is yet scarcely understood" by that small successful business and professional class. But Ovington was also unwilling to be too hard on middle-class blacks, for she knew the possible insult or hurt they faced even in success. Income and intelligence and access to the culture of the city "do not bring to the Negro any smug self-satisfaction," she continued, "only a greater responsibility toward the problem that moves through the world with his dark face." And then she came back with a reminder of a point she had made earlier, that for the Negro, there was no escape from the group and the achievements and problems of that group. There was no preaching and no condemnations in her prose, but reading carefully, one finds a clear argument across race lines for "workers of the world unite."

There was no quagmire into which Mary White Ovington did not delve in this book, and yet each time she gracefully sucked her boots back out. In the chapter called "The Negro and the Municipality" she covered access to public facilities, police behavior, court records, riots, machine politics, and vote buying. She joshed that choosing candidates "based on the argument of a two-dollar bill or the promise of a job" was a "selfish and unpatriotic attitude, not unknown perhaps to white voters," but weren't these citizens after all putting the ballot to its primary use, protection of their interests? The greatest need in New York was for steady, decent work; it made sense to go after it.

Ovington concluded her book with a sensitive examination of herself as a white American writing to white Americans about black Americans, not as individuals, but as a group. She illustrated the dilemma of such external analysis with a popular children's book, Lucy Pratt's *Ezekiel*. In Ovington's reading of the book, little Ezekiel Jordan was a child full of temperament, a dreamer, affectionate and friendly, "in his queer, unconscious way something of a genius." But unlike other storybook boys, Ezekiel had a double being: he was himself, and to white teachers and neighbors he was also "a Representative of the Negro Race":

When he arrived late to school, he was a dilatory representative; when, obliging little soul, he promised three people to weed their gardens all the same afternoon, he was a prevaricating representative. He never happened to steal ice-cream from the hoky-poky man or to play hookey, but if he had, he would have been a thieving and lazy representative. Always he was something remote and overwhelming, not a natural growing boy.

The position of Ezekiel "is that of each Negro child and man and woman in the United States today," Ovington wrote. Her book was a case in point, for, as she herself recognized, "we white Americans do not generalize concerning ourselves, we individualize, leaving generalizations to the chance visitor."

Let us try, then, to be just, she implored; let us try to look at the other "with the same impartiality and the same understanding sympathy with which we look upon our own race." In order to do this, she saw two things to keep in mind. First, it was not possible, in 1911, to evaluate the capability of Negro Americans, since there had not been equal opportunity. It would be as unreasonable as measuring men's ability to govern against that of disfranchised women. Second, dominant white Americans might not be the persons best fitted to judge the Negro: She concluded, "In moments of earnest reflection may it not occur to us that we have not the desire or the imagination to enter into the life emotions of others?"

These questions of judgment came to her intensely when she read the current expository literature. She found Matthew Arnold's quote apt when he said: "My brother Saxons have a terrible way with them of wanting to improve everything but themselves off the face of the earth." Ovington believed strongly that whites needed instead to contemplate the possibility that there were important things they could learn from the standards of other races.

Half a Man was positively and widely reviewed when it appeared in 1911, and has been reprinted three times. Reviewers noted that it was highly readable, compiled of material of various kinds, from statistical tables to anecdote with dialogue to literary and folk allusions, and sprinkled generously with wit. In her lengthy positive review in the *American Journal of Sociology,* University of Chicago professor S. P. Breckenridge suggested that in its unusual honesty of observation "warmly tinged with sympathy," the study could serve as a model for studies of other cities such as Chicago. Du Bois wrote in the *Crisis* that it was "one of the finest human studies done in America, done by a woman who knows her subject and has digested it."[68]

In 1969, when it was reprinted for the third time, it was possible to see past the book's specific information to its philosophy and wisdom. The *Manchester Union Leader* called it "a social work classic." *Choice* and *Library Journal* pointed out what a rare work it was in the Progressive, muckraking period: painstaking research on and long experience with a neglected topic. *Integrated Education* called it a pioneer study with unvarnished factual presentation. *Kirkus Reviews* found it "rather quaint but far from outdated" and called Ovington unique among the reformers of her time.

Half a Man: The Status of the Negro in New York stands halfway in Mary White Ovington's life. As she wrote it, forty-three of her allotted eighty-six years were spent. Within its 230 pages are flashes of her happy childhood; her college training; her settlement work; her fortunate introduction to and passionate involvement in "the Negro world" of America, South and North; her travels to Jamaica, Italy, Germany, and England; her love of the classics of American and European literature; her up-to-date readings and reviews of worldwide economic and sociological and historical studies of the Negro; her affection for the theater and for laughter; her strong convictions but kindly treatment of those who disagreed; her love of children; her joy in story, in conversation, in people of all kinds in all kinds of places—all melded seamlessly into prose at once lithe and learned, and a philosophy both idealistic and realistic.

In many ways, this book presaged the latter half of her life: the love of unconventional people that would keep her traveling to NAACP branches across the country, rather than sitting in the increasingly bureaucratic New York office; her belief in the laboring class that would keep her faithful to socialism-communism through two world wars; her eventual worry that the NAACP bolstered only the middle class and failed to bring Negroes into the workers' movement; an unwavering belief in racial integration as the ideal, even when practical progress might involve segregation, as in training black officers in World Wars I and II; writing for children, particularly black children, so that their lives might be enriched by literature as hers had been; support and promotion of black writers during "The Harlem Renaissance" and after, with hundreds of perceptive reviews in her syndicated "Book Chat" column; a steady conviction that feminism failed wherever and whenever it failed black women; an ability to look at another person and see possibility and promise, not error and fault, and to relate to the former and not get bogged down by the latter.

Mary White Ovington was forty-five years old when she found and created an organizational frame for her energy, her curiosity, her love of people and of fun, and her commitment to help those less fortunate than herself. The NAACP, in its first few years just a struggling coalition of like-minded but conflicting and individualistic activists, would grow and would frame and inspire the rest of her life.

6

Growing Pains

LIKE CLOCKWORK, November and December of 1913, 1914, and 1915 saw the top men at the NAACP in turn lashing out, huffing off with resignation letters, fighting the early morning and late afternoon New York darkness with increased self-importance and demands for recognition. Like a game of monotone musical chairs, Oswald Garrison Villard, Joel Spingarn, and W. E. B. Du Bois fought for position. Each received the ministrations of Mary White Ovington, always with her eye on the main chance of keeping Du Bois and the *Crisis* going, a task that also required money and readers.

Villard and Spingarn in turn feuded with Du Bois. Villard had never been a big Du Bois supporter, and their similar personalities clashed. They circled each other like lions, Villard with his tall, haughty figure and domineering manner, raised chin, and rimless glasses; Du Bois beginning to bald, with dark, intense eyes, a Vandyke mustache and beard, and a short man's defensively disdainful manner.

Villard resigned on November 19, 1913, after sparring with the *Crisis* editor on editorial freedom and responsibility and discovering that Du Bois was writing a book on what the chairman thought of as NAACP time.[1] Du Bois met with Ovington and the Spingarns to suggest ways out of the quagmire: possibilities included separation of the *Crisis* and the association; Ovington as chairman and a "young colored man to be selected as secretary and organizer"; or Archibald Grimke as chairman and Ovington as vice chairman. The solution he would accept in an emergency included the resignation of May Childs Nerney and his taking over both the jobs of executive secretary and director of publications and research.[2]

Villard reacted with the first of many "Du Bois or me" power plays. He told the board that he had taken the chairmanship only on the assumption that it held all the power of an executive position, including full authority over the *Crisis*. But now Du Bois had questioned Villard's control of the magazine, so Villard removed his name from the *Crisis* masthead. He could not continue as chairman under those conditions.[3]

Villard explained himself to Ovington in revealing detail. He would be happy to continue on the Finance Committee, "so as to carry on the fight which I have begun." He recommended one of the lawyers or Joel Spingarn in his place. "Again, I have had no support whatever on the financial side from other members of the Association," he claimed—amazingly—"and I could see myself again drifting into a position of having to carry the organization alone."[4]

It had to be irritating to hear Villard claim he did everything; to her other tasks, she had added two committees dealing with the difficulties between Villard and Du Bois.[5] But no irritation showed in Ovington's answer, which began by saying she had gone to her office on Sunday to have quiet time to think about it.

Ovington gently suggested that Villard had created an authoritarian hierarchy from a collegial situation. She laid it out: "Does the chairman . . . need to be an executive?" "Couldn't you continue in your office and have a vice-chairman or leave all the executive work with Miss Nerney, giving her a chance to show whether she can do it or not?" Finally she made a suggestion, which Villard took, and which she herself would later use to leave the board chairmanship. "By the way, there is a nice position open for you if you *really* don't want to carry an executive one—Treasurer! And if you follow precedent, you won't have to raise money. Sincerely and regretfully, Mary White Ovington."[6]

The letter was quickly followed by another indicating that she would have to send out notices for a meeting to consider his resignation. "I am sick at heart over it," she lamented, and then expressed her real concern: what did this say about the races working together?

To you it means just Dr. Du Bois and Mr. Dill, but to me it means a confession to the world that we cannot work with colored people unless they are our subordinates. And everyone who believes in segregation will become a little more firmly convinced that he is right. And when we demand that some colored man be put in office and be given a place in which he will be the equal of a white man, we shall be told, "You cant [*sic*] give a nigger a big job. Haven't you found it out yourselves?"

It puts us back five years.[7]

As if to say that he alone had not carried the organization either financially or administratively, as chairman of the Office Committee, Ovington notified Villard at the end of December that the NAACP and the *Crisis* were moving into new quarters at the Educational Building at Fifth Avenue and Thirteenth Street (70 Fifth Avenue). They would be out of his building by February 1, 1914, she told him.[8]

Joel Spingarn was elected chairman and Villard treasurer of the board at the annual meeting in January 1914. Seventy-seven people heard addresses by Belle La Follette of Wisconsin, Charles Edward Russell, and Du Bois, and many attended a dinner at the Rand School on East Nineteenth Street. Ovington left for Algeria later in the month and returned in time for the April board meeting, when Du Bois submitted suggestions for reorganizing the NAACP.

Du Bois's suggestions were sent to committee, and were acted on in July, in his favor. The new bylaws adopted then, with Du Bois's suggestions an adopted amendment, increased his authority as director of publications and research, and decreased the power of the treasurer and chairman. The holders of those three positions, plus the secretary, would form an executive committee that reported to the board.

But Du Bois undercut his success in gaining increased organizational power by continuing to offend various people, on and off the pages of the *Crisis*, throughout 1914. He attacked the *Survey* because it did not publish an article it had asked him to do. (Ovington continued doing book reviews for the publication.) He attacked Negro newspapers and, when Robert Ogden died, flailed him and all other white philanthropy. The colored clergy were denounced in a "Church Number" of the magazine, and Wilberforce University, just made a state school, objected to Du Bois's suggestions that it was a vast improvement over the older, church-affiliated institution (at which, in the last century, he had taught and which he had hated).[9]

In December the board reversed the July action that had favored Du Bois. It abolished the Executive Committee, made the chairman of the board the executive officer, with full authority over heads of departments (of which Du Bois was one) between board meetings.

Joel Spingarn, passionate and unrelentingly candid, swung the December vote by telling the board that the problem was Du Bois himself—that he was childish and insubordinate. Ovington and three others voted with Du Bois against the majority, but she went home and immediately wrote Spingarn, "I should not have said that under any given conditions, I, or anyone else, would leave the Association." "It sounds foolish and like a threat," she added. She thought the events at the meeting were exceedingly unfortunate:

> I have steadily worked, for five years, against what happened to-day—the lining up on lines of personality. When our vote came the debate made a personal matter of the situation—whether we should accept the arrangement of Du Bois or not—and some of us could not decide to agree in the judgement that had been passed upon him. I can only hope that your judgement is wiser than mine has been and that this bringing of all these matters before the Board may make us more united instead of splitting us in two. It is certainly taking the Board into our confidence.[10]

Chairman Spingarn was grateful for her note. "Your unfailing and unselfish devotion to our cause has been a beacon light spreading hope when every other light seemed dim." But she did, he told her, misunderstand his purpose in speaking openly. It was not a split he intended, but to destroy "forever" the division that had been there all the time, "nursed by trifling differences and unexpressed suspicions."

Spingarn described at length the realities he felt must be faced: Du Bois's extensive unpopularity in the colored world; the precedence of the NAACP over the *Crisis;* the question of authority; and, finally, the crux of the matter. He did not agree with Ovington (as he put it) that Du Bois was so delicate in temperament that he always had to be coddled and indulged. Du Bois had never been required to work with others because "you and a few other idolaters (pardon my frankness) have refused to consider it either necessary or possible." Couldn't she, Spingarn asked, persuade Dr. Du Bois and his friends to accept subordination to a worthwhile, principled organization and cause?[11]

Ovington answered Joel Spingarn's letter immediately. They had in mind the same goal—unity of effort—but their approaches differed:

Now, if your way succeeds, if you can make unity by telling the Board that there is friction and that this centres about a single individual, you will be doing a great service. But the effect of what you said upon me was to make me very angry so that I was guilty of so silly and unkind a remark as that I could get on with Du Bois if others couldn't. And I don't believe I was the only one made angry by hearing a man of 47 of international reputation described as childish and insubordinate. Doubtless he is, but I wouldn't suppose that exposing of him in that way, would make him be good.

If she "coddled" Du Bois, she wanted to define it her own way, as "looking at the best in people and letting them always feel that I believe in that and *see* that." Pointing out an adult's faults didn't work for her—she lost all influence for good with someone she criticized.

Finally Ovington dealt with the "charge" of her idolatry. "I do worship genius," she confessed. She had felt that way, she wrote to Spingarn, twenty years earlier when she first read Du Bois's "What It Means to Be a Problem" in the *Atlantic Monthly*, and, to her, the rest of them were just able journeymen,

> but Du Bois is the master builder, whose work will speak to men as long as there is an oppressed race on the earth. . . . Perhaps this master builder can rear but one cathedral, but if power is to be given him to do more he must be placed where he can work naturally and happily.

Ovington then explained how she could get along with people who were not easily accessible, enjoy them, encourage them, and bring out the best in them:

> My own life has been so happy, so full of pleasant happenings, that I feel singularly drawn toward people whose lives turn crisscross, whose spirits are harassed. And an harassing temperament is the most trying thing a man can own. You can't change it. You might as well tell Miss Nerney that you won't keep her as secretary unless she can grow three inches taller as to tell Dr. Du Bois that he can't edit the Crisis unless he ceases to be obstinate. You've just got to use his obstinacy.[12]

A year later, at the November 1915 meeting of the board, a motion to restrict Du Bois's duties simply to editing of the *Crisis* was replaced by a delay of the discussion until December, with a committee appointed by Spingarn to make recommendations. In December, that committee suggested new limits on Du Bois's power: that he could have duties assigned him by the board in addition to his editing, and that the *Crisis* finances be placed in the hands of a business manager responsible to the board. The proposal failed by a vote of twelve to two, appearing in the minutes as a positive vote that it was "not expedient" to take it up.

Du Bois responded with the first of many "white papers" appealing to a larger constituency in his conflicts with the board. He had had his resignation ready at the December meeting if the vote had gone against him. In the "Statement," written after the vote went his way, he said Villard and Spingarn had asserted claims as chief executive officer that he could not accept. He wrote that four times he had been prepared to leave the NAACP because he couldn't "in justice be asked every year or so to face the momentous question of a change in my means of earning bread and butter." He would remain only if he were "recognized as an executive officer directly responsible to the Board and independent of other executive officers."[13]

Du Bois had won a reprieve, but Joel Spingarn had lost by an embarrassingly lopsided vote. He did not take it well, and threatened resignation. "Thoroughly taken aback by the Board's adverse decision," wrote Joyce Ross in her close study of his career with the NAACP, "Spingarn displayed his major weakness as an administrator—the inability to gracefully accept the majority opinion when it was opposed to a view he strongly advocated."[14]

After the meeting Ovington wrote the chairperson: "Now that this vote is over won't you forgive us all around?" It was painful to have him walk in and turn away from "our section of the room as though we were under suspicion." She hoped that he would tell her what he was feeling about any injustice she had done, so they could shake hands on the matter and get on with the work.

That work would be none too easy. Nerney's report on the fieldwork had given Ovington the blues since Nerney had come to the board sounding as if she believed colored people had made a mess of all the branches, "and she spoke of them with quite brutal frankness." Creating and running and getting money from the branches of the organization had seemed to be Nerney's chief accomplishment as secretary, "and now she tells us it is a questionable one," Ovington wrote. "Who is capable of handling it if she isn't?"

And if Spingarn was now unwilling to continue in the chairmanship, and Villard wouldn't take it back unless Du Bois was eliminated, who would there be to take the job? The only choices were radicals (though she didn't say it, like herself). They would be in a bind even if Du Bois suddenly became cooperative and collegial and Nerney lost all her jealousy, because they would still lack someone effective in the field-work. She could only hope that the occasion would find the leader as it had found Spingarn earlier, she told him.[15]

Spingarn responded so generously that Ovington expressed her own desire "to have [the chairmanship] for a short time." The other viable candidates, Villard and Grimke, were too often out of New York. (Grimke agreed, writing Du Bois that if Spingarn left, he would support Ovington.) She spelled out her thoughts about leading, a combination of strong ideas and a willingness to work through the group.

> It is impossible for any one to have worked as long for the association as I have without forming many plans for it. These plans I could only put into execution as chairman. . . . If the board was not sympathetic with my ideas I could resign and have some one else take my place.

Her plans were to make New York the fund-raising locale, with a Washington, D.C., office headed by Grimke as the center of legal and political action. It would be easier to get money, she thought, if they were effectively acting on specific legal and political issues.

Spingarn said he wanted to move to black leadership. But couldn't they subordinate the New York office, Ovington asked him, and have Grimke leading in Washington? Lines other than color had been drawn, Ovington pointed out to him: "Perhaps, by putting a woman between a white chairman and a colored chairman you may be making the needed link!"[16]

Joel Spingarn made noises about resigning as the sun dipped lower each fall in 1916 and 1917. The unexpected death of Booker T. Washington in November 1915 gave him a new lease on leadership life. Using his contacts, his enthusiasm, and his Ductchess County estate, Spingarn put together a gathering of Negro leaders from all camps in August 1916, known as the "Amenia Conference." In April of 1917 he essentially took leave of the association by volunteering for, and being commissioned as an officer in, the U.S. Army. Ovington was

Silent Protest Parade in New York City against the East St. Louis riots, 1917. (Library of Congress)

Flag flown from NAACP headquarters at 69 Fifth Avenue in New York City during the antilynching campaign. (Library of Congress)

NAACP staff in 1920s: William Pickens, field agent; unknown; James Weldon Johnson, executive secretary; Walter White, assistant secretary; and unknown. (By permission of Archives of Labor and Urban Affairs, Wayne State University)

The national office of the NAACP in New York City, 1920, when Mary White Ovington became chairman of the board of directors. (By permission of Archives of Labor and Urban Affairs, Wayne State University)

Twelfth annual conference, NAACP. (Library of Congress)

NAACP colleagues W. E. B. Du Bois, Lillian Alexander, Mary White Ovington, Amy Spingarn (Mrs. J. E. Spingarn), and unknown. Snapshot from Lillian Alexander, probably from early 1930s. (By permission of Archives of Labor and Urban affairs, Wayne State University)

NAACP Christmas card showing integrated children's choir, no date. (Library of Congress)

made acting chairman. Leadership cockfights quelled for a time, as the mother hen came home to roost.

WHEN D. W. GRIFFITH's *Birth of a Nation* flashed on the theater screens of the nation in 1915, extra work and an extraordinary confusion of ideals had hit the new emancipators at the NAACP. Thomas Dixon, on whose fictional *The Leopard's Spots* (1902) and *The Clansman* (1905) the story was based, arranged for showings for his friend President Woodrow Wilson, his cabinet and staff, the chief justice of the Supreme Court, and congressmen. Griffith himself appeared for the screening at the White House, the first ever shown there. At the conclusion of the film, which dealt so eloquently with the Civil War and Reconstruction, Wilson wiped away tears. "It is like writing history with lightning," the southern president said. "And my only regret is that it is all so terribly true."[17]

Mary White Ovington agreed with the first part of Wilson's reported assessment. The narrative enticed and stimulated an audience with villains and heroines and battles and rescues and love. Griffith created artistic film techniques that have been used ever since: cutting to simultaneous events; symbolic realism, or single instances to stand for a large event; unusual camera angles; juxtaposition and contrast.

Ovington appreciated the power of theater to move an audience. Film processed and canned that power, made it repeatable and permanent and widely accessible. In less than a year, *Birth of a Nation* was shown 6,266 times in New York City alone. This was indeed "writing with lightning." Film had inestimable power, she believed, for good or ill.

But she and the NAACP disagreed vehemently with Wilson's second statement. *Birth of a Nation* did not show either historical truth or fictional "truth of the human heart" as she saw it. Yes, she knew, the villain was modeled after a historical character, Thaddeus Stevens, a U.S. legislator in the North until 1868. Yes, the Ku Klux Klan, heroes of the film, who save the heroine and civilization much like the knights of the Middle Ages, did spring up like parasitic poisonous mushrooms. Yes, there were Negroes elected to southern legislatures during Reconstruction.

But in filmmaking and history writing, angle is everything, and Dixon's and Griffith's angles of vision on the American past had a definite southern bent. They believed in the plantation tradition—or illusion—that the pre–Civil War South was a golden age populated by wealthy, leisured, kindly slave owners, and loyal, obedient, happy slaves. In the film, this supposed antebellum "Eden" is contrasted with the cold, hypocritical North, which corrupts free blacks and mulattoes (all played by whites), turning them into sexually dangerous animals. Quickly, this film influenced millions of people in their view of American history. One New York reviewer told parents they must take their children to see it or they would be "committing an educational offense."[18]

The problem for the NAACP was how to fight something that is so bad because it is so good. In a speech as NAACP board chairman, Joel Spingarn warned that full censorship was not the route to take, not only because it was dangerous to the free expression of art but also because it could work against *Uncle Tom's Cabin* as quickly as against *Birth of a Nation*.

However, Spingarn reported, he had asked the powerful National Board of Censorship in Moving Pictures to remove the more objectionable scenes of the film. But they took no substantial action. As Spingarn saw it, they evidently thought it "of higher importance to stop a play in which a young woman shows too much of her hosiery than one in which the character of 10,000,000 Americans is virtually assassinated."[19]

Ovington had gone to see *Birth* . . . immediately upon its opening in New York City, and was shocked to see how the audience lapped it up. Children came out despising Lincoln and the Congress for freeing the slaves—just as the movie intended. She attended a hearing in which city officials promised to cut some scenes, and went back to see the film again the following day. The offensive scenes remained intact. Other NAACP officials had less interest in the medium of film than she did. Oswald Villard, for example, though he refused to accept ads for *Birth* . . . in the *Evening Post* had still not seen it by March 9.[20]

Ovington traveled to Boston to appear at one of the municipal hearings the NAACP forced in several cities. Her testimony was carefully selective, aiming not to censure the South's sectional history, false though it was to her, but zeroing in on characterizations she found dangerous.

Two Negro characters, she thought, were created to play upon white sexual fears. The educated Silas Lynch, who is elected lieutenant governor of South Carolina by the newly franchised ex-slaves, "makes himself obnoxious" (Ovington's words) to the white girl, Elsie Stoneman; and the brutal, ignorant black man, Gus, pursues another white girl, Flora, with "lust portrayed in his face and in his grasping hands." Ovington objected to the suggestion that the free Negro, treated as a citizen, had "one paramount desire: to possess a white woman."

In the second instance, the film claimed that the South Carolina Reconstruction legislature, dominated by blacks and northerners, in Ovington's words, "was disgusting in its uncouth manners and ignorance." Third, it gave the impression that the Ku Klux Klan was made up of "noble, humane youths" who "rode out to rescue maidens in peril and to restore good rule to the State of South Carolina."

In Boston, Mayor Curley, then at the beginning of his long career, ran the hearing. Only one other person there besides Ovington had seen the film, although Moorfield Storey and others spoke against the *Clansman*, which they had read or seen in play form. She decided to emphasize the film's treatment of the Negro as a "dangerous, half-insane brute":

> If I could show . . . that the method of presentation might injure the Negro in the city where it was shown, if it was so bestial as to create antagonism, even violence, then it should not be produced. I made my plea on this line, dwelling especially on the flight of the white girl whose pursuer, his great clutching hands repeatedly pictured, was enough to make a Bostonian on Beacon Hill double-lock the door at night.
> "Was it as bad as *Macbeth*?" Mayor Curley asked.
> I thought of Lady Macbeth washing her hands of imaginary blood, and said, "Much worse."
> "As bad as *Othello*?" the Mayor persisted.
> "Yes worse than *Othello*."

In the movie, Flora escapes Gus, her would-be rapist, only by throwing herself over a cliff to her death. As a result of Ovington's testimony, after which Mayor Curley said he could cut but not stop the production, all but the beginning and ending of the scene was omitted in Boston, and the audience was left wondering why the girl was found dead!

In New York City, a sentence was added. Gus was made to say to the child he later pursues: "I'm a captain now, Missy, and I want to marry—." In a letter to the mayor, Ovington pointed out the ineffectiveness of this minor change. "It makes no difference to the girl," she wrote, "and the pursuit and the fall from the cliff are exactly as before." She got a runaround; her letter was referred to the License Department for "immediate attention." By the time of the NAACP board meeting two weeks later, nothing had been changed. "The Commissioner of Licenses who now has the matter in charge says that the law gives him no authority to compel the owner to make further changes in the film," Spingarn reported.[21]

The association succeeded in cutting scenes in some additional cities—St. Paul, New Haven, Providence. In some places the movie was outlawed as a result of NAACP activity: in the states of Ohio and Kansas, for example; and the cities of Albuquerque, Gary, Tacoma; and Wilmington, Delaware. Griffith aroused local ire, too, as with A. E. Pillsbury, NAACP member and former Massachusetts state attorney general, who argued that the film was unfair to Negroes and also to his state.[22]

At a special meeting of the board of the NAACP on March 23, 1915, Lillian Wald suggested, and Ovington moved, that a "dignified procession" be arranged of all interested organizations, to march to the mayor's office to protest the film. The committee to enact it included Ovington and Wald, Du Bois, Paul Kennaday, a social worker and journalist on the board, and Verina Morton-Jones, the physician with whom Ovington founded Lincoln Settlement. Ovington and Jones concluded, "It would be a great mistake for white women–colored men to walk in the parade—that the papers would simply feature 'niggers and white women,'" say nothing about the film, and author Thomas Dixon would clap his hands in glee. "The parade should either be all men or all colored people," Ovington told Nerney, having learned well the lessons of the Cosmopolitan Dinner in 1908 and the unchanging sensationalism of newspapers when dealing with race issues. The parade was all men, marching at eleven o'clock from Union Square to a meeting with the mayor at noon on March 30.[23]

Although Ovington participated in the NAACP tactics seeking to cut or ban *Birth of a Nation*, she concentrated her activity on researching, writing, and promoting material designed to counteract the effects of the film. She wondered about the actual history of the Reconstruction legislature in South Carolina, especially after learning that the father of board member William Sinclair had been one of its representatives and had also been lynched.

Her first discovery was that it was almost impossible to find out what had happened when the northerner and the Negro held power under Reconstruction. She could not find the proceedings of the legislature in the New York Public Library or the Library of Congress. She was ready to go to South Carolina—until Sinclair told her that the records wouldn't be there, either, for whites had destroyed all copies, even coming into Negro homes to take them off the shelves. Ovington finally found copies of the legislation, though not the debates. It did show positive activity: the beginning of public school education and the care of the aged.[24] She wrote a pamphlet of historical corrections: the positive legislation; the real roles of the Ku Klux Klan and the Black Codes—laws that restricted freedmen's civil, economic, and social rights. Arguably more effective than protests or censorship, copies were distributed in cities where the film was being shown—eight thousand in New York City alone.[25]

During the first sensational run of *Birth of a Nation*, Ovington published "The White Brute" in *The Masses*.[26] Editor Max Eastman thought it "a classic and more terrible than anything but truth." The reception to it bore him out. The NAACP distributed thousands of copies of it—hundreds were handed out at depots by Boston musician John Orth. ("One gasps to think of a passenger on a train," Ovington said, "going probably on some pleasant journey, having to read this terrible tale. But then, he could throw it out of the window.") "The White Brute" and her poem in response to the lynching of the innocent Leo Frank, a Jew, for the murder of Mary Phagan, published the same year in the *New Republic*, were her two most remembered works, Ovington believed.[27]

She tried yet another tack: fighting film with film. She set up a meeting with novelist-scenarist James Oppenheim and attorney Arthur Spingarn to talk about creating a rival film to respond to Griffith's behemoth, and then discovered that Villard's thinking had been following the same course. He had already enlisted the assistance of Universal Film Company, one of three large companies planning to produce a film rivaling Griffith's.[28]

Ovington served as chairman of a committee authorized by the board to work on an alternative film; the other members were Nerney, William English Walling, and John Underhill. The scenario was by Elaine Sterne, according to Ovington "one of our most artistic and successful moving picture writers." The film would be a short four reels unless enough money could be raised to match the twelve of the Griffith film. The situation was urgent, Nerney argued, for Griffith might at any moment bring out another film to capitalize on the controversy over *Birth of a Nation.*[29]

Ovington pursued this project with a great deal of hope and enthusiasm. Nerney was the only other real enthusiast, but as secretary she questioned the wisdom of putting in a lot of time on it since she felt that the interest of Negroes on the NAACP board was lukewarm. Villard did not even have time to hear the work he had originally commissioned, and Lillian Wald, the initiator of the protest march, was unwilling to do any work to reach New Yorkers with this more creative option. Nerney and Ovington tried to enlist the active support of Joel Spingarn, who was tucked away at his Troutbeck estate. People were not interested until they saw the script, they told him.

Ovington went back to Boston the last week of May, this time with Miss Sterne, to read "Lincoln's Dream" to the Boston Branch, including historian Albert Bushnell Hart from Harvard, who checked the work for accuracy. Arthur Spingarn and Dr. Underhill told Nerney and Ovington that with legal precautions in place there was no reason not to go ahead. NAACP staff publicity person Charles T. Hallinan outlined to Arthur Spingarn and Ovington an ambitious publicity campaign based on the projected film.[30]

In attempting to get Villard's support at least to the extent of hearing the scenario, Ovington described why she thought it would be successful and why it was important.

Miss Sterne has written a very good thing. She has the requisite number of thrills and two pairs of white lovers, but through it all is a colored youth and his mother, the boy struggling up from slavery, a fugitive, then a soldier in the 54th Mass., and last an educator in the reconstruction days. You see him helping the weak, defending the white home against gorilla [*sic*] warfare, teaching in the first schoolhouse under the trees; and every now and then on the screen is the picture of his mother, in the log cabin, waiting for her son, and at last rejoicing in his return. It tells the story we want told, and it will reach hundreds of thousands where the word we may be able to write will reach so few, and those few not the thoughtless, growing boys and girls who are learning from history through Dixon's eyes.

It seems to me this is the one big constructive piece of work that has been given us to do, nothing else has come near it in importance.[31]

Money proved to be an insurmountable problem. A good film could be produced for $50,000 and a magnificent one, for $100,000. Ovington took the skeleton plan and fleshed it out in a "Confidential" communiqué mailed rapidly to likely partisans. All Universal needed was a $10,000 loan that would be returned, evenly divided with the company, from the first profits until paid back. But pledges were not forthcoming. By October, Ovington suggested to the board that prominent white people write to Universal asking that (the yet-unproduced) "Lincoln's Dream" be shown in their cities. In November, she had to report for the scenario committee that the Universal Film Company had not yet finally decided to bring out the film, but that the attempts to influence them were ongoing. Though the committee continued to meet, that was pretty much the end of "Lincoln's Dream"—and of Mary White Ovington's.[32]

Had "Lincoln's Dream" been produced, could the film have rivaled *Birth of a Nation?* Our guess that this film would have "worked" must be based upon Ovington's knowledge of the genre as well as her description of the plot line. She was increasingly interested in the art of filmmaking; she had always been interested in theater's "sugaring the pill," to use George Bernard Shaw's description of the way knowledge or inspiration could be made entertaining; and she subsequently defended art that was realistic and hence exciting versus propagandistic and hence dull and ineffective.[33]

In a time of political correctness and hate speech rules, Mary White Ovington's voice in the wilderness rings truer than ever. She held firm to the principles of freedom of speech and freedom of the press. She also displayed a remarkable belief in the power (for evil or good) of the new medium of film. Holding those convictions together was her faith in the enduring ability of informed citizens to separate the Golden Rule of American liberty from the dross of race prejudice. "Don't you think anyway that we can't stop Dixon and his ilk from talking?" she asked a potential wealthy supporter. "We can only tell history from the other side," Ovington concluded, "and then let the public weigh the issue."[34]

BY 1917, MILITARY matters and domestic responses intruded into everything in the United States, including the NAACP, even before the United States' declaration of war against Germany in April. In a debate that would recur at the civil rights organization at the beginning of World War II in relation to segregated Air Force training for Negro pilots at Tuskegee,[35] both pro and con lined up around the plans of Major Joel Spingarn to train Negro officers. In seeming conflict with Spingarn's belief that segregated officer training was better than none at all, after war was declared, the board of the association passed a resolution to "oppose and take every feasible step to prevent any discrimination against Negroes in any volunteer or compulsory military act which may hereafter be passed."

Even pacifists had to face the discrimination issue. Oswald Garrison Villard made clear that his vote for the resolution "in no way implies support of conscription." Mary White Ovington left the chair to speak for it, making clear that "while she was absolutely against war and compulsory military service" she felt that the association and every branch of the association "must fight against allowing the Negro to be put in any position less than that of a citizen." The fight was crucial since the South, she said, was "determined to prevent the Negro from wearing the uniform of a Federal soldier which is prima facie evidence of citizenship."[36]

The real NAACP dilemma centered on what one might call "segregation for access." If the only way to obtain officer training for Negroes was through a segregated camp, should it be promoted? Ovington realistically supported Spingarn but placed her backing carefully in an antiwar context. "It seems to me that you are entirely right in your position," she told him, but "how I wish all this wonderful enthusiasm for the upholding of our 'National Honor' could be roused for home matters." Before war was declared, while German submarines were already sinking American ships, Ovington said:

> To me it is far more dishonorable to submit to seeing the poor of New York underfed, and the very rich growing richer, than to submit to Germany's killing a few American citizens; but the only people who will fight on the first issue are the women of the East Side.[37]

In *Four Lights*, she published a free-verse poem, "Gretchen Talks to Her Doll" in the month war was declared. "It must be a comfort . . . to be stuffed full of sawdust," Gretchen told her doll. "You don't mind going without butter on your bread— / And such nasty bread, too." When would the war be over? "When all of the children are hungry, hungrier than I am. . . . When the babies cry all night long. . . . Then, Mother says, the war will be done, and all our foes will be conquered." Meanwhile, Gretchen said, "My throat aches down to my waist. / I wish I were like you and stuffed full of sawdust."[38]

Ovington held to a middle path on the issues of war and peace, and segregation or resistance. She did not end up with Villard and Lillian Wald and Jane Addams on the dangerously subversive lists, but she did appear in the New York State Lusk Committee report as one of the people who contributed to the NAACP's "decidedly radical stand" as a socialist sympathizer.[39] She did not desperately dump the Socialist Party as did NAACP founders William English Walling and Charles Russell to take, as the latter said, "a stand against German autocracy and barbarism."[40] Ovington remained invisible—and probably more effective—as she had so many years earlier in promoting W. E. B. Du Bois over Booker T. Washington.

An indicator of Ovington's ability to express herself strongly and yet not alienate friends was her correspondence with Major Joel Spingarn. Even in wartime, she did not burn bridges as Villard and Du Bois and even Spingarn often did, but communicated across chasms of calling and opinion.

She joked with Spingarn that he and Royal Nash, the NAACP secretary who briefly succeeded May Childs Nerney before he volunteered for service, were "like men who once having expressed themselves freely on world topics have retired now into monasteries where freedom of speech and thought has disappeared, and authority alone rules."[41] Seeing Joel in his uniform, she went on, was comparable to his walking into the NAACP offices to find Mary White Ovington the Unitarian dressed in the garb of a "Sister of Charity, saying my beads, and if questioned declaring my acceptance of the supreme authority of the Roman Catholic Church."

She did not feel this way about all soldiers, but, as she told him, she had a problem with Spingarn's decision because he "loved to teach youth freedom . . . of thought, intellectual and moral audacity . . . , disobedience to forms." Now he would instruct young people in the emptiest of disciplines: "how to kill their fellows, and how to stand for their country, right or wrong."[42]

Well, it was a more pleasant title she used to address him now, Spingarn responded—for teaching unquestioning obedience he was called major; for teaching youth to think, what would he be dubbed, ex-professor? ("I shall see that the right title goes on all new stationery," wrote Ovington.) But, seriously, he would maintain his humane enthusiasms, Spingarn assured her. She clarified her point for Spingarn. Of course, Ovington conceded, great soldiers had often been humane men—General Robert E. Lee, for example—but Lee had chosen wrong, so she could not admire him: "You know I think a man's choice is his life." She got no thrill out of military virtues, they might be quite real, but they, she wrote to Spingarn, "belong to a despotism. . . . The best army is the most autocratic, since war is built on autocracy."[43]

The thing that drove her "almost to madness" about war was simply "its stupidity." Europe would probably never recover, she mused. One didn't have to believe in eugenics "to know that if you spend four years killing off your men with sound hearts, clean bodies, good eyes, good hearing, normal brain power, you will have a poor race left with which to breed." History's cycle of empires lent little hope for her. When a power like England became kinder and gentler, Ovington observed, "then the fresher, more virile, more brutal nation comes and beats it to pieces."

And now, if neither the British nor the German empire won, with American children taught to worship nationalism and citizen armies, Ovington believed that the United States would also have its turn at world domination, only to eventually give way to some other power.

Would American nationalism, too, be so selfish that we would perish from our very strength? Ovington hoped not, but her hope was feeble. "I trust that yours is strong," she wrote her man in the service.[44]

She saw three glimmers of hope: the revolution of workers; the potential of women; and the beauty of nature. It gave her some encouragement that "I've lived to hear Trotsky's cry, and though it was only answered by a few strikes in Austria and Germany, in which, I love to think, the women were prominent, the cry did sound out through the world." Now, ten years after the clear decision she made to focus her concern for the laboring classes on black civil rights, she made an assessment.

> Sometimes I wish I had had the courage really to join the labor movement, to forsake father and mother and sister and brother and live the life of the working class. . . . These folk who play with unionism or socialism until it hits their little world and then drop it returning to the viewpoint of their class, are of little use. At any rate I knew enough to know that and so went in for the Negro, where I could use what I had. But it troubles me sometimes lest we are only helping to make a black bourgeoisie.[45]

In a public letter she expressed the same judgments. She complimented the black radicals A. Philip Randolph and Chandler Owen on their magazine the *Messenger*, which made Negro support for the solidarity of labor its cornerstone. As a longtime socialist, she had previously looked in vain, she told them, for Negro college graduates with a revolutionary spirit. She believed that only class consciousness and internationalism could save the black races of the world. Indeed, the war showed that those two things were the only hope of mankind, she concluded.[46]

Spingarn, in their epistolary discussions, claimed that the ignoble side of human nature was more evident in peace than in war. Ovington was not so sure, although the gruesome details of the lynchings she knew would balance war's atrocities. But, she wrote him, "perhaps women mind cruelty more than men." Slowly starving a city in a siege "is quite as ignoble to me as usury. I can't view all those dead babies in Poland with any less repugnance than I view the private firm that poisons the soldier with decayed meat." In fact, "nobly" giving one's life for his country was not at all what a soldier was supposed to do. She wrote:

Every dead soldier is that much loss to the country. What the country wants is that the soldier should kill, not be killed. If he is killed at the onset he is of no use. He must kill, he must torture, he must maim, he must starve the enemy. That is his job.[47]

She drew sustenance from the natural world. In July of 1917, when the strain of the city hit her together with dread of family idleness at Bar Harbor, she went to a Long Island farm to live by herself and work.[48] Amid unflinching thoughts about war, in her correspondence with Joel Spingarn, Ovington turned, often, to nature—"Well, this is a pretty good world despite everything. There is the returning spring, and childhood, and the simple, real processes of life." In early 1918, Ovington retreated to the Pine Tree Inn at Lakehurst, New Jersey, to write. Joel Spingarn was close by at Fort Dix. She could hear the firing from the soldiers' camp; she believed then, too, that he must be able to see her sunsets.[49]

———————

DURING THE wartime absence of Spingarn, Acting Chairman Ovington demonstrated her leadership ability and style in both planned and unplanned activities. Two days before Independence Day, on July 2, 1917, the war came home to Negroes in East St. Louis, Illinois, and to their friends at the NAACP, like a predawn prelude to "The Red Summer" of 1919. This industrial center across the Mississippi from St. Louis had attracted a heavy Negro influx from the South as a result of floods and boll weevils in the cotton fields, wartime lack of immigrant laborers from Europe, recruitment by agents of northern industry, abuse and mistreatment by southern whites.

Ovington believed this Great Migration of the Negro, from the southern country of his fathers and mothers into the urban North, was a story that needed to be told, an epic as dramatic as the flight of the Israelites out of Egypt:

Who shall sing the story of the flight from Hattiesburg, Mississippi? How the marvels of the North fired the imaginations of the black dwellers in alleys and on farms. How the flame of enthusiasm grew until it swept through the church meeting and carried the minister along with it—a black Moses to lead the way with his children. How the day was set for the disposal of possessions and what a pitiful price was received for beds and chairs and cherished household goods. How trains were boarded and crowded to suffocation. How, through all the discomfort, there burned the glorious hope of a great deliverance, of a land ahead overflowing with milk and honey. How, the Ohio river crossed, men and women got out, kissed the ground and returned to the train, to sing of "Beulah Land." How, Chicago reached at last, the townsfolk clung together, took possession of four blocks, opened their church again, and brought Mississippi en masse to Chicago's South Side. The Negro poet has yet to come who shall recite this song.

The other part of the song was recited by screaming headlines. White and black clashed with increasing virulence in a city like East St. Louis, not quite South, not quite North. Conflicts raged out of control on July 2, spurred by rumors of Negro crime and claims that Republicans had imported Negroes to vote in the 1916 election. City officials could not cope with the initial violence and called in the militia, who apparently forced some Negroes into the hands of a white mob.

Hundreds of Negroes were shot or burned alive in their homes; an official figure could not be reached, for so many were tossed into unmarked holes or the nearby river. Nearly six thousand lost homes. American whites needed no lessons in barbarism from Germans. Nevertheless, Negroes were charged with inciting the riot and with murder.[50]

Acting Chairman Ovington acted quickly to coordinate NAACP response to East St. Louis. Du Bois and his assistant, Martha Gruening, went to investigate, and the *Crisis* published a twenty-page supplement. Lawyer Arthur Spingarn, brother of the chairman and head of the Legal Committee, joined with Ovington and Du Bois to hire a private detective and to decentralize the defense of those arrested. The St. Louis Branch of the NAACP collected data while the Washington, D.C., Branch pushed resolutions calling for a congressional investigation; the Chicago Branch monitored the state investigation and prepared personal damage suits for dependents of victims. And in the ironic way in which disaster brought money, contributions poured in to the special defense fund, including from, as Ovington reported to the board in

September, "several of the great Negro secret and fraternal organizations which heretofore have held themselves somewhat distant from the Association."[51]

In New York City, the skilled diplomatic hand of James Weldon Johnson shaped the Silent Protest Parade that astounded Fifth Avenue onlookers on Saturday, July 28. To muffled drums, ten thousand black men, women, and children in white marched with banners protesting lynching and mob violence.[52] It was "a very big thing," Ovington wrote Joel Spingarn, "and our men lead it." She told his brother, Arthur, that it was "the most encouraging thing I have seen for years." The acting secretary pulled the whole thing off impressively, and also, "as the result of great diplomacy," Ovington told Villard, created a Harlem Branch out of the organization that handled the parade. "This means that we have a Branch including almost all of the prominent Negroes in New York City, something which former secretaries have tried for in vain."[53]

Even while the office scrambled to respond to the riot, Oswald Garrison Villard claimed there was too much "inefficiency." When Secretary Roy Nash resigned in September, Villard began pushing Owen Lovejoy, general secretary of the National Child Labor Committee. Ovington had in mind for secretary a woman who had done "national suffrage work" and "suffered in the cause of the Negro," Mary Ware Dennett. The acting chairman did not think they could afford so expensive a person as Lovejoy—it would throw off the other salaries, and be unfair to small contributors. And she suspected a hidden agenda. It looked like Villard himself "wants to return to control things," Ovington bemoaned to Joel Spingarn. She grew worried when she "saw determination" in Villard's eye.[54]

She told Spingarn that "I always am annoyed at criticism from those who do nothing," and with typical honesty, she also told Villard, albeit more diplomatically. "I confess that there is one thing since I have been in social service work that has always greatly irritated me:—the criticism of work by those who are not actively engaged in it, nor closely in touch with it," she said. Lovejoy would not have been able to accomplish more than they had that week, she continued in her letter to Villard, and added a list of everyone's activities. But, more to the point, she worried that such a man would "assume command," and "alienate the colored people whom it has been so difficult to win."

Didn't they need to accept the fact that "the white people on the Board have never won the support of the colored people?" A white secretary would have to have, she continued, "great tact and must be able to work with his colleagues [on the basis of] equality, otherwise we shall lose, not only the office force, but the Branches which have been so admirably built up in the last year."[55]

With her letters, she effectively eliminated Villard from active participation in the NAACP for some time. I can see I am no longer useful, he shot back. He would not lend his name as treasurer to the association, he told her, unless the whole operation became more efficient, and he firmly believed the first step in that direction had to be the removal of Du Bois as editor. But almost as if *she* controlled *him*, Villard asked Ovington twice in the same letter that he be "allowed to leave."[56]

Through the war, Ovington nudged the NAACP toward diplomacy and decentralization in reacting to the unexpected. She also hinted at the way she believed things should be done with the seventh annual NAACP conference, The Negro in Wartime, held in New York City December 27 to 30, 1917. It was an ambitious plan, she told Lillian Wald, to make sure the out-of-town people had a good time.[57] The holiday season was chosen so more people could come and because it was "the most interesting and pleasant time to visit the great metropolis," as the announcement touted: "Those who have not seen the city during the winter season have not, in fact, seen real New York."

Delegates were guests of the association for lunches, for *The Servant in the House* at the Lafayette Theater in Harlem, and for a dinner. Afternoons allowed sightseeing. A Committee on Accommodations helped those who were new to New York, and another group acted as guides, but programs were very specific with directions for use of subway, elevated train, bus, or surface car.

For Ovington, the meetings were like an NAACP homecoming, a gathering of people she worked with in New York and a reunion with those she knew from across the country. With the association between secretaries, much of the work fell to her. She didn't mind because that meant she could make it the kind of event she had liked ever since her first Niagara Movement meetings at Harpers Ferry in 1906.[58]

War raged abroad and echoed throughout the United States. Ovington rehearsed for her upcoming role of chairman of the board of the

NAACP by responding thoughtfully and collegially to uncontrolled events and by planning creatively for events to further the cause.

———————————

SERVING AS acting chairman prior to the appointment of John Shillady as secretary in January 1918 had its benefits for Mary White Ovington, as did the freedom that followed upon the arrival of the tall, graying but youthful, broad-shouldered Shillady. While the organization was between secretaries, she had taken over speech-making, and found she enjoyed it. In fact, she had just come back from presentations at Boston and Hartford, Connecticut, right before the Mid-Winter Conference.

When Shillady arrived, she was no longer seated at the front table at meetings and gatherings. At an Urban League dinner early in 1918 she at first felt left out. But then she noticed a small table for two by a window, with one seat occupied by a tall, elderly gentleman with a high, old-fashioned collar. She asked if she might join him. When he assented, she sat down to what would be the most pleasant dinner of the year.

Her companion, it turned out, was real estate expert John E. Nail, father of James Weldon Johnson's wife, Grace Nail Johnson. Nail, Ovington discovered, was an "old-time New Yorker, who knew his New York as Dickens knew his London." As they swapped stories—Ovington telling about her great-grandfather's factory on Houston Street which had been called "Ovington's Folly" because it was four stories high—she looked up at Shillady's broad shoulders squeezed in at the speakers' table, and "lost all envy." It was good, she concluded, to be near the crowd, and yet not be of it.[59]

At the NAACP offices, Shillady's rapid acclimation meant she could stop stamping letters and receiving guests. His tenure as secretary was great for the organization—branch membership grew from nine thousand to forty-four thousand in one year, and the national office moved to large attractive rooms on the sixth floor at 70 Fifth Avenue. But Shillady's driving power left Ovington with no vehicle for her energy.

"The love of the place had grown on me," she realized, so she looked around for a task no one else had time for: coordination among the branches.[60]

After a writing break at the Pine Tree Inn, interrupted only by a return to New York on February 25 to the surprise fiftieth birthday dinner for W. E. B. Du Bois,[61] Ovington planned the first of her extended trips to visit branches, starting with her presentation of the Spingarn Award to William Stanley Braithwaite in Providence. As secretary, Shillady initiated the Moorfield Storey Drive to raise funds in honor of the NAACP president, and Ovington tailored her travel to support this campaign.

In June she felt "quite professional" as she headed west, adding to her usual suitcase a briefcase and a typewriter.[62] Her first stop was Pittsburgh, where she marveled at the vigor demanded of branch members without cars on the hilly streets. But her welcome made up for it, and the grime was not much worse than New York's. Here she first met Mrs. Daisy Lampkin, who would become an NAACP field secretary and a fast friend.[63]

In Chicago she spent a lot of time with the branch head, dentist Charles E. Bentley, going over the relationship of finances between the large affiliates (Chicago had a thousand members) and the national office. Bentley "didn't jump," she said, when she proposed that branches pay for their copies of promotional literature. As the Fourth of July, which she dubbed "spread Eagle time," approached, she realized that they should have printed thousands of copies of "What the Association has done for the Colored Soldier," but they couldn't afford it.[64]

Back in New York, W. E. B. Du Bois picked up the virus of patriotism from Joel Spingarn and proposed that he keep his *Crisis* job (and salary) while he took up a military commission in the Intelligence Bureau. In the July *Crisis,* he published a "Close Ranks" editorial supporting the war, and some quickly assumed that with his pen he had paid a bribe for the appointment. Stifled hostility for him exploded over the issue, and she heard much of it in her travels.

She told Du Bois that she thought "Close Ranks" "roars like a nightingale" because she found that the editorial's beauty paradoxically dominated its militarism. Laconically she added: "It must be comforting if you can really believe what you write, though I confess I find it almost impossible to think that you do." To this Du Bois replied with equal pith, after the board voted on July 8 not to support his plan, "I am meaning these days everything that I say in THE CRISIS, but I am not saying all that I would like to say." The following spring, he would write "Returning Soldiers" with drums of militancy replacing the bird-song echoes: "We *return*. We *return from fighting*. We *return fighting*."

Would Ovington have supported Du Bois had she been there for the vote in the hot summer of 1918, or was she beginning to find him less essential to the success of the NAACP? Du Bois told the board that both Ovington and Spingarn "agree with me that it would be wise to accept this offer," but of course that did not mean she thought the NAACP should keep paying him, too. Knowing her strong interest in the matter, John Shillady wired her of the outcome. "I am most relieved," she told Du Bois, "and I think you are probably glad of it." To that the editor responded simply: "I have decided not to go to Washington." As for reaction in the branches to the noncommissioned Du Bois, she found some who endorsed his stand, but mostly there was (choosing her words carefully) "a measure of criticism."[65]

Ovington spent the Fourth of July on the sweltering Iowa prairie outside Des Moines, attending two picnics before she had what she called the sad task of speaking to the Negro soldiers at nearby Camp Dodge. The ride to the camp was hot and dusty. Returning in a pouring rainstorm, she saw Iowa's rich, stoneless soil turn to mud, which kept the car stuck for an hour—though even then it was "jolly," in the back seat with two charming women, Mrs. Rush and Mrs. Hall.

At Camp Dodge she confronted directly the situation of the Negro officers and troops, speaking face to face with some of the 50,000 Negroes who did combat service in France (another 150,000 were in the service battalions—stevedores, butchers, and laborers). Ovington found she agreed with James Weldon Johnson that "military drill is a great thing for the race." The educated officers were given the worst of unlearned recruits. The first group Ovington saw was from Alabama, the next from Tennessee. When she saw how ignorant they looked in contrast to their charming, able young leaders, it made her realize the terrible neglect with which the United States treated its black children. In no other group in the country, she thought, would one find such a difference between the educated and the uneducated.

It seemed horrible to her that they were sent off to fight for the country in France "when they had had little of democracy or education to count at home." Three soldiers at Camp Dodge had been hanged in military discipline, even though, according to Ovington, there were extenuating circumstances. The three had gone singing to their deaths, however, leading her to comment that "I am so glad that, unlike the Calvinist, the Negro dwells not on hell but on heaven. Perhaps because he gets hell enough on this earth."

Ovington was so impressed by the officers that she modified her views on the military. They went far beyond their duty in training the uneducated troops, working from sixteen to eighteen hours a day, holding night school when the day's work was done. She wrote:

> Some time I hope the story will be written up for I imagine it is unusual in army annals. Certainly in the regular army you would not find an officer paying the slightest attention to his men when his regular work was done. If all officers had the spirit of the colored officers we need not so much dread the military caste.

The irony of black men serving their country abroad while they were being persecuted and killed at home continued, however. She noted that President Wilson, in his Fourth of July speech, had not spoken out against lynching, as the NAACP had been pressuring him to do. But before her trip ended, as she turned to head back east toward Omaha from Colorado Springs on July 26, the president finally did speak out, calling on governors, law officers, and men and women of every community to cooperate "not passively merely, but actively and watchfully" to end lynching. It was a "stupendous denunciation," Ovington told Shillady—a monument to him and to James Weldon Johnson.

> It's such a splendid thing that I feel as a general must feel who sees his side win a great victory. Only I should put myself in the position of a private. I hope that we shall have a great many letters of thanks go to Wilson. One doesn't want the twelve prayers and one thanksgiving.[66]

She and the NAACP needed that taste of victory, for as she traveled, the war kept intruding. In Minneapolis, she addressed men going off to Camp Dodge, and in Chicago she found families holding their breaths for the next casualty lists, for the rumor was rampant—and accurate—that the 370th Infantry, the old Eighth Illinois, which carried a full staff of colored officers, was in the front of the fighting at the Argonne offensive and was nearly wiped out.[67]

On the other, life-enhancing side of experiences, her 1918 trip was the first time Ovington had been farther west than Chicago, and she was struck by the beauty and fertility of the plains. Peoria, Illinois, astounded her—why hadn't anyone told her that it was one of the most beautiful cities in the country? Here the weather was wonderful, too, cool with puffy white clouds, nothing to mar the landscape spread before her.

In Moline, on the western side of the state, she stayed with the secretary of the branch and was given the best room in the house, looking directly out into peaceful woods. (Her hostess and host had moved out of their room for her; wherever she stayed, she knew when this happened, because other things might be removed, but always there was a line of neckties strung against the wall!)

When the weather turned hot, her travel became more difficult and tiring, but still she reveled in the land stretching out from the Mississippi River valley, all at its best, the grain about to be gathered and the corn just high enough to take on vivid green hues. The contrast between these vast expanses and the small patches of fertility she had seen before, hugging the fjords in Norway or the rocky hills of New England, was enormous. It became incredible to her that anyone in the country should be hungry. And in the towns and around the farmsteads, she found magnificent trees. The beetles that had hit the East had not yet reached the Midwest, so giant, stately elms lined the trails of the towns.[68]

Everywhere she went, from Colorado to upstate New York, she found wonderful hospitality from old friends and new, from NAACP branches and others she knew through her college and social work and socialist and library connections. In Omaha she found a socialist friend who subscribed to the *Messenger*—they got together for breakfast to "talk all the wild stuff we want."

"If I were royalty I could not be treated with more consideration," she marveled, "but if I were royalty I certainly should not have half so good a time." She did more motoring than on any other trip, saw more cities, and found people she would always remember for their charm and courtesy. Somehow she had expected the Midwest and North would show less hospitality than the South—but perhaps it was the size of places that made the difference. At any rate, she was repeatedly glad that she and Acting Secretary Johnson had shown the delegates to New York such a good time the previous Christmas.[69]

Ovington earned her way both in money collected at meetings to pay her traveling expenses and in NAACP members recruited and two new branches created—in Omaha and Colorado Springs. It was hard sometimes to be enthusiastic in a stifling church, with the audience waving fans gently, looking as though they would like to go to sleep (though none of them did). If she was the first speaker, or the local leaders did not much like speaking or praying, it was not so bad, but sometimes others wore the group out before she was announced. She was relieved when there was no program because she could reach the audience while they were fresh and stop when they were tired.

The various ways she was introduced delighted her. In Des Moines, the son of one of her heroes, James Baird Weaver, Populist candidate for president in 1892, compared her to all the great women of history, including Harriet Beecher Stowe, and in Moline, she was both a second Stowe and a female Abraham Lincoln.

The trip was delightful and worthwhile. She brought back some useful thoughts about policies and activities. First, she made sure that thank-yous went out as the contributions to her trip came in. Second, she had learned that it was a disincentive to the branches to be able to keep only fifty cents of each contribution-enrollment, no matter how large. Denver, for example, was not going to be happy at all being able to keep only fifty cents of Mr. Phipps's one-hundred dollar subscription! Maybe they could, she suggested, take fifty-five cents on the one-dollar memberships to make up what they would lose on the larger ones. Out in the country such a change in board policy would be quite an item. The third conclusion she had reached from the trip was that they should be working on developing college branches.

Fourth, she proposed that some branches would benefit from a pamphlet on legal redress work. Although branches formed organically, on their own, when education took place, what would they do once formed? The brochure could be short, practical, and specific, written by one of the lawyers or by the Legal Committee, using successful examples from places like Detroit. Fifth, she wanted a geographically rotating forum instituted, including a detailed program of six monthly meetings devoted to specific subjects affecting the Negro.[70]

Ovington came back to New York City in August newly energized for national and international challenges. Quickly, she made decisions as acting chairman to send the newly hired Walter White into the South for six weeks; to financially support Du Bois's travel to Europe for the Pan-African Congress in Paris and to investigate the treatment of the black soldier in the war; to hire additional staff, including a man she had been delighted with in Detroit, Father Robert Bagnall; and to move the association into larger quarters. Some established activities continued: resistance to the resurgence of *Birth of a Nation* segued into a battle against Negro caricatures on patriotic posters.[71]

Ovington wanted to add branch secretary to her acting chairman position, at least for a year, with an honorarium of one hundred dollars per month ("about half the money I am worth"), with the understanding that she might keep irregular hours. She would require more office space and a stenographer. But she wanted Shillady to decide if he wanted the chairman around doing the specific job of branch secretary—she didn't know if she would go for it were she in his position.

In contrast to the authority coveted by previous holders of the chairmanship, Ovington sought consensus and collegiality. The position of secretary was becoming under her leadership the executive position: "You are the real boss of this concern," she told Shillady,

> the one who has to bear the responsibility for the work, and I want to do what will make the work most efficient—I apologize for that word—but also most human, most in sympathy with this immense mass of people who are beginning to rise and who need every ounce of power that we have to give them.[72]

She did not get paid half of her worth; in fact she got nothing. But that didn't stop Mary White Ovington from becoming in January 1919, both chairman of the board and director of branches of the NAACP.

In February 1919, the National Association for the Advancement of Colored People reached its tenth birthday, having survived a difficult birth, a shaky infancy, family feuds, and world hostilities. It was on the verge of fame, if not fortune, with strength in numbers to do ever more of the work it had set out to accomplish, work that the country still demanded if it were to truly be the land of the free.

7

Chairman of the Board

AT THE BEGINNING of 1919, as the NAACP gathered for its annual meeting, the war was over, but Major Joel Spingarn, who had been chairman of the board of the NAACP since January of 1914, was still in France. W. E. B. Du Bois, editor of the *Crisis*, was in Europe, too, investigating treatment of Negro soldiers. Three other key players from the organization's first ten years were also across the Atlantic as investigative journalists: Oswald Garrison Villard, William English Walling, and Charles Edward Russell.

At the United Charities Building in New York City, the remaining group held the annual meeting on January 6. Mary White Ovington, in whose mind the organization had begun, who was the only woman to sign the incorporation papers, whose energy and interpersonal skills had nourished the struggling, growing association, was, at last, elected chairman of the board. Unpaid secretary in 1911–1912 and 1916, acting chairman since May of 1917, director of branches by her own request, she was also the only woman among the national salaried and elected officers.[1]

"Well, I am Chairman now," Ovington wrote Spingarn, "and I am trying to put in a few more hours each day that I may not have any of our supporters regret the Board's choice." She told Du Bois she felt "very grand" in her new position. Ovington had ambitious plans, but she also had to budget her energy and time in caring for her mother.

James Weldon Johnson spoke at the Carnegie Hall mass meeting that followed the business session. The next day, his mother died, and Ovington grieved with him:

I thought of you so often last night when I had my own mother at the meeting looking down at me and knew that your mother had looked at you for the last time on earth. I wish I might have known her. I am sure that I should have loved her. It's a hard world. Even for those whom life touches gently it's hard for the years are so few, but it's the love in it that keeps it dear to us and makes it worth while. And it's a great comfort, isn't it, that no circumstance can ever take this away—neither poverty nor persecution, nor death itself.[2]

Ovington had to drop some activities. One, the Lincoln Settlement in Brooklyn, which she had founded with Dr. Verina Morton-Jones in 1908, and whose board president and chief fund-raiser Ovington had been ever since, had to find a new leader in 1920 when it merged with the Brooklyn offices of the Urban League so as to concentrate Negro social service organizations in one place.[3]

She decreased the time she could contribute to groups such as the board of the Circle for Negro War Relief and increased her financial donations. Her monetary contributions throughout the 1920s show her interests as a radical, a writer, and an environmentalist. She gave to Near East Relief; Wilberforce and Calhoun Colored School; the American Friends Service Committee; the Cooperation League; the American Civil Liberties Union; the League for Industrial Democracy (grown out of the Intercollegiate Socialist Society); the League for Mutual Aid; the Women's International League for Peace and Freedom; the Sojourner Truth Home; the Authors' League and the New York Drama League; the Penguin Club and the Dickens Fellowship; the Teachers' Union, and the American Forestry Association.[4]

In addition to the NAACP, Ovington stayed active in the Civic Club at 14 West Twelfth Street. Along with several others, including her brother Charles and sister-in-law Elizabeth, she had founded this retreat in 1916. Immediately, it attracted 427 other liberals who liked fellowship and discussion of social problems. Even during the war, the club had maintained full freedom of expression in its programming. Its 950 members in 1921 included many NAACP workers, and Gertrude Stein, Elmer Rice, Roger Baldwin, Paul Kellogg, Helen Hull, Margaret Sanger, Caroline Pratt, Countee Cullen, Rosamund Johnson—writers, publishers, activists, and artists involved in civil liberties or birth control or education.

Throughout the 1920s, the twenty-dollar annual fee provided Ovington and her friends with a place where they would not be hassled for their race or gender; where current issues and books could be freely discussed; where interracial dinners could be held with elegance, as was W. E. B. Du Bois's fiftieth-birthday dinner in 1918; and where NAACP personnel could go for lunch. A large, airy, two-level dining hall welcomed Civic Club members, and its Belgian chef, Achilles, held his own with the best in New York.[5]

———————————

As new chairman of the NAACP board, Ovington introduced People Care/Paper Accountability to the rapidly expanding organization.[6] They went together. Personal support encouraged high productivity and clear records of daily activities—phone calls, correspondence, meetings—meant that when someone was overloaded or ill, a colleague could step in and pick up the work. When Ovington told Secretary John Shillady and then James Weldon Johnson that they had to take a vacation, the work did not stop. Johnson wrote Du Bois in 1924, "I do not believe the services of any single individual are now indispensable to the NAACP."

By 1919, the office was big and bustling, with Miss Stowe in charge of office staff, Richetta Randolph as full-time secretary to the secretary, and stenographers for Chairman Ovington, Assistant Secretary Walter White, Field Secretary James Weldon Johnson, and bookkeeper F. M. Turner. Alice Brown, who would soon become a secretary to Ovington, operated the switchboard; an office boy and a filing clerk were soon added. The *Crisis* offices, completely separate, also had extensive staff.[7]

Organization and expansion were not ends, but means. In a *Crisis* article in the same issue as the one announcing her election to the chairmanship, Ovington outlined her plans for "Reconstruction and the Negro."[8] Oppressed groups around the world, Ovington wrote, workingmen, women, small nationalities, and the so-called inferior races, were struggling to secure something of value in postwar chaos. None had more of an uphill climb than the American Negro, oppressed by both class and race.

Given that hill, what did she propose for climbing gear, for vehicles, for sustenance? She used an analogy between President Woodrow Wilson's Fourteen Point peace plan, and fourteen points desired by the

Negro. She asked the practical question: How shall we go about securing these wishes?

Agitation alone would not do it, she wrote. A program was essential.
Some demands in the program were applicable to all working-class
Americans, such as removal of peonage; reform of penal institutions; securing of better wages, education, housing, and sanitary conditions.
The best way to achieve these demands, Ovington suggested, was, to
"join with the progressive forces in the general community and to work
with them." Interracial effort was not impossible, even in the South,
she believed, and had been enhanced by cooperation on the war effort.

She was most concerned with those demands that applied specifi-
cally to the Negro: the ballot, the right to travel as others travel, to live
as others live, and "to enter without question into the life of the
American citizen." Unfortunately, as she saw it, no help could be expected from the president whom Negro soldiers had faithfully served
abroad. Since 1913, segregation had increased under the administra-
tions of southerner Woodrow Wilson. "The railroads are operated by
the United States," she wrote,

> but colored soldiers are Jim-Crowed as they return to their homes, are
> denied the right to sleep in Pullmans, are refused food at railroad res-
> taurants. Since 1912 the Negro federal employee has been subjected to
> many petty acts of discrimination that have aroused race antagonism
> and created antipathies that never existed before.

But legislatures could change rapidly, and the Negro, in organized
numbers, could elect friends to push his cause. Here, Ovington proposed, the NAACP was crucial. Membership had grown in a year from
ten thousand to forty-three thousand, meaning, she wrote, that there
were "groups of men and women, throughout the whole country, who
at a given moment could act unitedly for the benefit of the race. This
is the first great force to be used to secure the franchise, fair trial by
jury, anti-lynching." Victories came slowly, Ovington pointed out in
her article. A decision by the Supreme Court followed years of work.
And large victories came from small successes. Grassroots branches
won daily skirmishes that aided in the larger battle:

> It may be rescuing a woman from being convicted as a vagrant under the
> "work or fight" law in Georgia; it may be securing the right to sit in the

orchestra of a theatre in a northern city; but each time it is a bit gained in the great movement for the destruction of racial discrimination in a democracy that has preached to the world freedom and justice to all.

Finally, Ovington turned to America's shame: sixty-four people were lynched in 1918, 40 percent more than in 1917. The deaths were increasingly brutal, she wrote, as in the case of Mary Turner in Valdosta, Georgia:

> After her husband's death, [she] mourned and loudly proclaimed his innocence. For this she was slowly burned to death, watched by a crowd of men and women. She was pregnant, and as she burned, the infant fell to the ground and was trampled under a white man's heel. White children were held up in their fathers' arms to witness this brutality.[9]

How could these ghastly events be prevented, Ovington asked. The two causes she saw, ignorance and the "despotic power of one man over the life of another," had to be confronted by education and civil power. By disfranchisement and legislation, the South had rendered the Negro helpless. It was clear to Ovington that those who acquiesced in their powerlessness were not lynched, but those, like Mary Turner, who questioned or rebelled, were tortured and destroyed.

Alluding to her 1911 book, *Half a Man*, Ovington concluded that it was clear throughout the world that "there is no half-way status—a man must be a man or a slave. When he ceases to be a slave, he can never be a safe element in the population until he becomes a man." She saw lessons around the world and had hope that the United States could live up to its world rhetoric at home.

———

BETWEEN JUNE and December of the first year of Mary White Ovington's chairmanship, whites in the United States lynched seventy-six Negroes—some soldiers still in uniform—and twenty-five race riots flared across the United States. Riot statistics revealed something new—white injuries and deaths—as Negroes began to defend themselves and their property. Ovington began calling the riots "wars," and took grim pleasure in the new militancy.

Reflecting that militancy, Jamaican American poet Claude McKay penned his fighting sonnet:

> If we must die, let it not be like hogs
> Hunted and penned in an inglorious spot,
> While round us bark the mad and hungry dogs,
> Making their mock at our accursed lot.
>
> Like men we'll face the murderous, cowardly pack
> Pressed to the wall, dying, but fighting back![10]

The NAACP planned—and reacted. Chairman of the Board Ovington and Secretary Shillady maintained a friendly rivalry in their planning of the two conferences of 1919. Shillady's antilynching event at Carnegie Hall in May surpassed her tenth anniversary Cleveland conference in luminaries, Ovington joked, but hers was longer, a full week, and gave more people a chance to speak.

NAACP membership was now at 56,345, from 220 branches, and the *Crisis* went out to 100,000 readers. The NAACP had become the premier group fighting for Negro rights. The June conference in Cleveland was the largest yet, and the first to include labor issues. The mostly Negro representatives came from thirty-four states and set a pattern of open representation at annual meetings.

In commenting on the primarily Negro delegations to the conference, Ovington said she was disappointed only that more whites were not around to see this shift to black leadership in the branches. She and Shillady found the meetings a welcome contrast with previous NAACP gatherings and with social work organizations, where, she said, "it was the wisdom of the well-to-do, the philanthropically-minded," discussing what should be done for the poor and sick and disinherited. She amplified:

> But at the Cleveland conference, we white delegates were working *with* the people we were trying to help, were discussing not their economic problems but their status as citizens, and were constantly learning from them. . . . Few are interested in others' problems. White people were in-

terested in a story of distress . . . but philanthropy and justice often stand apart. The very recognition of the need of philanthropy denies justice.

Ovington arranged for informal interactions at lunches in churches and dinners in homes—a prudent as well as sociable way to handle meals, as it turned out, for James Weldon Johnson was refused service in a Cleveland restaurant. So with large numbers and intimate bread-breaking, stirring rhetoric and quiet tribute, the tenth-anniversary conference ended its week singing "God be with you till we meet again," as every representative from Los Angeles to Bangor resolved to carry on the work and win more men and women to the cause.[11] Their resolve would be tested by bloodshed to come in the following three months.

On July 19, in Washington, D.C., supposedly after an assault on a white woman, police searched and questioned Negroes found on the streets after dark. White soldiers and sailors wandered through the southwest district, shooting and entering homes. Finally, Negroes organized, secured guns, and patrolled Washington streets, and some, including Ovington, believed that this response is what kept casualties down. Order was eventually fully restored by the United States Provost Guard.

Chicago exploded on Sunday July 27, when Negroes crossed an imaginary color line at a Lake Michigan beach and whites pelted one of them, a seventeen-year-old boy, with stones until he drowned. A Negro was arrested and onlookers attacked the arresting officer. Violence increased and spread the following days, particularly against Negroes in white districts. Mobs pulled trolleys from their tracks, dragged out Negro passengers and beat, stabbed, or shot them. By Friday, aided by heavy rain, the militia quelled the riot. The total casualties stood at 38 dead (15 whites and 23 Negroes) and some 537 injured.

Chicago was a prime magnet for Negro migrants fleeing violence in the South. Ovington wanted national NAACP people there quickly; she did not trust the response committee of the local branch, which she described as a "very conservative" group that included Graham Taylor and Robert E. Park, who, according to Ovington, was "an old Booker Washingtonite, who never did an aggressive thing in his life."

It was "fortunate for the Association and for the Negro," as Ovington told him, that Joel Spingarn, the past chairman, was in Chicago when the riot occurred. She sent Assistant Secretary White and prevailed upon Charles Edward Russell: "You went to Russia for the United States, surely it is worth while going to Chicago for the Negro." The honor of the association and every northern city was at stake, she believed—she was sure the South was "chuckling with pleasure" at the news of a race riot in a major northern metropolis. Ovington wrote Shillady on vacation: "I greatly wish you could go directly to Chicago. . . . White is not experienced enough to handle this matter."[12]

The secretary immediately made plans to travel to Illinois, but first arranged with Ovington to continue from Chicago to Austin, Texas, where the branch was being accused of dangerous equality talk. The attorney general claimed they were operating illegally and demanded their books. What should we do? branch officials asked.

Ovington and Shillady talked it over at 70 Fifth Avenue. Texas had twenty-nine branches—including Dallas and San Antonio with paid-up memberships of 1,000 and 1,500. If Austin went, what would keep closures from spreading? Surely, she thought, if the secretary explained to the attorney general of Texas that the NAACP was legally incorporated in New York State, the problem could be resolved.

"Do you think there is any danger?" Shillady wondered about the situation in Texas. Ovington thought carefully. There might be danger if he were Negro, but assuredly not for the dignified white Shillady, meeting top officials of Texas. "Not to you," she told him.[13]

John Shillady reached Austin on August 20, and went the next day to the statehouse. Finding the attorney general and governor absent, he met with the acting attorney general to explain his mission and was told that "niggers" were dangerous if they got the idea that they could break down segregation. Shillady then headed toward the office of the captain of the state rangers, only to be touched on the arm by a constable, served with a subpoena, and hauled before a secret Court of Inquiry by the justice of the peace, the Travis County attorney, and the county judge.

The questions turned hostile, about the antisegregation resolutions of the Cleveland conference, the *Crisis*, and support for social equality, all the way to "Would you want your daughter to marry a nigger?" and "Why don't you stop at a nigger hotel?" There had never been a lynching in Travis County, Shillady was told. In fact, Texas had a good record on "niggers": just as many whites and Mexicans were lynched.[14]

The following morning Shillady visited a branch official. Returning to the downtown Hotel Driskill, he was once again tapped on the arm. He turned, expecting another subpoena, but was struck in the face by one of a group of six or eight, including the judge and constable. With additional toughs waiting in a nearby car, these men swore at him and beat him until his face and chest glowed with blood and bruises, and then, as he lay close to unconsciousness, told him to get out of town.

Shillady struggled onto a train through a menacing crowd, and the porter rushed to help him. As he lay high-pillowed, watching the monotonous landscape slide by, suddenly the curtain of his berth was drawn aside. He grabbed his typewriter for defense, but was greeted by an Associated Press reporter.

Back in New York, Ovington and staff were finishing a day's work when someone reading the paper cried, "Mr. Shillady has been attacked in Austin!" There was no further word for twenty-four hours, until Shillady reached St. Louis. Ovington was alarmed, and his wife frantic. When his train arrived at Pennsylvania Station, Ovington and others waiting heard the cry, "Shillady!" and dozens of Red Caps rushed down the platform to greet the man who had suffered in their cause. The procession to the NAACP offices was triumphant.[15]

John Shillady's face was wounded, but not badly scarred. His spirit was quite different, however. Ovington compared him to a shell-shocked soldier. James Weldon Johnson said Shillady never recovered "spiritually" from the attack. The board gave him a six-week paid vacation. By the end of December it looked as if he was back at work full force, and by March of 1920, he appeared to Ovington to be once again his old self, making decisions and seemingly happy at his work.[16]

But in April, the "bomb fell." Shillady notified Ovington of his impending resignation, and it went to the board in May. Ovington felt it keenly. She had sent him to Austin and assured him he would be safe. More than that, she hated to see him give up. It made any prosecution of the Texas officials impossible, and it was a discouraging model. In his resignation letter he wrote that he was "less confident than heretofore of the speedy success of the Association's full program."[17]

Tending the injured secretary was one failure; dealing with the state of Texas was another. As chairman, Ovington immediately sent a telegram to W. P. Hobby, asking what was being done to punish the offenders. The governor replied: "Shillady was the only offender in connection with the matter referred to in your telegram and he was punished before your inquiry came."[18]

The honor of the South was somewhat redeemed the following year. The large representation from the southern states at Cleveland led to an invitation from the mayor, the chamber of commerce, and governor of Georgia to hold the next convention in Atlanta. Some were hesitant after the Shillady attack, but Ovington saw it as a "gesture of defiance." ("We arranged for three days of meetings" instead of a week, "so that we could get away early," she joked.) Shillady, in his final weeks at the NAACP, did not go. He confessed to Johnson, who took Shillady's place in giving the keynote address as he would take his place as secretary, that "I think I have the moral courage, but I find that I have no physical courage."

Atlanta correctly believed that the whole region was on trial. Policemen, streetcar conductors, and anyone else who might come into contact with delegates were ordered to be courteous and to stretch the usual racial bounds. There were precautions taken. Ovington did not appear at the first day's mass meeting, which was, according to Johnson, the most tense. But "Atlanta treated us royally," Ovington said, and noted that whites attended meetings and that the press featured the organization on its front pages.[19] For the first time, the NAACP met and stated its principles openly in a southern city.

Ovington summarized the lessons of 1919 in an article in the *American City*. "The Gunpowder of Race Antagonism" pointed out that blowups such as those in Washington and Chicago could not occur from a single grain of gunpowder. "Unless a train is laid to some powder magazine, the result is only a slight flareup," she wrote. How, then, was the train laid in those cities, and "are we laying any lines of gunpowder in our own communities?"

She saw four causes for the racial violence. One of these, press dramatization of alleged Negro assaults on white women, had been crucial in Atlanta in 1906. In 1919, that cause was more evident in Washington, D.C., than in Chicago. The other three causes of violence, particularly in Chicago, were housing, corrupt politics, and conflict between organized and unorganized labor.

She observed that "few of us looking at our own cities can fail to see that we are dropping some inflammable material along the same lines." She suggested that one of the things that could be done immediately was to correct the misleading press coverage. Identification of Negroes by race in crime stories led readers to believe they were especially given to violence, yet statistics showed that "the white woman is in less danger of assault from the black than from the white man."

She called for careful study of conditions between the races in America's cities. "Only when there is indifference to the welfare of a group mass in the community can such race riots as those of Washington and Chicago occur." Those cities that had waited tensely through the summer of 1919 should take note. Gunpowder exploded only when it was laid out in a train visible to the concerned observer, she concluded.[20]

THE STORY OF the NAACP has often been told with emphasis on big issues, campaigns, and victories while smaller struggles and achievements have been overlooked. Not often noted is the extent to which Mary White Ovington brought women into power and empowered them, beginning with those who signed the Call in 1909. Those women came from Ovington's networks in social work, settlement work, and libraries, positions where white women had or created opportunity from 1900 to 1910.

Between the Call and the second decade of the NAACP, Ovington articulated her definition of feminist goals and actions in "Socialism and the Feminist Movement," published in the *New Review* in March 1914. Her actions in relation to women and power were not accidental, but built on careful analysis and continual action. She criticized the Socialist Party for failing to embrace women's suffrage and noted a "strange apathy" among writers and leaders on "the woman question." To her the women's movement went beyond the ballot:

> I believe that women for a long time to come, whether they have suffrage or not, will need to be banded together against oppression. . . . Doubtless Socialist women will be in the forefront of the battle, and their Socialism will give them courage for the conflict. But they will also recognize that as women they have their obligation to stand with all other women who are fighting for the destruction of masculine despotism and for the right of womankind.[21]

Ovington believed that inclusion for women had several dimensions. The goals of feminism had to go beyond suffrage, she thought, a position not otherwise widely articulated before women received the vote with the Nineteenth Amendment to the Constitution in 1920. Suffragists needed to include working women in their organizations, she maintained, and the male-dominated party of the working class, the Socialist, needed to support women's rights. Finally, Ovington fought subtly and strongly for the inclusion of black women in her own organization, the NAACP.

She was effective in this effort partly because of the strong friendships she developed with black women of all social classes. Ovington counted as lifetime friends Washington, D.C., activist Mary Church Terrell, and also Richetta Randolph, whom Ovington hired as a typist in 1905, and to whom she would dedicate her autobiography, for "the good days we spent working together." Mary McLeod Bethune, college founder and president, was a much admired ally; equally important was Carrie Overton, first employed as a typist at the NAACP in 1924, who devotedly managed to help the aging Ovington publish her life story in 1947. NAACP board member and doctor Verina Morton-Jones was a fast friend even after the two went on to other activities, as was secretary Alice Brown, whom Ovington helped support with loans, gifts, and extra income as an agent selling her books.

In the national office during her tenure as chairman, Ovington hired, befriended, and tended to the needs of office staffers. They were exploited, she said, "as all people in their group are exploited, and they have no one as far as I can see but myself to think about them." Across the country, Ovington lunched with, stayed with, and became friends with the black women who worked for the NAACP branches. She noticed over the years of increasing New York City–centered bureaucratization, that "no one pays attention" to the branches "except to beg them for money," and that when branches *were* recognized, "the showy people are noticed, but not the hard workers."

In her NAACP recruitment play, *The Awakening*, Ovington suggests another comment on work and historical credit. At one point, the committee to look into joining the NAACP is told: "I see you are not feminists. You appointed a man to do the work [as chair]." The female protagonist responds: "No we didn't. We appointed the man for the place of honor and the secretary, Thelma, did the work."[22]

Many of Ovington's ties to black women came through the National Association of Colored Women (NACW). A trip to Denver in early 1919 had been centered around speaking at their annual convention, and she was especially close to its president, Mary Talbert.

Ovington observed the black women's group through the lens of her mother's Brooklyn Woman's Club, a "frankly cultural" group that gave women who had had little opportunity for education something to study and talk about besides household affairs. Her daughter's generation, with more education, made fun of those half-hour discussions of Roman history or one-session histories of painting.

But the Negro women's group was different. They engaged in the kind of work the "liberated" college women of Mary White Ovington's generation did: they started kindergartens and day nurseries and looked after old people, and to do so, raised astounding amounts of money. In *Half a Man* Ovington had pointed out that black women much more often had economic responsibility for themselves and their families than white women did. Now she found that the volunteer work of black women who were freed from earning a living differed, too; it was much more directed at service than at personal enrichment. Greeting the group at its twenty-fifth anniversary in 1920, Ovington reaffirmed these conclusions: "There is an earnestness and a disinterestedness about your work that to my mind contrasts very favorably with the Woman's Club movement amongst the whites."[23]

The motto of the NACW was and is "Lifting as We Climb." The implications of that alone impressed Ovington—not a philosophy of "kicking down the ladder as soon as a slight social eminence was reached," but rather reaching down to help the one below. She observed:

> I never saw anything like it before, and I have never seen anything like it since. . . . I wish their story might be written some day and given to the world. Negro work built up by some individual has been frequently featured, individual Negroes have been honored, but the white world and, white women especially, have no appreciation of the amount of social service work that colored women, without wealth or leisure, have accomplished.[24]

Picking up the *New York Times* soon after her return from the Denver NACW meetings, the new chairman of the NAACP saw a quotation attributed to Alice Paul, leader of the militant Woman's Party fighting for woman's suffrage. In the heat of the battle for Senate support, Paul said all the talk about colored women in South Carolina intending to vote after ratification was "nonsense." Since Negro men couldn't vote there, how could Negro women? Paul asked.

That was not all. There was a movement afoot to meet southern objections by substituting for the Susan B. Anthony amendment to the Constitution a resolution by Senator A. A. Jones of New Mexico that would confer the right of suffrage on women only to the extent that men were permitted to vote in each state. A representative of the Woman's Party, John Milholland's daughter Vida, claimed that the Jones Amendment would not alter the Anthony resolution, that it was only a face-saving device.

Ovington knew better, as did the NAACP board. We absolutely must not write into the Constitution the right of the state to determine who shall vote, she told Milholland. Of course the southerners were attempting to disenfranchise Negro women—why else would they want the Jones Amendment? The Fifteenth Amendment said citizens could not be deprived of the ballot on the basis of race or color, and yet the southern states had found ways to do just that on other pretexts. The Jones proposal would in effect legalize those nullifications. Black men were about to make a determined effort to vote in parts of the South. "Don't let the white women turn against them to get suffrage for themselves," Ovington pleaded.

Ovington pressured Paul to publicly retract her statement. Paul claimed her words had been misreported and that she would clarify the matter at the party's Carnegie Hall suffrage meeting on March 8. When that was not done to Ovington's satisfaction, she brought forward at the NAACP board's March 10 meeting a strong resolution: Resolved,

> That the National Woman's Party be asked if, in its fight to remove the barrier of sex in voting in the United States, it thus intends to leave its professed stand of justice and democracy, and consent to the non-enfranchisement of the nearly 5,000,000 of colored women, and thus say to the world that the National Woman's Party does not believe in democracy to any greater extent than to secure the franchise for a part of the womanhood of that United States and not for all of it, and

whether the National Woman's Party will publicly repudiate the statement accredited to Miss Paul.

Mary White Ovington saw the Woman's Party's compromise as a double desertion: "If only you dear people could realize that every time you compromise with the conservative southerner, you not only hurt the Negro but you hurt the radical southerner." She cited the example of a meeting of the National Conference of Charities and Corrections in Memphis, when Graham Taylor of Chicago allowed Negroes to be segregated in the gallery. A southerner, Mr. Weatherford, moved his sessions to a church so that colored and white could sit together. His position was doubly difficult, he told Ovington, because of Taylor.[25]

Ovington's approach to women's suffrage was to keep an eagle eye out for any attempt to sell out black women, black men, and white radicals, even when others were willing to hush it up. Her advocacy for black women continued after enfranchisement. The NAACP expanded its voting-rights campaign to black women. Ovington continued pressure on the Woman's Party to include black women; extended her persuasion to the League of Women Voters, which grew out of Carrie Catt's National Woman's Suffrage Association; and kept a watchful eye out for discrimination in groups such as the YWCA.[26]

The NAACP devoted a day of its thirteenth annual convention in Newark in 1922 to women, culminating in Ovington's presentation of the Spingarn Medal to NACW leader Mary Talbert—the eighth medalist and first woman. Speakers included Hallie G. Brown of the National Association of Colored Women's Clubs; representatives of the Woman's Peace Party, the National Council of Jewish Women, the New Jersey League of Women Voters, and the New Jersey Federation of Women's Clubs. Such concentration on women at the height of the Dyer Anti-Lynching campaign came from the NAACP's woman leader.[27]

As chairman, Ovington wrote to President Warren Harding about a published rumor that he was going to appoint Senator John K. Shields of Tennessee to the Supreme Court, a prospect, she said, "seriously disquieting to those Americans, both white and colored, whose hope is a better relation between the races in this country."

Shields had said he was opposed to the ballot for "nigger women": "You see, we couldn't treat the wenches as we do the men; we just club the niggers if they come to the polls." "It is almost unnecessary to point out," she told the president, "that a confessed violator of the United States Constitution" who spoke of such violation with "ruffianly approval" could "only increase disrespect for law and government in the United States Supreme Court as he has already done in the United States Senate." Shields was not approved.[28]

A further example of Ovington's vigilance on the inclusion of black women came a couple of years later in a letter to Mrs. Franklin D. Roosevelt, chairman of the Platform Planks of Special Interest to Women on the Democratic National Committee. Ovington wrote to Eleanor Roosevelt early in, or perhaps at the beginning of, Mrs. Roosevelt's career of support for black women: "We should like to present a plank emphasizing the importance of colored women's voting throughout the United States, and demanding their protection in so doing in whatever part of the country in which they may live."[29]

Mary Talbert traveled extensively for the NACW and the NAACP, forming branches of the latter in hostile areas, particularly Texas. She also fund-raised for both groups: for the NACW she helped save Frederick Douglass's Washington, D.C., home; for the NAACP she raised prodigious amounts for the antilynching campaign.[30] Ovington often stayed with Talbert in Buffalo when she traveled, and warm correspondence flowed between them. Their friendship helped coordinate progressive action, as in the joint meetings of the Conference of Social Work and the NAACP at Cleveland. In sessions on cooperation between national agencies in work for the Negro, Ovington and Talbert, as leaders of the NAACP and the NACW, took their places with representatives of the Urban League, the YMCA, and the YWCA.[31]

Ovington's admiration grew during the antilynching campaign begun at the Newark conference. Talbert and the Anti-Lynching Crusaders made a dream come true: a full-page ad in the *New York Times*. Ovington said:

> We opened the morning paper to see THE SHAME OF AMERICA staring at us in great capitals, and below the story of lynching and America's shame. A full page! It was a proud moment when we could reverse the usual crime story in the press and show the crime of the white against the black.[32]

Ovington worked to get Talbert an NAACP vice presidency. First she appointed a black chairman of the Nominating Committee, Hutchins Bishop. When Talbert was not nominated as Ovington suggested, she sent the list back with the note: "No woman's name." Talbert was added, and elected in 1920. Other black women were promoted in the NAACP at the same time. Nannie Burroughs of Washington, D.C., became a board member. Addie Hunton was hired as a fieldworker after Ovington said "the next person we hire must be a woman."[33]

Ovington also demonstrated concern for probably the most unrecognized women in America: rural southern blacks. In 1928 she visited rural Mississippi to study the impact of the Sheppard-Towner Act, which had made federal funds available for the training of midwives. Southerners were filibustering against the act's renewal, and Ovington wanted to place an article called "Catching a Baby" in *Good Housekeeping,* where it might influence the debate.

Dr. Felix J. Underwood of the state board of health had done something remarkable with the federal aid. Most of the population of Mississippi, black and white, was brought into the world by 4,209 midwives, 99 percent of them Negro. As Ovington described it,

> unfortunately, most of these midwives were old and illiterate. They appeared before county registrars in old woolen dresses topped by dirty hats. They took snuff or smoked a pipe. Their superstitions were many, customs from the far past. Thus it was well [*sic*] to have a sharp instrument under the mother's bed at the time of birth, a scythe or an axe, to cut the pain. . . . Bathing was dangerous and fresh air poison. Some tried to hasten birth in risky fashion. A fair proportion knew that drops should be put in the baby's eyes and nearly all were familiar with the birth certificate. . . . But the work was by rule of thumb. And yet was it not the most important health work in the community?

The state took the unusual approach of licensing and training the practicing midwives. To see the results of this six-year experiment, Ovington visited a meeting of the Mississippi Mid-Wives Association and went with a visiting nurse to the log home of a trained midwife. She was astonished at the empowerment that came from respect, education, self-direction, and the bringing to the fore of "natural leaders."

She described the evening's demonstration:

> A colored woman of middle age, with soft brown skin and tender brown eyes, rolls up her sleeves and with deliberate thoroughness washes her

hands and arms. You see her for five minutes go over and over her warm skin. Her movements are leisurely but sure. In her white dress and white cap with its midwife's pin she is a person to inspire confidence. You feel glad for the mother into whose home she will come at that critical time, always associated with uncertainty and pain. You feel too, that the religious spirit of the Negro which purvades [*sic*] the meeting will bring to the mother relaxation, a lessening of natural terror.

The final event of the meeting was the inspection of the midwives' bags. Once they would have held soiled, infected items wrapped in newspaper. Now each woman had a washable satchel, clean dress and cap, soap and Lysol, scissors, eyedrops, and birth certificates. This was, Ovington wrote, the "visible sign of the profession, the equipment that is necessary for maternity work, and it deserves the same religious care as the surgeon's shining implements." Finally, the women took their leave of the meeting by singing a full eight verses of "The Midwives' Song," to the tune of "John Brown's Body."

Visiting one of these newly trained and empowered midwives later, Ovington saw the positive impact. She wrote:

Her enthusiasm for her club is not an affectation to please the nurse and me. It is an expression of genuine happiness at being part of something bigger and better than her narrow home. Had Aunt Phyllis gone to school she would have walked out of the log cabin before this, seeking a place in the world. Now the world has come to her, bringing a greeting once a month. Through the reading of the simple manuals and the nurse's visits she finds herself not an isolated unit but one of a great army to bring better conditions to the state. Her life is dignified.

Ovington's unpublished article reveals much about the innovative program and her sensitivity to the poor, black, and rural. It was one thing to read about the southern filibuster sitting home in New York; it was quite another, as Ovington put it, "to come up against the reality on that Mississippi road."

As Ovington and the nurse drove back to Tougaloo they talked of the things that had to be covered without federal help: battling pellagra and hookworm, treating syphilis, trying to abate malaria, and training children in hygiene in the public schools. Without federal help, there was nothing for maternity work. Ovington left Mississippi on a fine smooth road, easy on the car. It was preposterous, she thought, that the nation would help the state build such a road but would fail to protect babies from life's hard bumps.[34]

Ovington's promotion of, and energy and encouragement from, black women was pervasive both personally and professionally for forty years, and was not limited to the NAACP or other organizational work. In reviews, in personal interactions, and in lending out her Riverbank retreat, she complemented her watchdog purview of white women's groups and of the NAACP with the personal touch and care that was her style in chairing the NAACP board. It was activity with rich rewards both for them and for her. As she would repeatedly say, anything she did was more than amply returned to her by the enduring friendship of numerous black women.

WHILE THE CHAIRMAN of the board of the NAACP sent telegrams to Texas after the assault on Secretary John Shillady in 1919, news hit of a riot beginning September 30, 1918, in Phillips County, Arkansas, in the rich Mississippi bottomlands below Memphis. Negroes led by a white man, reports said, were shooting landlords, seizing their property, and taking control.

Ovington saw differences in this situation from other "Red Summer" reports. The Progressive Farmers and Household Union of America was said to be holding meetings where they sang "Organize, Oh, Organize." The white man was attorney U. S. Bratton from Little Rock, eighty miles west. Rioting had spread from a Negro church at Hoop Spur. She suspected that Negro farmers had joined forces to improve their condition by legal means, or why would they involve a lawyer? The rioting could very well be the white response to this unusual occurrence.

Ovington used NAACP and Intercollegiate Socialist Society connections to ferret out the truth. The price of cotton was high in 1918 and 1919, but tenant wages remained low, so the farmers formed a union and sought out Bratton to tell, as Ovington said, "an old story, a well-known form of peonage," in which charges at the company store were always a little more than the value of the crop.

It was to raise Bratton's fifty-dollar fee that the September 30 Hoop Spur meeting was held. White men fired into the church, putting out the lights. In the panic that followed, both sides fired, and two white men were killed. Headlines proclaimed that the Negroes of Phillips County had organized to kill, and whites roamed around the river town of Elaine, killing Negroes on sight. Estimates gave a death toll of two hundred. Bratton's son, who had gone in his father's place to meet the farmers, was saved from lynching only by jail.

The governor of Arkansas appointed seven white men to investigate and assured the mobs that justice would be done. Within a month, seventy-nine Negroes were arrested for murder and insurrection, tried (with no defense), convicted (in a five-minute jury deliberation), and sentenced, twelve to death, and sixty-seven to prison terms ranging from one to twenty-one years. To the threatening mob outside the courtroom, the execution date was announced: December 27. Ovington declared it a classic "lynching by law."

She had sent Assistant Secretary Walter White (who could pass as white) to investigate personally; he left on October 8, and his findings were reported to the board on Ocotober 13. He did all right posing as a northern reporter in the more progressive Little Rock, even receiving Governor Charles H. Brough's autographed picture after interviewing him. But when White arrived in the bitterly prejudiced village of Helena and headed for the jail to visit the condemned prisoners, a large black man whispered, "turn to the right at the next corner." White did so, and was told to get away—fast. He jumped on a train for Memphis and, when asked for his ticket, said he had been called away suddenly and had not purchased one. The conductor made change and conversation: "There's a damned yellow nigger down here parading for white and meddling in our affairs. He won't pass for white any more when the boys get through with him."[35]

Attorney Bratton, with a history of taking such cases, was safer in the North, too, and became a drawing card for raising defense money. The impact of antilynching meetings waned, and other ways had to be found to bring in funds. Shillady feared the cost of the Arkansas cases, but Ovington saw the dramatic appeal—it was easier to raise money for a case than a cause. As she said, these were hardworking "men with no other crime than that they had opposed their landlords. They had not killed white men but they had been active in trying to kill their own status as peons which held them in wage slavery. What more popular appeal could anyone make!"

Bratton headquartered in the NAACP offices, where Ovington and the staff got to observe him. (This was a reasonable precaution; according to Arthur Spingarn, unethical or racially biased lawyers sometimes tried to "fleece" them.) Ovington found Bratton to be honest and sincere in his desire to help the convicted Negroes. But if his testimony were used publicly to raise money, he would not be able to return to Little Rock.

So she set up confidential meetings with him at the home of Agnes Leach (Mrs. Henry Goddard Leach) and at the *Survey* offices with Paul Kellogg in New York City, as well as in Boston and Philadelphia. She sent fund-raising appeals across the country and, on January 5, 1920, worked with the Committee for Justice to the Negro on a big mass meeting at Cooper Union. "What makes it so immensely interesting is that we have testimony from a Southern white man," she told prospective contributors; "it is very wonderful to have a southerner who is such a splendid radical on this matter."

But in November darkness she confided to Archibald Grimke: "I doubt if you ever saw three more utterly weary people than Mr. Shillady, Mr. Johnson and myself." "It is a pretty terrible world just now, isn't it? I do not like to look ahead." She was very anxious

> not to let so terrible a condition as this in Arkansas continue (they will doubtless go on convicting more and more Negroes for standing up for their rights) and they will think no one cares. . . . It is hard to have much hope but when you meet with a man who has sacrificed very much for your cause and who is ready to tell his story you feel that the least you can do is to give him the chance to interest others.

Ovington moved quickly on the Arkansas cases because of the need to prevent the executions, because of her frustration with Texas over the Shillady beating, and because of her strong commitment to labor issues and worker organization. Ten years later she would hesitate in the more famous "Scottsboro Boys" case.

The regular November 10 board meeting included a Justice Department report that the farmers had not planned to massacre whites, but had simply sought to legally test the system of exploitation by landowners, their agents, and merchants. After the speedy convictions of the farmers, more had to be done and fast. She called a special meeting in late November to back up her decisions with board action; the board would otherwise not meet until December 8, fewer than twenty days before the execution.

In addition to Ovington, only Joel Spingarn, W. E. B. Du Bois, Shillady, Walter White, and James Cobb from the District of Columbia Branch were at the meeting on November 24, 1919; only the first three were board members—evidently no one called for a quorum. Ovington reported that the condemned and imprisoned men "had been practically railroaded to death and to the penitentiary," and presented a memorandum already sent by Shillady to Bratton, outlining the terms under which the association would hire Colonel G. W. Murphy of Little Rock to represent the interests of all the defendants for a total of three thousand dollars. After discussion the commitment was approved, with the added statement that "special efforts" would be made to raise funds for this case.[36]

The following years provided cliff-hanging drama in real life, demonstrating skill, courage, determination, and faith. Colonel Murphy fortunately hired as assistant Scipio Africanus Jones, a Negro lawyer from Little Rock with a high reputation for a clear mind, tenacious memory, and an orator's persuasiveness. The first success was a delay of the executions. Then in March 1920, six men were given a new trial in Little Rock, and the cases of the other six were reheard at Helena, where, since Walter White had been driven out, four out-of-town Negroes had been killed and no one indicted. Colonel Murphy became ill, and Jones handled the week-long Helena trial himself, slipping unannounced into a different Negro home each night for protection. He lost and appealed to the Supreme Court.

In Little Rock, he tried to get the other six cases taken directly to the Supreme Court as well, but the necessary writ of certiorari was denied. On the day of the denial, Colonel Murphy died, and Scipio Jones was on his own. Murphy's law firm demanded exorbitant fees, and when the NAACP did not produce them, the firm resigned from the case. The Little Rock Branch of the NAACP then hired Jones to continue, and formed a Citizens Defense Fund Commission to raise money for the convicts.

In December 1920, Ovington was delighted to recieve a telegram from Scipio Jones announcing that the Arkansas Supreme Court had reversed the cases of the Helena Six, granting a change of venue and a new trial. But the governor, responding to demands from planters, the Rotary Club, the American Legion Post, and the press, had set the date of execution for the Little Rock Six for June 20, 1921. (The NAACP asked the American Legion if it was their policy "not only to exclude colored veterans of the World War from membership but to publicly urge the execution of colored men whose cases are before the courts.")

On June 19, the condemned men were ushered into the jail yard where six coffins lay: "You'll die there tomorrow," the jailer said. "No," they responded. "Scipio Jones won't let us die!" A zealous Chicago newspaper the next day printed a full account of their execution—but they had not died. Once again, Scipio Jones had pulled it off with a writ of habeas corpus issued by Chancellor John E. Martineau. But the Court of Chancery does not have criminal jurisdiction, ruled the Supreme Court of Arkansas, and once again the governor set an execution date: September 23. Finally, on the presentation of new evidence—that some of the defendants had been tortured into testifying against the others—an appeal was granted to the Supreme Court of the United States.

Ovington wrote to Moorfield Storey expressing her hope that certainly he would want to argue the case before the Supreme Court. She put him in contact with Jones and Bratton. Given the Court's decision in the case of Leo Frank, which had ruled that community mob pressure had not adversely affected the trial, Storey did not think they could win. Meanwhile Ovington continued in her efforts to raise the fifty thousand dollars needed to try the case, going after big bucks from Julius Rosenwald and Mrs. Emmons McCormick Blaine.

Before the decision came down from the United States Supreme Court, the Helena Six were freed. Scipio Jones whisked them to Little Rock, where homes had been found in the black community. On February 19, 1923, Justice Holmes spoke for the majority of the United States Supreme Court on the case of the Little Rock Six, holding that, as Ovington summarized it,

> If in fact a trial is dominated by a mob so that there is an actual interference with the course of justice, there is a departure from due process of

law; and that if the State, supplying no corrective process, carried into execution a judgement of death or imprisonment based upon a verdict thus produced by mob domination, the State deprives the accused of his life without "due process of law."[37]

The cases were remanded for a new trial, but it was never held. On January 14, 1925, over five years after some of the tenant farmers had been condemned to death, and the others to long prison terms, Scipio Jones wired the NAACP that the last of the "Arkansas peons" had been freed. The association claimed it to be the greatest victory of its kind ever. Men unjustly accused and convicted were freed and the riot was shown to be a carefully manufactured plot to suggest organized violence among the Negroes. The case had exposed peonage, economic exploitation, and the devices that left the Negro (and poor whites) helpless.

Louis Marshall, who had been unsuccessful in arguing the Frank case, promptly sent the NAACP a substantial check and joined its committee of lawyers, congratulating them on achieving what he had not been able to: the forbidding of "legal lynching."

In Arkansas, the lengthy case had "wearied the Negro haters," Ovington observed, and whites who stood for order and justice were encouraged—they even elected Martineau, the judge who had stayed the executions, as governor. Scipio Jones came to New York NAACP offices with a picture of the twelve men. Ovington kept the photograph as an encouraging remembrance. Not one, she saw daily, had the least resemblance to a criminal. "They were hard-working farmers who tried to better their conditions, came up against a powerful, vicious economic system, and escaped with their lives," she affirmed about the long case carried through successfully under her watch. It was her kind of case.[38]

The Arkansas peonage case is one of many NAACP efforts about which full-length studies have been written. Political scientist Richard C. Cortner, in *A Mob Intent on Death: The NAACP and the Arkansas Riot Cases,* emphasizes the importance of *Moore v. Dempsey* (the title under which it was won), a case much less known than, but equally important as, the 1954 NAACP victory in *Brown v. Topeka Board of Education. Moore v. Dempsey,* Cortner says, "established what came to be regarded as milestones both in the modern development of the Due Process

Clause of the 14th Amendment and the law governing the writ of habeas corpus in the federal courts" (p. 192).

Cortner refers to Mary White Ovington throughout the book only as an NAACP board member, never as the chairman of the board, who called the emergency meetings and was in charge of raising funds. The NAACP was founded in 1909, he says, "by a small group of blacks and white civic leaders, such as John Haynes Holmes, Rabbi Stephen Wise, and Oswald Garrison Villard."[39] We know better. This was a "hands on" case for the NAACP's prime founder.

Day-to-day involvement in the two activities that for Ovington represented the most exciting time yet in the history of the NAACP—the Arkansas peonage cases and the Dyer Anti-Lynching Bill—was neatly divided between Ovington as chairman and James Weldon Johnson, the first black secretary of the association and successor to John Shillady. The former connected strongly with the economic and labor issues Ovington had long studied; the latter became the NAACP's first concerted lobbyist of the U.S. Congress, a task for which both Johnson and his choice for assistant secretary, Walter White, were well suited.[40]

Ovington was painfully concerned about the failure of the states to control mobs. The "Red Summer" of 1919 had seen a dramatic increase in lynchings and made the year's figures the highest since 1908 and the Springfield, Illinois, riots that had served as the bloody impetus to the founding of the NAACP.[41] The first order of action, as Chairman Ovington had described it in her "Reconstruction" article, was to bring it to the front pages of the nation's conscience by any means necessary—protests, publicity, publications. This the antilynching meetings had done effectively, but spreading the word had gone only so far.

No amount of protest would change the acquiescence to lynching among the educated, powerful whites who controlled the governments of the South, she believed. Illegal death for Negroes and legal impunity for white killers would continue until, she wrote, the "despotic power of one man over the life of another" was brought down by the ballot, the legislatures, and the courts.[42] Ovington would likely have preferred a voting-rights campaign, but she knew that to solicit money the organization needed something more dramatic. Thus was born the NAACP campaign for the Dyer antilynching bill.

All efforts to draft a bill ran into the difficult question of constitutionality. NAACP president Moorfield Storey, constitutional expert, had real problems with this, for federal antilynching legislation would essentially take away States' rights as defined in Article IV of the Constitution. Lawyer Arthur Spingarn, too, was horrified by the initial draft of the Dyer bill. Eventually they based the NAACP's argument on the Fourteenth Amendment, prohibiting the states from violating due process or equal protection under the law.[43]

Ovington's question about what form the bill should take was practical: what could they hope to actually get passed? She thought the initial draft had too punitive a tone to pass. "It reads like a bill that a man would bring up to please his Negro constituents, going in for anything that sounds rousing, and expecting to have the bill turned down," she sagely observed.

She wanted a positive approach:

> Can't a bill be framed that reads as though it were not so much for the Negro as for the honor of the United States? We do want to get something through but I don't think that our representatives are ready to vote to punish white men because they have lynched black men. If they are going to punish them it will be because they have disgraced the country. The bill might do pretty much what this bill does and yet give that impression, might it not?[44]

The Dyer antilynching campaign consumed Secretary Johnson. Ovington supported him by raising money and watching out for his health. She was a key link with the Anti-Lynching Crusaders, who, with five hundred dollars in "seed money" from the board, had pledged to raise a million dollars.

For Secretary Johnson's health, she did several things. Her supportive letters and telegrams flowed to him in Washington and linked him with Storey in Boston. When money came in, as did a two-thousand-dollar donation in June 1922, Johnson was the first to know.[45] When she saw his fatigue, she came back from her own summer rest in September 1922, and promised not to go away until after the board meeting—"if that will be of any help to you." "It is the Bill that is always on your mind, I suspect," she wrote to him. By March 1923, when the bill had failed in the Senate and the congressional session ended, Ovington brought concern about Johnson's health to the board, which commanded him to take the vacation he had skipped the two previous years. By fall, he had still not taken time off, so she provided and insisted on the means: her Berkshire cabin.[46]

The Dyer Bill's only victory had come in January 1922, when the U.S. House of Representatives had passed it. Between the exhilaration of that event and the discouraging failure of the Senate to pass it fourteen months later, Chairman Ovington had placed on the record her priorities and preferred plans of action.

Instead of concentrating so much leadership energy and so much organizational money on antilynching, she had said at the February 14, 1922, board meeting, it was time to move to education. Slogans and campaigns lost their effectiveness after a time. The minutes recorded that Ovington "felt that on the subject of education there were two ways of getting action,—first, through political action and secondly, through a campaign of publicity to show the unfair treatment of colored pupils in Southern states." From a practical point of view, she believed it was important to intertwine antilynching and education strategies. Branches in the South, she said, could not directly and safely attack lynching or Jim Crow railroad cars or disfranchisement, but they could work on education and live to tell about it. Why not ask them to collect a body of data on which to base an education project?

The board voted at the 1922 meeting that "the NAACP take up the matter of education as a part of its campaign for 1923," and authorized a committee to be appointed by the chair. Ovington immediately appointed Florence Kelley and Du Bois. The topic came up again in 1924, when Ovington succeeded in moving Secretary Johnson away from the defeated antilynching campaign to work on education: the two of them formed the committee that brought to the board suggested changes to the Sterling-Towner Bill.[47]

During the first years of the NAACP leadership under Ovington as chairman of the board and Johnson as secretary, two big cases had dominated. The Arkansas peonage cases had led to the United States Supreme Court's outlawing of "legal lynching" by mob-frightened juries and judges and governors. The Dyer antilynching campaign had led to a decline in macabre American scenes of burnings of human beings. Ovington believed that, even though the bill ultimately failed to become federal law, the public notoriety the Dyer campaign lent lynching was a prime cause of the drastic drops in these horrible numbers after 1924.[48]

Just as Ovington's feminism focused on more than the ballot, so in fighting legal and illegal lynching, she examined contexts of white behavior and black vulnerability. Education was the key, in her mind, to opening rooms where decision-making power resided to change human behavior for the better.

8

Catalyst to the Harlem Renaissance

WHILE MARY WHITE OVINGTON served creatively as chairman of
the board of directors of the NAACP, she maintained, sometimes amid
difficult family demands, a complementary personal life and contributed to the larger cause of literary and artistic endeavors.

She imbibed sustenance, as in her childhood and youth, from the
natural world. Through happy happenstance, at the Civic Club one
evening early in 1920, Ovington heard a teacher, Isabel Davenport, say
that she had a little summer home in the Berkshires for sale, at Alford,
outside of Great Barrington, Massachusetts. Her ears perked up and
she checked her bank account. For $650, she could have a little build-
ing, but more important, four acres of terraced land, dropping down to
the Green River.

Ovington saw it in May, when the apple trees bloomed and willow
and black alder laced the river. A soft haze enveloped the rock-ringed
swimming hole at the curve of the stream. The "cabin" was no Berkshire "cottage" (read mansion), but a barn left when the house had
burned down. It would need a lot of work, even for her planned simplicity, and the grounds had plenty of burdock to battle.

She finalized the purchase July 7, 1920. This was now her own se-
cluded refuge, and easier to get to from New York City than her family vacation house in Bar Harbor, Maine. She named it Riverbank,
after Ratty's home in Kenneth Grahame's *Wind in the Willows*. She
could entertain anyone she wanted and offer a haven to which she

could send friends for rest. Riverbank would be her sustenance for twenty years of demanding NAACP work and writing.

Alford Township was sparsely settled in 1920, its earlier dams and mills marked only by swimming holes like the one on Ovington's land. Her nearest neighbors, the Delleas, whom she soon came to know, were engaged in dairy farming, the predominant industry. Their wide front veranda commanded the hill across the winding river as she looked out from the west side of her rooms. Their barns lay across the highway to the east; early and late, she could hear John Dellea and his sons trekking to milk the cows.

The most spacious homestead in the neighborhood belonged to Laura Williams Millard, who had gone to school with "Will" Du Bois. Ovington's contrasting modest acreage had been part of Millard's property until Davenport had purchased the land from Millard and another woman in 1914. Ovington sold Riverbank to Violet Heming, a British actress, in 1941; it was subsequently sold to Elizabeth Madden, an editor at Doubleday, and then to Irene Rheinsham and Madden's aunt, Dorothy Poplowski. Mrs. Poplowski, who still lives nearby, suggests that the manageability of the place—small, simple, and convenient as well as beautiful—made it attractive to single women.

In 1920 Ovington's expenses for the property's upkeep rose to eight hundred dollars by the time she paid for the lawyer, insurance, repair materials, and help from her teenage niece and nephew, Betty and Ted Kingsbury, and Richetta Randolph. Most of the cleanup and another nine hundred dollars, she left until the following summer, hiring local construction people and neighbors to fortify and remodel the barn, to plow for vegetable and flower gardens, and to even out and mow the meadow. She loved buying curtains and linen and kitchenware for what became a comfortable three rooms. By 1923 the major jobs on the place were done. Her annual expenses, under two hundred dollars total, were to pay a neighbor to open the house, for seeds, for the phone, and for fire insurance. She did not count the high cost of "motoring," which she placed under "amusements." From the first there was a small return from sale of hay and apples—enough, by 1925, to buy rosebushes.

The largest return was intangible and more important. In Riverbank, Ovington had a piece of the natural world for herself, her colleagues, and her friends. She tested racial tolerance immediately by offering a resting place to two young black women while she and her mother went to Maine. "To the honor of New England," Ovington found, "no one was unkind." Mrs. Millard's daughter Josephine took the young women on drives, and racial antagonism came only from city people in the expensive cottages of the developed Berkshires.

A long list of NAACP people enjoyed Ovington's Berkshire barn. Assistant Secretary Walter White wrote his antilynching novel, *The Fire in the Flint,* in its quiet seclusion, "with no greater atrocity to stir his emotions than a robin eating a worm," according to his hostess. Fieldworker Robert Bagnall and his wife became expert at driving out rats. Richetta Randolph came frequently. Herbert Seligmann, the only white salaried worker after John Shillady's departure, brought his bride there and painted one of its seven wall murals, as did Laura Wheeler Waring.

Ovington was a generous hostess; her account books show expenditures for food and even gifts for visitors. With cots in the loft and pull-down beds in the living room, the little remodeled barn could sleep eleven—just how the chemical toilet handled that many is not clear! In 1926, she bought a tent for additional sleeping space.

Ovington's visitors Grace Nail and James Weldon Johnson eventully bought their own Alford Township home. From the time Chairman Ovington ordered overworked Secretary Johnson to take a break in 1923, until 1926, the Johnsons vacationed at Riverbank. Then they found Five Acres nearby, another little barn, which they turned into a bright, rose-entwined cabin on the Alford Brook. Thus for the crucial period of the late 1920s, the two top officials at the NAACP cemented their friendship, and renewed their energies as neighbors in the wooded hills and rippling streams of southern Berkshire County.[1]

It was only a thirty-mile car trip for Jim Johnson and Ovington to Joel and Amy Spingarn's estate in Dutchess County outside Amenia, New York, where they could meet NAACP people coming by train from New York City. The contrast between the country places of two white leaders of the NAACP is instructive. On the one hand was tiny Riverbank, like the poorest of country people's well-loved plots. On the other hand was Troutbeck's eight hundred acres of lake and stream and woods—roughly the size of Central Park—along which the Spingarns' other dwelling, a double town house, stood. An oak-paneled library with a fireplace, a conference room with a terrace, thirty bedrooms

The bridge on Highway 71, and the old swimming hole in the Green River at Mary White Ovington's summer cabin, Great Barrington, Massachusetts.

Winter photo of Mary White Ovington's cabin Riverbank taken by her young friend Monaver Bechtold and used by Ovington as a Christmas card in the 1930s. (Courtesy of Monaver Bechtold von der Heydt)

The family of young
Ovington friend
Monaver Bechtold on
their first visit to
Riverbank, Great
Barrington, Massa-
chusetts in 1932.
(Courtesy of Mon-
aver Bechtold von
der Heydt)

Mary White Ovington's summer acreage Riverbank, as it looks today.

welcomed guests at Troutbeck. Here one might meet neighbor Lewis Mumford, or a visiting Sinclair Lewis, G. A. Borgese, Van Wyck Brooks, or the Mexican artist José Orozco. Joel Spingarn's daughter, Honor Spingarn Tranum, once said that becoming involved with black civil rights was the only selfless thing that her father had ever done. The Troutbeck estate confirms the enormous independent wealth with which he could do as he wished.

The names of Mary White Ovington and Joel Spingarn are often linked in histories of the NAACP as "wealthy white liberals," but it is edifying to remember these country homes that reveal their very different financial circumstances and passions. (One could point out the same greatly contrasting means between the two founders, Ovington and Oswald Garrison Villard.) But one must add that Ovington was in a unique social position to appreciate both her farm neighbors and Joel and Amy at their abode of gracious remove. Mannerly but not formal, interested but not overpowering, kindly and conversational, she seemed to bring out the best in all people.[2]

OVINGTON WAS A talented and prolific writer throughout her life, and Riverbank inspired her. Much of her early published work in periodicals, as well as her 1911 *Half a Man,* was in lucid expository prose. But "The White Brute" and many unpublished stories revealed her continuing interest in writing fiction as well, including work for young people.

In 1913 the Crisis Publishing Company, which Ovington created with Du Bois, had published her appealing children's book titled *Hazel.*[3] "When I was a little girl, my favorite books dealt with children whose lives were like my own," Ovington wrote in the preface. For some time, she had thought that black children had to be tired of always reading of faraway places and people, and so, she told the reader, "out of my years of experience among these soft-eyed, velvet-cheeked small friends, I have written this story."

She had purposefully avoided dialect in the book, since English spelling was hard enough anyway, but she did try to express the flavor of southern speech. It was her hope that "my colored friends will smudge my pages. And if the white child stops to read, I trust that she will feel an awakened sympathy for the dark-faced boys and girls whose world is outside her own."[4]

Ovington's plot was appealing in its blend of geography, history, maturation, contrast, climax, and happy closure. Hazel Tyler of Boston is sent by her widowed mother, for reasons of health, to stay with her paternal grandmother in Alabama over the winter. The rural world of Granny and her neighbors is of course much different from her own, and Hazel gains much besides her health. She also brings much, particularly to a boy her age, Scipio, whose drunken father and numerous younger siblings have forced him to mature rapidly, without schooling. She teaches him to read and opens his world.

Hazel discovers that her grandmother, born a slave, has never had a birthday or a party. So with the help of candles ordered from Boston, a cake baked secretly, and many lessons on how to sing "Happy Birthday," she leads the neighbor kids in throwing a surprise party on a certain April day. Before Hazel returns to Boston, she has inspired the community and even directed some northern missionary money toward Granny's corner of Alabama.

Similarities to Eleanor Porter's hugely successful *Pollyanna*, which appeared the same year, might occur to the reader. Both books featured as protagonist a young girl who comes from the outside and transforms a community in a positive way. But it would be hard to make the same accusation of saccharine sweetness about Hazel Tyler as has often unfairly been made about the glad tomboy Pollyanna. Ovington's book realistically exposes segregated rail travel, "separate but equal" schools, and wealthy white prejudice.

Ovington also had a light touch with language and a love of humor. She had a quick, watercolorlike ability to evoke a scene, as this passage illustrates:

> Granny's house was fenced in and within the enclosure was her garden and a little outhouse in which was a small cooking-stove and a loom. The garden showed a few late vegetables and in the front of the house roses climbed upon the porch, and grew in the bushes by the fence.
>
> The landscape dipped at the back of the cabin, and Hazel looked over fields of corn and stubble and dry cotton stalks. A number of cabins were dotted about among the fields. In front, across the road, was a

hill, half covered with pines. No house was visible from the road, but among the pines, to the left, was a chimney from which smoke issued. Hazel felt that she was a long way from trolley and library, from rattling carts and loud-voiced children, from school and playground.

Ovington conveyed both humor and a nondialect evocation of southern speech in her description of Granny as she first sees her birthday cake with its seventy lit candles:

> "Baby," Granny said holding [Hazel] tight. "It's the prettiest sight these eyes has ever seen. Scip," she called suddenly, "don't you let those candles burn down. Everybody's got to see my cake."
> "And now, Granny," Hazel said when the candles were blown out, "you must cut the cake for the children."
> "Cut the cake for them tricks," Granny cried excitedly. "No, indeed. The children can have corn-pone. Everybody has got to see my birthday cake. Where did you buy it, honey?"
> "I made it," Hazel answered, and that completed Granny's amazement and Hazel's happiness.

For a week the cake stayed on the table, and the candles were lit over and over for neighbors to troop in and see:

> At length, when the candles had burned to their sockets, Granny cut through the icing and gave a slice to Hazel and one to herself.
> Hazel ate and said nothing, but she was glad it had not been cut before. Staleness might seem to account in part for the very heavy character of the half-cooked dough.
> But Granny ate her piece as if it had been ambrosia, the food of the gods.
> "That are splendid cake," she exclaimed. "That icing are as sweet as you are, sugar, and I can't say more."
> And she took another slice.

A play version of *Hazel* had been performed at the YWCA in Brooklyn in 1916 by children from the Lincoln Settlement,[5] and Ovington had been pleased with reactions to both book and play. One of Joel and Amy Spingarn's young daughters met the author with, "Is this Miss Ovington? I so enjoyed reading *Hazel*." Ovington encouraged her friends to see the play, simply because the children and young people acting it were so engaging.[6]

IN "THE WHITE BRUTE," Ovington turned upside down America's assumptions that blacks were the brutes. In *The Shadow*, one of two books she had published in 1920, and her first and only adult novel, Ovington had twisted another staple character in American fiction: the "tragic mulatto."[7] Whereas "passing" usually referred to blacks like blue-eyed, blond Walter White who could move in society as white, the real-life basis for Ovington's novel was, from all indications, a young woman with golden-red hair and white skin who "passed for Black."[8]

The Shadow's protagonist is Hertha Williams, a white baby left at the doorstep of a black minister. She is raised by respectable, ambitious people, who give her an education and train her in kindliness and good manners. When grown, she finds that she is actually Hertha Ogilvie and is forced to leave her family to enter the white world.

Ovington's fascination with film inspired her romantic plot and descriptions. All of the reader's senses are engaged, and settings subtly convey character and action. One can almost see the camera shots juxtaposing white and black worlds in the South with the laboring world in the North. She opens with a graceful periodic sentence depicting the vehicle of exile and return.

> In the far south of the United States, where through the winter months the sun holds in warmth the blue encircling sky, opening the buds of the roses in December, where palmetto and white sand meet deep green swamp and heavily scented magnolia, there flows a great river. (11)

As the novel begins, Lee Meriwether, heir of a diminished plantation at the river's edge, has returned from college to restore the gardens of his ancestors.

Before the spacious mansion stretches sand dotted with grass tufts and fallen leaves. "The glory of the open space is the live-oaks," immense spreading trees with roots twisting into the sand, with small, darkly rich green leaves, and bunches of hanging white moss. Ovington wrote of the moss clumps:

> On a still day they are motionless, but the slightest breeze sends them softly waving, and in a storm they swing back and forth, the wind tearing through their long, thin strands, dragging off a bit here and a bit there, but in the end leaving them still companions of the live-oak.

To the sides of the manor lie orange groves, and "back of the groves comes the second world, the world of the black folk" (13).

In antebellum log shanties on legs, with chickens pecking underneath, surrounded by weeds, red roses, violets, cosmos, and zinnias— under the pines, the widow of the black preacher, Mrs. Williams, lives with her ambitious daughter Ellen, her unambitious daughter Hertha, and Tom, sent off to school by his aspiring oldest sister. Tom's departure at the river's edge leads to an evocative separation from the gentle Hertha, who has cared for him from babyhood.

Hertha is also very close to her mother, a "salt of the earth" woman who thinks or says no evil. Ovington attempts to duplicate the unschooled sound and tone of her language. "You don' know what it means . . . to part a mudder f'om her only son," Mrs. Williams, known as Aunt Maggie, tells her daughter Ellen.

Hertha's job as companion to Miss Patty, sister of the old, widowed Meriwether, Lee's father, gives her a choice of routes daily, either past the cabins or through the pines to the orange groves, the latter not permitted to her darker-skinned family. Hertha prefers the orange-tree route for its beauty. It is there, in secrecy from both families, that Lee Meriwether falls in love and entertains her with Cinderella stories. Soon she, too, is in love, and is torn between passion and chastity, as Meriwether asks her to meet him there in the night.

Ovington skillfully evokes the image of Hertha lying awake, stretched on the rack of illicit desire:

> With her eyes fixed on the dim window square that saved the room from utter darkness, she dreamed of his near presence, feeling his breath upon her cheek, until, her whole body swept with emotion, she clenched her hands and pressed them to her lips to keep back the welling tears. (38–39)

The situation worsens as her love and his requests escalate:

> If for a moment he had been rough, if he had endeavored to take by force what she hesitated to give, she could have resisted him; but his gentleness was his power. . . . Would he remain faithful if she failed to give him all that he desired? . . . To hold him and yet not to sacrifice herself.

Finally Hertha goes to meet him, running "across the open yard, bright in the moonlight, to the darkness of the trees."
Meriwether does not come.

> Returning to the gloom of the cypress she put on her coat and waited, slow-ticking minute following slow-ticking minute, until the young moon set and the chill wind made her shiver and crouch in terror and loneliness and miserable shame. (73–74)

The climax of "The Pines," the book's opening section, finds Hertha learning of her white heritage and inheritance. She must leave her black family, and she determines to go north. At a farewell breakfast in the pines, her mother tells her:

> Keep us in you' heart, but don' try ter lib in our worl', not at fust. It ain't gwine ter be so easy, allus ter remember as you's white. . . . When yer gits yer place firm in de white worl', den yer kin turn back ter look at de black. But not now, dearie, not now.

"Kathleen," part 2, is set in New York City, where Hertha has struggled to find a home with a militant and gentle Irish nurse, and a job at the Imperial shirtwaist factory. Ovington uses sound images to convey the shock of city and factory noises for one accustomed to the soughing of air in the pines. One can easily imagine the rapid bombardment of visual images a "silent" film would use to convey the sounds. In her factory seat, Hertha "started her own thundering whir" on a beetlelike machine, devouring and disgorging miles of muslin through its needle jaws. During her short lunch break, heavy cups and saucers hit hard marble, knives and forks and spoons fall on platters, and plates smash into the dumbwaiter. Walking home, she endures motorcar squeaks and croaks, police whistle shrieks, trains crashing overhead. In her third-floor Lower East Side tenement apartment, she goes to bed with the aggressive grind of the trolleycar wheels against axle and rail and the constant vibration, rumbling, and roar of the elevated train.

In this section, Ovington uses the shirtwaist-makers' strike of 1910 as the background setting. The Jewish girls in Hertha's factory walk off the job to support strikers in a neighboring one. Hertha is caught in the middle. She admires the dedication of the immigrants and is suspicious of the employer-trusting stance of the "Americans," but she is not forceful, decisive, or militant.

Finally Hertha joins the walkout, but despite her housemate Kathleen's castigation, refuses to picket. Meanwhile, she has met in the library a young, ambitious southerner who falls in love with her. The third section, "Dick," begins when Hertha follows his lead in moving to a boardinghouse in Brooklyn, and uses her inheritance to learn stenography. Her classes do not go well, and Dick's desire to take care of her becomes more and more tempting, thanks in part to the help of their motherly southern landlady, Mrs. Pickens.

But one day Hertha sees her brother Tom running an elevator in New York. As they keep in contact, Hertha runs up against her white world's attitudes toward her black family, leading up to an encounter in Brooklyn's Prospect Park, when Tom comes to tell her their mother is dying, and Dick sees Tom place his hand on her arm.

Several other young white men join Dick in threatening Tom. The only way Hertha can stop the attack and protect Tom is to cry "He's my brother! I'm colored!" The man she had almost married turns on her with revulsion. "Damn you. . . . You damned white-faced nigger. I'll teach you to lie to a white man. You hear me? You've had your play with me, and by Christ, I'll have mine now." One can imagine the appeal of the melodramatic twist to a movie audience, with the reversal of the rape threat counteracting the implications in *Birth of a Nation*. As Ovington had learned, women had more to fear from white men than from black men.

Hertha knows now that saying she is colored is a test of character and friendship. She gets Tom to the hospital and, beaten and bruised, finds her way back to Kathleen's apartment. "You don't want to know me, you don't want to be near me. I'm colored," she cries. But the working-class Irish nurse passes the test with flying colors:

> With a sob Kathleen drew the girl close in her arms. . . . With her strong, capable hand she caressed the girl's small head and kept repeating, "My

darling, as though that mattered!" and "Why should you be thinking anything of that!" and "As if that mattered, mavourneen!"

Part 4 of *The Shadow* brings us back once again to the South, with Hertha beside her mother. "She slipped her hand into the black one lying on the bed by her side. Holding it close she drank in the look of deep, unstinted love on the dark face." As Aunt Maggie slips away, Hertha is illuminated with the golden radiance of a dream:

> She heard the requiem of the despised. From across the deep spaces of the universe voices sang to her of the poor in spirit. The great majestic syllables throbbed through the little cabin, carrying their triumph to her listening heart.

Hertha now tells her sister of Lee Meriwether's failure to meet her in the orange grove, and Ellen clears up the confusion. A landed-class southerner has passed the race test, for Meriwether had refrained from seducing Hertha before she was an Ogilvie, when she was a Williams, colored.

The penultimate paragraph of Ovington's novel reunites the lovers in the orange grove, with Hertha looking forward to life as the favored daughter in a beautiful old house. Yet the ultimate paragraph suggests a darker thread:

> But as she moved through the sunshine to the broad steps of this stately home her thoughts went back to the dark pines, the home of her past, and a throb of pain smote her heart. For on ahead, through the long, happy years, she saw a black shadow, a shadow of man's making, lying beside her path.

What is the meaning of this shadow, and what has Ovington achieved through reversal of the tragic mulatto theme and a focus on labor issues? The shadow cannot be race itself, for that is not man-made. The shadow is a strange and pervasive notion among some white Americans that race alone makes the difference, not kindness or honesty or learning or hard work. That the shadow is in the minds of the viewers is established by Ovington's choice of a character who possesses not even one-sixteenth black blood—what it took to define one as "colored" in southern states—but one with no black blood at all.

Attitude toward race is Hertha's litmus test of friendship; it is also the first item on Ovington's questionnaire on American character. In the book, some southerners pass; others fail miserably. Some northerners, too, fail, while others pass. Characters who flunk are otherwise good, decent, even kind people. The shadow becomes a powerful image for the unpredictable and inexplicable specter of racism in American life. Significantly, the person with the highest score on the test of race attitude, Kathleen, is a nurturing immigrant woman who was sent to the mills as a child and a strong union member.

In combining a happy ending for Hertha Williams Ogilvie with the evocation of "The Shadow" of her title, Ovington straddled the ongoing debate in black literature about "defeatist" endings. Happy endings whitewashed American reality while tragic ones admitted the powerlessness of black victims. She also carefully intertwines the race and labor questions. In Hertha Ogilvie's reluctance to picket, Ovington suggests that the race issue had to be resolved before other forms of liberation could take place. Here Ovington reflects her own decision from 1908 that she would work to make it *possible* for black people to join the workers' movement. "I wouldn't picket," Hertha tells Kathleen, "but that wasn't my conflict. It wasn't mine until it came to Tom."

Ovington's book was serialized in England, Ireland, and the United States.[9] Reviews praised its realism, its construction, and its plea for tolerance. *Booklist* admired the equal treatment of black and white characters, which opened the way to future fictional portrayals. The reviewer in the *Freeman*, perhaps having in mind Ovington's reviews in that magazine, thought she saw more as a sociologist than an artist, but that that would not trouble the average reader.[10]

The book reveals something of an inner life about which Ovington was otherwise reticent. She was clearly no stranger to love, physical passion, and moral decision—Hertha's intense feelings are very real. Nor was she against marriage between compatible social sensibilities. Most important, Ovington clearly suffered pain from negotiating between the white and black worlds. As she had written to W. E. B. Du Bois early in the century, she was ashamed of her own race. She identified, rather, with the despised. In choosing to explore the outer and inner worlds of a woman white on the outside, black on the inside, Mary White Ovington mapped her own psyche.

Ovington tried very hard to get the book filmed. Elmer Rice, a fellow Civic Club member, conveyed it to the story committee at Hollywood's Goldwyn Pictures, who found it to be meritorious and suitable. Their rejection was based entirely, she was told, on business considerations. It would not go over in the South and perhaps not even in the rest of the country as the "general aversion to stories dealing with propaganda or controversial themes" would damn its showing. Rice himself thought the book to be one of the most "tolerant stories dealing with a complex and controversial theme that I have ever read."[11]

THE UPWARD PATH, which Ovington edited, was also published in 1920. The anthology sprang from a suggestion by Harcourt, Brace and Howe, the publishers of her novel, who wanted an all-Negro, no-dialect reader for Negro high schools. Ovington was a good choice for editor; she knew the literature, had extensive contacts with possible contributors, and was genuinely interested in publications for young people.

She had no trouble finding published biography, travel, folklore, and poetry, but suitable short stories posed a problem. She found one by Angelina Grimke, whose play *Rachel* Ovington had helped Lillian Wald produce—a story called "The Land of Laughter." She chose Paul Laurence Dunbar's story "The Boy and the Bayonet" as the first selection in the anthology. Then she turned to the NAACP offices. She knew of Augusta Bird's writing from their contact at Lincoln Settlement, so she asked her for a story. The story Bird provided, "Anna-Margaret," is delightful, written from the point of view of the baby of a family struggling to show she is independent. Anna-Margaret has her mother tie her shoes and wants to tell her older sister that she did it herself:

> "But tell 'er I did, won't you, Muvver," she pleaded.
> "Anna-Margaret, I can't do that because I would be telling a lie. Don't I whip Ruth and Edith for telling lies?"
> "Tell a lie, Muvver, tell a lie, *I won't whip you.*"

Ovington convinced another member of the office staff, Lillian Witten, to write two high school stories with morals, "Cooperation and the

Latin Class," and "The Knighting of Donald." Walter White provided a rousing college football story, in which the protagonist sacrifices a game in order to win at "the game of life" in controlling his temper at a crucial moment. What other small office could have shown so much talent, Ovington wondered.[12]

There was even more talent there in works already published that Ovington also used. From Du Bois's *The Souls of Black Folk* she took the story of "My First School." From James Weldon Johnson she included a humorous, mock-heroic, first-person story full of variations on old proverbs and biblical and classical allusions, "Behind a Georgia Mule." The speaker, trying to get a borrowed mule to move forward, resorts to having it back up all the way home:

> I began to coax my mule with some words which perhaps are not in the Sabbath School books, and to emphasize them with the rising and falling inflection of the stick across his back; but still he moved not. Then all at once my conscience smote me. . . . I listened almost in expectation of hearing him say, "Johnson, Johnson, why smitest thou me 3,333 times?"

Lest a reader get the wrong impression of Johnson's seriousness Ovington also included three of his poems, the now well-known "O Black and Unknown Bards," and two others, "The Young Warrior," and a long poem written for the anniversary of the Emancipation Proclamation, "Fifty Years: 1863–1913."

> This land is ours by right of birth,
> This land is ours by right of toil;
> We helped to turn its virgin earth,
> Our sweat is in its fruitful soil.[13]

From Jessie Fauset, who had become literary editor of the *Crisis* in 1919, Ovington used a happy nature poem, "Rondeau." The *Crisis* also provided the source for other poems and stories by Alston W. Burleigh, Fenton Johnson, C. Emily Frazier, Lottie Dixon, Roscoe Jamison, and Ruth Anna Fisher.

Poetry was the easiest to find; nearly a third of the book is made up of poems from known and unknown writers, from Dunbar's nondialect work ("Ere Sleep Comes Down") to Edward Smyth Jones's "A Song of Thanks." There is also a goodly sample of four poems by H. Cordelia Ray. Thematically, the poetry selections reflect inspiration and thanksgiving, including the inspiration of the soldier; Christian themes; and nature in its comforting qualities.

It is in the other material, which Ovington said was the easiest to find, that much of the interest in the book lies—biography and autobiography, which make up another third of the book, and essays of various kinds. A selection from Booker T. Washington's *Up from Slavery* describing his entrance to Hampton Institute was included, as well as a piece about Washington. The other famous nineteenth-century black leader was represented with both his own "Incident in the Life of Frederick Douglass" and a piece on him by Ovington's acquaintance from Atlanta, W. H. Crogman. From an autobiography she reviewed in the teens, she selected William Holzclaw's "The Beginnings of a Mississippi School." Lesser-known or unknown people were also represented, for example, in another education autobiography, Lieutenant Henry Ossian Flipper's "The Colored Cadet at West Point," and an anonymous letter home from a Negro soldier in France, "November 11, 1918."

Women were represented in the life stories with a short piece by Leila Pendleton on "A Negro Woman's Hospitality," describing the kindness of an anonymous African villager. There were two pieces describing white male heroes, Benjamin Brawley's essay on David Livingstone, and William Pickens (also from the NAACP offices) on Abraham Lincoln.

There were numerous life stories of black male heroes, many of them soldiers, but some from other disciplines, such as city planner Benjamin Banneker, described by Benjamin Brawley, and Matthew Henson's own description of his experience from twenty-three years as the companion of Admiral Robert Peary, "A Negro Explorer at the North Pole." Actor Ira Aldridge was characterized by William J. Simmons, and Du Bois wrote about a historic struggle for independence in "Haiti and Toussaint L'Ouverture."

The essays ranged widely in their subject matter. Some selections covered aspects of nature, of agriculture, and the environment; there was even a short selection on how to treat animals kindly. Housekeeping and hospitality were examined in Azalia Hackley's "The Home of the Colored Girl Beautiful." Many selections were on Africa: William Henry Sheppard's "Animal Life in the Congo" and "A Great Kingdom in the Congo"; L. J. Coppin's on South Africa and a description of folk customs in Liberia by George W. Ellis.

Shorter selections rounded out *The Upward Path:* "nuggets of wisdom" culled from various writers; parables or allegories, including one using the African Brer Rabbit; and one a kind of *Pilgrim's Progress* voyage through temptations. The illustrator Ovington engaged, Laura Wheeling Waring, was particularly inspired by the more imaginative fairy tales and poems; four of the five full-page drawings are richly elaborated, evocative renderings.

Ovington chose as epigraph to the book a quotation from a Booker T. Washington book she had reviewed in 1911, a passage she had also quoted approvingly then:

> The man who is down, looking up, may catch a glimpse now and then of heaven, but the man who is so situated that he can only look down is pretty likely to see another and quite different place.

She closed the book with the "Oath of Afro-American Youth" by Kelly Miller:

> I will never bring disgrace upon my race by any unworthy deed or dishonorable act. I will live a clean, decent, manly life; and will ever respect and defend the virtue and honor of womanhood; I will uphold and obey the just laws of my country and of the the community in which I live, and will encourage others to do likewise; I will not allow prejudice, injustice, insult or outrage to cower my spirit or sour my soul. . . . I will in all these ways aim to uplift my race so that, to everyone bound to it by ties of blood, it shall become a bond of ennoblement and not a byword of reproach.

The Upward Path is an excellent anthology, even by contemporary standards; it holds up well against William Bennett's *Book of Virtues*. Its thematic emphasis is uplifting—courage, honesty, dedication, inspiration, and hard work—and its form interesting. Simultaneously, Ovington introduced students to a wide variety of authors, known and unknown, male and female; a variety of genres, in addition to the standard poetry or story; and a wide variety of topics.

Although Mary White Ovington clearly did the editing work on *The Upward Path,* as evidenced by her writing and office diaries,[14] the publishers listed Myron Pritchard, principal of the Everett School, Boston, as her coeditor, perhaps for consultation, and perhaps to lend the book legitimacy and assure its use in schools.

———————

IN ANOTHER WRITING venture in the 1920s, Ovington undertook the ambitious project of a book review column syndicated through the NAACP news service. This was not an entirely new activity, as she had published many reviews in the previous fifteen years. But in 1921 the scope and impact of her "Book Chat" column were greatly expanded. It was picked up by many black newspapers, from the Albany, Georgia, *Supreme Circle News* to the Chicago *Broad Ax* to the *AME Christian Recorder* to Marcus Garvey's *Negro World*.[15]

Visits to NAACP branches had convinced her of the need for such a column. Blacks hungered for knowledgeable access to books, and libraries were not used as much as they could be. Black writers needed black readers. By 1920 the publishing market had opened, but the reading audience was still white; agents trying to sell *The Shadow* told her "that the colored people are not accustomed to spending money for novels."

There was much published in the following years to provide material for her column. Fiction began with Walter White's 1924 *Fire in the Flint*—written, as we have seen, at Ovington's Riverbank.[16] James Weldon Johnson's *Autobiography of an Ex-Colored Man*, published anonymously in 1912, was reissued in the 1920s with the author identified. In her review, Ovington recalled that when the novel first came out, there was criticism of the portrayal of the Negro as at times "leading a naughty life"—gambling and dancing. "We hear the same criticism today," she continued, "but with less certainty." She wrote that the realization that a work of art should not be

> a Sunday School treatise is growing with colored readers. Propaganda, if it is to appear at all, must be subtle. But while the "Autobiography" depicts the underworld it does it with the restraint of the days before the war, not with the gusto of these bootlegging times.

Of a book that definitely had the gusto of bootlegging—Claude McKay's *Home to Harlem* (1928)—Ovington wrote that it was no wonder that "the little brown girl, who has tinted her leaf-like face to a ravishing chestnut," falls for the amoral hero, Jake, who is "no stilted philosopher." Ovington believed that McKay—by then essentially in permanent exile in Europe and Africa from his adopted United States as well as his native Jamaica—was homesick, and hoped that he would "soon be on Lenox Avenue watching the show that he describes so brilliantly." But even more, she hoped that he would write of his roots—that he would

> for a time forget the revolution that has so savagely torn at his life and tell again of life close to the soil, life that has within it dignity, permanence. I wish that his imagination might hark back to his golden hills and that he would show us, though it would seem to him today only a dream, the sturdy life of the black peasantry among whom he was born.

In another review, Ovington described Rudolph Fisher as the writer who "correctly interprets the Negro of today—his habits, his ways of thought, his idiosyncrasies," and illustrated with what Fisher called the "marked racial tendency to make light of what actually was grave." She enjoyed Fisher's satire of the dance of the "General Improvement Association," where "everyone gets a dig," from the wooden white "uplifter" to the "dicties" in the balcony boxes. Concluding her review, Ovington hoped tongue-in-cheek that the absence of cabaret scenes, murder, and prostitutes wouldn't hurt the sale of Fisher's *The Walls of Jericho* (1928) too much. "The taste in Negro literature today seems to be for the highly spiced." Ovington, with this book, singled out for special praise and promotion the book with the proletarian hero that critic/historian Nathan Huggins described in his 1971 book on the Harlem Renaissance as "the only novel in the decade that exposed class antagonism among Harlem blacks."[17]

Nella Larsen's *Quicksand* (1928) and *Passing* (1929) drew raves. ("We in New York" know the author as "Mrs. Imes, librarian," Ovington added as an aside.) In works free from propaganda, with "keen insight into the race problem," Larsen wrote with "a finished style, beautiful in its choice of words and its sureness of imagery." Ovington especially liked Larsen's women. "We see them as they move through their days, doing quite simple things, but vibrant with emotion."

Ovington also praised Zora Neale Hurston's first novel, *Jonah's Gourd Vine* (1934), although she felt that Hurston had a ways to go to make full use of her rich folk material:

> Zora Hurston is still very young. While a college graduate she has yet lived among all sorts of people and has been able to throw herself into the life of the rough Negro worker as no other writer has done of whom I know. She has magnificent material. But as yet, she is a looker-on. When she lives her book, lives it intensely, she should produce something for the world.

By the time of this review, Ovington had met and worked with Hurston in Florida, and so knew that this young writer—Hurston was twenty-seven in 1934—had the potential to do what Ovington predicted in 1922: use the material collected and written by Negroes themselves, not white onlookers, in creative, artistic, nonpropagandistic forms.

The poet who depicted lives of ordinary people was Langston Hughes. Ovington ended her first review of his collected poetry in 1926 (*The Weary Blues*) asking for more of his "vivid bits of life," which, she wrote, made Hughes "very much a modern." "He only gives us tidbits of all that must be rushing through his mind. We have sat down to the *hors d'oeuvre* and they have whetted our appetite for more. May the next course come soon!"

It came the next year in *Fine Clothes to the Jew*, which caused Ovington to comment on Hughes's appeal in the context of the reading audience for poetry:

> Those who buy verse in America could all be lodged in one of New York's towering hotels and leave plenty of space for the poets who came for shelter on a stormy night. To reach this small group and have them ask for more is something to be commented upon.

In this book, too, she found powerful pictures of Negro life:

> No work of fiction that we have shows so naturally and with such sympathy the unsophisticated colored folk as they move through their city streets, into their homes and cabarets, or take to the open road. The girl whose man has left her, the boy trudging up from the Mississippi town, these touch our hearts.

In her *Portraits in Color*, Ovington quoted liberally from Hughes's poetry to show him as "the vagabond of Negro poets," who loved "the untrodden road, the joy of the unexpected," who knew the people of whom he wrote by having worked and lived with them. "No other Negro writer has done so much to reveal the humble people of his race as Langston Hughes, unless we except Paul Laurence Dunbar." But Dunbar, she wrote, "lived in another age . . . and wrote of another Negro."

In 1933 Ovington summed up the experience of knowing and reviewing the work of so many young writers over the previous dozen years. She felt that Negro writing had unfortunately entered the American literary scene at an awkward period in its evolution, that, as a pioneer, the Negro writer had "faith and energy and laughter," but was publishing at a time of frustration and ennui.

Even with that limitation, there had been considerable success for many authors. When two friends spoke to Ovington about Jessie Fauset's third novel, *Chinaberry Tree*, she knew there had been progress. "You must realize that I am accustomed to speaking first of Negro books, and when a white friend tells me emphatically that I must read one, I am more than pleased," she exclaimed.

Her enthusiasm over black literature took its energy not solely from art but from interracialism. She was insistent about whites and blacks "meeting on the high plane of endeavor," she said, because it was the "only way this question can be settled right. Whether the contact comes through the workers meeting for a decent wage, or the poets gathering to chant their songs to one another, prejudice disappears in a common interest."[18]

By 1933, she was happy to say that spurred, perhaps, by her own example, black newspapers were themselves doing so much reviewing that the need for hers had diminished. She was also delighted that there was by then so much material that she could no longer cover it single-handedly.

Early in her writing of "Book Chats" Ovington began to receive appreciative responses that encouraged her. For example, one woman, Cornelia Cook, wrote her from Ocean City, New Jersey, that the column was "pure inspiration," a "wonderful service to the unborn children of the colored people." "You rare, wonderful woman!" she concluded her letter.[19]

IN HER COLLECTION of biographical sketches, written during her mother's final illness and published in 1927, the twenty *Portraits in Color*, Ovington included writers and artists and achievers in all areas of human endeavor. She wrote only of people she knew and had talked with, undertaking extensive travel to do so. At first she thought of it as mostly for a white audience—her dedication is to NAACP president Moorfield Storey. It would be, she thought,

> indirect propaganda, for I feel that there is nothing more important than that the white race should think, not of the Negro race, but of the individual Negro. And as we always measure our own race by its highest men and women, we ought to measure another race in the same way.

After the book's appearance, however, she saw its need among blacks as well.

> The more I travel, . . . the more I find that colored people do not begin to know of the achievements of their own race. I think they need to know this not only for their own self-respect but because they find such information valuable in refuting the careless arguments of white people regarding racial inferiority.

Portraits remains to this day an engaging and useful book. Some of the sketches are of people who have unfortunately been forgotten and whose stories are hard to find—Max Yergan, Scipio Jones, Roland Hayes. Those about the famous—Paul Robeson, George Washington Carver, Marcus Garvey—bear Ovington's personal interactive stamp. "To write wholly dispassionately," she thought, "means to be dull—a much greater sin than partisanship." More than any of her writing, she loved this book because, as she said, it belonged not to its author as much as to those written about, and throughout her life, she received thank-yous for its inspirational models. One young musician wrote that the Robeson and Hayes biographies had "the effect on me that a bugle call has on a soldier."

Gwendolyn Bennett, in *Bookman* (January 1928), called the collection an "invaluable service" to the reading public and wrote that the portraits argued "the Negro's case in the name of humanity" better than any amount of "propaganda and invective." The *New York Herald Tribune* (November 1, 1927) thought Ovington's characterizations "vivid and dramatic, sympathetic and wise." They put "to shame many of the more ponderous biographies that flood the book stores today." It was even rumored that Ovington almost won the Pulitzer Prize for *Portraits*.[20]

In 1930, after the death of her brother, Ovington stayed at Tuskegee Institute in Alabama to research and write *Zeke: A Schoolboy at Tolliver*, a boy's book to match *Hazel* for girls. She learned there about chicken-raising, and her niece Betty helped with the baseball parts. Carefully, Ovington studied the way her characters would talk, coming from rural Alabama to an English class at Tuskegee. How would their speech change? What corrections would a teacher attempt to instill, and how?

The book was exciting and realistic enough to force Ovington to change the name of the school to Tolliver—no young men played cards in the bell tower during chapel at Tuskegee, she was informed, even though she had seen them with her own eyes. "So the children were too naughty, I am tempted to say, too real, to please the principal of Tuskegee and the publicity department?" she joshed with C. Lane Imes of Principal Robert Moton's office and his long list of complaints about the "unwholesome" picture of Tuskegee.

"You dear people I see still want your children always described with their faces washed. . . . I'm afraid I couldn't do that in a boy's story and have any boy read it." And then Ovington broadened her response to encompass one of the big debates of the Harlem Renaissance: "Sometime you and I must have a talk about this matter of using the Negro as literary material. The Negro intelligentsia must assume the responsibility for much of the muck that is written if they cannot accept realism."[21]

It is of course impossible to gauge the influence of Mary White Ovington and her writing on the many writers and artists she appreciated, described, recommended, and imitated. Significant encouragement can be small and subtle. But, perhaps more so than any other participant in the rebirth of creativity in the 1920s, Ovington assisted at the first as well as the second genesis. What is very clear is that her life was enriched and ennobled by art in its many forms.

THROUGHOUT THE years of her demanding work at the NAACP and the creative work of writing, Riverbank refreshed Mary White Ovington, her family, and friends of all races. Integration of public and private roles seemed to come naturally there.

From the time of her father's death in 1909 to 1927, Ovington cared for her mother. Their health intertwined. Ovington would pick up a cold on a trip and soon Louise Ovington would have it. The daughter would tend her mother's flu bed, only to catch it herself. There were happy times, too, such as opening gifts on Christmas morning with her brother Charles and his wife Elizabeth, whose apartment was in the same building.

Riverbank was a refuge from the city for them all. Charles and Elizabeth boarded with the Delleas before the barn was remodeled and with their mother hayed and milked cows, motored through the hills, and thoroughly cleaned out their city-soaked systems. Ovington's doctor-enforced New Year's resolution in 1922 was no tea, no coffee, no cigarettes, nothing with cane sugar, no breakfast, no starches eaten with protein, and only one serving of protein a day. "I am leading the simple life," she wrote to Joel Spingarn; "it's strenuous, but I enjoy it." Riverbank made it easier.

When James Weldon and Grace Johnson came to Riverbank in 1923, Ovington and her mother made the long trip to their Seal Harbor, Maine, vacation home. The Ovington Gift Shops had an extension there, and President Charles Ovington had a summer home on Gotts Island. The five hundred miles by chauffeured car (Ovington did not drive) or train was difficult for the ninety-year-old Louise.

Care for her mother wore down the daughter, too. Already in 1923 Ovington considered resigning from the NAACP board chairmanship but was talked out of it.

By 1926, with her mother too weak to make the long trip, Ovington happily gave up Maine. She attended the annual NAACP conference in June in Chicago and presented the Spingarn Medal. During May's absences, her mother would stay with Charles and Elizabeth or sister Helen Kingsbury in Massachusetts, or someone would move in with her. That year, Ovington came back from Chicago and the two women headed joyfully to the Green River. It would be her mother's last visit.

The daughter was confined to the small acreage, "taking care of my baby, which is what a very old person sometimes becomes." There were no trips with the Johnsons to Troutbeck, just the six miles to the doctor and hospital in Great Barrington. At least confinement was less confining than in the tall apartment building on Eighty-sixth Street, for "after all of one's travels," she told Joel Spingarn at his huge estate, "nothing is so emotionally satisfying as one's own brook and meadow and garden."[22]

In the city in January 1927, Ovington canceled meetings because of her mother's illness, but still talked about what she would do "when" her mother "recover[ed]." But by February she confessed that "I have daily to watch and care for my mother's serious and helpless illness." She was working only on *Portraits in Color*, "not even lending my name to any organization that I cannot serve." To friends she confided that "my mother is well physically but has almost entirely lost her mind. It is hard to think of anything more pathetic. I have all the nursing help I need, but the thing is on my mind a good deal. One's friends are a great help at a time like this."

The loss of one's mother is a crucial transition in a woman's life, and when the parent loses senses and memory the child grieves. Louise Ovington's mind was gone for some time before her death, and, presumably, recognition of the daughter who cared for her. That daughter undoubtedly began mourning before her mother's death.[23]

Louise Ovington died at their apartment on April 4, 1927. A small funeral was held at Ovington sister Adele Merritt's home at 3 Monroe Place, Brooklyn. One of the letters daughter Mary treasured was from a relative, Fannie Geery, who told her that no one could have been more devoted—May was the best daughter in the world. But the loss of one's mother was something one never got over, Geery went on aptly, "for no one can do for you quite as a mother can." In response to an expression of sympathy from her old friend W. E. B. Du Bois, Ovington wrote that "now that the end has come I am glad I did act like an old-fashioned daughter, though there were times when I wanted to run away."[24]

After her mother's death, Mary White Ovington moved out of the apartment they had shared, put her things in storage, and, following a month's bout with illness, took off on an extended southern and western trip. She had two consistent ways of recuperating: Riverbank and travel.

Very near the end of her five months on the roads and the rails came a blessing of providence in Seattle. After sunny California the chill of the northern Pacific gave Ovington a cold, but she kept as many engagements as she could, speaking her last Sunday at three black churches, dining with friends, attending a reception, and talking to a large white audience in the evening. When the branch secretary asked her to listen to a young pianist named Lorenza Jordan Cole, Ovington at first declined—saying she needed sleep—but then consented.

Such requests were not unusual, and she expected an aspiring, mediocre performance. But from her reclining position in a pleasant room, Ovington sat up when the young woman began. Cole had studied with Madame Liszniewska at the Cincinnati Conservatory of Music, a great teacher, and was a spirited worker.

"The afternoon was glorified," Ovington exclaimed. "To hear great music under the pleasant surroundings of a private home is a gift rarely bestowed upon the ordinary mortal." Cole had been recommended for a scholarship at the Juilliard School. Ovington promised to raise money for a school year if the young woman could get herself to New York City. "Lorenza fell upon my neck, and I became a patron of the arts—the first and only time I have had the means to occupy this position." The year's commitment became three, and "I found myself assuming the responsibilities of a parent."[25] Losing a mother and gaining a child balanced pain and joy; the loving and talented Lorenza Cole brought Ovington deep pleasure over the following years, showering her with letters to "My dear Miss O." "My darling," "My sweet Miss O.," and with music, music, music.[26]

In August 1928, Ovington moved to Greenwich Village, close enough for Jim Johnson, as he said, to "drop in . . . at times and have a cup of tea with you." He was recuperating at Five Acres and had checked on Riverbank. The lawn was fine, the flower garden had gone to seed, and the burdock was flourishing, he assured Ovington. He was sure she would have a "poetic spot," in the Village, and indeed, she did—as nearly like Riverbank as could be found.

Number 4 Van Ness Place was probably the most difficult address to find in New York City, a few houses hidden in the old footpaths of the Village. Reading the card she printed to guide them, her guests "felt as I do about directions in knitting—the thing printed can't be done," she laughed. She had the third floor of an old house with square, old-fashioned rooms and a "darling kitchen" where mice sometimes ran across the floor but into which the sun poured. She could see trees and grass from her windows as she faced the chaos of packing boxes. She never wanted to move again.

Helping Lorenza sometimes exhausted all of Ovington's energy. The compensation was that the pianist came regularly to practice on the Steinway Ovington rented. She never tired of listening to Lorenza play—music offered her a sense of communion with the ineffable, similar to her previous epiphanies in nature.

Ovington's brief two years at Van Ness Place were her happiest in New York City since the Tuskegee Model Tenement in 1908. She could have visitors of any race she pleased, without difficulty over doormen and elevators. "In Greenwich Village, at the buzz of a bell, I had only to push a button and my door opened on a stairway to be used by all visitors, icemen or millionaires."[27]

She put the Maine house on the market in March 1928 and sold it in November. Figuratively, it reflected the status of the Ovington family as class structures changed. When Ovington's parents had bought it, comfortable, upper-middle-class families summered there. But by 1928, Seal Harbor was the playground of John D. Rockefeller Jr. and Edsel Ford. Though swimming pools and tennis courts were supposedly open to all cottage holders, she recognized that it would not be easy to sell at a profit (even though she had added a two-car garage), "because it is not elaborate enough for the rich nor inexpensive enough for the few poor who still go there."

Of her net profit of $9,000 ($2,000 less than she asked), she donated $500 to the NAACP. Fifty to $100 a month was going to Lorenza, plus piano rental at $30, and furnishings and repairs and moving costs for the new apartment were about $500. Rent at Van Ness Place was $125 per month. Ovington put $8,000 into the Ovington Gift Shops company; its dividends had contributed $4,000 to her income in 1928.[28]

For all too short a time, her finances and her living situation were secure for Mary White Ovington in the last years of the 1920s. She came back from major addresses to the League of Women Voters and the NAACP twentieth-birthday celebration in 1929 to what was to have been a three-and-a-half-month cruise to Scandinavia with her brother, his wife, and friend Corinne Bacon.

It started out happily on June 29 on the Hamburg-Amerika *Reliance*. Just the word *Iceland* was attractive in the June heat. She was glad she was going with family—it helped her resist adding to her intinerary Prague and the conference of the Women's International League for Peace and Freedom. Frantically, she made arrangements with Arthur Spingarn for a leave for Jim before tending to herself, but she was in no better shape. "I am about as exhuasted [*sic*] as it's possible to be and pound a typewriter, inverting the letters for diversity, but when the boat leaves the dock I shall be a lion again in strength."[29]

Charles and Elizabeth began the trip with zest, even though he had been running a fever since a tooth extraction. The seas were smooth, with just a bit of afternoon fog. Some of the four hundred passengers were gift shop customers Charles knew.

Iceland's bleak landscape was relieved by charming village churches, fish stacked in fields like great haycocks, visits at the National Library in Reykjavik, and daylight until eleven. And then they were off for the Ice Barrier and North Cape, as close to the North Pole as a big ship could go. There were the usual ship's entertainments, including a spelling bee in which May understandably went down in the first round—too bad you weren't here for it, she told Richetta Randolph back at the office. They traveled down the coast of Norway, in and out of the spectacular fjords, stopping at shops with polar bear skins and eiderdown quilts, waterfalls and cathedrals.

Charles Ovington kept up a good front at first, but by the time they had eased their way down the coast of Sweden and headed north through the Baltic toward Stockholm at the end of July, he was obviously not well. He had no energy and wanted only to sleep. Elizabeth and Mary decided to cut the cruise short and head for Hamburg and a good doctor. Ovington wrote Richetta Randolph that if the doctor's report was bad, they would cable her to contact their sister Helen in Massachusetts. Meanwhile, Ovington tried to keep from worrying by salvaging some adventure out of the change in plans: she had taken a "little fly around Hamburg," she told Randolph, with one of the German pilots who "are the best in the world."

Hamburg doctors were of no help, nor was Charles any better, so plans were cut short and the quartet headed back home. In New York he entered the Medical Center for tests in late August. By mid-September, Ovington was helping Elizabeth handle the couple's business matters; it broke her heart, Ovington said, to watch her sister-in-law.

Like Jim Johnson, the more tired she became with worry, the more she felt compelled to keep nervously busy. May admitted, finally, that her brother was "dangerously ill." Ovington kept up something of a good front herself during the months of her brother's last illness, particularly in her letters to Johnson. It wouldn't help much, after all, to have him go away for recovery only to receive letters of worry from friend May.

The weather that October 1929 was gorgeous in New York City. The air "tingles with ozone," she told Jim. As she enjoyed her sunny rooms, she imagined him "smiling your very nicest at the great men you are meeting at the conference, and making excellent points during the discussions, and having good times when the work is over." She signed her letters to Jim Johnson, "Always yours devotedly, May Ovington."[30]

Charles K. Ovington died on January 9, 1930, at his apartment, of septicemia, or blood poisoning. His estate, with a net value of $118,119, went to his wife.

Mary White Ovington felt the loss of her older brother keenly; he was the head of the home, and it seemed everything would fall to pieces without him. Discouraged for a time, she wondered if it made any difference, for "we're all getting old." Her one consolation was a new baby whose bassinet was moved into his great-uncle's bedroom, the first of the next generation of Ovingtons. Charles Ovington Callin was born to Adele's daughter Louise, who had come to New York City for the event.

Again and again, Ovington knew how to tap the reserves that after each loss could bring her back to full strength. At Riverbank, she could don her purple swimsuit and slip into the cooling Green River; she could nestle bobolinks in her lap and listen to her dog Chubby's excited yapping as he raced to the river. Across the country she could visit and be embraced by the courageous frontline fighters for education and for justice, and again find inspiration for her writing.[31]

9

Rifts and Evolution

MARY WHITE OVINGTON and W. E. B. Du Bois's relationship deteriorated after she became chairman of the board. She had defended him previously as essential to the organization, but in the 1920s the difficulties he created seemed to outweigh his contributions. The change had much to do with her increasing closeness to the genteel and talented first black executive secretary, James Weldon Johnson. He and the chairman of the board skillfully divided the work and worked together. As neighbors in rural Berkshire County, Massachusetts, they shared passions for nature, writing, poetry, music, and theater. Johnson's leadership style, which she had initially feared would be too mild-mannered, soon impressed her as highly effective in winning over neutral or hostile audiences.

As the NAACP changed in the 1920s from a small, radical, mostly white, mostly volunteer organization to one that was national, mostly middle-class, mostly black, and run by salaried staff, Du Bois and Ovington found themselves moving in different directions. The *Crisis* editor was no longer the NAACP's primary employee, nor was his magazine its prime symbol. The chairman of the board was no longer the top executive, but shared and then ceded that place to the executive secretary. The founders handled marginalizing differently.

Chairman Ovington returned from California fund-raising in 1921 to escalating money requests from Du Bois and continuing complaints about his autocratic behavior. She supported his plans for the Second

Pan-African meetings, but suggested economies such as less expensive quarters on the ship to Europe.

But she put her executive foot down on Du Bois's treating the *Crisis* and his lecture and writing time as his to use at will, even while the NAACP paid for his trips and the magazine paid his salary. The editor must be held accountable as other executives were, she mandated—in short, "all special privileges will cease."

To Arthur Spingarn, she traced their long relationship:

> I have worked with Dr. Du Bois and I know that he is a slippery customer, ready to take advantage of any false step the other side may make. I know that he is relying in this emergency on the power that he has over white people. . . . Were the matter in hand to go before the colored members of the Board, men and women, the decision would be less lenient than the one I have agreed to. Were I as chairman to permit such a decision as you have reached, and the decision were ever known, it would be put down as personal liking for Dr. Du Bois on my part, as an unwarranted retaining of a man who had forfeited his right to remain in the high position he now has.[1]

Du Bois was also attacked by militant black leaders outside the NAACP: editors of the *Messenger*, A. Philip Randolph and Chandler Owen from the left; United Negro Improvement Association (UNIA) head Marcus Garvey from the right. Du Bois's differences with the latter provided the most newsprint.

The high points of Garvey's black nationalist, back-to-Africa movement and Du Bois's Pan-African meetings coincided, with both groups meeting in August and September of 1921. There similarities ceased. The UNIA filled Madison Square Garden and Liberty Hall with American blacks; the Pan-African group met in London, Brussels, and Paris. Garvey's procession, in Ovington's words, "surpassed anything Harlem had seen" in gold braid and brass buttons.

> Garvey led on his horse, robed in the colors [black, red and green] of United Africa. Following him came the knights and nobles; then the grand, resplendent Army. Banners waved bearing victorious slogans: "Africa Must Be Free." "The Negro fought in Europe, he can fight in Africa." "Africa a Nation, One and Indivisible." "Garvey, the Man of the Hour." Best of all, trumpets blared, and drums beat their magnificent music.

Du Bois's meetings of 113 prestigious personalities from the United States, the Caribbean, Africa, and Europe adopted mild-sounding resolutions calling for Africa to be assimilated with full equality into "two or three of the great world states," or, that failing, for the rising of "a great black African State founded in Peace and Goodwill."

Du Bois attacked Garvey and the legitimacy of his Black Star steamships in the January 1921 *Crisis*. Garvey sued, and the NAACP settled out of court with a retraction. By 1923, Garvey was saying that

> in his fifty-five years Du Bois personally has made a success of nothing. In all his journalistic, personal and other business efforts he has failed, and were it not for [his white associates], Du Bois, no doubt, would be eating his pork chops from the counter of the cheapest restaurant in Harlem like many other Negro graduates of Harvard and Fisk.

But by then, Garvey himself was close to failure. He was well on his way to federal prison, having been sued by a stockholder for fraud and convicted for using the United States mails to do it.[2] Ovington was intrigued by Garvey's appeal. In October 1926, she interviewed him at length at the federal prison in Atlanta for *Portraits in Color*. There was no hope for the Negro in white America, he said. Africa was the place for a Negro state. The American Negro "should study to fit himself for this great task. He should know how to build the bridges, how to clear the land, how to found the cities that are to be." Ovington dwelled on Garvey's best quality: his unwavering concern for black people. Though he was defrocked, nationalism did not die, she believed, "for the call of race is a real thing."[3]

More revealing was her handling of attacks on Du Bois from the socialist and communist side. Owen and Randolph criticized in print Du Bois's coolness to the Russian Revolution and to labor unions. Ovington's stance was much more radical than Du Bois's on these issues. She castigated the liberal press for "casually dismiss[ing] what Russia wants" in writing of peace prospects in early 1917 in a letter to the *New Republic*. And in the *Liberator*, Max Eastman's successor to the *Masses*, she published "Bogalusa," the story of black workers unionizing under the Industrial Workers of the World (IWW) in Louisiana, with white workers coming to their support.

Ovington's leftist beliefs often departed from NAACP policy, but she was much more careful than Du Bois in separating personal expression from official representation. She signed her published letters "Mary White Ovington; New York City" and her articles with her name only. The press did not always cooperate in maintaining her separation of personal and official opinion, and that created problems. The *Messenger* took advantage of Ovington's and William Pickens's support by quoting their letters in ads and adding their NAACP affiliations.[4]

This brings into focus the crux of the ongoing NAACP dispute with Du Bois. Was the editor and originator of the *Crisis*, particularly in editorials, an employee of the NAACP, subject to the same restrictions as other employees and board officials? Or was he exercising rights of freedom of speech and the press, whether or not he agreed with, or brought difficulties to, the organization?

Du Bois argued the latter and even seemed to go out of his way to undercut the NAACP. But he could validly argue independence only if the *Crisis* was self-supporting. If its existence depended on the association, could not the association legitimately place limitations on his editorial freedom?

Du Bois's arguments suggested that indeed he was a "slippery customer" as Ovington had described him. He had a *Crisis* fund for his travel expenses, but pocketed resulting lecture fees. He defined funded trips broadly as keeping in touch with "aspects of the Negro problem in the different parts of the United States." For "NAACP trips," he claimed payment from the general fund. Thus his expenses were paid and his lecture and writing income enhanced. Moreover, no matter how many *Crisis* subscriptions resulted from volunteer travel by Mary Talbert or Ovington, or paid travel by Johnson or Walter White or Pickens, Du Bois thought the *Crisis*, and not the NAACP, should get ' _ full subscription amount.[5]

Conflict intensified as circulation passed its peak after 1921, Johnson began the Dyer antilynching campaign, and Ovington struggled to raise money for the Arkansas cases. She worried about *Crisis* debts and believed that "now that we have begun to do work in Congress, the Crisis must represent to some extent, the policy of the Association."[6]

Du Bois's resistance increased as Johnson's star ascended. They were the same age, and their careers equally distinguished. Johnson excelled in administrative, negotiating, people, and language skills, conversing in French or Spanish on his trips to Haiti or Nicaragua. He was also as black as Du Bois[7]—and that meant the editor lost leverage that he used in conflicts.

With Johnson's rise, the necessity to keep Du Bois on board diminished, and he felt it. He took great offense in 1923 when, from his point of view, he was not asked until the last minute to be on the Kansas City convention program, and then was told by Ovington that they could not pay everyone's way. She cleverly suggested that "I hope you will feel that it is of sufficient value to the *Crisis* to meet your expenses and that we may have you with us."

It was just a ruse, Du Bois claimed. For years, he said to Johnson, "I seemed to sense on the part of you, Miss Ovington and Mr. White a feeling that I was not needed longer in this capacity and that my gradual elimination as a speaker on the platform of the NAACP was desirable." The next year Du Bois told Johnson that if his service was not necessary in Kansas City, no one would be able to convince him he was wanted at Philadelphia. Getting kicked once, he added, was not a person's fault, but anyone who kept letting himself be kicked must be dead of spirit.

Johnson responded by reminding Du Bois that the *Crisis* could have paid his way to Kansas City, and that he had the choice spots on programs and committees at Detroit and Newark. Du Bois felt he was not wanted, but, Johnson wrote to him, "the question with us here in the National Office has been that you appeared unwilling to allow us to make fuller use at the conferences of your abilities and prestige." How could not being taken to Kansas City and being urged to go to Philadelphia both be "kicks"? No one was indispensable. Only at the end of his long letter did Johnson express his personal surprise and hurt from the "implications that I have conspired against your prestige in the Association."[8]

Du Bois might well have been jealous on another score: Johnson supplanted him in Mary White Ovington's admiration and affection. The secretary's takeover of the limelight of her regard was evident in her 1927 *Portraits in Color*. Three things were immediately evident, none of which reassured Du Bois.

First, Ovington saw black leadership passing to women who had not been adequately recognized. Lucy Laney, founder and principal of the Haines Institute, "would rather teach than eat," Ovington wrote. "Her school has been her meat and drink for forty-five years." Maggie Lena Walker ran a successful insurance business and bank in Richmond, Virginia. Janie Porter Barrett, with the founding help of the NACW, "has made the Virginia state farm for colored girls not a reformatory but a home." And Meta Vaux Warrick Fuller, a pupil of Rodin, was a notable sculptor.

Second, by 1927 Ovington could pick subjects for her book from among many black male leaders. From 1900 to 1915 two black males had dominated leadership in the black community: Du Bois and Booker T. Washington. Now Ovington wrote of an array of prominent achievers. There were Johnson and Garvey and Christian Communist Max Yergan; Mordecai Johnson, president of Howard University; attorney Scipio Africanus Jones of Little Rock, Arkansas; the young Walter White; Robert Abbott of the *Chicago Defender,* who "made the colored newspaper a popular institution"; Eugene Kinckle Jones, who had led the Urban League to prominence; Louis Tompkins Wright of the Harlem Hospital medical staff, later to become NAACP board chairman; Ernest Everett Just, biologist and first recipient of the Spingarn Medal; George Washington Carver and his quiet, practical agricultural chemistry; Langston Hughes, much-loved poet of the people; Roland Hayes, whose musical nobility "has taught the world to forget race"; and the radical Paul Robeson, astounding achiever in just about everything, including athletics, music, and theater.

Third, Du Bois was supplanted by position in the book itself. Ovington placed James Weldon Johnson first, praising his music and theater work with his brother, John Rosamond, his poetry, his consular activity in Venezuela and Nicaragua, and his work with the NAACP. In her foreword, she also thanked Johnson for proposing and titling the book.

The Johnson brothers' "Lift Ev'ry Voice and Sing" was a favorite of hers. Composed in 1900 for a chorus of black schoolchildren and Lincoln's birthday, its creators forgot about it, Ovington wrote, but not so the teachers those youngsters became. "Now it is sung all over the United States and has been rightly called the National Negro Anthem." She wrote:

> One should hear this song given by thousands of voices at a Negro convention. The music is sonorous, with a deep beat that follows majestic words. In swing and fervor and high patriotism it is far superior to any other anthem America possesses, unless we except "The Battle Hymn of the Republic."

Jim Johnson's outstanding trait was charm composed of friendliness, kindness, "an unconscious self-respect," she wrote. As a result, he received "more consideration than any other Negro of as dark a skin as he."

> And whether he walks down the street with the stride of the actor, his hat a little on one side, whether he stands before an audience reading from his last and best book of verse, *God's Trombones*, or whether he greets an acquaintance with his disarming smile, he is always the gentleman. One knows him to be one reared in gentle ways, endowed with graciousness.[9]

James Weldon Johnson was Ovington's lead portrait; W. E. B. Du Bois was tucked into the middle. She emphasized Du Bois's "genius as a writer," which "forces Americans to face the Negro problem." "Among the distinguished Negroes in America, none is so hated by the whites" for a good reason, she stated: "he insists on making them either angry or miserable." He is "a master of invective. . . . But he has a mass of facts behind him. No white man who reads can doubt that the punishment is deserved." Ovington highlighted Du Bois's early and, to her, best writing, *The Souls of Black Folk*, and his early battles. His "scholar's work was for the most part over" when he began editing the *Crisis*, she wrote, and he became "a propagandist for a new social world." This was written before Du Bois's *Black Reconstruction* of 1935, a work of scholarship that Ovington would praise highly.

Her personal description of Du Bois revealed a new distance, particularly in contrast to her comments on Johnson. "There is a cruel look in Du Bois's sensitive, poet's face," she said.

> [I]t lurks somewhere about the mouth—a half-sneer, a scorn. . . . Life's greatest spiritual gift to him may have been his dark face. His passion has been turned against the most glaring of America's sins. . . . Du Bois counts . . . discriminations one by one, and then hurls his scorn at those who perpetrate them. And his aim is straight.[10]

From half of the subjects of her sketches Ovington received not even an acknowledgment of the very attractive purple and gold volume sent them. One person was, in fact, "openly indignant at not having been praised fulsomely enough," Ovington said.[11] One suspects that that person was next door in the *Crisis* office.

As Du Bois felt himself marginalized in the NAACP in the 1920s, other founders and original officers disappeared. John Milholland died in 1925, and the remaining faithful contributed to a bust in his honor. Henry Moskowitz, one of the three people who had gathered in 1909, wished that he had more than his social worker's income to contribute. Moskowitz nicely summed up the changing context of twenty years. John Milholland, he said, "stood for race fellowship when it was not so easy. He had the courage of the pioneer for he fought race prejudice when its acceptance or acquiescence was a mark of respectability. Thank God he was never respectable."

Moorfield Storey, the association's first president, died the day before the stock market crash in 1929. He "would not have understood the era which followed," says his biographer, and, indeed, did not much appreciate his last decade, despising motorcars and corruption and sham prosperity. Happily, Ovington had organized a tribute to Storey and the old ideals of humanitarian reform while he lived, in a bas-relief by Meta Fuller. The chairman also represented the NAACP at their president's simple, impressive funeral.[12]

Also dying during 1929 were Paul Kennaday, director of the Foreign Press Service, who had been with the NAACP from the beginning as an incorporator and a board member, and Dr. Charles Bentley of Chicago, a Niagara Movement man and an early president of the Chicago Branch. Louis Marshall, a late but important recruit to the legal forces, responsible with Storey for five U.S. Supreme Court victories, died unexpectedly in Switzerland. Ovington represented the NAACP at two services for this second of their prominent constitutional lawyers to die within weeks. The list of casualties was a veritable history of the organization and Ovington's career.

Ovington, too, was ready to leave, but for two years delayed her departure for Johnson's sake. She intended to refuse reelection in January 1929—and then Neval Thomas of Washington, D.C., created havoc with attacks on the secretary. She couldn't pull out in the midst of a dirty battle in the ranks, only to see a man she loved destroyed and an organization she had begun ripped futilely into warring camps. As leader in the 1920s, she had had to extinguish plenty of brushfires, but this threatened total conflagration. So on January 7, 1929, she was reelected as chairman.[13]

This twentieth birthday year began of necessity with fund-raising. A total of fifty thousand dollars came into the coffers in 1928, mostly from branches. The goal in 1929 was to quadruple that amount, and the only way Ovington could see to do so was to add "larger contributions from whites in this great money center" of New York City. "There are great groups of people who are able to give who evidently do not know about our work," she concluded. And founders could be brought back.

She began with Charles Edward Russell. Couldn't we have a chat sometime, she asked:

> I know that during war times we thought very differently, but it would be a pleasure now to feel that our deep interest in the same cause of the colored people could make all past differences of opinion forgotten. After all, how stupid it would be if we all did think alike.

She told Oswald Garrison Villard frankly that she had done some research on issues in the *Nation* and noted that it was "lacking in Negro material." Wasn't it time he came back to the cause?

> Do you realize that it is twenty years, or will be next Feb 12, since you wrote and published our first Call for a conference on the Negro? That was a great document. We are going to celebrate our twentieth anniversary and you ought to lead us.

Villard pledged the last thousand dollars of the first hundred thousand—now all she needed was pledges for the last thousand of the first twenty-five, and fifty, and seventy-five.[14]

The NAACP at age twenty had 325 branches in 44 states, 18 of them new that year. Executives of the association addressed 530 meetings in 25 states, including 8 by Ovington. She was the only woman executive between the time of Addie Hunton's leaving in 1924 and the hiring of Ovington's NACW friend Daisy Lampkin as regional field secretary on January 1, 1930. Six women sat on the thirty-five-member board in addition to the chairman: Jane Addams, Lillian Alexander, Florence Kelley, Ella Rush Murray, Maggie L. Walker, and Nannie Burroughs. Chairman Ovington served on four standing committees: the Committee on Branches, the Crisis Committee, the Anti-Lynching Committee, and her creation, the Committee on Administration. On three of these, she was the only woman.

The NAACP's twentieth-anniversary conference was held in Cleveland, Ohio, from June 26 to July 2. In her chairman's speech, Ovington looked back on the organization's history, which she described as "a history of the Negro race." The association had touched every life phase of the American Negro, she told her audience:

> It has assisted him in his education, disclosing the discrimination against him in the distribution of school funds in the South, and has prevented many segregated schools in the North. In housing, it has repeatedly affirmed the Negro's right to live where his money will take him and this affirmation has been made effective by Supreme Court decisions. It secured the verdict that Dr. Sweet could defend his home.
>
> The Association has greatly lessened the crime of lynching. It has made dents in the doctrine of "white supremacy," securing the Supreme Court decision against the Texas White Primary.

She looked ahead with hope not so much in the national office but in the faithful and unheralded workers across the country:

> What will [the NAACP] do in the next twenty years? Probably its work will be along much the same lines as now. An oppressed minority has a slow task to win to full citizenship. It will gain its rights only inch by inch. I like to think that we are the torch-bearers. Work is doubly hard, if it is done in the dark. Then, too, we furnish the tools of warfare in our peaceful conflict. More and more we can say that every city of any size in the country where Negroes dwell has its company of "trained troops." They have come with their ammunition to this Conference. They are earnest and they will not lay down their arms until they see that color is obliterated, the full rights of citizenship belong to black as well as to white in these United States.[15]

Ovington had intended this speech to be her "swan song," but, she said, "I stayed on as chairman another year because of the Neval Thomas mess but this is positively my last appearance." But financial matters at the *Crisis* were again in crisis, with a loan from the American Fund for Public Service (the Garland Fund) needed to keep the magazine going. Under the increased tension, Johnson worked harder. Ovington observed that "the tendency to feel that he alone can do the things that have to be done grows on the man as he loses in strength." She was terrified at the state of his health; he seemed near a breakdown.

Ovington insisted that they get Jim "away from the whole thing *at once*" for two weeks, no matter who was left in the office, with it understood that under no circumstances would the secretary be phoned.

As for Johnson taking a year's leave with an offered Rosenwald Foundation Fellowship, that was something he had to decide. Personally, she was "always rather inclined to believe in changes because I don't like the idea that anyone is indepensable [*sic*]. When a person dies the work goes on and it will go on if one goes away—not so well, but if the cause is worth much it will go on." But if Johnson left, she gave assurances that she would not give up the chairmanship, since she and Arthur Spingarn would be the only "regulars" to keep the machinery running. If she were deciding just for herself, she would exit.

> I am not of much use except as a cheerer on. None of the crowd likes to do something that another person suggests. They don't cooperate, at least with me. They are always pleasant and friendly, but new suggestions generally mean more work and that's against them, but more than that the crowd is in a rut. See how alike one conference is to another. I only say this if next year I do not seem to do any work, because I have wasted an awful lot of time sitting around there (I haven't many years more of work) enjoying our little talks, signing checks, but really doing nothing constructive.[16]

Ovington liked work and, even in her sixth decade, sought change. She rejected being a figurehead, or a pampered, aging founder, or a repository of power without responsibility. Her position was different from anyone else's, paid or volunteer. Like an entrepreneur who created a business from passion and devoted untold energy without thought of return, she saw the NAACP "succeed," to be taken over by paid staff who had a job, not a mission. Other volunteers came and went; she had been there from day one.

The Crash in October 1929 escalated money troubles. Contributions for which Ovington had received commitments did not materialize; Acting Secretary White could not keep up with his personal bills, let alone handle the NAACP budget with frugality; and the *Crisis* lost more every month, coming to the general fund for handouts and loans.

But there was an upside to fund-raising at the end of the anniversary year, too—perhaps there is always a silver lining that is less visible when clouds gather than when they break up. Throughout the Depression, Ovington promoted benefit parties and pageants because people would always pay for entertainment. The first occurred on December 8, 1929, at the Forrest Theater, with Heywood Broun as master of ceremonies, and stars led by Duke Ellington, his Cotton Club Orchestra, and the entire floor show of the Cotton Club.

Writers Carl Van Vechten, Arna Bontemps, Nella Larsen, and Cecil Mack contributed poems and prose to the souvenir program; Miguel Covarrubias, a Mexican artist, and Aaron Douglas did drawings and the cover. The Woman's Auxiliary of New York City sold the tickets and boxes.[17]

The commemoration of the NAACP's twentieth-anniversary year continued into 1930, partly because the NAACP name and the *Crisis* had begun in 1910, and partly because Mary White Ovington was having to deal with the illness and death of her brother, Charles. Though she was able to conduct some NAACP business from his sickbed, she had to ask the acting secretary to extend the anniversary fund-raising drive for six months. She suggested ways the bulletin could feature a successful branch each month. They could "get a sense of competition that is good," and "it would also help the branch that was used as an example." She had great hope that Daisy Lampkin's work out of Pittsburgh, which began on January 1, might "develop new things." Branch notes in the *Crisis* should be "popular and optimistic. All the success psychology possible," she recommended.

Her communication to Du Bois was trickier. She wasn't antagonistic to him in regard to the *Crisis* and its receipt of NAACP funds, she told him. But, she asked, since the magazine would need a regular subsidy, couldn't that be "recognized as a fact . . . and provided for" in the budget? Problems of "ill feeling" on the board came with the kind of "S.O.S. call that we had before."[18]

Du Bois did not go along with the suggestion, and last-minute *Crisis* money demands continued through 1930. As November and December days shortened, battles heated up and came to a boil. Many ingredients simmered: Director of Branches Robert Bagnall and Field Secretary William Pickens questioned Walter White's administration and receptivity to their ideas. Isadore Martin did not like their "tone": "If I had made as poor a showing as these two men have made this year in the way of raising money, I should keep quiet and feel thankful that the Board of Directors did not take me to task."

The protest fight over the Supreme Court nomination of Judge John J. Parker of North Carolina, which White handled, and the subsequent attempts to foil the reelection of senators who voted for Parker,

Mary White Ovington in her late years. (Library of Congress)

The Twenty-third Annual Conference of the NAACP at Harpers Ferry, West Virginia, May 22, 1932. (Library of Congress)

Group panorama photograph of NAACP personnel at the Thirty-first Annual Convention, Philadelphia, Pennsylvania, June 18–23, 1940. Included are Mary White Ovington; Walter White; William Pickens; Daisy Lampkin; and attorneys Arthur Spingarn, William Hastie, and Thurgood Marshall. (Library of Congress)

PILGRIMAGE OF THE 23RD ANNUAL CONFERENCE OF THE N.A.A.C.P. TO HARPERS FERRY, W.VA. MAY 22 1932
SCURLOCK PHOTO

...NAL CONVENTION ...ADVANCEMENT OF COLORED PEOPLE ...23. – 1940. – PHILA, PA.

was questioned by board member Joseph Loud of Boston who feared playing "partisan politics." Relations with Herbert Hoover's Republican administration were soured by the Parker matter.

In December, Joel Spingarn was elected to the presidency heretofore held by Moorfield Storey. Black newspapers were outraged because this was the man who had worked for segregated training for black officers. Spingarn responded that there were a thousand black officers in the United States military who would not be there had he not developed the officers' training camp. He had left his NAACP position to do it and had had the support of James Weldon Johnson, Du Bois, William Pickens, and Storey himself.

Ovington had to call a meeting in late December to deal with Johnson's resignation. He had been gone for a year on official leave, and that had led to his decision to take the less stressful position of professor of creative writing at Fisk. He had served the NAACP for fourteen years; he was praised effusively and elected a board member and a vice president. Though Walter White had enthusiastically held the position of acting secretary, he was not, to his disappointment, elevated to secretary at the meeting.[19]

Before the special meeting, Du Bois, perhaps anticipating White's imminent promotion to secretary, threatened his own resignation. In two letters dated the same day, the first typed by a secretary, the second handwritten, the editor first tried to get *Crisis* budget matters together at the last minute by asking for an immediate meeting between the Spingarns, Ovington, and his current business manager, Miss Malvan. The second letter to Joel Spingarn began: "After further thought I have decided that unless the present constitution of the Crisis Editorial Board is changed, I shall withdraw from The Crisis and the NAACP."

Ovington tried to redefine Du Bois's assignment, writing to him after a December 19 conversation. She had not made a copy, she told him, and had not told anyone else about her suggestion. She indicated that he would probably never again hold the high position he had had in the past, when the *Crisis* was really more important than the association, and more unique and important to Negro progress and radical Negro thought. At that time, when there had been controversies about his handling of the magazine, he generally won, she remembered. Now it seemed to her that the publication could be that important only if there were a source of huge capital available, which was highly unlikely.

No matter who became secretary, Ovington wrote, the magazine would not offer Du Bois the position he had once held. He would have less control and would enjoy it less than before, she thought. Given this situation, she suggested that he consider becoming a member of the staff, writing for the *Crisis* and lecturing for the NAACP, with pay based on the work done. Though his income would be smaller, she acknowledged, there would be fewer clashes with the other executives, and a chance for Du Bois to speak to branches more than had been the case for some time. If he was interested, they could talk, Ovington concluded; otherwise he should just tear up her letter.

Du Bois ripped up her suggestion, not the letter. Not for a moment would he consider her idea. If the *Crisis* was not necessary to the association, he should be allowed to run it independently, he asserted. If it was necessary, he should be able to remain as editor under a reasonable amount of control. Du Bois kept the thread unraveling and the board and the secretary in tumult for another year and a half before he had to accept for a time the offer Ovington first suggested in her late 1930 letter.[20]

These letters make for sad reading. Ovington wanted to give Du Bois options, as he had no financial alternatives to the NAACP. But he could not admit or adjust to the new situation. In her realistic though kindly tone, and in his black-or-white, either-or, intractable response are the sources of his attack on her a year later. Perhaps no person who is unable to compromise and negotiate can stand the kindness of one who can. And since receptivity to thoughtfulness is not an option for such a personality, there is an ironic tendency to find a way to lash back. It took Du Bois another year, but he managed to find a way to make Mary White Ovington, chairman of the board, sting with pain.

The new year of 1931 opened for the NAACP with a twenty-second Annual Mass Meeting on Sunday afternoon, January 4, at St. Mark's M. E. Church in Harlem. Ovington presided. James Weldon Johnson, Walter White, and Joel Spingarn spoke, as did the U.S. senator from New York, Robert Wagner. The audience, led by the St. Mark's choir, sang "Lift Ev'ry Voice and Sing," and the choir as well as a cello-violin duo performed Negro spirituals: "My Lord, What a Mornin'"; and "Stay in the Field." W. E. B. Du Bois was not on the program.

At the annual business meeting held the next day at 69 Fifth Avenue, Mary White Ovington was reelected chairman of the board of directors for the last time. On January 9, Mr. and Mrs. Walter Wh..e sailed for Haiti, leaving Robert Bagnall as acting secretary through January and February. In White's absence, Du Bois succeeded in having the board repeal a 1929 resolution making the secretary the executive officer of the association, so that when Walter White was finally elected in March, salaried officers were no longer "subject to his authority."

But White was not timid. Even before March, signing himself as "Secretary," he told Du Bois, on the "instruction" of the Committee on Administration, that the editor would have to rapidly revise his annual report. All references to conflict over internal administration of the magazine were to be removed, he told Du Bois:

> It would be to the disadvantage of the *Crisis* as well as of the Association for there to appear to be any dissension. Since there is no dissension, and since there have been various opinions regarding the future of the *Crisis* which members of the Board have naturally and intelligently given voice to, the Committee on Administration feels that it would be most unfortunate to give the public the idea that there is any dissension.

So much for anything that might be called dissension! On to the "tone" of Du Bois's report. "The Committee feels," White told him, that the editor's report "seems not so much as an officer reporting *for* the NAACP as that of a critic of its policies, and that an annual report is not the place for such criticism."[21]

The new year started dramatically, spurred by external events. On March 25, 1931, nine of the two hundred thousand people who made the rails of America their home were pulled off a Chattanooga-to-Memphis freight train where it dipped into Paint Rock, Alabama, near the town of Scottsboro. White hoboes reported that they had been beaten and forced off the train by "a bunch of Negroes," and a search by quickly deputized Jackson County white men turned up nine black males as the possible culprits. To the searchers' surprise, they also turned up two white girls wearing men's caps and overalls.

The nine were brought to the county jail in Scottsboro while Ruby Bates, the younger woman, said they had raped her friend Victoria Price. Within hours, the rumor was embellished until several hundred armed whites gathered to lynch "the black brutes" who had "chewed off one of the breasts" of Ruby Bates. Immediate lynching was prevented by the National Guard. The prevention of an ultimate "legal lynching" became an international cause célèbre and a complicated battle between the Communist Party's legal arm, the International Labor Defense (ILD), and the NAACP.[22]

Essentially the NAACP botched the Scottsboro Case. Although the responsibility has often been laid at the feet of Secretary White, an examination of the internal NAACP battles suggests there was more going on. In historical discussions of the contest between the NAACP and ILD, it is assumed that what Du Bois wrote in the *Crisis* in 1931 was a position of the NAACP, not usually a safe assumption even though the NAACP openly subsidized the magazine.[23] The Scottsboro Case was Walter White's first big chance to make a name for himself, and Du Bois was not anxious for that to happen.

Scottsboro changed everything at the NAACP offices and board meetings except Du Bois. The accused included Charlie Weems, age twenty; Ozie Powell and Clarence Morris, in their late teens; Olen Montgomery, blind in one eye and with bad vision in the other; Willie Roberson, ill with syphilis and gonorrhea; Haywood Patterson, age nineteen; Eugene Williams, age thirteen; and the brothers Andrew and LeRoy Wright, who were nineteen and thirteen, respectively. They were indicted by a hastily called grand jury, tried, and all but the youngest, LeRoy Wright, sentenced to death within two weeks. On April 13 the NAACP board referred any action on Scottsboro to the Committee on Administration, authorizing that group to send someone immediately to investigate.[24]

The events of the next few months were confused and confusing. Walter White was dispatched to Scottsboro, where he interviewed the "boys" in prison and reported to the board at its May 11 meeting. Meanwhile, NAACP Field Secretary William Pickens, on the road in Kansas City, saw the announcement in the *Communist Daily Worker* of April 16 that the ILD had stepped into the Scottsboro case. Since as far as he knew, his own organization had not yet done anything, he sent a letter of support to the ILD together with a contribution. The *Worker* promptly took the opportunity to tweak the NAACP by printing a photostat of the Pickens letter accompanied by an article criticizing NAACP officers.

Pickens thought there was more going on, that someone within the NAACP was leaking information from the Committee on Administration in order to create dissension with the ILD. He had received a three-page telegram from "some white person in New York," about a rumor that SOME ENEMIES OF THE ASSOCIATION AND OF MINE were engineering controversy, "and that they expect our office to 'bite,'" he told Du Bois. Additionally, nonpublic information was finding its way quickly out of the Committee on Administration into Harlem, Pickens noted.

The leaks gave the ILD a lot of ammunition. Pickens told Ovington that he believed the motive of the *Daily Worker*

> in publishing, without my knowledge or consent, my generous letter acknowledging what I read of the Labor Defense plans, and at the same time publishing, on the same page, their ungenerous sentiments about officers of the Association, is plain: to offend sensitiveness and create dissension among us. That is cunning: somebody who knows something about our organization must have advised that.

Dan Carter, in his thorough study of Scottsboro, says that "there was a certain Machiavellian touch to the Communists' use of the Pickens letter, but their campaign to discredit the NAACP lacked craft or duplicity." Rather, it had, as one Negro columnist said, "all the finesse and subtlety of an enraged rhinoceros." Looking closely at what was going on within the NAACP between Du Bois and everyone else, it is tempting to conclude that the Machiavellian touch in the use of the letter might have been inspired by the resident NAACP prince.[25]

Ovington probably sought to soften the board's ensuing censure of Pickens, in accord with her previous defenses of, and her own sympathies toward, the ILD. She expressed her disagreement with Du Bois vehemently, apologizing after the May 11 meeting for "irritating" him. "But we do seem to have a good many bouts these days," she noted. "I suppose with years and the philosophic mind, my capacity for hero worship has left me."

She went on to express the pleasure and encouragement she received from traveling, particularly from meeting college students, and implied that Du Bois's role might better be served outside the office, too:

> But if my hero's clay feet show to me, I think my evaluations count for more, and I shall always think of you as one of the really great influences in these times. I felt it so much when I was recently at Morgan and Howard. The youth of the Negro race believes more in itself because of you.

Du Bois's response was not in kind. The problem wasn't their personal differences, he said, but that she violated every rule for running a meeting. She shouldn't "monopolize the speechmaking," he lectured. She should give up the chair if she wanted to speak. "It seems to me that you continually violate this very old and clear conception of a chairman." Period. End of letter.[26]

One can follow the progression of the Scottsboro case through the NAACP legal files in Arthur Spingarn's papers. White's first mistake seems to have been dealing with the "boys" rather than with their parents. They were minors and thus their signatures were not binding. Moreover, convincing them to accept NAACP defense was predicated on criticizing the parents, who had been effectively massaged by, and had signed on with, the ILD.

None of the groups involved agreed with the others: not the local attorneys, the NAACP, or the ILD. Roger Baldwin at the American Civil Liberties Union tried to negotiate between them. Disputes over money proliferated with the original lawyers and with Clarence Darrow, brought in by the NAACP. When he was no longer in the case, the stock market crash made it impossible for him to return his two-thousand-dollar advance. The ILD claimed it was "whitewash money" the NAACP was collecting but not using on Scottsboro.[27]

Walter White, if he did not mismanage Scottsboro, appears at least to have overmanaged it, with little understanding of the increasing appeal of the Communists as the Depression deepened. Dan Carter says the NAACP moved too cautiously in the initial stages, and relied on old tactics. "For better or worse, the politics of the nation had shifted to the left; the National Association for the Advancement of Colored People had not." Richard Cortner says that NAACP handling of both the Arkansas peonage cases and Scottsboro suffered from the lack of an organized litigation department and the condescension of several of the men toward uneducated blacks—Shillady and Johnson in the earlier case, White and Pickens in the Scottsboro case.

Ovington did not get very involved with Scottsboro, although it was the big case of her last year as chairman. Reasons emerge from contrasting it with the Arkansas peonage cases that heralded her chairmanship a decade earlier. At first blush, three issues raised by Scottsboro—"radicalism, racism, and the operation of the Southern court system"—would seem to be foremost among her concerns as well as keys to the Arkansas cases. Why then did Scottsboro not arouse her active passion the way the earlier cases had?

"Radicalism" for Ovington meant "Workers of the World Unite"—what the Elaine, Arkansas, farmers were attempting to do. The "Scottsboro Boys," on the other hand, might indeed have been traveling on that freight train to look for work, but when the ILD called them *workers*, the use of the term was strained. It was clear, at least, that they were not in the business of organizing as workers, nor were they prosecuted because of any challenge to white business owners.

Second, "racism" led to violence in both cases, but the sexual hysteria of Scottsboro was very difficult to alleviate with a legal defense. Establishing guilt or innocence in rape is never easy, and in fact Ovington took the blame for the NAACP's having delayed until they could be sure of the young men's innocence.

Undoubtedly she was shocked back to the Atlanta riots of 1906, when she saw firsthand how any southern white woman's word, even when the woman was a prostitute, as with Victoria Price, was taken as gospel truth against the word of any black man. On the other hand, the fact that the South (and to some degree, the North) was wide open to false "rape" charges against black men did not mean that rapes did not occur, and one could not automatically assume that an accusation by a white woman was false. Sensational publicity about Scottsboro made it almost impossible to determine guilt or innocence initially. Once the *legal* injustice had been committed with an inadequate trial, however, different questions came into play; that is when the NAACP tried to step in.

Ovington knew firsthand from her visit in 1926 that many things in the South had not changed, and for that reason she did not get passionately involved in the Scottsboro case. She had long known what most whites were just learning in 1931 about race and sex in America, and she did not believe that increased agitation was going to solve the problem. She knew that smothering ingrained feeling under negative publicity simply forced it underground—into the psyche or into a dormant state, ready to rise again when conditions were right. Ovington knew firsthand the sickness of the white man's fear of black sexuality; she did not think the publicity surrounding the Scottsboro trials would cure it.

Of the three issues of Scottsboro, "the operation of the Southern court system" caught Ovington's interest the most. Of all the outsiders who converged on Alabama after March 25, 1931, Mary White Ovington was probably the most informed on the issues involved, and, what's more, she understood something of the unhelpful context created by the Communists' media blitz. Whites who wanted to "do the right thing"—and she knew there were some—were hindered by blanket accusations about southern justice.

Ovington attended the second set of trials, in Decatur, Alabama, in 1933. The courtroom was small and silent, 425 seats, three rows of whites and one of Negroes. The twelve men of the jury—attentive, sober citizens, she thought, with "less intermixture of race" than would show up in the North—sat in front of the first two benches and in front of them, Samuel Liebowitz for the defense, and two lawyers for the prosecution.

Haywood Patterson was being retried, and his fate would determine that of the others. Little in his appearance pled his case. Two years of prison left only defiance and eyes bleary from lack of sleep. The tall and lank Judge James Edwin Horton Sr. entered, and the trial began. Ovington had heard much of him and had met his wife. His fairness made him hated, and Mrs. Horton believed his life was in danger. But Ovington saw no nervousness as he took his seat. The first trial had been mob-ridden, but Horton's "was as orderly as a High Church service."

By chance she hit the most dramatic day. Lester Carter, a white boy who had claimed to have been thrown off the train, now said the Negroes were innocent. Victoria Price and Ruby Bates had gotten on the train and had sexual intercourse with him and his friend Orville Gilley.

Liebowitz announced that the defense rested—with reservations. As he sat down, a messenger came to him with a note and he approached the bench to confer with Judge Horton, who called a brief recess. Tense excitement filled the courtroom; Liebowitz had planned his star witness for the last possible moment.

Guards opened the back doors and a perspiring matronly woman walked down the aisle, in back of her a pretty girl in a new spring hat and dress. "It's Ruby Bates!" the audience gasped. Bates recanted her former testimony. But victorious as she looked for the press, she was not convincing to the jury, and Patterson's case was again lost. "The wreckage of civilization [is] seen in both those witnesses" Ovington thought.[28]

"Scottsboro, Too, Is Worth Its Song," wrote Countee Cullen to the poets of America who had spilled ink on the murder trials of anarchists Nicola Sacco and Bartolomeo Vanzetti in 1921. But at the NAACP in 1931, everyone, including Walter White, was hamstrung by the internal problems of Du Bois and the *Crisis*. There were few resources left to sing the song of Scottsboro with any energy or clarity.

As usual, hostilities heated up in November. Du Bois reported: "The *Crisis* must have January 1, $1,500 to balance its accounts properly." White said impossible—that the association had a $12,000 deficit. It was the secretary's "duty," Du Bois shot back, to remind the NAACP that despite "the extraordinarily difficult financial condition," there had to be added to NAACP red ink the *Crisis* deficit of $1,500. The board would have to decide whether the *Crisis* would cease or White curtail his expenses.

White told Joel Spingarn, president, that the *Crisis* deficit was "a burden too great for us to bear." The board could decide to continue pouring money into the magazine on demand, but it would be left to Secretary White and his staff to raise the funds. White wanted to "merely mention" that already he had gone without vacations and worked on Sundays and holidays. He was conveying the situation also to Ovington and Arthur Spingarn.

Du Bois then wrote of his side to the Spingarns. The *Crisis* was going to have to borrow five thousand dollars or cease publication. Of course someone would have to cosign, and "there would be some risk for the endorser." But if the "general situation begins to mend" in the next two years, he wrote, "we can probably handle this indebtedness."

At the December 14, 1931, board meeting, Budget Committee head Charles Edward Russell (whom Ovington had succeeded in reinvolving) presented its report in executive session while the executive staff was asked to withdraw. Du Bois was the only executive staff person who was also a board member, and he was not present. The board recommended severe retrenchment: reduction of printing, postage, and mimeographing; laying off a clerk, a special legal assistant, and Mr. Pickens's secretary; reducing salaries by 10 percent (those $1,250 and up) and 5 percent (those between $1,000 and $1,250); turning over all business affairs, including the *Crisis*, to the association. They didn't get through the full agenda at the meeting, so Ovington called a Special Meeting for December 21.

She was not pleased that for forty minutes they debated whether or not to get rid of Pickens, a costly field-worker, "but in two minutes the board voted to dispense with his secretary," she noted, "a dark-skinned girl who will find the greatest difficulty in getting another job." It was a symptom of larger problems with the organization and her role.

She was not bothered by the change in the responsibilities of the chairman, which had begun with Shillady and continued with Johnson. But to them, she had still been useful. They respected and used her judgment. "But Mr. White does not care to ask another's opinion, certainly not mine," Ovington wrote to Joel Spingarn right after the first December meeting. She liked Walter White—he was "a dear fellow"—and thought he liked her. But clearly he would rather be without the "slight power the chairman very, very occasionally uses." "I do not always feel that he is just to others"—but she had long since ceased to offer him advice. Her work, she wrote, "largely resolves itself into settling an occasional squabble among departments," or "perhaps someone comes in to see me who hopes I will use my influence regarding a salary." She was ex officio on all committees, but didn't like to attend meetings unless invited, and she never was. She had not even met new members of the Legal and Crisis committees. "Is a chairman needed any more except to preside at meetings? . . . Is the Chairmanship, as it once was, something to be quietly dropped by dropping the present occupant of the position?"

She could simply refuse to be renominated and in fact had considered that ever since Jim Johnson left—except for matters like the carelessness regarding Pickens's secretary. "While to the inner group of executives and board members I am no longer needed, the people in the outer office feel that I belong especially to them," she observed. And to Ovington "the outer office" included volunteers in the NAACP branches across the country. She had long noted that no one paid attention to them except to beg for money. When she went out into the field as chairman, people liked knowing she represented their interests in the national office.

She had an idea to try out on Spingarn. With his move from treasurer to president, there was no good candidate for the place he vacated. Both Villard and Spingarn had moved from chairman to treasurer. What did he think of her doing that, too? That would keep her among the important officers to represent the "outer office" across the country, and it would give her more of a voice at board meetings. She had broached the possibility with White and Russell. Russell was adamant that she not give up the chairmanship, but she could see that White, as well as the two attorneys, Arthur Spingarn and Charles Studin, hoped that she would.

That Ovington turned to Joel Spingarn as her sounding board on this important decision is indicative of their closeness. "We think alike about a good many things," she told him, and "you have helped me more than anyone I know to preserve such idealism as I have." Spingarn shared her sensitivity to practical means and overall goals. "I don't want to make a mistake this time," she told him, knowing he would both believe and understand, as some would not, what she said next: "I want to do what means not the gratification of any ambition, but the finer life. One way or the other must be the better service."

Spingarn composed a very careful response. Her becoming treasurer and his chairing meetings as president, with a change in the constitution, or as chairman, combining it with the presidency, was "an almost ideal solution." They needed a treasurer who had the complete trust of both white and colored people. She would have more input, for the keeper of the treasury was always listened to. Spingarn told her he saw no weakening of ideals involved, but rather, a matter of her accepting the duty for which she was most needed. Whatever she decided, she would have his full and continuing backing, sympathy, and admiration.

Ovington was relieved. "Shan't I enjoy having a vote," she exclaimed. Before the second December meeting, she told Isadore Martin, chairman of the Committee on Nominations.[29]

It is not clear if Du Bois knew of Ovington's decision. After the first meeting a comedy of errors ensued in an office murky with fears of layoff. Russell had been delayed by dense fog, went directly into the meeting, and had to use Ovington's copy of the budget report. Then he went off unintentionally with it. Du Bois the next morning asked Richetta Randolph for a copy. She had not seen it. He then demanded it from Ovington and she said there was no copy in the office—perhaps Russell had it. Smelling a conspiracy, Du Bois wrote to Arthur Spingarn asking whether Ovington had the right to withhold the report from him as a member of the board. Spingarn replied of course not. Walter White, too, had been frantically trying to find the report; it had, at last, been located in Russell's pocket.[30]

Not knowing what was in the report that might affect him, Du Bois wrote a proposal to Russell that any scrutiny of *Crisis* finances be matched by an examination of Walter White's shop. He wanted three people from outside the NAACP to do it. If a "proper" committee were constituted, and it went over the two offices "carefully," Du Bois said he would be willing to follow its judgment.[31]

What pushed Du Bois to his next step is not clear. Perhaps he saw that an outside investigation would not fly unless he raised suspicions about White. He wrote a statement accusing White, with the complicity of Ovington, of dishonestly managing finances and of mismanaging relations with staff. Then he got signatures from Field Secretary Pickens; Herbert Seligmann, director of publicity; Roy Wilkins, assistant secretary; and Robert Bagnall, director of branches.

The special meeting started out smoothly enough, with the board modifying its salary cuts, at the suggestion of White, to ensure that two of the clerks who were just above the cutoff line be reduced only 5 percent. It also passed Du Bois's motion to retain Pickens's secretary through the month of January.

Then came the bombshell. Du Bois took the floor and read his statement, signed by all the executive staff except White. The final paragraphs read:

> It is our solemn and carefully considered opinion that unless the power of the Chairman of the Board over the appointment of committees is curtailed and unless Mr. White is going to be more honest and straight-forward with his colleagues, more truthful in his statement of facts, more conscientious in his expenditure of money, that the chief question before this organization is how long he can remain in his present position and keep the NAACP from utter disaster?
>
> We make this statement with our free will and at the solicitation and suggestion of no single one of us; and with a full realization of the gravity of what we say and the utmost willingness to abide by the consequences. We have all had considerable and varied experiences, but in our several careers, we have never met a man like Walter White who under an outward and charming manner has succeeded within a short time in alienating and antagonizing everyone of his co-workers, including all the clerks in the office.

Ovington, White, and everyone else were totally taken aback. Since she was implicated, she could not rule as out of order Du Bois's request that it be entered into the minutes, with a copy to every board member.

Joel Spingarn saved the day with a substitute motion. It gave Du Bois extra time by calling for the appointment of three "outside experts" together with two board members and one more person, presumably staff, to "investigate the expenditure of funds by the National Office of the Association and the *Crisis*." The group was to be appointed not by the chairman, but by the president.

Spingarn regarded Du Bois's action as cruel and indefensible, but with executive staff signatures on the accusation, all he could do was order the investigation, although after the meeting he quickly checked and informed the editor that it was unconstitutional for him as president to appoint the committee. John Haynes Holmes thought Ovington, particularly, had been "unjustly assailed" and attacked. He told Spingarn "I deeply deplore Dr. Du Bois's attitude."

Ovington was less hurt by the charge from the executives than by the thought that the clerks had joined in the cabal. Quickly she wrote to her longtime friend Richetta Randolph, head of the office staff and secretary to White. When Du Bois read the statement, she wrote,

> charging the Secretary of extravagance and the Secretary and Chairman of dishonesty, he read the names of those who signed it and then added that it was also the opinion of all the people of the outer office. . . . It is incredible to me that this should be true of all the outer office but you did not deny it.

Randolph's response was immediate. To the executives who had signed the statement she wrote, "I am not sure just how many of us in the outer office . . . you classify as clerks, but I do want you to know that I personally do not subscribe to the . . . statement." To Ovington she said it was a "dirty deal." It was not right of Du Bois to include the reference to the clerks, who were not part of the protest against White. Pickens even told her that it was not fair that they had been mentioned in a complaint they hadn't signed. As for her feeling toward Ovington, "there has been no change in that feeling since I met you in 1905."

Pickens wasn't the only one with second thoughts. Wilkins and Seligmann sent letters to White and Ovington withdrawing all statements and offering to resign. Seligmann was the most abject, apologizing for both "substance and manner." He sent copies to all who were at the meeting. Ovington thanked him, and he replied on Christmas Eve with gratefulness for "the beautiful spirit of your letter."

Bagnall was stunned to find the "ranks had been broken." Not able to reach Du Bois, he found Pickens, and they decided that they had no alternative but to "withdraw personal charges" but "hold to field work contentions, as it had been agreed before—'all or none.'" Bagnall wrote to Du Bois, saying, "You must be wondering 'why these things'" and going on to explain that no one had been coerced to withdraw, and no one was fearful. "They just came to the decision they had made a mistake and so changed," he explained. He did not think White would "be so difficult to get along with as in the past."

Pickens, meanwhile, had had a "long and frank and understanding" talk with White and clarified his concerns about fieldwork. In his retraction, he said that since all had signed the document together, they all should drop it together and the matter should be closed; he had not originated the idea, and he wished it had never been done at all.

Just after Christmas President Spingarn told Du Bois that since the memo "has now been completely and unreservedly repudiated" by everyone else who signed it, the editor should also "retract every charge or innuendo against the character, honesty, or motives of the Chairman and the Secretary." As long as the charges stood with Du Bois's name attached, Ovington insisted that the investigation go forward. Wouldn't it be better to drop it all, and let the new chairman appoint an impartial outside expert? Spingarn was blunt:

> I must tell you frankly that your friends have only too often been pained by your habit of casting aspersions on the character or motives of all those who happened to differ with you on questions of policy or opinion. In this case, I hope you will do the manly thing, and make a complete retraction, so that the Board may not be forced to take some form of action which will grieve your friends, among whom you must surely know that I am included.

Du Bois's response, on New Year's Eve, was much shorter and much more blunt: "I will not retract or change a single word in the statement I signed and read before the Board." Thus ended 1931 at the NAACP. If anyone entered the New Year concentrating on Scottsboro and its song and the increasing loudness with which the ILD was making its voice heard, it would have to be considered a little-known Christmas miracle.[32]

At the January 4, 1932, meeting of the board of directors of the NAACP, Mary White Ovington was elected treasurer. Joel Spingarn was made both chairman of the board and president. W. E. B. Du Bois was not at the meeting. At its February 8, 1932, meeting, the board resolved:

Mary White Ovington is one of the two or three people in whose brains and hearts the National Association for the Advancement of Colored People was originally conceived and out of whose conference and cooperation it was born nearly a quarter-century ago. She has served as a member and an officer from the beginning and as its chief executive in the capacity of Chairman of the Board of Directors from 1919 to the end of 1931.

Through all this period she has given unselfishly and unsparingly of her thought, her active services, and her means, to the success of the Association's work,—and through all this time and years before she interested herself in the welfare of the American Negro. She will abide in our histories and in our recollections as the "Mother of the New Emancipation."

10

Traveling Fund-Raiser

MARY WHITE OVINGTON was not joking when she said she left the NAACP's board chairmanship at the beginning of 1932 for the "more arduous" job of treasurer. Though the men who had made this move did pull away from close involvement, committees and check-signing did not satisfy her. "I must do more or less," she decided, and the former won out once again.

As the years had passed and aging and loss, both personal and professional, wearied Mary White Ovington, she had repeatedly found invigoration among extraordinary ordinary people in the hinterlands. She loved to get out of New York City to the Midwest, the West, and the South, to places both famous and obscure. Her goals were various: raising money and fighting fires for the NAACP; receiving and sharing education on race issues; research for writing; and personal energizing. John Shillady and James Weldon Johnson had professionalized the national office. Ovington found unpaid work forming branches and encouraging branch workers.

Her first major fund-raising trip had been in 1921, with a first stop in Kansas City, Missouri, and its twin city in Kansas. Pollution made her lungs "as grey as the dingy curtains" in hotel windows, but her speeches to churches, chambers of commerce, and Rotary Clubs, brought in donations. "If I can't get the idea of the Association over well enough for people to be willing to give something to it, I have not gotten it over at all," was Ovington's brass-tacks attitude. Black

259

communities "overflowed with kindness," showering her with receptions and bouquets.[1]

Following the westward route of the first settlers stirred her imagination. Between Denver and Salt Lake City she thought of the Mormon pioneers who had crossed the badlands, found the green, rippleless Great Salt Lake with nary a tree, and stayed to make it bloom. Their religious views (especially regarding women) might be awful, but she found them hardworking and fun-loving, traveling with a brass band and dancing every night. Once her niece had said to her: "I believe, Aunt May, you like everything that is unpopular." Ovington was sure her mother would think of that when her daughter wrote that she had grown to respect the Mormons.

In Stockton, San Francisco, and Berkeley, she made many presentations and was presented with innumerable lunches and receptions by white groups: the University of California at Berkeley, Mills College, civic centers, and churches; she even enjoyed a picnic and a midnight party, and could have gone to many more had time and energy allowed. Her first speech to an NAACP branch was in Oakland. She tailored her message to her audiences, knowing that repetition, even if it pleased them, would bore her.

She found that white audiences needed education about race conditions in the United States. Negroes, on the other hand, as one man said, "know the colored problem so well that we can anticipate every sentence that will be said on it." To them she told of the NAACP's beginnings, of Richetta Randolph and Frank Turner, of the role of each executive; and "our few big results." She did not have James Weldon Johnson's or William Pickens's oratorical bombast, but she thought her speeches brought branches "right up in enthusiasm and loyalty." "This is the first time we have had a clear exposition of just what the Association was doing at headquarters" she was often told.

Ovington grew to love speaking. There were no distracting microphones then, "no photographers creeping and crouching along the edge of the platform to snap pictures," she remembered. One minister roused concern about her gentle, interactive style by glancing often at the clock. But when she finished, he said: "I wondered how long Miss Ovington could hold her audience, using a conversational tone. She did it for an hour and ten minutes. Now if Brother Moore . . . or I had wanted to hold your attention for that long, we would have had to go in for some skyrockets!" Never had she thought that she could get such rounds of applause, such bouquets. To her mother, back in their New York City apartment, where her brother Charles or his wife, Elizabeth, could look in on her daily, Ovington wrote that the trip was "very gratifying . . . and makes me know we are on the right track and that it was a good thing for the NAACP to have been born."[2]

In 1928 she had been thrilled to present the Spingarn Medal at the Los Angeles NAACP annual meetings to a favorite author, Charles Chesnutt, and had paced the lonely beach at Carmel and talked into the night with Lincoln Steffens and his wife, Ella Winter, about the achievements of the Soviet Union. To Grace Johnson back at Five Acres, Ovington wrote that California's climate had given her back her youth, and back east again, in her New York City apartment and at Riverbank, she had adopted the casual California style, where meals became happy picnics. "Life like this tends to break down caste," she believed.[3]

Much of Ovington's travel in the 1920s was to the South, where she saw much change since her first trip in 1906–1907. Increased prosperity had followed massive exoduses to the North, with shops where one could "even buy books," paved streets, clean hotels, and good roads. She found train stations had "known the mop of the cleaning woman" and saw fewer rags and more mail-order clothes on both whites and blacks. "Even the hogs have changed," she wrote in an article Du Bois requested: "The razor-back is less common on the highway and in the field, giving place to his better-bred brother in the pig-pen."

The effects of the Interracial Commission, begun in Atlanta after the 1906 riots and expanded after World War I, both encouraged and frustrated her. Executive Secretary Will Alexander did good work in bringing educated whites and Negroes together, as in a program called Adventures in Good Will. George Washington Carver, for example, lectured at a white college. Students leaned in around this elderly, unassuming, industrious man, fascinated. "They have seen a great scientist and he is black. A man who was born a slave," Ovington said. "Without saying a word on the subject of race, Professor Carver is the best propagandist for the doctrine of good fellowship that the Interracial Commission knows."

But the Augusta Interracial Commission had actually hindered black progress in schools, Ovington observed. "Wide awake, able" Negro members "are told to trust the whites and be sure not to vote against bond issues," she wrote. Thus the most aggressive Negroes could be silenced by putting them on the commissions, making promises, and warning them that complaining would hurt the group's work.

Segregation in facilities in the new South was a shock. "Only a white person who has been accustomed to move freely among Negroes," she saw, could appreciate the COLORED and WHITE signs that hit her at every turn: the drinking fountains in an Arkansas courthouse; train stations where Negroes were "shunted off to an inferior waiting room." She bought her ticket at a separate window and rode on a separate coach. On streetcars, hers was the front seat. A white person was told over and over without the option of dispute that the Negro belonged with "the untouchables." The effects were terrible on both races.

> To grow up in this atmosphere means to be painfully conscious when in the presence of any Negro who is not a servant. It means too the besmearing Negroes with the stigma of "colored" wherever they may travel, from the North pole to the equator. The southerner's idea of segregation is to deny the educated Negro the right to remain anywhere where he, the southerner, has decided to put his foot.[4]

In all her travels, Ovington often spoke to college classes, white and black, on race relations, black history and literature. History professor Merle Curti had her lecture in a course called Political and Social History of the United States in Recent Times at Smith College. "I wanted my class to understand racial inequality and prejudice," he recalls.

He was impressed that she distinguished among black classes—tenant farmers, sharecroppers, and working-class, professional, and intellectual groups—and the ways they experienced "white people's intolerance, prejudice, and dominance." "Even the Southern girls were much impressed," he told her. She was "mellow and sympathetic," but not sentimental, and her "combination of conviction and quiet charm" was engaging. In response to questions he thought her "unpretentious and gracious," and overall she "probably made a deeper impression on the students than W. E. B. Du Bois might have done."[5]

In 1928, Ovington gave several lectures on The Negro as Literature at Tougaloo College in Mississippi. Through her hundreds of "Book Chat" reviews, her knowledge was extensive. She even recommended anthologies—Countee Cullen's poetry collection *Caroling Dusk*, for example, was up-to-date, but had some serious omissions that would have to be dealt with in a classroom. English teacher Bernice Davies used her notes for course development.[6]

Valiant blacks across the country invariably renewed her faith. "I suppose there are other national organizations in the United States as remarkable as the NAACP," she said after repeated trips:

> I suppose so, but I don't really believe it! . . . When people will hang together, decade after decade, supporting an ideal, . . . when they save from their small earnings to send a member to the national conference, when they respond to every appeal to action, then surely they are better than any other organization going![7]

WHEN SHE LEFT the chairmanship and became treasurer in 1932, her fund-raising intensified because she was very much attuned to triple demands on the budget. Secretary Walter White had expensive tastes: "I happen to be a rather finicky person," he said to explain taxis and meals, and "I cannot eat food unless it is in a clean atmosphere, free from odors." Monthly demands from W. E. B. Du Bois and the *Crisis* escalated. What should have been first ended up last: programs and legal cases, including the Scottsboro case.

Layoffs and salary cuts dragged at the bottom, and accusations flew at the top between the secretary and the editor as to whose shop was more profligate. "It's beastly being in debt, isn't it," Ovington said to White as she borrowed and made settlements and payments: "It makes people haggle so."[8]

She started planning trips immediately, even writing a play, *Phillis Wheatley*, to use on the road. To make sure she would raise more money than she would cost, she paid half her expenses herself. Now in her late sixties, she also had to plan for staying well. Short stops were the most tiring, so wherever possible she wanted to spend several days in a city. Then she welcomed all the entertainment a branch wished to provide.[9]

But the first year, illness and income kept her in New York City, with doctor visits in February, April, November, and December, and "grippe" at the beginning of 1933. She completed her "Reminiscences," published weekly by the *Baltimore Afro-American* beginning in October. Her income had dropped precipitously; she needed the two hundred dollars she received for these newspaper memoirs.[10]

By March 1933, she was on the road to Ohio, Indiana, Tennessee, Georgia, Alabama, and Virginia. She reached Columbus Sunday morning in time to be introduced at the Baptist church, and addressed an audience of a thousand people there that afternoon. Her stops followed a pattern: she stayed and dined mostly in black homes, visited with people she knew from other parts of her life, talked and listened to new groups and individuals, and enjoyed some purely social times.[11]

She was shocked by the effects of the Depression. Banks were closed and people had nothing to give. One after another, the citizens of Zanesville, Ohio, told her they had no work. In Kokomo, Indiana, plate-glass workers were unemployed. Later she said she spent her first week doing jigsaw puzzles after finding it impossible to raise money.[12]

But she saw hope in the young. She spoke often in grammar schools—five in Indianapolis alone—where she told of Roland Hayes or George Washington Carver. In a high school journalism class or assembly she might talk about her own books, if asked. She lectured to Charles Johnson's class on The Negro in America at Fisk and to two hundred students in a History Club at Tennessee State; Talladega students wanted to discuss Scottsboro.

To parents and community groups she pointed out conditions in de facto segregated schools. Kokomo's was "a disgrace to so progressive a community and such progressive colored people." There she rallied YWCA women as well as the NAACP board. "It was a matter that could create great excitement if tackled," she found. She talked education, too, with state leaders such as Governor McNutt of Indiana— "quite the handsomest governor, I am sure, in the U.S."

She conveyed suggestions back to the national office: that the upcoming Chicago conference give a day to the youth movement and that they prepare a national youth movement program and establish a lending library. She retracted a statement from her "Reminiscences," that "the youth of the race does not seem eager to support us," for she was met at every turn by "students eager to know of the work of the NAACP" and who wanted to form branches.[13]

The illness of her sister Helen Kingsbury and the death of her sister Adele in a sanitarium in California forced Ovington to cut short her 1933 trip, and made what she described as "a sad break in my home life." Only when she got home did she realize how tired she was. After a quick business/pleasure trip to Philadelphia at the end of May, writing an NAACP pageant and motoring to Valley Forge, she ended up sick herself through most of June. "I would like to lie off somewhere and do nothing for a while," she said. That meant Riverbank.[14]

The board meeting of January 8, 1934, kicked off the NAACP's twenty-fifth anniversary year with an ambitious fund-raising campaign planned by Treasurer Ovington and Field Secretary William Pickens. His idea was to raise a penny for every Negro in the United States. "You've got a bully idea," she told him: "I will help . . . to the best of my ability."[15]

For the *Crisis*, Ovington wrote "The Year of Jubilee" review of NAACP history. She praised others, beginning, as did the NAACP's official birth story, with Oswald Garrison Villard's penning the Call, and continuing with the *Crisis* and Du Bois, where she emphasized the preceding Niagara Movement. She described many heroes: Mary Talbert and James Weldon Johnson and the antilynching campaign; Scipio Jones and Moorfield Storey and the acquittal of the Arkansas "peons"; Walter White and the defeat of Judge John J. Parker; Charles Houston and William Hastie, "our young colored lawyers . . . who are now so splendidly and unselfishly defending our cases in court." Much of her space went to unnamed branch workers—"from zero in 1909, the branches number 378" in 1934.

Even the "most sanguine" among the signers of the Call did not expect to see in twenty-five years such a far-flung, aggressive association, with cases before the Supreme Court and literature all over the world. "We formed our little group almost in desperation," she recalled, "feeling someone must voice opinion against the lynchings and riots and the constant taking away of privilege." If much had been accomplished, much was left to do, she concluded. "Discrimination, discrimination and again discrimination must be fought over and over again. We have just begun."[16]

In February 1934, W. E. B. Du Bois stunned *Crisis* readers with an editorial promoting segregation as the way to advance the Negro cause. Ovington, on the road and on the overseeing Crisis Committee, exclaimed, "*I had not laid eyes on it*" before its distribution. *What* it said was "bad enough," but tragically, she also thought it "spiritless." She could see the truth in Du Bois's analysis as applied to the South, as she noted that "every Negro who has made a reputation here has made it through segregation." But she would have preferred a defiant statement that said, simply, if you won't let us work with you, then we'll do it on our own.

The dispute gave her speeches a new urgency. "Segregation. That is a word that brings instant attention in a colored audience today," she would begin. But whites did not do all the segregating. "For twenty-five years I have watched the NAACP become more and more an organization manned by one race only," Ovington said. She could see no advantage in excluding whites. Why make no effort to enlist those whites who were in sympathy with the minority's goals? she asked. Of course Negroes wanted to *lead* the organization, but wouldn't they find, when they got to work, that they needed "white friends on the bench, in the jury box?" Why then not educate whites, she argued, especially given their "abysmal ignorance." "Don't blame people too much for being indifferent to your ills when you don't ask them to drop their indifference and join with you," she pleaded with her black audiences.[17]

It was the ideal time to involve whites in the NAACP, she thought. It seemed to her that the Communist Party had had such success of late because it joined forces with Negroes without inhibitions or patronage. She had also noted fewer calls to get white teachers out of black schools, and that black students were seeking and benefiting from contacts with white students. Yet, at the NAACP, they seemed to be going the other way, with fewer white volunteers and no white person on the executive staff.[18]

She traveled to Baltimore and Washington, D.C., then Charleston and Savannah, the only city in the far South where the Negro who met her could go with her through the train station. In Georgia "the food's bad," "the people are mean," and "they haven't even got a good movie." Florida was "indifferent or cruel or both," with "the Negro . . . cheated every way he turns," including in federal projects.

It was hard in a state so disorganized as Florida for a white person to do anything, she found. This made her admired friend Mary McLeod Bethune, of Bethune-Cookman College, indispensable to the NAACP. Only such a powerful personality stood a chance of breaking through the "colossal indifference" of the whites, Ovington thought.

Ovington took a twelve-day vacation at Winter Park, staying with her niece, Betty Kingsbury, who was then teaching ornithology at Rollins College and engaging in "tremendous hikes through swamps and sand looking up birds," as her Aunt May described it. This gave Ovington a chance to observe interracialism in the best of the South. She spoke to Professor France's class in economics, and Professor Clark's class in sociology, and found the students very liberal, outspoken, and stimulating in their questions.

Ovington then wended her way north, noting at a Methodist school that the students were "demure as little nuns." "One might be in the convent in Cradle Song for all the fun I can see that they get out of life," she thought, one of her steady concerns over the years. Certainly their food was no fun—"were I a millionaire I would get French chefs to teach cooking in Methodist schools," Ovington laughed.

She moved through North Carolina in a straight line, through Charlotte, High Point, Salisbury, Greensboro, Durham, Raleigh, before moving up to Virginia to Norfolk and Hampton. Palmer Memorial Institute in Sedalia, the little crossroads outside of Greensboro, was a special weekend visit with Charlotte Hawkins Brown. Ovington added fascination with the school to her previous captivation by Brown herself.[19] Spending time with Bethune and Brown led Ovington to conclude that "a courageous woman can do more with the white south than a courageous man."

She brought in two or three times her expenses, and had never before felt so good about bringing the NAACP to the people. But she was less encouraged, though much better informed, about progress in race relations, having spent time with both whites and Negroes. To the chairman of the Legal Committee, Arthur Spingarn, she said that she now believed she was mistaken "in thinking that the NAACP had overemphasized the individual case." In the South she saw that that was what they stood for, and without increased staff, that was about all they could do.

Her letters sound discouraged on the issue, but prescient about later decades.

The hardest thing to bear as one views things here is the cowardness [*sic*] of the white . . . , [who] gets the apple and the Negro the core. . . . I want the NAACP to be a voice, as always, crying in the wilderness, but

I don't see accomplishment in the deep South, except occasionally to defend life, and always to give publicity to things. But constructive work will have to originate down here.[20]

She saw clearly on this trip the incompatibility in the South of her larger and smaller loves: the labor movement and the NAACP. Doctors and undertakers who wanted to start a branch were most anxious not to get mixed up in labor disputes, and no one from the outside could come into a southern community and touch a labor subject.

The "NAACP Marching Song" (to be sung to the tune of "Marching through Georgia") appeared in the *Crisis* at the beginning of 1934 under the heading: "25 Years of the NAACP: Issued by the Anniversary Committee, William Pickens, Chairman; Mary White Ovington, Treasurer."

Twenty-five full years ago we started on our way,
Bound to give the colored man his place before the day—
Everybody knows that we are here and here to stay
  As we go marching together.
Hurrah! Hurrah! We'll shout the Jubilee!
Hurrah! Hurrah! For the NAACP!
East and West and North and South unite for victory
  As we go marching together.

As Ovington came back from her last marches through Georgia and Florida and Indiana and Ohio for the NAACP, approaching her seventieth year, her voice was still strong in celebration and dedication.

———————

IN THE SPRING and early summer of 1934, the board of directors of the NAACP became entangled in the issue raised by W. E. B. Du Bois's prosegregation editorial the previous February. They passed a resolution of "unyielding opposition to any and every form of enforced segregation," and President Joel Spingarn ordered a literal obedience with complete disassociation from black schools and colleges. Du Bois took another delighted swipe at the hornet's nest in May with a piece he called "Segregation and the Board of Directors." One reader reported nausea "to see Du Bois literally 'spank' the Association."

It is not hard to imagine Mary White Ovington going home from the May board meeting with a disappointed confirmation of thoughts coming out of her extensive travels. The board was not representative of either the problems or the possibilities she saw in the larger America of 1934.[21]

Du Bois resigned in the summer, and the way was cleared to move forward with a new burst of time and energy and money. The effect was immediate at the July board meeting. The Committee on Segregation was abolished and its duties merged with those of the Committee on Program.

The Budget Committee was able to recommend salary increases and the hiring of a mailing clerk in the final six months of 1934. Roy Wilkins was made managing editor of the *Crisis* until September, with extra compensation, and the magazine would have two hundred dollars per month from association funds during the transition months.[22]

Ovington initiated several of the actions that propelled the association forward, and saw opportunity in Du Bois's departure. Since the departure of James Weldon Johnson, Secretary Walter White had drawn Du Bois's fusillades, with Ovington in the crossfire. Now that White was in command, she was anxious that he be helped to do the best he was capable of. Ovington knew, she told Arthur Spingarn, that the executives were far from ideal. There was a lot of jealousy and secretiveness, she recognized, "two traits horribly common among Negroes and doubtless hangovers from slavery." She couldn't help but note that "there aren't many Jim Johnson's [*sic*] but his very freedom from his race's fault made him rather apart from his race."

Nevertheless, after the years of consideration showered on Du Bois, shouldn't they encourage White, she asked. She showed her support for the secretary:

> If we are to gauge men by their value to the community, I think for the past fifteen years White has been of a great deal more value to the community and to the race than Du Bois. And while we want to be grateful for what men did in the past, we have to judge their usefulness by what they do to-day.

White had pulled them through their financial difficulties because he was an "indefatigable worker, a worker who counts the cause he serves as his religion."

For four years, she had heard Du Bois praised over and over again and had seen his opinions treated with the utmost care, perhaps, she thought, because people were afraid of him. But now that Du Bois was out of the picture, she hoped that White would receive some encouragement. She had recently realized, seeing him at the annual conference, why he was so egotistical in his talk:

> He is a small, insignificant looking man, and with a poor delivery. I never yet have known a conspicuously short man who did not seem conceited. . . . I'm afraid they can't help it—they must learn it as boys when they have to stand up against bigger boys.

Ovington praised the efficient, self-effacing style of newcomer Roy Wilkins. He never gave the impression that he was doing anything much. Yet when she compared his work with that of his predecessors, who both were good at making themselves noticed, it seemed to her that such things as conference routine and publicity were taken care of as well as ever.

She put people into two work-style categories: those with "an immense amount of energy" who "give the impression" of accomplishment and those who worked "at a different pace," who "believe in loafing when they can and sometimes have a trying way of seeming to do nothing at all." Into the latter category she put Arthur Spingarn and Wilkins. Not being herself at all of that temperament, she laughed, "I of course, greatly admire it! We busy, energetic folk, always in people's way, can be a terrible nuisance."[23]

In a fitting conclusion to the Du Bois era of the NAACP, Oswald Garrison Villard, who had left in 1916 with a stubborn "him or me" stance, returned. "Du Bois and the failure of the directors to uphold me in my proper authority as chairman drove me out," he told Ovington (again) in July of 1934. As for Du Bois's departure, he could only say—and did say—"I told you so." Villard doubted Walter White's being "sufficiently big" to run the association.

Again, Ovington argued in support of the virtues of the secretary: "It has been very hard for him since the depression and Du Bois has made it infinitely harder." But, she added, "now we are rid of our octopus, for of late he has been draining our strength, I hope we shall do better work."[24]

On April 8, 1935, the NAACP board passed the following resolution:

The National Association for the Advancement of Colored People, founded twenty-six years ago, was visioned by Mary White Ovington, devoted friend of the Negro, and through all these years Miss Ovington has given, without stint and without thought of self, of her time, her strength and her means to the success of the organization.

The Board of Directors of the Association, with deep appreciation of all that she has meant to the cause of the Negro, greets Miss Ovington on her seventieth birthday and extends to her its best wishes for many more years of life and happiness.[25]

Ovington had planned to celebrate quietly with her "oldest friend," Corinne Bacon, in New Britain, Connecticut, while also speaking at nearby Hartford. But the day before she came down with a "bad eye" and had to delay her trip. Her ocular misfortune was fortunate, for otherwise she would have missed a wonderful day during which the apartment she now shared with her widowed sister-in-law, Elizabeth, at 12 East Ninety-seventh Street was filled with roses and jonquils and sweet peas and tulips—and telegrams.[26]

Greetings poured in from chapters around the country, and longtime associates added their congratulations. From Charles Edward Russell: "You have been, for many years, the most conspicuous and inspiring example of devotion, unselfish and unsparing, to a great cause." From Circuit Court Judge Ira Jayne in Detroit: she would not be living on borrowed time because she had "built up a surplus of many years of useful living" to draw on. From John Haynes Holmes at Community Church: "All the Negroes of this country should arise, and I hope will arise, to call you blessed. I count you in the great succession of the sainted abolitionists."

To Jane Addams, whose death would shock Ovington in just over a month, she responded: "These are such strange times compared with the nineties when I began my social settlement work. I feel sometimes that I hardly know how to live in it." But, she added, she wouldn't have missed it for anything, and her optimism continued. "I hope yours does," she concluded in what was the last correspondence between these two innovative, dedicated women.

Congratulations also came from other organizations, such as the YWCA: "Not only for Negroes but for all humankind your courage and your ideals shall go far in the great struggle for a better world." And good wishes came, too, in painfully handwritten letters from prisons, answered in kind: "I cannot find adequate words to express my profound appreciation of your excelling services render us. You have been permanently with the same activity from 1909. . . . I trust it will be proven to you that your interest in us have not been in vain."

Ovington issued a press statement of thanks through the NAACP. She compared herself to the hero of the Broadway play of the season *Rain from Heaven*. A polar explorer given a Fifth Avenue parade can only think of the absurdity of cheering him for doing what he most wanted to do. So with myself, Ovington wrote: "Why should I be cheered for doing what I most wanted to do, exploring among a people whose keen minds, fine artistic feeling, and wealth of affection has made my life richer than it could have been on any other road."[27]

On May 8, sister Helen's son Ted picked her up to motor to Riverbank. The people who had honored her on her seventieth birthday didn't realize the effect it would have on her, she joked with Richetta Randolph. "As long as they think I've done something worth while with my life, why now I am going to stop all work except just what I like." What she liked that summer was writing for young people once again, and the result was a manuscript of a Berkshire adventure story, "The Pokam River Mystery."

She replaced the tent that had been stolen the previous year. Summer melded into a cold but golden fall and her apple trees produced pies and a bit of extra cash. Her Pokam River manuscript was rejected by Knopf. She entertained the Johnsons for Sunday supper before they went back to the city for the winter. Mrs. Amy Spingarn came over from Troutbeck for a walk in the woods up the hill past the Delleas. The wife of her longtime friend Joel was very interesting, Ovington found, "when you get her alone."[28]

Even though Mary McLeod Bethune was to receive the Spingarn Medal, Ovington did not break the resolution she had made after the tiring 1934 Oklahoma trip not to attend the next annual convention in St. Louis. She wished that her place could be taken by some other white woman who would be entertained and enjoy things as she so often had. She definitely did not like the feeling that Mary White Ovington was unique.

Mid-October meant the city again, and a renewed interest in involvement. Would you like to have me help with branch work? she asked William Pickens. And to several NAACP staff and board members she sent her ideas about "the program of work" for 1936. "My effort is to consider the state of the finances as well as the many things we desire to do."

Ovington's suggestions have an elegant simplicity that cuts through hopeless campaigns and encourages forward-looking ones. The plans she promoted became the major thrust of the NAACP in the following decades. In the hopeless category she put "work that involves the support of Congress and the Executive," including an antilynching bill. "Let us," Ovington proposed, "in as dramatic a manner as possible and with all the publicity possible, call upon the South to get the legislation. Publicize those societies that have been with us, and ask them to go ahead."

Ovington's chosen thrusts for the NAACP program were in intertwined areas: education and legal defense. Publicize illiteracy and the breakdown of the schools in the South, she advised, the way lawlessness had been exposed in the antilynching campaign. In a positive way, take up the question of textbooks in New York and with the American Education Association. Consider working for a secretary of education in the cabinet. And start a legal defense fund the first of January, saving some money from the budget, raising money from lawyers and others.[29]

In December the treasurer reported two significant donations. James J. Ryan had given money for the Costigan-Wagner Anti-Lynching Bill, and the Joint Committee of the American Fund for Public Service had contributed ten thousand dollars plus five thousand for publicity for an education campaign. The largesse led her to suggest that Charles Houston, who had just been hired full-time as special counsel, begin raising money immediately for a legal defense fund.

Jack Greenberg, in his 1994 *Crusaders in the Courts,* credits Houston with the notion of a litigation campaign and with paving the way for the NAACP Legal Defense and Educational Fund, Incorporated, created March 20, 1940. (Thurgood Marshall, Houston's protégé, "sat down" in 1939 "and with his own hand wrote out the charter.") "Houston's most important conception may have been the step-by-step assault on segregation in education, which he began in the mid-1930s," claims Greenberg. But Ovington was there earlier, both in recommending and raising money for the fund and in pushing the organization toward its attack on unequal education.[30]

The NAACP, in its second quarter-century, and Mary White Ovington, in her eighth decade, were aging—and were still growing. There were always problems to be found in the United States, but now news from Germany, her favorite European country, once again challenged faith and hope and idealism. There was no rest, even for the elderly and the weary, and no stopping time's inexorable momentum.

Even as she read of Adolf Hitler's rise, even as she saw how much was yet to be done toward achieving racial equality in the United States, Mary White Ovington still believed that social ideals could accomplish things new and enduring. For a time new ideas might be "crushed by old fashioned tyrants," she concluded, "but I'm an incorrigible optimist and believe the tyrants can't last for very long."[31]

11

"Lift Ev'ry Voice and Sing"

THE TELEPHONE SPLIT the air like a rocket from the future tearing the past to jangling shreds. In the rough-walled cabin, it did not take May long to reach it. Tent caterpillars had denuded Berkshire County trees that early summer of 1938, and storms swelled the twisting streams over their banks and carried away soil in brown fury. But Sunday, June 26, had been quiet until the phone rang.

Mary White Ovington, age seventy-three, had driven earlier from her own Riverbank to James Weldon and Grace Johnson's Five Acres. They were returning from Maine, and Ollie Sims, Jim's nurse and all-around-helper, was outside in knickers picking up tangled sticks and refuse. "After a time nature will heal a good many cavities," Ovington had told Grace. "We are all looking forward to seeing you before long."

But the phone brought the news that in driving rain at a train crossing in Wicasset, Maine, James Weldon Johnson had been killed at age sixty-seven, and Grace, considerably younger, seriously injured.[1] Of all the deaths in Ovington's seven decades, James Weldon Johnson's was the most traumatic; she never recovered. He brought together the disparate pulses of her heart. A writer and administrator, a smooth and ever-sensitive mover between the black and white worlds, between the powerless and the powerful, Johnson was her ideal. She loved him.

A deep void replaced the Jim who came smiling around the corner while Grace parked the car, the Jim who sat under the evergreens on the river's bank reading Shakespeare aloud, and the Mr. Johnson who

275

strode jauntily down city streets and confidently onto a stage before hundreds. Two days after his death Ovington hoped to get a message to Grace. She wrote:

> Please give her my dear, dear love. She is very precious to me, and however terrible the present she has had the expressible happiness of living with one of the finest, clearest minded and most loveable men in the world. You see, I feel that he is in the world. He has left an imprint that cannot die.[2]

The next year moved rapidly, as external time is wont to do as the internal clock ticks more slowly. Ovington tried to revive Grace's energies, traveling to visit her in the hospital and writing newsy letters. She raved about Ethel Waters's debut as a tragedian in *Mamba's Daughters,* telling Grace she would have to see it.[3]

Ovington kept busy with work, too. As NAACP treasurer, she sought money and authorized its spending. She was on the Committee for Administration, which was in effect the executive committee, and the Crisis Committee. She bombarded Secretary Walter White, Assistant Secretary Roy Wilkins, and legal counsel Charles Houston with ideas for changes and activities—about building an integrated concert hall in Washington, D.C., after Marian Anderson was denied access to Constitution Hall, about a Negro Building at the New York World's Fair; about having several NAACP branches in the larger cities, with more chance for more people to be involved.

By 1939 Ovington was struggling with that stubborn, unpredictable, uncontrollable beast, age. She commiserated with Grace over the "wearisome task of disposing of extra possessions." Cleaning closets she found "one just has to be hard hearted," but she admitted was "not quite equal to it."

A checkup at Roosevelt Hospital found her blood pressure at an alarming 240/130, but a month of "cabbage-life existence" at Riverbank brought it down by 70 degrees.[4] She had not had great concerns about sickness since her bout of typhoid fever in 1903—just the normal flu and colds when she became exhausted. But now her health had grown precarious. She counted the years she might have left, and wondered what she might hope to accomplish.

In July she saw that Riverbank, too, was a possession that would have to go. Travel there had become too difficult, and the upkeep expenses too much of a drain on her pocketbook. Highway 71 had been widened so that its paved edge was only two feet from her outside wall, but the grounds were prettier than ever. There wasn't a lot of river property available, so she thought she might do well with the sale price.

The buyer was a stranger who did not keep it long. Violet Heming, an English actress, planted hundreds of daffodils in the grass and irritated the neighboring farmers by regarding their fields as open to her wandering, while her own space off limits to their children—a real "humdinger" of a neighbor when compared with "Miss Ovington." Ovington got only six hundred dollars in 1940 for a property that fifty years later would be assessed at over sixty-five thousand dollars when Alford Township, following the rest of Berkshire County, became fodder for summer residents rather than cows. The Dellea farm where Charles Ovington helped milk and hay, where Mary Ovington visited the baby on the porch, would sell in pieces for a million dollars.

There were not a lot of things to move besides books; she had never done much cooking there, though she had introduced the young Catharine Dellea to chocolate mousse. But usually when neighbors and friends came, it had been "pot luck." But books overflowed space and time. Frank Santoni trundled to the Delleas with a wheelbarrow full.

Disposing of possessions is one of the most difficult things we have to do, Ovington mused.[5]

AS OVINGTON CULLED her possessions and withdrew from physical involvement with the NAACP offices and from travel for the organization, she intensified her thinking and debating about its history, its accomplishments, and its goals. She wrote long letters to lawyer Arthur Spingarn, and to Secretary White and Assistant Secretary Wilkins.

She thought the NAACP's problem by 1940 was confusion about its role. "We are faced with the fact the [*sic*] we want to do practical things and yet are impossibleists," she wrote Spingarn, adopting the term that had been applied to socialist purists who refused political compromise. In middle age she had forgone chunks of the "impossibleist" ideals she espoused—socialism, feminism, pacifism—to attempt what in 1909

Charles K. Ovington, Mary White Ovington's brother, in his later years. Photograph by Alice Boughton. (By permission of Archives of Labor and Urban Affairs, Wayne State University)

Elizabeth Graham Ovington (Mrs. C. K. Ovington), Mary White Ovington's sister-in-law, around 1905, with whom she lived after her brother's death. (Courtesy of Joan Callin Foster)

Elizabeth Kingsbury Friedmann,
"Betty," Mary White Ovington's niece.
(Courtesy of Elizabeth Kingsbury
Friedmann)

Carrie Overton, secretary and close
friend to Mary White Ovington in her
late years. (By permission of Archives of
Labor and Urban Affairs, Wayne State
University)

had seemed achievable: extend the protections of the country's Declaration of Independence and Constitution to its black citizens.

Having sunk thirty years into that practical goal only to discover that large pieces of it, too, were seemingly impossible, she did not try to justify her decisions by exaggerating the role of the "possibleist" or vilifying that of the "impossibleist." She recognized the need for both. "We are an association a generation old," she wrote.

> Our first days, as with all organizations formed to right human wrong, were our easiest. Like the Abolitionists our effort was to rouse the people to a sense of the iniquities practiced againt [*sic*] the Negroes. We set forth facts and Du Bois's editorials [in the *Crisis*] were bitter and soul-stirring. Fortunately we had legal work as well as propaganda.
>
> Your brother [Joel Spingarn] used to like to call our movement the "new abolition," and I think it is not a bad parallel. The Liberator [William Lloyd Garrison's abolitionist newspaper] showed the horrible, the detestable character of slavery and the abolitionists continued to the end to decry any comprimise [*sic*] with slavery and call the constitution a covenant with death and an agreement with hell. They consistently used propaganda and only propaganda to the end. Others wanted to do something, went into politics, started the free soil party, that went into the republican party, and with each move came more and more compromise. Revolution came in the end but not without an attempt to prevent it. The only thoroughly consistent people were Garrison and Phillips and their followers. . . .
>
> There is no right or wrong in this matter. You cannot truthfully say that Garrison was right and Lincoln wrong, it is a matter of judgment. History seems to show that both types of people are needed.

Idealism and realism were both needed, but an organization had a hard time aspiring to both. Isn't it true, she asked Arthur Spingarn, that you can't be at the same time the Abolition Society and the Republican Party?[6]

Ovington repeatedly came down on the "possibleist" side. Something was better than nothing when it was clearly impossible to get all of what one wanted. Shouldn't the NAACP "carefully consider what work we can embark upon with some hope of success and what in all probability is doomed to failure"?

They had begun antilynching work in 1910 and thirty years later were still at it. "If our next piece of work is to take thirty years more of our best strength surely we ought to consider it and not find ourselves in it without our knowing how our entrance happened." Throughout the 1930s the NAACP had "made out elaborate programs," particularly in economic areas—here she refers to studies done under the dual pressures of the Great Depression, which of course hit black America with particular vehemence, and the increasing co-opting of NAACP legal and moral battles by the Communist Party. But their studies had been "so comprehensive that they have never been referred to after adoption."

Ovington's suggestion was "practical." "Let the Board now see what work it is already committed to, and then, if there is money and time for anything lese [*sic*] decide what that shall be, allot money and time, and put it through."

During World War I Ovington the integrationist and pacifist had had to admit that the segregated training supported and promoted by the board chairman, Joel Spingarn, and the war participation promoted by W. E. B. Du Bois, no matter how abhorrent in principle, had practical value for black advancement. During World War II she adopted that compromise again, against Walter White's doctrinaire opposition to any segregation. She said to him:

> I think that carrying the fight against discrimination into the field of education, in this case education of the soldier and his officers, and preventing that education's proceeding as fast as possible is a tragic thing for the black man. What he needs is power, and fighting in this war will give him more power and a greater sense of power than staying at unskilled, uneducative tasks at home, or attached as a laborer to the army. . . . It isn't the intellectuals who will win the battle for the oppressed, whether black of [*sic*] white. They don't think in terms of reality when they come up against prejudiced stupid men. They think in terms of dogma.

Her main interest was in legal work, she told White, where propaganda was found wanting.

> In legal work we have to meet men and work hard to convince them. It doesn't do to say to the court "Negroes should not be discriminated against. They should have the same salary, when teachers, as white teachers have." Lawyers have to do a lot more than that and often accept compromises. Mind meets mind in a law court.[7]

Even after she had ceased to do direct battle with Secretary Walter White on the issues, she continued discussion of the segregation issue with Roy Wilkins:

> I who have found that I am a dialectic materialist, believing in no absolute truths and that man's progress, when he makes any, is not the result of slogans but of work, still wonder whether each issue that comes would not be carefully studied and decided not on the merits of publicity, but, shall we say, on the merits of the greatest good to the greatest number.
>
> I would oppose turning down a fine technical school, let us say, that the government might open for Negroes in the South on the grounds that it is segregated. But we have done just that in the great schools of the army. The Negro needs power and he doesn't get all the power he should in this war through military training.[8]

An interesting example of Ovington's practical action had appeared in the mid-1930s. Her last official communications with James Weldon Johnson were about education: she chaired and wrote the report of the NAACP Committee on Textbooks and Current Literature. She had received Johnson's response—"the whole thing constitutes a big job, but I believe that with correct data at hand we can make some headway"—just two months before his sudden death.[9]

The "Report of Miss Ovington on Textbook investigation by Mr. Reddick" that she sent to Johnson on April 11, 1938, was a fascinating precursor of revisions in the study and teaching of American history usually credited to the advent of Black Studies on university campuses in the late 1960s and 1970s. In some textbooks, Ovington and L. D. Reddick, the paid investigator, found, slavery was treated "in a manner fairly favorable to the Negro," but "Reconstruction is distinctly southern in its bias," with justification of the Black Codes, depictions of northerners as scalawags and carpetbaggers, attacks on the Freedmen's Bureau, and statements that "almost justified" the Ku Klux Klan.

About one high school text Ovington said:

> It is surprising to discover the way in which the author, who seemed reasonably fair in the discussion in social and economic questions, apparently follows the traditional treatment—pro-southern—in dealing with politics of the slavery and Reconstruction periods.

Another book, while it did not display any "considerable anti-Negro bias" had "simply absorbed a great number of stereotype mental patterns current in American writing," including clinging to "an old-fashioned Booker T. Washington-is-the-greatest-Negro conception."

Much of Ovington's report was directed at how to remedy sins of commission and omission. Publishers could be pressured. "Slight changes might be quite possible," for example, describing what Matt Henson actually did when he accompanied Peary to the North Pole, instead of calling him a "faithful colored servant." "Those who have read Henson's life know that he was an experienced explorer," she wrote. Esteban, or "Little Steven," could be mentioned among the explorers. If the Boston Massacre was mentioned, then Crispus Attucks's name should be given. The part the Negro played in the Civil War needed to be included.

More difficult were the overall attitudes about American history. She thought the big problem was that both the South and the North were "interested apparently in sliding over the slavery question." They did

> not mention the slave ship or the riches that came to the North because of this trade. The most offensive part of the treatment of slavery in most of the books is the representation of the Negro as happy and contented, laughing while at work. This I would think would have a bad effect on the white children and would be mortifying to the colored children. It might be possible to have this omitted.
>
> When we come to Reconstruction, we have a much more difficult task. The textbooks reflect the history of today and today's history is written in favor of the South. We have, however, Du Bois' volume [*Black Reconstruction*] which can and should be used.

Ovington included suggested subjects for Ph.D. dissertations that she had solicited from Arthur Spingarn, many of which have since been done, with results filtering into textbooks. She added, "I myself would like to suggest a study of the populist movement in the South and its relation to the Negro." It is safe to say that, had Mary White Ovington had the chance to complete a degree and thesis, this would have been her topic.

As a special student at Harvard Annex, she had discovered that formal education failed to deal meaningfully with present problems. At the height of populism, nary a word was spoken of it. And only the top of history's heap was studied; books on the Peasant's Revolt said not a word from the point of view of the peasant. In a dissertation on "the populist movement in the South and its relation to the Negro," she would have looked freshly on history from both angles.[10]

As OVINGTON MULLED over history and goals, she was working her way toward her final published work, her autobiographical history of the NAACP, *The Walls Came Tumbling Down*. She still needed to earn an income through her writing, but she continued to feel that a straight autobiography would be self-indulgent and not very interesting. For twenty years she had come to the same conclusion: "If someone could convince me that it was really worthwhile I should undertake it. But it is hard to know what is most worthwhile, isn't it?"

But the need for historical tracers had increased—no one knew that better than the chairman of the Textbook Committee—and she was particularly suited to provide them in regard to the NAACP, its historical context, and all it had attempted and stood for. Later she would write plaintively to Walter White, "You are *making* history and I am only *recording* it, but I want to finish my job before it finishes me." The transition was not a simple one. Age made it a necessary one.[11]

Little by little, letter by letter, Mary White Ovington inched toward re-creating her life. After Riverbank was sold, she spent two summers at Two Lights, in Cape Elizabeth, Maine, boarding with the H. E. Maxwell family. It was beautiful by the eastern sea in June of 1942, but she envied Richetta Randolph and the others who were in Los Angeles for the annual conference. And this second world war in her lifetime was never far from her thoughts. "At times the house shakes from the Portland guns and bombers fly over us."

Back in New York City, the winter hit her with two bad sessions of grippe, she moved out of her NAACP office, and decided not to go to the annual conference in Detroit. She also tried to sell some stories. The following summer, her sister Helen said she would stay with Elizabeth in New York for six months so that May could go to a warmer climate the following winter. From Maine at the Maxwell's, she began trying to find a place.

Hotel prices had doubled in Florida, and Ray Stannard Baker in Winter Park knew of nothing. The southern schools she had so often visited were overrun with soldiers. Finally, Mrs. Thomas Elsa Jones found that Fisk would not be feeding soldiers, only housing them, so that there would be room for Ovington at the Fisk University Inn.[12]

While she planned for a trip to Nashville, news reached her of the August 1943 Harlem riots, and again she felt the irony of American violence. As she wrote to Wilkins,

> riots are terrible things but they certainly supply publicity. . . . The Treasurer hears of so much money to-day that it seems incredible, and like all people who have had little seems impossible to last. But I feel sure we shall never be unknown again. Splendid publicity and circumstance have made us of deep national significance.

Nevertheless, she cautioned frugality.[13]

Mary White Ovington began the project of an autobiographical history of the NAACP with enthusiasm and energy in the fall of 1943, even distributing a questionnaire to the staff—when had they first heard of the organization? seen the *Crisis*? was there a branch in their hometowns? what was the most important thing the group had done? hadn't done?

She arranged her travel to Nashville; as long as she didn't have to change trains, she didn't care how long it took to get there. She went with her trunk to the Joneses for a few days, and from there to a large three-windowed room with an adjoining bath (which she would share with "an occasional transient female") at Fisk University Inn, 1002 Seventeenth Avenue North.

At the university Christmas party, Arthur Croley, the organist at Fisk, invited her to have meals at his home while his housemate, David Stone, was away. She had a delightful time, for Croley had a "grand cook"—"a little inclined to grease but on the whole, excellent." Stone returned and she planned for Jubilee Hall, only to receive a call from him inviting her to continue to eat with the two of them. "Wasn't it nice of them?" she wrote Grace Johnson. "I am regularly in the family and we divide expenses."

The soft coal that fueled Nashville winters in 1943 was an unending source of fine dust and conversation. One tasted coal, one had to scrub hands and face hard to get it off, and Ovington's snowy white hair became clouded with it. But as long as she felt good, even there May Ovington found a bright side. "It's so full of soft coal that the air is weighted down with soot," she told Arthur Spingarn—"and gives us grand sunsets."[14]

Socializing energized her, as did the inevitable invitations to speak. She opened the Nashville NAACP membership drive in November ("It seemed to me that I closed it, for they did not introduce me until quarter to ten," she joked). In January, at Fisk Chapel, she tailored her speech to students who were very practical, making her appeal from what was for her a "new angle, the selfish one." Why should they join the NAACP? What would it do for them? She asked for Wilkins's ideas, which he sent in a telegram. She discovered and heartily approved the new generation's approach to civil rights, writing Richetta Randolph of the "efforts . . . on the part of a few young people toward interracial cooperation. The older people, except for a few exceptions, try to crush anything of this sort."

Most important, from October to February, her writing of the book progressed. Congestion in the wartime mails gave her an excuse not to send so many Christmas cards—she wrote only to those she never heard from otherwise—and that gave her more writing time. "This is certainly my swan song and I only hope it wont prove a cackle," she told Wilkins. In upbeat letters she asked office staff for copies of her "Book Chats" from the 1920s; her Christmas story of the teens; her recruitment play, *The Awakening;* the leaflet she and Martha Gruening had done of the Reconstruction South Carolina legislature's acts unjustly ridiculed by D. W. Griffith's 1915 movie, *Birth of a Nation;* and *all* the branch reports—"not just the high lights but each little place in the union." "I want to show a picture of vigilance," she told secretary Lucille Black, "first in New York and Washington . . . and then all over the nation. It might be very impressive."

The writing jogged her memory in evocative, unpredictable ways. The 1919 annual conference, for example, she remembered "as wonderful but I don't remember details":

I remember an awful thunderstorm—a dramatic story but I think that was Detroit. There was the man who used to bring his little son. I think that conference was as earnest a one as we ever had. I do remember Archibald Grimke. Were we singing "Lift every voice and sing" by that time?

Richetta Randolph, who had also been there with the NAACP from the beginning, was indispensable. The previous year, Ovington had organized a testimonial for Randolph's thirtieth year of service. Randolph had in that time missed work only three times, those for sickness and death in her family, and had reported on every annual conference but one. "My dear, you don't mind writing my book, do you?" Ovington asked her, and then joked that "you've done beautifully so far." Randolph graciously responded, "Just because you—the only living person living who can do so—are doing this History of the NAACP, I want to do all I can to help."[15]

Arna Bontemps had come to Fisk with his wife and five children to take up his long-term position as librarian. He was a godsend of a reference source. More important, he liked her manuscript. There were long months beginning in February 1944, when that alone sustained her.

For then, the body that had cooperated to get her to Nashville and to within a month of her seventy-ninth birthday rebelled. It first opened its doors to a nasty flu virus. March came, and she was temporarily better, and enjoyed the return of spring. Then, large portions of her eyesight began to disappear; she could not read or write, though she could hear the cardinals and the mockingbirds.

Judge Bill Hastie was in Nashville and stopped to see her—the NAACP staff was worried. Visitors and doctors kept asking her if she had suffered any loss of speech and the repeated question haunted her with the thought that she might want to say something about her book and would not be able to. But seeing Bill Hastie was "almost as nice as Jim Johnson would have been." She would not remember it, but she was taken to the hospital in Nashville with her blood pressure at 220; blood clots blocked her vision.

When her eyesight returned a little, she managed to send the partially finished manuscript to Arthur Spingarn to read and to Carrie Overton to type; she wanted it passed on to an agent suggested by Bontemps. Once she got back to Maine for the summer, she hoped she would have strength enough to finish it.

She clung to Arthur Spingarn's kind, helpful letters. "It is this loss of strength that makes me throw myself upon you and the NAACP."

Nashville was "jolly," but she was looking forward to getting back to New York City; she would be there early Wednesday April 19.[16]

Ovington was very ill when she arrived. The suggested agent did not take her manuscript, but, she wrote Spingarn shakily in early May, she would have been more disappointed "had I not known that I cannot possibly finish it." She had been in a bad state since she came home. "I tried to tell Mr. White that I need the NAACP, but I doubt if he understood. . . . I need the sense of not being so terribly aone [*sic*]. I don't believe I've ever had to do anything really hard and I have not much courage." As for her partial manuscript, "Meet the Negro," she thought that it might be of value as a record and that the NAACP should keep it.[17]

There is no writing by Mary White Ovington from June to October 1944, and no entries in her otherwise meticulous expense journals. Her sister-in-law took over her affairs and told the inquiring that Ovington was "very ill . . . with cerebral hemorrhages."

Sometimes depressed, sometimes nervous and excited, she was taken to the Institute for Living in Hartford, Connecticut, on August 20, where she was given shock treatments. She was not aware of William Pickens, worried why he hadn't heard from her, nor of Walter White telling her about the best annual conference ever, with 25,000 to 40,000 people at Washington Park on July 16.

By early October, there was slight improvement, but doctors did not predict recovery. And then, unbelievably, by November 1 Ovington was giving her own version of events. "How do you do? Wouldn't I like to be at the November Board meeting?" she scrawled to Spingarn, Dr. Louis Wright (now chairman of the board), White, and Wilkins. She had been "unlucky," what with strokes, loss of sight, shock treatments, and recently a fall and broken wrist. But now, "I am very much better, my wrist will be out of its bandage in a few days, my mind is quite clear, and I have a prodigious appetite. As to my eyes, the less said about them the better."

Her young physician ("a Mexican, whose soulful eyes must have wrought havoc with the Mexican ladies") suggested that she try to get in writing "an idea of the cooperation I can expect from the NAACP on my new book." Had they heard about it? she asked. Arna Bontemps liked it. Could she maybe get stenographic help and someone to read to her? Could it be pushed in NAACP publicity, and sold through NAACP agents? It might not add to her prestige as an author, but "it should add to the contents of my pocketbook. A comparatively helpless old age will need money which I must earn by my books. And if I make my fortune, I will also be adding to the noble balance now in our treasury."

She was sending her scrawled letter to Randolph to type, with a note that her recipients should "consider the signature as really mine, and know that as always my heart is in our work which has progressed so gloriously since its humble beginning thirty-five years ago." And just then Elizabeth called with the news that the NAACP board had voted her a two-hundred-dollar-per-month stipend, retroactive to June; a check for eight hundred dollars was on its way. Ovington was blank. Should she have known this? she asked. "But how wonderful of the Board to do such a thing! I cannot thank them enough."

She had thought she would be out in early November. "When I do return I hope to serve the Association," she told White midmonth. Her loss of memory, though mostly pleasant, made her wonder if she owed that money. It was her "great hope" that she would be able to pay it back from royalties.

Looking at a blanket of fresh snow, she composed a holiday greeting:

Old age comes and knocks me on the head,
Blackens my eyes and plugs up my ears,
Yet he isn't so bad as he at first appears;
He counsels indolence, and slyly says:
"Let your friends take the buses and the subway trains,
You stay at home while it snows and it rains.
Send them calendars, let each choose a date,
(Evening preferred) so they come at any rate."
Though youth lie dying and weary age thrive,
Here's to ageless friendship in 1945.

But soulful-eyed Dr. Gardo said no way could she send out blanket invitations, nor could she leave for at least another month.

But that didn't faze her. She kept the cards for the next year, writing on the back:

The doctors saw this card and said: "No go:
New York and you at present may not mix."
This might be true in '45, I know

But isn't true in 1946.
So I'll be home at any time you fix.[18]

The eighty-year-old Mary White Ovington bounced back to finish her book before it finished her. She put "the writing first *and last*" (her emphasis). "Evidently I was so ill—I remember nothing of it—that it takes some time for me to get back all my strength," she told Grace Johnson.

The past jogged current action, too. On a peppy day, she told Walter White that she wanted to create a restaurant near association headquarters. And when Roy Wilkins had a breakdown, she helped locate a rest home in the Berkshires.

It was a strange sensation, being captured by the past while the work went on without her. Her body seemed trapped in worry and caution while her mind raced. "I know how busy you must be and how thrillingly interesting the NAACP is today," she wrote Wilkins. "The end is in the clouds with all other great social problems, but we've gone a good piece of way on the earth."

It was impossible getting the younger men at the NAACP to understand what she needed. She required so much help with reading. Cheap yellow wartime paper hurt her eyes. Hadn't the board promised assistance? "Is it not legitimate to put this work of mine not as something to be given help at odd minutes . . . but as something to be provided for as promised and without question?" she asked President Arthur Spingarn. Her doctor told her not to get excited—"what a bore, looking out for one's health"—"so I'll end by saying I know everything will be all right. How can I think otherwise after all the Asscn has done for me?"[19]

It was a time of difficult dealings with three old NAACP stalwarts. Richetta Randolph had retired to half-time on January 1, 1945, and spent one day a week on her own time helping with the book. Ovington repeatedly offered to pay her, while Wilkins and Spingarn insisted that the NAACP cover the twenty-five dollars per month. But Secretary White saw a chance to pay back Ovington for slapping his fiscal hand over the years, and disapproved what he called Randolph's "increase in salary." "You've socked the oldest employee and the oldest member of the association in the jaw," Ovington told him, in some of the strongest language she ever used. "Well," she went on, when I was in the dentist chair this spring my doctor—who is a grand person and knows all about us—said when he understood my present physical handicaps: "Well, hold up your chin, so they can sock it." I shall hold it up hoping that some time you may feel a little interest in what I am doing.

White brought the matter to the board in July, claiming he was simply "obeying the explicit mandate of the Board." After the board approved the expenditure, Randolph, also smarting in the jaw, refused to be considered for the work, and on August 1, resigned completely from NAACP employ and was voted fifty dollars per month for three years. Ovington was saddened by the mode and finality of Randolph's departure. "I hate, hate to think of the NAACP without you in it." "I won't talk about it. There is little to take me there now." Randolph was the strongest link to the core of her life. "You won't forget me I know," Ovington told her.

Ovington shared with Randolph how difficult everything was in the fast-moving crowds. In May, she took a sentimental journey to Great Barrington and had a very hard time. She waited twenty-five minutes for a taxi, for there was no doorman at her building. She stood fifteen minutes at Penn Station before an elderly redcap took her bags. In July, for the much longer trip to Maine, she had to plan not only how to get to the station with her trunk, but needed a "strong arm" to help with her small suitcase on her overnight in Boston. "I am an experienced traveller, but these days are like nothing I ever knew before," she admitted.

Safely ensconced in her deck chair on the Maxwells' sunny porch, she wrote better, even though worrisome news came from New York. Elizabeth Ovington spent a month in Presbyterian Hospital with life-threatening pneumonia and had to be nursed around the clock back at their apartment. May Ovington was not immediately informed, and their doctors agreed that she could not return until the nurses were gone. "I am of no use now, on emergency," she lamented.[20]

Du Bois's renewed relationship with the NAACP was an unwelcome reminder of the tangles in which his ego had embroiled them before he left in 1934. The "blunt truth" about his return, White said later, was that "he was offered a job by the Association because we did not want to see him at 75 years of age without financial security"; that they had paid him a salary, supplied a research assistant and other help totaling ten thousand dollars a year; and that he had been left free to "come and go as he pleases, to write books and articles and to fill private lecture engagements."

A decade away had not changed Du Bois, from the perspective of the NAACP officials. He signed himself, unauthorized, as the "Director of Research." He demanded more office space. He made political statements supporting Henry Wallace in his own voice while being identified with the NAACP. He leaked internal NAACP matters to the newspapers. And he formed an Emergency Committee for W. E. B. Du Bois and the NAACP with signatures from all over the country and press releases full of one-sided "reports"—after the board in September released him for his "refusal to work as a staff member and observe routine organizational procedure."[21]

These years did see a touching rapprochement between the two founders, however. Ovington initiated it. In April of 1945 she invited Du Bois to dinner with Thurgood Marshall and Albert Kennedy of the National Federation of Settlements. Du Bois had told her that he would like to read her manuscript, and she wanted him to know he could get the carbon from Arthur Spingarn. She would appreciate his opinion on whether she was in the story too much, she told him. Shirley Graham (Du Bois's future wife) had said Ovington wasn't there enough. Only able to work three hours a day herself, Ovington marveled at what a lot of work Du Bois was able to do.

In May of 1946, Du Bois and his first wife, Nina, who lived in Baltimore, celebrated their fiftieth wedding anniversary. Ovington wrote:

> I remember when I first met you both at Atlanta. The University was new to me then and I felt strange. You told me to come to your rooms whenever I wished and if you were not there to stay and enjoy the library. I appreciated the invitation and took advantage of it. One must think with affection of the past, but I believe the granddaughter, Du Bois, will find a kinder world than ours was, though for everything we get we lose something. Secure in the past, may the golden wedding day be bright in the immediate present.
>
> With affection, Mary White Ovington.

Her assessment of Du Bois in *The Walls Came Tumbling Down* was more complimentary than the sketch in *Portraits in Color* in 1927. She concluded by quoting from his "Credo," which had given her heart such a leap in the first decade of the century. Despite their difficulties and falling out during Ovington's years as chairman of the board, on balance the forty-year relationship of Mary White Ovington and W. E. B. Du Bois was amazingly supportive and productive.[22] They both had problems with the NAACP in their late years. But, from a larger perspective, these two were the NAACP.

———

IN EARLY 1946, Mary White Ovington wrote to Walter White: "Everything I do grows increasingly difficult for me and I have to be very methodical about the few things I do. I try to go to the bank once a month. Sometimes my check comes in the middle of the month, sometimes at the end." She hated to fuss, but could her NAACP honorarium be sent always at the same time?

Able to work only three, and then two, hours a day, she was sustained by public and private love and encouragement. Praise that she would be too ill to appreciate after publication in 1947, and which would be nearly absent at her death in 1951, came in 1945 and 1946.

In May of 1945, the month after her eightieth birthday, radio station WFIL in Philadelphia broadcast "America's Other Voice," based on her life.

"How goes it, America?" the program began. America's first answer is full of postwar pride and praise. "We showed 'em" in Europe, didn't we?" . . . We're the greatest country on the face of this earth . . . the strongest, the richest, the wisest, the most understanding, the very best."

Then the voice of conscience filters through: "Come clean now. Be honest with yourself. . . . What do your people say?" In answer, we visit a southern voting booth: "You heard what the white man said . . . move along there. There's no votin' here for black men." We learn of public schools: 41 percent of Negroes with less than a fifth-grade education; only 5.7 percent completing high school; 1.2 percent finishing college.

And then we learn of Ovington. "Ain't you the Miss Ovington that's the daughter of the big department store Ovingtons uptown?" asks a slum tenement agent. "Movin' in here with 'em to live. . . . Well, that just ain't done," she is told; "because, mam, these people in this whole block a' tumble-down tenements is Negroes . . . that's what."

> That is why I've come here, sir. The Negroes of this city are subject to the worst indignities of any group . . . and just because no one else sees fit to do anything about it is no reason why I won't. I'm going to move right in with them . . . and become familiar with their problems first hand!!

She walks into the office of publisher Oswald Garrison Villard. "Let's get as many humane leaders of the nation together as we can. . . . Then after we get it established among the white leaders of America, invite the colored leaders . . . all over the country" to join, and to set up branches.

"I felt good on that day thirty-six years ago," America's conscience reports, "when the first mass meeting of the NAACP was held in New York City. It was a good beginning."

And now it was time to do more. The play ends with the ironies of Negro Marines abroad, race riots, and discrimination at home in 1945.

The radio sketch gave a lively substance to a revealing abstraction: the life of Mary White Ovington as the "other voice" of America's conscience, the unflagging prod to make actions support words, to make the spirit of the Constitution as real as its letter.

In July of the following year, Henry Winfield Wheeler wrote of "The Guardian Angel of the NAACP" in his "The Spider's Web" column in the *St. Louis American*, asking the organization to declare a "Mary White Ovington Day" or establish a monument to a woman "who has done more to make America The Land Of The Free And The Home Of The Brave than any other living soul." "Blessed be the name of Mary White Ovington, originator and first member of the National Association for the Advancement of Colored People," he wrote.[23]

Ovington particularly appreciated young people's responses to her writing. *Portraits in Color* continued to inspire those who discovered it. In May of 1946, for example, she received a whole bundle of letters from the eighth graders at Howard Kennedy School, Omaha, Nebraska, and the following year the NAACP received a contribution in honor of a Toledo, Ohio, public school music supervisor whose interest in Negro children had been inspired by these biographies.[24]

Probably private communications gave her the greatest sustenance. Her friendships knew no limits of gender or race or class or age. Even as her abilities to communicate were constrained, she kept in touch.

From Angola, Portuguese West Africa, Beth Torrey sent her usual "big hug and kiss" and pages and pages of news. From Fisk University, Arthur Croley told of musical events and their mutual acquaintances. He and David Stone "got quite a kick out of proof reading" the parts of the book she had written there. Mrs. Maxwell in Maine wrote of family and hoped Ovington would return to her steamer chair, to dinners of crab and lobster and fresh beans from the garden, games of rummy and rides in the countryside. And from the village of Alford, poet Rosemary Ferrar discussed local events and mutual friends, as well as her latest reading and writing.[25]

No correspondence could have been accomplished without the lively young secretary, Carrie Overton. After Richetta Randolph's departure from NAACP employ, Walter White first sent Julia Baxter to help Ovington edit. Overton came with her to handle dictation and typing. By the end of 1946, Overton kept the book on track while also doing personal correspondence. She checked out facts and statistics. She typed and retyped.

Carrie Overton sometimes climbed to the apartment on Ninety-seventh Street just to read to the two elderly women. Mary would pour a fragrant Earl Grey tea from her place on a plush olive green velvet divan. Often the young woman was invited for dinner—usually roast duck, her favorite. Katina, the maid, lit candles in fine silver candlesticks from Ovington's Fifth Avenue and an Italian pewter oil lamp near the divan, turned off the lights, and slipped back in the shadows as Mary stood at the head of the table to carve. Conversations were always enlightening—about the latest art exhibit, books, and music.

With the book out of her hands by October, she wondered what kind of audience it might attract. She reflected that white readers would likely prefer "the Negro's own story." Nor did she anticipate its appealing to the Negro intelligentsia. The NAACP workers on the hustings were her real audience: "Mrs. Jones of Muskegee, Mrs. Smith of Keokuk. . . . There I have some publicity and there the style of writing, semi-biographical, will be liked." It was a group that had, she felt, "rarely been reached, but it should be reached."[26]

Just before Christmas 1946, she received Robert Giroux's letter from Harcourt Brace, accepting her book for publication. Writing with this news to all who had helped her, after turning her bedroom over to visiting niece Louise Callin, and struggling to send out Christmas cards and gifts of books and calendars, sleds and mufflers, she was hit by dizziness that left her shaky and took away a big chunk of sight. She tried to see brightness—"I should compare it with those who have none and then be thankful!" The next year would see her book in print, but her only celebration was in trying to recoup her energy.[27]

With the book finished, Mary White Ovington returned in mind and spirit to her early love, the workers of the world. From 1904 on, she had concentrated on equal rights for blacks, so that they, too, might join the cause of universal brotherhood and sisterhood. The years and decades flew, and though there was progress, full racial equality eluded America. After she completed the book that was her final effort in that cause, she scrawled pages upon pages that reveal her shift toward larger issues.

Contributions and letters also show the breadth of her late concerns. She supported Indusco, the American Committee in Aid of Chinese Industrial Cooperatives, and warned of the danger to wildlife of atomic experiments in the Pacific. With the Unitarian Community Church she shared money and time. With its radical minister, John Haynes Holmes, she debated issues of race and class, and political and social philosophy.

She believed ethics was relative just as physics was, she told Holmes:

Nothing is right to-day, yesterday and forever, at all times and places, and . . . many of the truisms that we have accepted as wellnight [*sic*] divine are only very human conclusions that are relative to the time in which they were made, and to the status of the people who made them.

Humans often carried good ideas too far, Ovington thought. The Reformation, for example, had positively freed the individual, but once overemphasized, individualism had encouraged nationalism, the cause of many wars.

She was not religious in the usual sense, she told her minister. She did not believe in "a power not ourselves that makes for righteousness," because history had shown that appeal to higher human nature did not prevent fighting. "The Christian life can't be felt out, it's got to thought out and in terms of man's animal background as well as in terms of his advancement beyond the animal."

She believed that we are on the earth to better it before we leave, that we are not divine, but human, that we can never achieve Utopia and the sooner we realize it the better, and that there is no absolute good. She once wrote:

For everything we get we lose something, and . . . the physical conditions under which men live, wealth or poverty, make different sets of values. . . . Those who live in security except they have amazing imaginations, never understand the values of those who live in insecurity. . . . The animal, man, has two intense urges, sex and acquisitiveness. . . . The only hope that men can ever cease to war upon one another, cease to strive to get something away from someone else is in a reasoned, intelligent form of society. That form seems to me communism.

Finally, in a manifesto that comes close to that demanded of the "haves" in her 1915 poem "Revolution," Ovington declared: "I am profoundly a communist though I know a communist state would destroy the basis of the civilization under which I live and under which I have had an unusually happy life." She would like to debate this with "some liberal Christian," she concluded to her minister. "The church should answer when it's challenged and communism challenges it."

Two decades earlier, she had written something very similar, about the horror expressed by the well-to-do that in revolutionary Russia, "the poor are fed first." That the producers of the food, who had formerly waited their turns, would suddenly take the best for themselves and leave nothing for the rich was considered anarchy. The scars of the war would fade, Ovington thought, but not the scars that the lower class leaves upon the upper class; those would remain open wounds. The real war of human history was class war.

Who would ever forget if he were forced to eat last, after his servant had dined? No one who has known plenty will forgive the iniquity of a time when the impoverished ruled, and *copying their betters*, dared to help themselves first to the food of the earth.[28]

On January 6, 1947, Mary White Ovington was in absentia reelected treasurer of the NAACP for the last time. The last board meeting she attended was in March 1946, when she had great difficulty getting home in New York's snowy darkness. No taxis were to be found and buses sloshed past her. She would not be there for the announcement of her book.

In Boston, subway posters cried, THE WALLS CAME TUMBLING DOWN. "Other people think it is an advance notice for some movie," her niece Betty wrote, "but of course it must be for your book!"

Ovington was ill, "out of the running," as she put it, but still got necessary permissions; checked galleys; corrected the Harcourt catalog (which said she was from Boston); compiled the index; and condensed Walter White's foreword. Her April birthday led her to tell him: "Even though I come from a long-lived family—the average age of my grandparents was 86, and of my parents 85—still that does not give me more than three or four years to be a nuisance! Old age *is* a nuisance."

In sweltering July, she sent off the final page proofs and promptly found regrettable omissions. On August 19, the dark blue book was in her hand. On the twentieth, she managed to get to the Harcourt offices to sign copies. The portions of Walter White's foreword she had edited gave an evocative description of Ovington at age eighty-two. This "exquisitely featured gentlelady" was "an exceedingly deceptive person," he found:

> Her delicately pale blue eyes, her placid and sensitive face, and her beautifully tailored pastel clothes leave breathless and defenseless those who meet her for the first time after becoming angered because of her views. When instead of the grubbily dressed, fanatic-eyed, loose-moralled female which neurotic enemies always picture in their minds as typical of those who speak out for minorities, such visitors to Miss Ovington's office find her quite different, it is usually some time before they can gather their wits together enough to launch the planned attack. When her cool and incisive wit and wisdom is brought into the discussion, Miss Ovington's erstwhile foes are changed into friends.

She had removed the verbal description, but her portrait on the back of the book jacket conveyed the same clear, direct vision in those worn eyes.[29]

Harcourt, Brace ran ads in the white and Negro press and cooperated with Wilkins at the NAACP on a circular for branches and correspondents. Macy's erected a prominent display of *The Walls Came Tumbling Down*.

Reviews were positive: "Miss Ovington at 82 writes with the zest and energy of youth" (*Booklist*); "an interesting study" of one woman in a "fight that has advanced immeasurably the whole perspective of genuinely-functioning democracy in America" (Harold Preece in *Christian Century*); "She writes objectively, without preaching or pointing," and "she is wise enough to realize that the documented facts alone are eloquent" (I. J. Trese in *Churchman*); "socially important; humanely interesting" (*Commonweal*); "this is an heroic account, told in the simplest of terms" (Henrietta Buckmaster in *Saturday Review of Literature*).

Personal reviews poured in, too, in a veritable retrospective of her life. From Mary Simkhovitch, director emeritus of Greenwich House: the book is "so like you in its simplicity, clarity, and power." From Charlotte Hawkins Brown, president of Palmer Memorial Institute in Sedalia, North Carolina: "How I'd love to pay your fare down here for these youngsters to see you—What a blessing you have been to them, to me and all my race!" From Dr. Louis Wright, NAACP board member, president, and Spingarn Medalist: "No comment of mine can properly tell you what a signal contribution to humanity that I consider it to be."

Oswald Garrison Villard thanked her for her kind references to him, "so characteristic of you." He bemoaned "the fact that Mary White Ovington is an old lady, as I am an old and back number man, for you have been a truly Christian leader in all our work, and if there were an ecclesiastical authority among the blacks to do it you should forever be their St. Mary."

Beth Torrey, home from Angola and studying at Yale, described her heart leaping up at Ovington's picture. "What a fine face!" a friend said. It was "the most encouraging book I have read in many a long time," Torrey continued. "Sometimes I get fed up with reading research books and calamity books and wishy-washy books. And here is yours—a clear-cut description of life as it was, and as it is, and by implication of what it will be." She said she had known only the "lovable and loving shell" of Mary White Ovington, with "the best part hidden way underneath."[30]

Sheer will had kept Mary White Ovington going. When she finished galley proofs, she also jotted the final, shaky entries in her meticulous account books: purchases of a dress, a book, food, travel, gifts. As the inevitable decline set in, her contacts narrowed to family and close friends.

Her nieces and nephews chatted about current events, often emphasizing interracial and other matters they knew would interest her. Betty raved about William Warfield in *Call Me Mister*. Ned Merritt examined his own urges to write and described his new Hudson Commodore Eight and his latest trek to the mountains. His sister, Louise Callin, responded to questions about genealogy records.

Older relatives such as cousin Florence Barlow recalled the past. The family tended long distance to "Aunt Georgia," widow of Ovington's cousin Edward, stranded in Paris in 1941. May and Elizabeth Ovington helped their cousin Harold organize shipments of food and clothing. The two New York women felt the inevitability of their own increasing need.[31]

By late October 1947, only a month after the book's publication, Mary White Ovington was in rapid decline. Words twisted illegibly; lines ran together. Dictated letters to Carrie Overton told how she felt. She had undergone a "sort of let-down physically" and was "entering upon a queer existence"; she didn't know herself. "All the old energy is gone and I can hardly remember it," she conveyed.

By Christmas she was weary and depressed. In January of 1948, the first year since its beginning in 1909 that the NAACP would hold elections without her name, Ovington was once again taken to the Neuro-Psychiatric Institute of Living in Hartford, Connecticut. By the end of the month, Psychiatrist-in-Chief C. C. Burlingame reported to John Haynes Holmes that she was less depressed and more interested in her surroundings. But just a few days later Ovington herself told Holmes not to write or come to see her. Sometimes she sounded like her old self: "These are difficult days but there is always hope."

Months passed and as another Christmas dawned, it was to her "dearest" Richetta Randolph that Ovington wrote with stories of her long-suffering roommate who didn't mind going out with her in the night, of a fall on a slippery bedroom rug (no bones broken). She didn't know if she was getting better or not; they move you about, she reported, but they don't send you home.[32]

Mary White Ovington was able to go back to New York City briefly in 1949 before she was taken to live with her sister in Massachusetts. "I have telephoned until I was tired," she wrote Randolph in a shaky hand in the spring. "Come to see me after work. Will be home whenever you say. Very lovingly . . ." At Christmas, Ovington sent "Greetings to a very old and dear friend." By the time of her birthday in April of 1950, she wrote from Massachusetts with thanks for Randolph's greeting and with descriptions of her flowers and cards and the delicious cake Helen had made. Come and stay with us, Helen wrote Randolph in June, telling her that Miss Ovington "tires easily and cannot converse too long at a time with anyone, but she has expressed a real desire to see you."

Randolph described her friend's last years as a change of personality due to the physical disabilities of advanced age and the corresponding psychological disappointment that she couldn't devote herself any longer to the things in which she was so interested. Depression, likely connected with the strokes that also affected her eyes, was a periodic problem for Ovington only after age eighty, so her close friends might very well have seen it as a personality change.

Richetta Randolph, friend and colleague of Ovington for forty years, thought it a shame that the stories of other social workers—Jane Addams, Lillian Wald, Florence Kelley—had eclipsed Ovington's. Miss Ovington was, in Randolph's estimate "the greatest! She was far ahead of them and her time. She was involved with the Negro while to the others the Negro and his problems were only secondary. . . . She was the wave of the Future and the prophet crying in the wilderness."[33]

Ovington's nephew Ted Kingsbury was appointed her conservator on the basis of her own trembling signature on January 17, 1950. The examining doctor found her "incapable, by reason of advanced age . . . of caring for her property." For some reason he crossed out "Mental weakness." Kingsbury, from Kennebunk, Maine, appointed his mother, Helen, in his place.

An inventory of Ovington's assets showed $2,403.78 and $965.06 in her checking and savings accounts; household effects valued at $1,000; and an undetermined "distributive share" in the estate of Elizabeth Ovington whose death had preceded her own.

Mary White Ovington died on July 15, 1951, at a small nursing home at 2 Raeburn Terrace, Newton Highlands, Massachusetts, though news reports all placed the death at Helen's home at 526 Auburn Street, Auburndale. She was eighty-six years, three months, and four days old. The cause of death was arteriosclerosis, generalized, and the normal process of aging. Her body was cremated at nearby Newton Cemetery.

Ted Kingsbury as executor appointed his sister Elizabeth as agent. Through the inheritance of Ovington Gift Shop money from her sister-in-law, Ovington's estate grew considerably between the writing of her will and her death, finally totaling $22,713.47, mostly to Helen Kingsbury, with the final distribution made in December 1953. To the young daughter of her Baha'i friend, Monover Bechtold, Ovington willed $100. The NAACP was to receive the rights to *The Walls Came Tumbling Down,* and her great-nephew Nicholas Noyes Kingsbury the rights to *Zeke: A Schoolboy at Tolliver.*[34]

Services in Ovington's memory took place at Community Church in New York City on Wednesday afternoon, July 18, led by Reverend Donald Harrington. Arthur Spingarn, NAACP president, described her as a woman "who hated nobody" although her zeal for equality for black Americans created many enemies. "What she hated was ignorance, poverty, the exploitation of the defenseless, injustice and hatred itself." Roy Wilkins added that "her most enduring monument is in the hearts and spirits of Americans of all races" who would for generations be "the beneficiaries of her crusade for equality and brotherhood."

Of the original fifty-three signers of the Call for the founding of the NAACP, only John Dewey, John Haynes Holmes, and W. E. B. Du Bois still lived—Du Bois was at the service with his new wife, Shirley Graham. Richetta Randolph and William Pickens were there; though Ovington "legally died" in July, the latter wrote, "she will never really die as long as many intelligent people of all races shall still live."

The *New York Herald Tribune* pictured her as an old woman but covered central events of her life, as did the *Times*. Carl Murphy of the *Baltimore Afro-American* reprinted the twenty installments of her 1932 "Reminiscences," beginning with a statement of "Why We Print This Story":

> She was no fair weather friend. The race problem was no fad with her. She shared the problems of the race from days when it was almost a crime for white people to associate with colored people. It has been said of her that "no person in America deserves the classification of a true and understanding friend of colored Americans more than she." ... *Afro* Editors believe Miss Ovington's story one of the greatest of the Age. It is the autobiography of a wonderful woman and the history of a great organization.[35]

Age always brings burdens but sometimes also brings wisdom, especially to those who have fought for truth and justice. How little the battles have changed since she first assaulted the walls that separate human from human. She suffered to share her life and wisdom; they are there for us to use.

Notes

CHAPTER 1

1. Except where indicated, sources for chapter are unpublished fragments, Mary White Ovington (MWO) Papers, Archives of Labor and Urban Affairs, Wayne State University (WSU); MWO, "Reminiscences," *Baltimore Afro-American*, September 17, 1932, 24; and MWO, *The Walls Came Tumbling Down* (New York: Harcourt, Brace and Company, 1947).

2. "Plans for Plays, MWO-HDO," MWO Papers, WSU.

3. Theodore T. Ovington to Louisa [Ketcham], 30 letters, 1854–1855; Louisa to Theodore, n.d., MWO Papers, WSU.

4. "Theo" [Ovington] to "Loo" [Louise Ovington], five letters, 1870, MWO Papers, WSU. In 1855, his salary was one thousand dollars a year, he stayed with his parents, and he worked until 9 P.M.

5. MWO, "Shopping Yesterday," MWO Papers, WSU.

6. Nancy Woloch, *Women and the American Experience* (New York: Knopf, 1984).

7. *New York Times*, March 3, 4, 1875.

8. MWO to Mother, June 26, 1883, MWO Papers, WSU.

9. Robert Brockway to MWO, September 17, 1947, MWO Papers, WSU.

10. MWO to Mother, n.d., and June 7, 1883, MWO Papers, WSU.

11. MWO, "Literature for Young Girls," n.d., MWO Papers, WSU.

12. Charles Ketcham Ovington, diary, 1885, MWO Papers, WSU.

13. Charles Ovington, diary and account books, MWO Papers, WSU.

14. Charles Ovington, diary, MWO Papers, WSU.

15. MWO to Corinne [Bacon], July 4 [n.d.], MWO Papers, WSU.

16. Charles Ovington, diary, MWO Papers, WSU.

17. Brooklyn *Eagle*, May 13, 1954; Alice A. Chadwick, pamphlet, May 18, 1895; brochure on Packer's Centennial, 1945, Brooklyn Public Library. Marjorie Nickerson, *A Long Way Forward: The First Hundred Years of the Packer Collegiate Institute* (Brooklyn: Packer Collegiate Institute, 1945).

18. Charles Ovington, diary, MWO Papers, WSU.

19. William Newell, founder of the American Folklore Society, became a good friend. See Newell to May [MWO], November 25, 1904, MWO Papers,

WSU. Mrs. James Lowell Moore (William Newell's sister), "The Fayer-weather House," *Cambridge Historical Society*, January 1939, 86–94, MWO Papers, WSU.

20. Robert Morss Lovett, *All Our Years* (New York: Viking Press, 1948), p. 51. Dorothy Elia Howells, *A Century to Celebrate Radcliffe College, 1879–1979* (Cambridge: Radcliffe College, 1978).

21. Radcliffe College Archives. Most did not complete degrees or certificates, and many did not finish even a single course. MWO, "The Harvard Annex," for *Packer Alumnae*, Winter 1892, MWO Papers, WSU.

22. Radcliffe College Archives; MWO, "Heroines of English Novels," n.d.; essay on Dickens, n.d., MWO Papers, WSU.

23. Byrd L. Jones, "A Quest for National Leadership: Institutionalization of Economics at Harvard," in *Breaking the Academic Mould: Economists and American Higher Learning in the Nineteenth Century*, ed. William Barber (Middletown, Conn.: Wesleyan University Press, 1988). Ashley's work after his nine years at Harvard parallels Ovington's, even to quoting Wordsworth, Browning, and Arnold.

24. Anne Ashley, *William James Ashley: A Life* (by his daughter) (London: P. S. King and Son, Ltd, 1932).

25. Radcliffe College Archives.

26. Dorothy Elia Howells, *A Century to Celebrate Radcliffe College*.

CHAPTER 2

1. *New York Times*, August 21, 22, 26, September 10, 1896.

2. Except where indicated, the following is from Mary White Ovington (MWO) Papers, Archives of Labor and Urban Affairs, Wayne State University (WSU); "Reminiscences," *Baltimore Afro-American*, September 24, 1932, 24.

3. Charles Pratt, "Morris Building Company: Astral Apartments, Greenpoint, New York" [10 pp. pamphlet], 1885, illus. In Brooklyn Historical Society Library.

4. Margaret Healy, "Neighborship Report," *First Report of the Pratt Institute Neighborship Association* (Brooklyn, 1895), 38–39.

5. Daniel Cryer, "Mary White Ovington and the Rise of the NAACP" (Ph.D. dissertation: University of Minnesota, 1977), 114.

6. MWO, "By the Playground," *Outlook*, vol. 77 (July 16, 1904), 648.

7. MWO, "The Price of a Coat," n.d., MWO Papers, WSU.

8. MWO, "Report of the Head Worker of the Neighborship Settlement," *Report of the Pratt Institute Neighborship Association, for the Year 1895–96* (Brooklyn: Press of George Mayer, 1896), 23.

9. Ibid., 31; *Brooklyn Eagle*, December 20, 1897, 12.

10. MWO, "The Penny Paper," *Outlook*, vol. 76 (January 30, 1904), 280–83. *The Weekly*, edited by Lyman Abbott, published Booker T. Washington's *Up from Slavery* in 1901, and by 1906 was attacking W. E. B. Du Bois vehemently.

11. Constitution, Social Reform Club, Leonora O'Reilly Papers, Schlesinger Library, Radcliffe College.

12. 1897 through December 30, 1898; Diaries of Leonora O'Reilly, Schlesinger Library, Radcliffe College.

13. See MWO to Booker T. Washington (BTW) [1901], BTW Papers, Library of Congress (LC).

14. "Booker T. Washington Honored," *New York Times*, April 3, 1901.

15. John White Chadwick to MWO, August 18, 1903, MWO Papers, WSU.

CHAPTER 3

1. Few settlements served blacks. See Judith Trolander, *Settlement Houses and the Great Depression* (Detroit: Wayne State University Press, 1975); Elisabeth Lasch-Quinn, *Black Neighbors: Race and the Limits of Reform in the American Settlement House Movement, 1890–1945* (Chapel Hill: University of North Carolina Press, 1993).

2. Ovington capitalizes "Negro." Where "negro" appears in Ovington's publications, it is not her usage.

3. Mary White Ovington (MWO) to W. E. B. Du Bois (WEDB), June 10 and 16, 1904, WEDB Papers, University of Massachusetts (Mass.).

4. MWO to WEDB, July 25 [1904] (in 1924 file), October 7, 1904, WEDB Papers, Mass. MWO to Mrs. Joel Spingarn, November 9 [1916?], Joel Spingarn (JES) Papers, Moorland Spingarn Research Center, Howard University (Moorland). MWO, "Reminiscences," *Baltimore Afro-American*, October 10, 1929, 24.

5. WEDB, "Credo," *Darkwater: Voices from within the Veil* (New York: Schocken Books, 1969, rpr. of 1920), 3–4; MWO to WEDB, November 4, 1904, WEDB Papers, Mass.

6. MWO to WEDB, October 27, November 4, 10, 1904, WEDB Papers, Mass.

7. WEDB to MWO, November 8, 1904, MWO Papers, Archives of Labor and Urban Affairs, Wayne State University (WSU). Where Du Bois's letters are duplicated in drafts on the backs of letters to him at Mass., only one source will be given.

8. MWO to WEDB, January 9, 25, 1905, WEDB Papers, Mass. To Archibald Grimke she wrote that "my own blessed minister" had died. He "never lost an opportunity in speech or in writing to show his full sympathy

with the colored man." Grimke Papers, Moorland. MWO, "John White Chadwick: In Memory," *Unity*, March 2, 1905. MWO Papers, WSU.

9. Mary Kingsbury Simkhovitch, *Neighborhood: My Story of Greenwich House* (New York: W. W. Norton, 1938), and *Here Is God's Plenty: Reflections on American Social Advance* (New York: Harper and Brothers, 1949).

10. Simkhovitch, *Here Is God's Plenty*, 87–89.

11. Greenwich House Papers (GHP), Tamiment Library, New York University (Tamiment).

12. MWO to WEDB, October 7, 1904, WEDB Papers, Mass.

13. GHP, Tamiment.

14. Ibid.; Franz Boas, foreword to *Half a Man: The Status of the Negro in New York*, by MWO (New York: Longmans Green and Company, 1911), ix. MWO to WEDB, October 7, 1904, WEDB Papers, Mass.

15. E. R. A. Seligman Papers, Columbia University Libraries, Rare Book and Manuscript Library, uncatalogued correspondence, passim.

16. MWO to WEDB, October 7, 27, 1904, January 9, 1905, WEDB Papers, Mass. MWO, *Half a Man*, 40.

17. MWO to WEDB, January 25, 1905, WEDB Papers, Mass.

18. WEDB to MWO, March 21, May 13, 1905, MWO Papers, WSU. MWO to WEDB, March 13, May 13, 1905; WEDB to MWO, on back of her letter of February 22, 1905. Program for the Tenth Atlanta Conference. WEDB to Horace Bumstead, June 7, 1907, WEDB Papers, Mass. MWO, *The Walls Came Tumbling Down* (New York: Harcourt, Brace and Company, 1947), 53. Ovington mistakenly gives the year as 1904 here.

19. MWO, February 24, April 6, November 8, 1905, MWO Papers, WSU.

20. WEDB to MWO, March 21, April 3, 1905, MWO Papers, WSU; MWO to WEDB, March 25, May 13, June 29, 1905, WEDB Papers, Mass. MWO, *The Walls*, 54–55.

21. MWO, "Atlanta: A City Nursing Dead Ideals," *Colored American*, July 1905, 389.

22. MWO to WEDB, January 9, 1905, WEDB Papers, Mass.

23. MWO to Mother, n.d. [Fall 1905], MWO Papers, WSU.

24. MWO, "The Settlement in America," *Colored American*, June 1905, 331–35. In November 1906 Ovington published again in this magazine. "A Life of Service" is about a young man, Lloyd Cofer, Jr., who had run a boys' club until his early death from typhoid fever.

25. MWO, "Fresh Air Work Among Colored Children in New York," *Charities and the Commons*, vol. 17, October 13, 1906, 115–17.

26. MWO, "Working Girls' Clubs," *Northeastern*, July 1906, MWO Papers, WSU.

27. *Analytical Guide and Indexes to the Voice of the Negro, 1904–1907* (Westport, Conn.: Greenwood Press, 1974).

28. MWO, "The Negro in the Trades Unions in New York," *Annals of the American Academy of Political and Social Science*, May 1906, 551–58.

29. MWO to WEDB, September 2, 1905, WEDB Papers, Mass.

30. WEDB to Paul Kellogg, back of Kellogg letter to WEDB, May 6, 1905, WEDB Papers, Mass.

31. MWO to Aunt Sarah, n.d. and November 15 [1905]; MWO to Mother, n.d. (two letters); Charles Ovington diary, MWO Papers, WSU. MWO to WEDB, April 13, 1907, WEDB Papers, Mass. MWO, "Reminiscences," *Baltimore Afro-American*, November 12, 1932, 21; Joan C. Foster to author, June 14, 1996.

32. *Dictionary of American Reformers;* Charles Edward Russell, *Bare Hands and Stone Walls: Some Reflections of a Side-Line Reformer* (New York: Charles Scribner's Sons, 1933), 231; John E. Milholland Collection, New York State Historical Association, Ticonderoga, N.Y. (THS). When Ovington first met Milholland, Meadowmount consisted of a huge rectangle of buildings (picture postcard of "Meadowmount," 1905, THS). Today it is a music camp.

33. John Milholland diaries, THS. Milholland to BTW, September 10 and 13, 1900, BTW Papers, LC.

34. John Milholland, diary, THS.

35. GHP, Tamiment.

36. Milholland diary, THS; MWO, "Reminiscences," *Baltimore Afro-American*, October 8, 1932, 24.

37. GHP, Tamiment; MWO to WEDB, February 22, 1905, WEDB Papers, Mass.

38. John Milholland diary, THS.

39. MWO to WEDB, December 18, 1905, and May 20, 1906, WEDB Papers, Mass.

40. Andrew B. Humphrey to BTW, May 4, 1904; BTW to Charles Anderson, [September 1905], BTW Papers, LC; Manning Marable, *W. E. B. Du Bois: Black Radical Democrat* (Boston: Twayne Publishers, 1986), 69.

41. MWO to WEDB, December 18, 1905, WEDB Papers, Mass.

42. Milholland to WEDB, January 7, 1906?, WEDB Papers, Mass.

43. *New York Times*, February 2, 1906.

44. Charles Anderson to BTW, March 6, 31, 1906, BTW Papers, LC.

45. MWO to WEDB, May 20, 1906, WEDB Papers, Mass; Minutes, Association of Neighborhood Workers, May 6, 1905, Kennedy Supplement Papers, Social Welfare History Archives, University of Minnesota.

46. D. Joy Humes, *Oswald Garrison Villard, Liberal of the 1920's* (Syracuse, N.Y.: Syracuse University Press, 1960), passim.

47. Oswald Garrison Villard (OGV) to BTW, July 31, 1906, BTW Papers, LC. Villard told Washington that Ovington was planning to stop "either going or coming" at Harpers Ferry, North Carolina, and Birmingham, thereby hint-

ing and obscuring her coverage of the Niagara Movement. By 1907, Ovington removed herself from the BTW reporter's subsidy. BTW to OGV, February 11, 1907; MWO to Mr. Pent, "Tues. morning" [February 1907], BTW Papers, LC.

48. MWO to WEDB, July 31, [August 5], 1906; WEDB to MWO, n.d., on back of her letter [August 5, 1906]; Program, "The Niagara Movement; Second Annual Meeting . . . ," WEDB Papers, Mass. In *The Walls Came Tumbling Down*, Ovington said that only Negroes could become full members; white men and women could be associate members. She seems to have said this, however, in order to indicate that "the direction of the movement belonged to the colored" (101). When Du Bois asked her to become a member, he did not indicate that it would be as an "Associate Member." WEDB to MWO, October 30, 1906, MWO Papers, WSU.

49. MWO, *New York Evening Post*, August 20, 1906, 8. Her first article appeared in the *Post* on August 17, 1906, 5. An unsigned article of August 18, 8, was also likely Ovington's. This piece, "The Spirit of John Brown: Still Beckoning the Negroes to Arise and Seek the Recovery of Their Rights," quotes a speech by Reverend Reverdy C. Ransom. The first *Post* report on the Negro Business League, August 30, 1906, 12, was also unsigned, "Address by Booker T. Washington at Atlanta, Georgia."

50. *New York Evening Post*, August 17, 1906, 5. MWO, *The Walls*, 101.

51. MWO, "The Negro in Business" (August 31, 1906, 7); "Negro Energy and Thrift: Testimony of Successful Men of Business" (September 3, 1906, 4—Editorial Page); "Negro Banks and Banking: Teaching Economy and Proper Acquisitiveness" (September 4, 1906, 12); "The Negro's Position: His Comparative Helplessness in the South" (September 7, 1906, 3) and "Race Feeling as an Asset" (September 8, 1906, 5), all in *New York Evening Post*.

52. MWO, "Reminiscences," *Baltimore Afro-American*, October 8, 1932, 24.

53. MWO to WEDB, September 10 and 20, 1906, WEDB Papers, Mass; BTW to MWO, September, 1906; MWO to BTW, September 10, 1906, BTW Papers, LC.

54. BTW to MWO, October 2, 1906; MWO to BTW, October 5, 1906, BTW Papers, LC.

55. BTW to OGV, September 6, 1906, OGV Papers, bMS Am 1323 (4098), by permission of the Houghton Library, Harvard University (Harvard). Washington consistently misspelled "Ku" as "Klu."

56. MWO to BTW, September 10, 1906, BTW Papers, LC.

57. MWO to WEDB, September 10, 20, 1906, WEDB Papers, Mass.

58. Peter Bergman et al., *A Chronological History of the Negro in America* (New York: Harper and Row, 1969), 347–48.

59. [OGV], Editorials, September 24, 25, 1906, *New York Evening Post*. MWO to OGV, October 3 [1906], OGV Papers, bMS Am 1323 (2921), Harvard.

60. Bergman, et al. *A Chronological History*, 348.

61. WEDB to MWO, October 6, 1906, MWO Papers, WSU.

62. WEDB, "Litany . . . ," *The Independent*, October 1906.

63. WEDB to MWO, October 30, 1906, MWO Papers, WSU.

64. Elliott Rudwick, *W. E. B. Du Bois: Propagandist of the Negro Protest* (New York: Atheneum, 1969), 69, 103–4.

65. MWO, "Atlanta Riots," *The Outlook*, vol. 84 (Nov. 17, 1906), 684.

66. Lyman Ward to MWO, December 4, 1906; January 18, 1907, MWO Papers, WSU.

67. WEDB to MWO, September 28, October 6, 1906, MWO Papers, WSU.

68. MWO, "Reminiscences," *Baltimore Afro-American*, October 29, 1932, 24; *The Walls*, 63.

69. MWO to WEDB, September 20, 1906, WEDB Papers, Mass. Ovington said "the Milhollands," but the family was not in New York City. Milholland wrote, "Miss Ovington came to luncheon and talk of the South" (Milholland diary, THS). Milholland had for some time wanted the "right man" to go south and get at facts. He would finance such a person for as long as it took to do the job. It required someone "brainy" and "judicially minded." Milholland to BTW, April 30, 1901, BTW Papers, LC.

70. WEDB to MWO, n.d., back of her letter, September 20, 1906, WEDB Papers, Mass; WEDB to MWO, October 6, 23, 1906, MWO Papers, WSU.

CHAPTER 4

1. Mary White Ovington (MWO), "Reminiscences," *Baltimore Afro-American*, October 29, 1932, 24; MWO, *The Walls Came Tumbling Down* (New York: Harcourt, Brace and Company 1947), 63.

2. MWO, "The Atlanta Situation. . . ," *New York Evening Post*, December 26, 1906, 5; MWO to Ray Stannard Baker (RSB), January 25, 1907, RSB Papers, Library of Congress (LC).

3. W. E. B. Du Bois (WEDB) to MWO, October 6, 1906, MWO Papers, Archives of Labor and Urban Affairs, Wayne State University (WSU).

4. MWO, "Reminiscences," *Baltimore Afro-American*, October 29, November 5, 1932, 24, 16; *The Walls*, 66–74; "A Woman Who Answered Prayer: Charlotte R. Thorn and the Calhoun School," *Woman Citizen* (March 1927), 18–19, 48–49. The following paragraphs are taken from these sources unless otherwise indicated. Thorn's colleague in founding the school was Mabel Dillingham.

5. Frances MacGregor Ingram, "The Settlement Movement in the South," Speech, Fiftieth Anniversary of University Settlement, December 4, 1936, Social Welfare History Archives, University of Minnesota.

6. Leslie Pinckney Hill to MWO, January 30, 1906 [1907], MWO Papers, WSU.

7. MWO, "A Day of Praise...," *New York Evening Post*, January 26, 1907, Saturday Supplement, 2. MWO, "Slaves' Reminiscences of Slavery," *Independent*, vol. 68 (May 26, 1910), 1131–36.

8. Lyman Ward to MWO, January 18, 1907, MWO Papers, WSU.

9. The following uses "Reminiscences" of 1932, MWO, *The Walls*, of 1947; and "Winston, the Free County of Alabama," MWO Papers, WSU.

10. Traveller [MWO], "The South's White Problem," *Post*, January 29, 1907. MWO, "The Sunny South and Poverty," *New Review*, March 15, 1913, 325–29.

11. MWO, "The White Brute," *The Masses*, vol. 6 (October–November 1915), 17–18. Reprinted in MWO, *The Walls*, 88–99.

12. MWO to Ida Tarbell [October or November 1906], RSB Papers, LC. A Baker biographer says the muckraker brought to the topic of the color line "a curious mixture of ignorance, idealism and prejudice," typical of the Progressive period. Baker chose the topic for its circulation potential. Robert Bannister, Jr., *Ray Stannard Baker: The Mind and Thought of a Progressive* (New Haven, Conn.: Yale University Press, 1966), 126–27.

13. MWO to RSB, November 12 and 14, 1906, RSB Papers, LC.

14. Ibid., December 26, 1906, January 18 and 25, 1907, RSB Papers, LC; RSB to WEDB, February 2, 1907, WEDB Papers, University of Massachusetts (Mass).

15. RSB, *Following the Color Line* (New York: Harper and Row, 1964; Doubleday, Page and Company, New York, 1908), 3–25. Originally in *American Magazine*, April 1907.

16. Ibid., 271–91. Originally in *American Magazine*, August 1907.

17. MWO to RSB, August 18, 1908, RSB Papers, LC.

18. Ibid., November 12, 1908, RSB Papers, LC. Baker's articles assured a solvent beginning for the new magazine. Dewey W. Grantham, Jr., introduction to *Following the Color Line*, by RSB, v–vii. John Semonche, in *Ray Stannard Baker: A Quest for Democracy in Modern America, 1870–1918* (Chapel Hill: University of North Carolina Press, 1969), says Baker "hit upon" the idea of the series in the fall of 1906. No one mentions Ovington's correspondence with Baker.

19. MWO, "Some Publications Regarding the American Negro," *Library Journal* (March 1907), 117, based on speech, New York State Library Association, September 1906.

20. MWO to WEDB (postcard), February 10, 1907, WEDB Papers, Mass.

21. "For the New York Age," Booker T. Washington (BTW) to Fred Moore, February 20, 1909, BTW Papers, LC.

22. John Milholland to WEDB, May 9, 1907; WEDB to John Milholland, May [18], 1907; MWO to WEDB, February 5, 1906; April 13, 1907, WEDB Papers, Mass.

23. MWO to WEDB, August 2, 1907, WEDB Papers, Mass. Background information following is from Elliott M. Rudwick, *W. E. B. Du Bois: Propagandist of the Negro Protest* (New York: Atheneum, 1969), 108–12.

24. August Meier, *Negro Thought in America, 1880–1915: Racial Ideologies in the Age of Booker T. Washington* (Ann Arbor: University of Michigan Press, 1963), 178–79.

25. MWO, "Negroes on Firmer Ground . . . ," *New York Evening Post*, September 3, 1907, 7; Manning Marable, *W. E. B. Du Bois: Black Radical Democrat* (Boston: Twayne Publishers, 1986), 70.

26. MWO to WEDB, October 8, 1907, WEDB Papers, Mass.

27. For a summary of Washington's tactics, see Marable's chapter, "Tuskegee and the Niagara Movement," in *W. E. B. Du Bois: Black Radical Democrat*.

28. BTW to Robert Moton, October 2, 1907, BTW Papers, LC. The letter has "Miss Overton," crossed out and "Ovington" written in.

29. MWO to WEDB, October 19, 1907, WEDB Papers, Mass.

30. MWO to WEDB, December 23, 1907, April 24, 1908, WEDB Papers, Mass; WEDB to MWO, April 16, 1908, MWO Papers, WSU.

31. MWO to Oswald Garrison Villard (OGV), May 29, 1908, OGV Papers, bMS Am 1323 (2921), Houghton Library, Harvard University (Harvard).

32. Elisabeth Lasch-Quinn's *Black Neighbors: Race and the Limits of Reform in the American Settlement House Movement, 1890–1945* (Chapel Hill: University of North Carolina Press, 1993), 42–46, describes Ovington as an exception to even the "most enlightened" representatives of settlements on issues of race, including Jane Addams. Ovington did not exhibit the same low estimation of black culture or the assumption of benefits of segregation. Yet Lasch-Quinn does not cite or recognize several of Ovington's achievements, including the founding and running of Lincoln Settlement. The *Handbook of Settlements* compiled by Robert Woods and Albert Kennedy in 1911, and published by the Russell Sage Foundation (Social Welfare History Archives, University of Minnesota), also leaves out Ovington's role, mentioning only Dr. Morton Jones.

33. MWO, "Reminiscences," *Baltimore Afro-American*, November 19, 1932, 24. (Ovington leaves out all references to founding Lincoln Settlement in her 1947 book.)

34. William Jay Schieffelin to J. G. Phelps Stokes, May 24, 1906, Stokes Papers, Rare Book and Manuscript Library, Columbia University.

35. Letterhead of the "Committee for Improving the Industrial Condition of Negroes in New York," June 1907, WEDB Papers, Mass; Nancy Joan

Weiss, *The National Urban League, 1910–1940* (Cambridge: Harvard University Press, 1974), suggests Ovington could have as easily made her reputation in the Urban League rather than the NAACP (20–25, 57).

36. MWO to BTW, October 5, 1906, BTW Papers, LC.

37. MWO to OGV, October 8, 1906, OGV Papers, Harvard.

38. MWO, *The Walls*, 43–44; "Reminiscences," *Baltimore Afro-American*, October 22, 1932, 24.

39. MWO to WEDB, April 24, 1908, WEDB Papers, Mass.

40. *New York Times*, April 28, 29, 1908; Daniel Cryer, "Mary White Ovington and the Rise of the N.A.A.C.P." (Ph.D. dissertation, University of Minnesota, 1977), 230–32. MWO, *The Walls*, 43–47; "Reminiscences," *Baltimore Afro-American*, October 22, 1932, 24.

41. MWO to OGV, May 29, 1908, OGV Papers, Harvard.

42. MWO, "Reminiscences," *Baltimore Afro-American*, October 22, 1932, 24.

43. There is indirect damning evidence in later Washington correspondence. BTW to Charles Anderson, January 21, 1911; Charles Anderson to BTW, January 19, 23, and 25, 1911; "Three Races Sit at Banquet," *New York Press*, January 25, 1911, 1, BTW Papers, LC. Louis Harlan, "The Secret Life of Booker T. Washington," *Journal of Southern History*, vol. 37 (August 1971), 393–416, concludes that Tuskegee engineered the 1908 coverage. But Harlan misrepresents Ovington as a "wealthy white settlement worker in the Negro slums," who "became an NAACP staff member," "a very proper old maid [who] was still upset by the incidents when she wrote her memoirs in 1947."

44. OGV to MWO, April 29, 1908, OGV Papers, Harvard.

45. WEDB to MWO, May 14, 1908, WEDB Papers, Mass.

46. MWO to Mary Church Terrell, May 18 [1908], Terrell Papers, LC.

47. Carolyn Heilbrun, *Writing a Woman's Life* (New York: W. W. Norton and Company, 1988), 49.

48. Ibid., April 24, August 29, 1908, WEDB Papers, Mass.

49. Ibid., August 29, 1908.

50. Ibid., January 29, 1908.

51. MWO to RSB, August 19, 1908, RSB Papers, LC.

52. MWO, *The Walls*, 49.

53. Ibid., 49–52.

54. Ibid., 47–48. Ovington did not "cease to work for socialism," in 1908; rather she sought to involve socialists in both black and feminist causes. She remained active in the Intercollegiate Socialist Society (see, for example, the "Notes on the Bellport Conference" of September, 1918" in *The Intercollegiate Socialist*, December–January, 1917–18, where she and Du Bois are quoted in the discussion of "The Negro and the Trade Union"). She was on the soci-

ety's Executive Committee in 1914, and wrote about the organization in the New York *Call*. After its formation, the NAACP advertised itself in the group's publication, *The Intercollegiate Socialist*. Ovington also published articles in other Socialist publications: the *New Review*, the *Liberator*, the *Masses*, and the *Messenger*.

CHAPTER 5

1. Peter Bergman, *The Chronological History of The Negro in America* (New York: Harper and Row, 1969), 352. Mary White Ovington (MWO), "How the National Association for the Advancement of Colored People Began," *NAACP*, 1914, 1940. Throughout the following, the Ovington pamphlet is used as a source, and will not be further cited.

2. MWO, "Reminiscences," *Baltimore Afro-American*, November 19, 1932, 24.

3. Ibid.; *The Walls Came Tumbling Down* (New York: Harcourt, Brace, 1947), 102.

4. William English Walling, "The Founding of the NAACP," *Crisis*, vol. 36 (July 1929), 226.

5. MWO, *The Walls*, 104.

6. Hamilton Holt to William English Walling, January 27, 1909; Walling to Holt, February 1, 1909, Walling Papers, Wisconsin State Historical Society, Madison, Wisconsin.

7. Charles Flint Kellogg, *NAACP: A History of the National Association for the Advancement of Colored People* (Baltimore, Md.: Johns Hopkins University Press, 1967), 12; MWO, *The Walls*, 103.

8. The people on Villard's but not Ovington's list are Reverend Walter Laidlaw; Mary Church Terrell; Mrs. Henry Villard; Reverend M. St. Croix Wright; Jenkins Lloyd Jones; Major Brand Whitlock; Ray Stannard Baker.

9. Allen F. Davis, *Spearheads for Reform: The Social Settlements and the Progressive Movement* (New York: Oxford University Press, 1967); Kellogg, *NAACP*; Wilson Record, "Negro Intellectual Leadership in the NAACP: 1910–1940," *Phylon*, vol. 17 (1956) 375–89; Guide to the Jane Addams Papers, Swarthmore College Peace Collection.

10. MWO, "The Status of the Negro in the United States," *New Review*, September 1913, 748. Ovington credits only the NAACP and the IWW with racial justice concerns.

11. Storey was in 1909 divided in his support for Washington and Du Bois, and would have difficulties working with the militants. William B. Hixson, Jr., *Moorfield Storey and the Abolitionist Tradition* (New York: Oxford University Press, 1972), 99, 124–25.

12. Kellogg, *NAACP,* 15.

13. MWO, in *William English Walling: A Symposium* (New York: Stackpole Sons, 1938), 80–81. Minutes of the Committee on the Negro, March 1909, NAACP Papers, Library of Congress (LC). Ovington wrote on stationery from 3 Monroe Place, Brooklyn, the home of her sister and brother-in-law. The minutes of April 27 and May 4, 1909, were also by Ovington.

Ovington earlier invited Baker to meet Irvine and "a few prominent colored people." (MWO to Ray Stannard Baker [RSB], April 10, 1907, RSB Papers, LC). To Du Bois, she described Irvine as a "Christian Socialist" who investigated southern peonage by working beside colored workers, and she recommended him as a speaker for the 1907 Niagara meetings. (MWO to W. E. B. DuBois [WEDB], April 20, 1907, WEDB Papers, University of Massachusetts).

14. Charles Anderson to Booker T. Washington (BTW), May 29 and 31 (telegram), 1909, BTW Papers, LC.

15. WEDB, "National Committee on the Negro," *Survey* (June 12, 1909), 407–9. Further references to Du Bois's account of the conference are also to this source.

16. *New York Times,* June 1, 1909.

17. MWO, "Reminiscences," *Baltimore Afro-American,* November 26, 1932, 24.

18. Ibid.; *New York Times,* June 1, 1909; "Then and Now: NAACP 1909–1959," pamphlet, Roy Wilkins Papers, LC; John Milholland, diary, New York State Historical Association, Ticonderoga (THS); MWO, "The NAACP," *Journal of Negro History,* vol. 9 (April 1924), 111. See also Leonora O'Reilly, diary, May 31, 1909, O'Reilly Papers, Schlesinger Library, Radcliffe College.

19. MWO, "Reminiscences," *Baltimore Afro-American,* November 26, 1932, 24.

20. Oswald Garrison Villard (OGV) to BTW, May 26, 1909; BTW to OGV, May 28, 1909, OGV Papers, bMS Am 1323 (4099), Houghton Library, Harvard University (Harvard).

21. "National Negro Committee" Broadside, NAACP Papers, LC.

22. MWO, *The Walls,* 106; MWO to RSB, July 2, 1909, RSB Papers, LC.

23. MWO to OGV, June 2, 1909, OGV Papers, bMS Am 1323 (2921), Harvard. MWO, "Reminiscences," *Baltimore Afro-American,* November 26, 1932, 24. Wells-Barnett, unfortunately, had a different reading of the compromise and Ovington's role. Ovington says she left the meeting in exhaustion, needing to be alone; Wells-Barnett describes her as sweeping by with a triumphant smile. The misunderstanding tainted their relations from then on. See Alfreda M. Duster, ed., *Crusade for Justice: the Autobiography of Ida B. Wells* (Chicago: University of Chicago Press, 1970), 325–29.

24. John Milholland, diary, THS.

25. MWO, "The NAACP," *Journal of Negro History*, vol. 9 (April 1924), 111–12.

26. John Haynes Holmes, *I Speak for Myself: The Autobiography* (New York: Harper and Brothers, 1959), 196, 199. Frances Blascoer to "Lady" [Isabel Eaton?], March 26, 1910, WEDB Papers, Mass.

27. William English Walling to WEDB, June 8, 1909, WEDB Papers, Mass. Kellogg, *NAACP*, 34–39. OGV to BTW, September 3, 1909, BTW Papers, LC. OGV's first public siding with WEDB came in a *Post* editorial April 1, 1910. WEDB to "Hope," January 22, 1910, WEDB Papers, Mass.

28. MWO, Review of Edgar Gardner Murphy's *The Basis of Ascendancy*, *Survey*, vol. 23 (November 6, 1909), 169–70.

29. Minutes, National Negro Conference, December 13, 1909, Minutes of the Committee of Forty, February 14, March 14, March [April written on] 24, 1910, and Minutes of Subcommittee February 23, 1910, NAACP Papers, LC.

30. MWO Papers, Archives of Labor & Urban Affairs, Wayne State University (WSU).

31. Untitled mailing on National Negro Committee letterhead from M. W. Ovington, n.d. [1910], WEDB Papers, Mass. Minutes of the National Negro Committee, April 7, 21, May 5, 1910, NAACP Papers, LC.

32. John Milholland to WEDB, May 20, 1908, March 4, 1909, May 25, June 20, 1910; Committee on the Permanent Organization of the NAACP [1910], WEDB Papers, Mass.

33. "Report of the Preliminary Committee on Permanent Organization," NAACP Papers, LC. For debates on organization, see Kellogg, *NAACP*, 42–44.

34. William English Walling to RSB, March 5 and 22, 1909. WEDB to RSB, May 6, 1909. RSB Papers, LC.

35. MWO to RSB, March 9, 16, July 2, November 9, 1909, and n.d. [1910], RSB Papers, LC.

36. RSB to BTW, May 13, June 20, 1910, BTW Papers, LC.

37. "Prof. Boas Predicts Race Amalgamation," *New York Times* May 15, 1910, 2.

38. MWO, *Survey*, vol. 24 (May 28, 1910), 343–45. She also covered the 1912 and 1913 meetings: *Survey*, vol. 28 (May 18, 1912), 318–20 and vol. 30 (June 7, 1913), 322.

39. Minutes, Executive Committee, June 28, 1910, NAACP Papers, LC. MWO to Joel Spingarn (JES), November 7, 1914, JES Papers, Moorland Spingarn Research Center, Howard University (Moorland).

40. WEDB, Oral History Interview, Columbia University.

41. WEDB to William English Walling, August 16, 19, 1910, WEDB Papers, Mass; MWO, "How the NAACP Began," 1914.

42. Kellogg, *NAACP,* 51. Minutes, Executive Committee, September 6, October 11, November 29, 1910, NAACP Papers, LC. *Crisis,* vol. 1 (November 1910).

43. MWO, MWO Papers, WSU.

44. MWO to RSB, n.d. [1910], RSB Papers, LC. MWO, "Reminiscences," *Baltimore Afro-American,* December 3, 1932, 24; MWO, typescripts, MWO Papers, WSU. Unless indicated, sections on Jamaica are based on these.

45. MWO, *The Walls,* 131. Kellogg, *NAACP,* 83.

46. "The Races Congress," by "Our Own Correspondent," *Crisis* (September 1911), 200–209. This unsigned article could very well be by Ovington, though it gets listed in Du Bois publications.

47. MWO, *The Walls,* 131–32; "The Races Congress,"; "List of Members of the First Universal Races Congress . . . ," (London: Watts and Company, 1911); *Record of the Proceedings of the First Universal Races Congress . . .* (London: P. S. King and Son, 1911). British Museum, London.

48. MWO, *The Walls,* 132–33; "Reminiscences," *Baltimore Afro-American,* December 24, 1932, 24; MWO to Louise Ovington, August 18, 20, 26, 31, 1911, MWO Papers, WSU.

49. MWO, "Revolution," *Independent,* vol. 75 (July 3, 1913), 20.

50. MWO to Arthur Spingarn (ABS), December 31, 1913; ABS to MWO, January 14, 1914, ABS Papers, LC.

51. MWO, "Algiers: In the Land Where the Sons of the Desert Are the Children of France," MWO Papers, WSU.

52. MWO, "On Christmas Eve," *New York Evening Post,* December 24, 1914.

53. MWO, "Reminiscences," *Baltimore Afro-American,* December 24, 1932, 24.

54. "The N. A. A. C. P.," *Crisis* (May 1911).

55. Board Minutes, April 11, May 16, 1911, NAACP Papers, LC; Kellogg, *NAACP,* 94; Charles Flint Kellogg Papers, WSU.

56. "Proxy. . . ,"; "Certificate of Incorporation. . . ,"; "NAACP Waiver of Notice . . . ," Minutes, June 20, 1911, NAACP Papers, LC.

57. Board Minutes, February 6, 1912, NAACP Papers, LC; Rosenwald Papers, University of Chicago.

58. MWO, "The Negro in America: Today and Tomorrow," *Survey* 28 (May 18, 1912), 318–20; *The Walls,* 125–27; *Crisis* (June 1912).

59. MWO, *The Walls,* 115–16; Kellogg, *NAACP,* 186–87; 205–6.

60. Board Minutes, November 29, 1910, March 7, November 14, 1911, NAACP Papers, LC.

61. MWO, *The Walls,* 108–9.

62. Ibid., 111–12; *Crisis* (January 1912), 110; "Notes on Lynching . . . ," ABS Papers, LC.

63. Board Minutes, June 6, 1911, NAACP Papers, LC; MWO, *The Walls*, 118–21.

64. Board Minutes, 1912, NAACP Papers, LC; MWO, "Mary Dunlop Maclean," *Crisis* (August 1912); MWO, "Protection" *Crisis* (July 1912), 144.

65. MWO, "Nativity," *Crisis* (December 1911), 76.

66. MWO, "Introduction," *Half a Man: The Status of the Negro in New York* (1911; rpt. N.Y.: Schocken, 1969), 3. Subsequent references will be indicated with page numbers in parentheses.

67. Not all prostitution was by choice. Ovington also describes slave traffic, black more than white.

68. Reprints were by Schocken Books, Preface by Roy Wilkins; Negro Universities Press, 1969; Hill and Wang, 1970, Introduction by Charles Flint Kellogg. S. Breckenridge, Review, *American Journal of Sociology*, vol. 17 (November 1911), 414–17. WEDB, "What to Read," *Crisis* (October 1911), 256–57; (January 1912), 123–24.

CHAPTER 6

1. Charles Flint Kellogg, *NAACP: A History of the National Association for the Advancement of Colored People* (Baltimore, Md.: Johns Hopkins University Press, 1967), 94.

2. W. E. B. Du Bois (WEDB), "Memorandum to Mr. J. E. Spingarn, Mr. Arthur Spingarn and Miss Ovington" [1915], Arthur B. Spingarn Papers (ABS), Library of Congress (LC).

3. Oswald Garrison Villard (OGV) to Board, NAACP, November 19, 1913, OGV Papers, Houghton Library, Harvard (Harvard).

4. OGV to Mary White Ovington (MWO), November 21, 1913, OGV Papers, bMS Am 1323 (2921), Harvard.

5. Board Minutes, April 1, 1913, NAACP Papers, LC.

6. MWO to OGV, "Sunday" [November 1913], OGV Papers, Harvard.

7. Ibid., November 25, 1913.

8. George A. Plimpton gave them two suites for a third of their worth. Board Minutes, January 6, 1914, NAACP Papers, LC; MWO to OGV, December 31, 1913, ABS Papers, LC.

9. Kellogg, *NAACP*, 98–99.

10. MWO to Joel E. Spingarn (JES) [November 4, 1914], JES Papers, Moorland-Spingarn Research Center, Howard University (Moorland).

11. JES to MWO, November 5, 1914, MWO Papers, Archives of Labor and Urban Affairs, Wayne State University (WSU).

12. MWO to JES, November 7, 1914, JES Papers, Moorland. See also MWO to OGV, August 10, 1915, OGV to MWO, August 11, 1915, OGV Papers, Harvard.

13. WEDB, "A Statement" [December, 1915]; WEDB to Board, December 13, 1915, WEDB Papers, University of Massachusetts (Mass.); Board Minutes, November 8, December 13, 1915; Report of the "Committee appointed for the purpose of defining and delimiting the work of the executive officers" [December 1915], NAACP Papers, LC.

14. Joyce Ross, *J. E. Spingarn and the Rise of the NAACP* (New York: Atheneum, 1972), 77.

15. MWO to JES, December 13 [1915], JES Papers, Moorland. More troubles: three-fourths of the January 1916 *Crisis* print run was destroyed by a printer fire, with no insurance. Who bears the cost? Du Bois asked—the magazine or the NAACP?; WEDB to Charles Studin and ABS, December 23, 1915, ABS Papers, LC.

16. MWO to JES, December 20, 1915, Joel Elias Spingarn Papers, Rare Books and Manuscripts Division, New York Public Library, Astor, Lenox and Tilden Foundations (NYPL); Archibald Grimke to WEDB, December 29, 1915, WEDB Papers, Mass. There would be a first black chairman of the board, almost right after Ovington's tenure: Dr. Louis Wright became chairman in 1934, after Joel Spingarn took the post briefly once again in 1932. Meanwhile, under Ovington's chairmanship, much authority passed to the executive secretary, to which position James Weldon Johnson was appointed as the first black incumbent in 1920.

17. Roy Aitken, as told to Al Nelson, *The Birth of a Nation Story* (Middleburg, Va.: Denlinger, 1965), 6; *The American Film Institute Catalog, 1911–1920* (Berkeley: University of California Press, 1988), 71.

18. "Zit," *New York Journal*, March 15, 1915, ABS Papers, LC.

19. JES, Speech, January 3, 1916, NAACP Papers, LC.

20. MWO, "Reminiscences," *Baltimore Afro-American*, December 31, 1932, 24. May Childs Nerney to OGV, March 9, 1915; MWO to "His Honor, John Purroy Mitchel, Mayor of the City of New York," March 31, 1915, NAACP Papers, LC; MWO, *The Walls Came Tumbling Down* (New York: Harcourt Brace, 1947), 127.

21. MWO, *The Walls*, 127–30; MWO to John Purroy Mitchel, March 31, 1915; Executive Secretary, City of NY to MWO, April 1, 1915; Board Minutes, April 13, 1915, NAACP Papers, LC.

22. A. E. Pillsbury to Boston *Herald*, n.d., ABS Papers, LC.

23. Board Minutes, March 23, 1915; MWO to May Childs Nerney, March 25, [1915]; Nerney to MWO, March 26, 1915, NAACP Papers, LC. After the East St. Louis Riots in July of 1917, the same precaution would be made, only that time the parade was all black.

24. MWO, *The Walls*, 130–31.

25. Kellogg, *NAACP*, 144.

26. MWO, "The White Brute," *The Masses*, vol. 6 (October–November 1915), 17–18.

27. MWO, "Reminiscences," *Baltimore Afro-American* February 18, 1933, 24.

28. MWO to OGV, April 17, 1915, OGV Papers, Harvard; Kellogg, *NAACP*, 144–45.

29. May Childs Nerney to MWO, May 15, 1915; May Childs Nerney to JES, May 21, 1915, NAACP Papers, LC.

30. May Childs Nerney to JES, May 19, 21, 1915, NAACP Papers; Richetta Randolph to ABS, May 30, 1915, and Charles T. Hallinan to ABS, June 1, 1915, ABS Papers, both LC. Ovington was very careful about spending NAACP money on the film project—she permitted the association to pay her expenses to Boston for testifying before the mayor, but not for reading the scenario to Hart (MWO to M. C. Nerney, May 20, 1915, NAACP Papers, LC).

31. MWO to OGV, June 6, 1915, OGV Papers, Harvard.

32. Board Minutes, October 11, November 8, 1915, NAACP Papers, LC.

33. MWO's best discussion of realism versus polemic and propaganda is in "Reminiscences," *Baltimore Afro-American*, February 11, 1933.

34. MWO to Mrs. William H. Baldwin, Jr., et. al., "Confidential" [June, 1915]. (enclosure promoting "Lincoln's Dream"), MWO to Mrs. Baldwin, June 8 [1915], Levi H. Wood Papers, Rare Book and Manuscript Library, Columbia University. David Levering Lewis says, "*The Birth of a Nation* and the NAACP helped make each other" through the mobilization of protest but Du Bois "quickly lost interest" in the alternative film project. *W. E. B. Du Bois: Biography of a Race* (New York: Henry Holt, 1993), 495, 509.

35. President George Bush attended a play about the Tuskegee program as the first bombs fell in the Persian Gulf War. The question in 1991 was whether the numbers of blacks in the military represented too much "equal opportunity."

36. Board Minutes, April 9, 1917, NAACP Papers, LC.

37. MWO to JES, February 28, 1917, JES Papers, Moorland.

38. MWO, "Gretchen Talks to Her Doll," *Four Lights* (April 21, 1917), MWO Papers, WSU.

39. Kellogg, *NAACP*, 290. *Revolutionary Radicalism*, Report of the Joint Legislative Committee of the State of New York Investigating Seditious Activities, part 1, vol. 2, 1318–21, 1476–1520.

40. Charles Russell to Graham Stokes, March 15, 1917. Stokes Collection, Rare Book and Manuscript Library, Columbia.

41. MWO to JES, July 5, 1917, JES Papers, Moorland.

42. Ibid., August 15 [1917].

43. Ibid., September 26, 29, 1917. MWO to JES, March 16, April 5, 1918, JES Papers NYPL.

44. MWO to JES, March 6, April 18, 1918.

45. Ibid., April 5, 1918.

46. MWO, "Letter," *Messenger* (July 1918), 114–15. Ovington did not use her title, but the editors added it to ads, getting her into trouble at the NAACP. William Pickens had the same problem.

47. MWO to JES, April 5, 1918, JES Papers, NYPL.

48. Ibid., August 15 [1917], JES Papers, Moorland. Letters are addressed "c/o S. H. Vollmer, Huntington, L.I."

49. MWO to JES, April 5, March 16, 1918, JES Papers, NYPL.

50. Kellogg, *NAACP,* 221, 224. Elliott M. Rudwick, *Race Riot at East St. Louis, July 2, 1917* (Carbondale: Southern Illinois University Press, 1964; reprint, Cleveland: Meridian, 1966) 59–60. MWO, *Portraits in Color* (New York: Viking Press, 1927), 142–43.

51. Richetta Randolph to William English Walling, July 20, 1917; M. Kendrick to MWO, July 23, 1917; James Weldon Johnson (JWJ) to MWO, WEDB and ABS, July 24, 1917, ABS Papers, LC. WEDB to William English Walling, July 31, 1917, WEDB Papers, Mass; Board Minutes, September 17, 1917, NAACP Papers, LC; MWO to JES, September 29, 1917, JES Papers, Moorland.

52. Kellogg, *NAACP,* 226.

53. MWO to JES, August 15, 1917, JES Papers, Moorland; MWO to ABS, August 17, 1917, ABS Papers, LC; Board Minutes, September 17, 1917, NAACP Papers, LC; MWO to OGV, October 5, 1917, OGV Papers, Harvard.

54. MWO to JES, September 26, 29, 1917, JES Papers, Moorland.

55. Ibid.; MWO to OGV, October 5, 1917, OGV Papers, Harvard.

56. OGV to MWO, October 6, 1917, OGV Papers, Harvard.

57. MWO to Lillian Wald, November 15, 1917, Lillian Wald Papers, Rare Book and Manuscript Library, Columbia University.

58. "The Great Mid-Winter Conference of the NAACP" Announcement; "The Negro in Wartime" Program; MWO to Lillian Wald, November 15, December 3, 26, 1917; Lillian Wald to MWO, November 20, 1917, Wald Collection, Columbia.

59. Board Minutes, December 10, 1917, NAACP Papers, LC; MWO, "Reminiscences," *Baltimore Afro-American,* January 7, 1933, 24.

60. MWO, "Reminiscences," *Baltimore Afro-American,* January 7, 1933, 24. Board Minutes, December 9, 1918; MWO to John Shillady, July 31, 1918, NAACP Papers, LC.

61. Ovington headed the committee that planned the surprise and solicited money for a loving cup: See WEDB to MWO, February 26, 1918, MWO to WEDB, March 4, 1918, WEDB Papers, Mass; MWO to JES, Febru-

ary 17, 1918, JES Papers NYPL; MWO to Archibald Grimke [Washington, D.C., branch president], January 9 and 18, 1918, Grimke Papers, Moorland. Her own fiftieth birthday in April 1915 apparently passed unnoticed at the NAACP and *Crisis* offices.

62. MWO, "Reminiscences," *Baltimore Afro-American*, January 14, 1933, 24. Ovington dates the trip as 1920, but parts are from 1918 and some from February, 1921; she did not travel west in 1920. The typewriter was a blessing. To Shillady she typed, "Let me congratulate you on your typewriting. I am certainly a bummtypewriter [*sic*]," but she knew it was better than her scrawl.

63. MWO, "Reminiscences," *Baltimore Afro-American*, January 14, 1933, 24. MWO to John Shillady, June 30, n.d. 1918, NAACP Papers, LC.

64. MWO to John Shillady, June 30, August 7, 1918, NAACP Papers, LC.

65. WEDB to MWO, July 11, 1918; WEDB to Board, July 2, 1918; MWO to WEDB, July 7, 10, 1918; WEDB Papers, Mass. Board Minutes, July 8, 1918, NAACP Papers, LC. V. Morton-Jones to WEDB, July 3, 1918, WEDB Papers, Mass, supported Du Bois's proposal.

WEDB, "Close Ranks" (July 1918); "Returning Soldiers" (May 1919), *The Crisis;* reprinted in Walter Wilson, ed., *The Selected Writings of W. E. B. Du Bois* (New York: New American Library, 1970), 170–72. MWO to John Shillady [August 5, 10, 1918], NAACP Papers, LC.

66. MWO to John Shillady, July 6, 27, 1918, NAACP Papers, LC. Peter Bergman, *The Chronological History of the Negro in America* (New York: Harper and Row, 1969), 385; MWO to WEDB, July 7, 1918, WEDB Papers, Mass. Kellogg, *NAACP*, 227–28.

67. MWO to John Shillady [August 5, 1918], NAACP Papers, LC; MWO, *The Walls*, 140, 142.

68. Ibid., July 4, 1918; MWO, "Reminiscences," *Baltimore Afro-American*, January 14, 1933, 24.

69. She also visited Lincoln, Denver, Minneapolis and St. Paul, Detroit, Syracuse. MWO to John Shillady, Sunday [July 28], and July 31, 1918, NAACP Papers, LC.

70. MWO to John Shillady, July 4, 6, 7, 12, 24, 27, 28, 31, 1918; Board Minutes, September 8, 1918, NAACP Papers, LC.

71. Board Minutes, October 14, November 11, December 1, 1918, NAACP Papers, LC.

72. MWO to John Shillady, July 31 [1918], NAACP Papers, LC.

CHAPTER 7

1. Minutes, Annual Meeting, January 6, 1919, NAACP Papers, Library of Congress (LC).

2. Mary White Ovington (MWO) to Joel Spingarn (JES), January 19, 1918 [1919], JES Papers, Rare books and Manuscript Division, New York Public Library Astor Lenox and Tilden Foundations (NYPL); MWO to James Weldon Johnson (JWJ) [January 7, 1919], JWJ Papers, Yale Collection of American Literature, Beinecke Rare Book & Manuscript Library, Yale University (Yale); MWO to W. E. B. Du Bois (WEDB), January 10, 1918 [1919], WEDB Papers, University of Massachusetts (Mass.).

3. Harold Connolly in *A Ghetto Grows in Brooklyn* (New York: New York University Press, 1977) cites Lincoln Settlement as the first social service organization in Brooklyn to deal comprehensively with the needs of blacks.

4. Arthur Spingarn (ABS) Papers, LC; MWO, account books, MWO Papers, Archives of Labor and Urban Affairs, Wayne State University (WSU). MWO to Grace Johnson, August 4, 1919, JWJ Papers, Yale.

5. MWO, office diary, 1920, NAACP Papers, LC. "The Civic Club," MWO Papers, WSU; MWO, *THe Walls Came Tumbling Down* (New York: Harcourt, Brace and Company, 1947), 193–98.

6. "Office diaries" list phone calls, letters, meetings; "Members of Speakers Bureau" form lists speeches. NAACP Papers, LC.

7. MWO to JES, January 19, [1919], JES Papers, NYPL; JWJ to WEDB, April 17, 1924, WEDB Papers, Mass.; Charles Flint Kellogg, *NAACP: A History of the National Association for the Advancement of Colored People, 1909–1920* (Baltimore: Johns Hopkins University Press, 1967), 51, n22.

8. MWO, "Reconstruction and the Negro," *Crisis* (February 1919), 169–73. Unless indicated, the following material is from this article.

9. MWO, *The Walls*, 152.

10. Claude McKay, "If We Must Die," in *Blackamerican Literature*, ed. Ruth Miller (Beverly Hills, Calif.: Glencoe Press, 1971), 334.

11. MWO, "Reminiscences," *Baltimore Afro-American*, January 7, 1933, 24; *The Walls*, 167–77; Kellogg, *NAACP*, 136–37, 236, 271; Kenneth Kusmer, *A Ghetto Takes Shape: Black Cleveland, 1870–1930* (Urbana: University of Illinois Press, 1976), 178.

12. MWO to JES, August 1, 1919; MWO to Charles Edward Russell, August 12, [15], 1919, NAACP Papers, LC. MWO to John Shillady, August 11, 12, 1919; Russell to MWO, August 14, 1919, in transcripts of NAACP material later lost, Arthur I. Waskow Papers, Wisconsin State Historical Library (Waskow).

13. MWO, *The Walls*, 171–73; "Reminiscences," *Baltimore Afro-American*, January 7, 1933, 24.

14. MWO, "Reminiscences," *Baltimore Afro-American*, January 7, 1933, 24; "Proceedings of a court of Inquiry. . . ," ABS Papers, LC.

15. MWO, "Reminiscences," *Baltimore Afro-American*, January 7, 1933, 24; *The Walls*, 172–75; MWO, "Is Mob Violence the Texas Solution of the Race Problem?" *Independent*, September 6, 1919, 320.

16. Kellogg, *NAACP,* 240–41; John Shillady, office diary, December 31, 1919, NAACP Papers, LC; MWO to JWJ, April 9, 1920, JWJ Papers, Yale.

17. MWO to JWJ, April 9, 1920, JWJ Papers, Yale; Board Minutes, May 10, 1920, NAACP Papers, LC; MWO, "Reminiscences," *Baltimore Afro-American,* January 7, 1933, 24; *The Walls,* 175.

18. MWO, "Is Mob Violence the Texas Solution of the Race Problem?" *Independent,* September 6, 1919, 320.

19. MWO, "Reminiscences," *Baltimore Afro-American,* January 7, 1933, 24; JWJ, *Along This Way* (New York: Viking, 1933; reprint, New York: Da Capo Press, 1973), 356–57.

20. MWO, "The Gunpowder of Race Antagonism," *American City,* vol. 21 (September 1919), 248–51.

21. MWO, "Socialism and the Feminist Movement," *New Review,* vol. 2 (March 1914), 143–47.

22. Carrie Overton to ABS, October 8, 1924, ABS Papers, LC; MWO, account books, MWO papers, WSU; Verina Morton-Jones to MWO, February 28, 1922, MWO to Alice Brown, November 14, 1927, NAACP papers, LC; MWO to JES, December 15 [1931], JES Papers, NYPL; MWO, *The Walls,* Dedication; MWO, *The Awakening,* 1923; reprint, Freeport, N.Y.: Books for Libraries Press, 1972, 58.

23. MWO, "Reminiscences," *Baltimore Afro-American,* January 14, 1933, 24; MWO to Mary Talbert, July 10, 1920, NAACP Papers, LC.

24. MWO, "Reminiscences," *Baltimore Afro-American,* January 14, 1933, 24.

25. MWO to Vida Milholland, February 26, April 8, 1919; Vida Milholland to MWO [March, 1919]; Board Minutes March 10, 1919, NAACP Papers, LC. Eleanor Flexner, *Century of Struggle: The Woman's Rights Movement in the United States* (New York: Atheneum, 1973), 276–313, passim.

26. In December 1920, Ovington asked the Woman's Party to include Talbert on its celebratory program and to establish a committee to work on enfranchisement of Negro women. The orderly process was too unsensational. "Had the colored women picketed the Woman's Party it would have been in the papers but their dignified hearing got no publicity." MWO, office diaries, NAACP Papers, LC; MWO to ABS, April 2 [1921], ABS Papers, LC.

27. "NAACP Holds 13th Annual Conference. . . ," Moorfield Storey Papers, LC. Ovington campaigned for Janie Porter Barrett, who ran a NACW reformatory for Negro girls, to get the Spingarn Medal, wanting to recognize a "social reformer." See MWO, "Janie Porter Barrett," in *Portraits in Color* (New York: Viking Press, 1927), 181–93. MWO to Oswald Garrison Villard (OGV), January 17, 1932, OGV Papers, Houghton Library, Harvard University (Harvard). By 1932, Ovington pointed out, Mary Talbert was the only woman recipient. Another Ovington suggestion, Mary McLeod Bethune,

received it in 1935. Adding Marian Anderson in 1939, three Spingarn Medals went to women from among the first thirty-one.

28. MWO to Warren G. Harding, October 31, 1922, NAACP Papers, LC.

29. MWO to Mrs. Franklin D. Roosevelt, May 28, 1924, NAACP Papers, LC.

30. MWO to John Shillady, July 6, 7, 1918, NAACP Papers, LC; MWO to WEDB, July 10, 1918, WEDB Papers, Mass. MWO, "Reminiscences," *Baltimore Afro-American*, January 14, 1933, 24.

31. "Itinerary of Miss Mary White Ovington," April 17–19, 1919; MWO to Mary Talbert, April 14, 1919; MWO office diary, Board Minutes, May 12, 1919, NAACP Papers, LC.

32. MWO, *The Walls*, 154.

33. MWO to JES, October 22, 1919; Board Minutes, December 13, 1920, NAACP Papers, LC; MWO to ABS, December 27, 1920, Richetta Randolph to ABS, December 30, ABS Papers, LC.

34. MWO, "Catching a Baby" [1928–29], MWO Papers, WSU.

35. MWO, *The Walls*, 154–57; "Scipio Africanus Jones," in *Portraits in Color*, 95–97; Kellogg, *NAACP*, 242–43; MWO to Mrs. Fannie Crowell, October 21, 1919, Waskow; MWO to Lillian Wald, ["Nov 1917"; should be 1919] Wald Papers, Columbia.

36. MWO, *The Walls*, 157–58; MWO to Lillian Wald, "Sunday" [1919], Wald Papers, Columbia; Memo on conference with U. S. Bratton, MWO, Shillady, Walter White (WW), and JES, October 31, 1919; MWO to Edith Wharton Dallas, November 11, 1919; MWO to A. H. Harris, December 12, 1919; MWO to John Milholland, December 17, 1919; MWO to William F. Fuerst, New York Foundation, December 11, 1919, Waskow. MWO to ABS, November 12, 1919; Agnes Leach to Mr. and Mrs. Spingarn, November 14, 1919, ABS Papers, LC. Board Minutes, November 25, 1919, NAACP Papers, LC. MWO to Archibald Grimke, November 13, 1919, Grimke Papers, Moorland-Spingarn, Howard University (Moorland).

37. "In *Frank v. Mangum*, 237 U.S. 309, 335, 59 L. ed. 969, 983, 35 Sup. Ct. Rep. 582, it was recognized, of course, that if in fact a trial is dominated by a mob, so that there is an actual interference with the course of justice, there is a departure from due process of law; and that 'if the state, supplying no corrective process, carries into execution a judgement of death or imprisonment based upon a verdict thus produced by mob domination, the state deprives the accused of his life or liberty without due process of the law.'" Quote from "Cases Argued and Decided in the Supreme Court of the United States," October term, 1922, in 260, 261, 262 U.S. Book 67, Lawyers' Edition, Rochester, N.Y.: Lawyers Co-Operative Publishing, 1924, p. 545.

38. MWO, *The Walls*, 159–63; *Portraits in Color*, 97–103; Kellogg, *NAACP*, 244–45; MWO office diary, December 6, 1920; MWO to Florence Kelley,

April 27; Moorfield Storey, October 24; William Graves, October 26, 1921, NAACP Papers, LC; Moorfield Storey to MWO, November 13, 1922; MWO to ABS, October 24, 1923; ABS to MWO, October 25, 1923, ABS Papers, LC.

39. Richard C. Cortner. *A Mob Intent on Death: The NAACP and the Arkansas Riot Cases.* (Middletown, Conn.: Wesleyan University Press, 1988).

40. For the Dyer antilynching campaign, see Robert Zangrando, *The NAACP Crusade Against Lynching, 1909–1950* (Philadelphia: Temple University Press, 1980), 33, and "The Dyer Bill," Charles Flint Kellogg Papers, WSU.

41. Robert Zangrando, *The NAACP Crusade*, 5–7, gives the 1918 total as 60. Ovington says 64. Zangrando's tables show the increasing race emphasis. When Texas claimed, after the Shillady attack, that they lynched as many whites as blacks, they were not far off; from 1882 to 1968, 141 whites and 352 blacks were lynched in the Lone Star state, after Mississippi with 581, and Georgia with 531.

42. MWO, "Reconstruction and the Negro" *The Crisis*, Volume 17 (February 1919), 173.

43. ABS to WEDB, February 9, 1921, ABS Papers, LC.

44. MWO to ABS, February 8, 1921, ABS Papers, LC.

45. "Agreement Between the Anti-Lynching Crusaders and the NAACP," [June 1922], ABS Papers, LC; MWO, *The Walls*, 154. MWO to Robert Bagnall, October 31, 1922; MWO to Moorfield Storey, January 26, February 7, May 29, 1922; MWO to JWJ, June 29, November 28, 1922; MWO to Richetta Randolph [1922], August 3, 1922. NAACP Papers, LC.

46. MWO to JWJ, August 7, 1922; Board Minutes, March 12, September 10, 1923, NAACP Papers, LC; MWO to ABS, August 24, 1923; MWO to JWJ, September 8, 1923, JWJ Papers, Yale.

47. Board Minutes, February 14, 1922; April 14, 1924, NAACP Papers, LC; "The NAACP Will Memorialize the United States Senate. . . ," ABS Papers, LC.

48. In the years from 1924 through 1930, the number of lynching victims was 16, 17, 23, 16, 10, 7, and 20, respectively. (Zangrando). Ovington supported a congressional inquiry, which White and Johnson eschewed. By 1947, she noted, lynchings nearly disappeared because of better roads, education, churches, and workers against lynching in the South.

CHAPTER 8

1. Mary White Ovington (MWO), *The Walls Came Tumbling Down* (New York: Harcourt, Brace and Company, 1947), 186, 238–42; James Weldon Johnson (JWJ), *Along This Way* (New York: Da Capo Press, 1973), 382–83; Court Records, Southern Berkshire County, Great Barrington, Massachusetts;

Interviews: Mary Dellea; Katherine Dellea Smith; Laura Keeney Tucker, Dorothy Poplowski, July 2–7, 1989.

MWO, Account Books, MWO Papers, Archive of Labor and Urban Affairs, Wayne State University (WSU). MWO, office diaries, 1920, NAACP Papers, Library of Congress (LC); MWO to Joel E. Spingarn (JES), January 11, 1922, Joel Elias Spingarn Papers, Rare Books and Manuscripts Division, New York Public Library, Astor, Lenox and Tilden Foundations (NYPL).

2. "Troutbeck" [brochure for Executive Retreat Conference Center], c. 1989; Interview with Jim Flaherty, June 14, 1989; Lewis Mumford, "An Old Neighbor," "The Story of Troutbeck" [1920s]; the author thanks Flaherty for these items; MWO to JES, July 6, 1926, NAACP Papers, LC. Charles Flint Kellogg, *NAACP: A History of the National Association for the Advancement of Colored People* (Baltimore: Johns Hopkins University Press, 1967), 62–65.

Daniel W. Cryer, in his master's thesis, Minnesota, 1969, "Mary White Ovington and Oswald Garrison Villard . . . A Study in Contrasts," makes much of their differing upbringing, describing Villard's hundred-acre Dobbs Ferry estate, its six living rooms, dozen dogs, liveried servants, stables (27).

3. "The Crisis Publishing Company" was first part of the incorporated NAACP; it was later legalized as separate and profit-making. See W. E. B. Du Bois (WEDB) to Charles Studin, August 21, 1914, Arthur B. Spingarn (ABS) Papers, LC.

4. MWO, *Hazel* (New York: Crisis Publishing Company, 1913), v–vi.

5. Leonard Archer, *Black Images in the American Theater: NAACP Protest Campaigns—Stage, Screen, Radio and Television* (Brooklyn: Pageant-Poseidon, Ltd, 1973), 112. Archer calls Hazel a nonstereotyped Negro child, the opposite of Topsy in *Uncle Tom.*

6. MWO to JES, August 15 [1917] (marked [1915]); MWO to Mrs. Spingarn, November 9 [1916], JES Papers, Moorland-Spingarn Research Center, Howard University (Moorland).

7. Ovington's Social Reform Club friend, William Dean Howells, used such a character in *An Imperative Duty* in 1893; Mark Twain, his protégé, played with the concept in *The Tragedy of Pudd'nhead Wilson* in 1894. T. S. Stribling helped set the Harlem Renaissance in gear with *Birthright*, which inspired Jessie Fauset to write *There Is Confusion*, to be followed by Walter White's *Fire in the Flint* and Nella Larsen's *Quicksand* and *Passing.* Charles Chesnutt used the mulatto for the irony of racial identity and the psychological implications of "passing," as did James Weldon Johnson in *Auto-biography of an Ex-Colored Man* in 1912.

8. MWO, "Reminiscences," *Baltimore Afro-American*, December 17, 1932, February 18, 1933, 24; MWO, *The Shadow* (New York: Harcourt, Brace and Howe, 1920; reprint, Freeport, N.Y.: Books for Libraries Press, 1972).

9. *Outward Bound*, 1921, publicized with big posters: ". . . The Most Thrilling Colour-Life Story since Uncle Tom's Cabin." *Irish Christian Advocate*, October 1924. MWO Papers, WSU.

10. *Booklist* (June 1920), 314; *Boston Transcript* (June 2, 1920), 4; *Freeman* (October 6, 1920), 93; *New York Times* (June 27, 1920), 25; *New York Evening Post* (May 1, 1920), 3.

11. Elmer Rice to MWO, May 29, 1920, MWO Papers, WSU.

12. MWO, "Reminiscences," *Baltimore Afro-American*, December 17, 1932, 24; MWO and Myron Pritchard, eds. *The Upward Path* (New York: Harcourt, Brace and Howe, 1920), 25, 109, 143–47, 153–59.

13. MWO and Pritchard, eds. *The Upward Path* (New York: Harcourt, Brace and Howe, 1920), 29–38, 66–72, 54–55, 208–209, 228–232.

14. MWO office diaries, 1920, NAACP Papers, LC.

15. MWO, "Reminiscences," *Baltimore Afro-American*, February 11, 1933, 24. Tony Martin, in *Literary Garveyism: Garvey, Black Arts and the Harlem Renaissance* (Dover, Mass.: The Majority Press, 1983), calls Ovington "a most unlikely regular reviewer" in *Negro World*.

16. MWO, "Reminiscences," *Baltimore Afro-American*, February 11, 1933, 24. MWO to Archibald Grimke, November 9, 1920, Grimke Papers, Moorland.

17. Nathan Irvin Huggins, *Harlem Renaissance* (New York: Oxford, 1971), 119.

18. MWO, "Reminiscences," *Baltimore Afro-American*, February 11, 1933, 24.

19. Cornelia F. Cook to MWO, n.d. [1922?], NAACP Papers, LC.

20. MWO, *Portraits in Color* (New York: Viking, 1927); MWO, "Reminiscences," *Baltimore Afro-American*, February 18, 1933, 24. MWO to Julius Rosenwald, December 7, 1927, NAACP Papers, LC; MWO to Oswald Garrison Villard (OGV), January 5, 1929, OGV Papers, bMS Am 1323 (2921), Houghton Library, Harvard University (Harvard). Ovington needed income. She bought copies from Viking, and sold them through agents, but took a loss in 1928, paying out $395 and taking in $255. Regular royalties totaled $210 in 1928. MWO, account books, MWO Papers, WSU.

21. Bess B. Walcott to MWO, September 5, 1930; C. Lane Imes to MWO, November 8, 17, December 16, 1930; MWO to C. Lane Imes, November 30, 1930, MWO Papers, WSU.

22. MWO to William Pickens, March 20, 1923; Richetta Randolph, July 23, n.d., September 4, 1925; Wilbur Lucas, April 12, 1926, Board Minutes, November 12, 1923, NAACP Papers, LC; MWO to ABS, April 4, August 24, 1923, ABS Papers, LC; MWO, account books, MWO Papers, WSU; MWO to James Weldon Johnson (JWJ), September 8, 1923, JWJ Collection, Yale Collection of American Literature, Beinecke Rare Book and Manuscript Library, Yale University (Yale); MWO to JES, May 9, August 13, 1926, JES Papers, NYPL.

23. MWO to Norman Thomas, January 26; Moorfield Storey, January 26; Henry Hunt, February 1; Daniel Kelley, February 1, all 1927, NAACP Papers, LC.

24. Fannie to "May," April 4, 1927, MWO Papers, WSU. MWO to WEDB, April 17 [1927], WEDB Papers, University of Massachusetts (Mass.). "Mrs. Louise Ketcham Ovington," [obit.] *New York Times*, April 5, 1927, 27.

25. MWO, "Reminiscences," *Baltimore Afro-American*, January 28, February 4, 1933, 24; *The Walls*, 215. Cole did not graduate from the Cincinnati Conservatory because she was denied access to required classes.

26. Ovington arranged lessons and concerts, and, finally, funding to send Cole to London, from whence come the fond and newsy letters. Lorenza [Cole] to MWO, November 20, 22, and 23 (2 letters), December 9, 14, 15, 1930, MWO Papers, WSU.

27. JWJ to MWO August 30, 1928, MWO Papers, WSU. MWO to Edith Morris Bourke, August 22, 1928, April 25, 1929; Eleanor [Bigelow], October 23; Nadyne [Waters], October 17; Corinne [Bacon], October 17; Marguerite Liszniewska, October 23; Max Yergan, October 24; Pauline [Newman], November 1, all 1928; NAACP Papers, LC. MWO, *The Walls*, 216–18.

28. MWO, account book, MWO Papers, WSU. MWO to John E. Nail, March 5; Bar Harbor Banking Company, October 29; Dora Smallidge, October 29; Charles Edward Russell, October 28, all 1928, NAACP Papers, LC.

29. MWO to [Mrs. Herbert Platt], June 22; Eleanor Brannon, June 22; Beth [Torrey], June 21; Walter White, June 21, all 1929, NAACP Papers, LC. MWO to ABS, June 28, 1929, ABS Papers, LC. Charles Ovington to "Ned" [Merritt], July 1, 8, 1929, MWO Papers, WSU.

30. Charles Ovington to Ned [Merritt], July 1, 8, 1929; Charles Ovington diary, MWO Papers, WSU. MWO to Richetta Randolph, July 16, 29, 1929, Richetta Randolph Papers, Brooklyn Historical Library. MWO to Alice [Brown], August 30; Clara Gray, September 13; Sue, September 13; Fannie [Geery], October 16, all 1929, NAACP Papers, LC. MWO to JWJ, October 24, November 12, 1929, JWJ Papers, Yale.

31. MWO to Walter White [January 5, 1930]; MWO to Daisy Lampkin, February 21, 1930; Richetta Randolph to Walter White, January 14, 1930; Board Minutes January 6, 1930, NAACP Papers, LC. MWO to WEDB, January 3 [1930], WEDB Papers, Mass. MWO to JES, January 20 [1930], JES Papers, NYPL. *New York Times*, January 10, February 2, 1930, April 21, 1931.

CHAPTER 9

1. Mary White Ovington (MWO) to Mother, March 12, 22 [1921], MWO Papers, Archives of Labor and Urban Affairs, Wayne State University (WSU);

MWO, "Reminiscences," *Baltimore Afro-American,* February 4, 1933, 24; MWO to Arthur B. Spingarn (ABS), April 2, July 24 [1921]; John Haynes Holmes to MWO, November 19, 1920, "Memorandum for Friday conference between Mr. Holmes and Dr. D.B." [July 29, 1921] ABS Papers, Library of Congress (LC).

"Memorandum to the Chairman of the Board on an estimated budget for the Second Pan-African Congress" [July 1, 1921]; [WEDB], "Memorandum on the History of The CRISIS. . ." [1921], W. E. B. Du Bois (WEDB) Papers, University of Massachusetts (Mass). Board Minutes, February 14, 1921, NAACP Papers, LC.

2. MWO, "Marcus Garvey," in *Portraits in Color* (New York: Viking, 1927), 18–30; Manning Marable, *W. E. B. Du Bois: Black Radical Democrat* (Boston: Twayne, 1986), 99–120; Board Minutes, February 14, 1921, NAACP Papers, LC; ABS to WEDB, February 9, 1921, WEDB Papers, Mass.

3. MWO, "Marcus Garvey," 18–30; Richetta Randolph to ABS, ABS Papers, LC.

4. MWO, To *The Masses,* January 1916, MWO Papers, WSU; MWO, "The Status of the Negro in the United States," *New Review* (September 1913), 744–49; MWO, to *New Republic* (January 27, 1917), 355. MWO, to *The Messenger* (July 1918), 114–15; MWO, "Bogalusa," *The Liberator* (January 1920), 31–33. MWO to William Pickens (WP), March 7, 1923, NAACP Papers, LC.

5. Later Du Bois argued for the agent portion of subscriptions obtained by NAACP officials and volunteers, going around the chairman. WEDB, "Memorandum to the Secretary and the Treasurer of the NAACP," May 11, 1922, MWO to ABS, May 29, 1922, ABS to MWO, May 31, 1922, ABS Papers, LC.

6. MWO to Joel E. Spingarn (JES), November 1, 1921, NAACP Papers, LC.

7. Garvey's attacks made an issue of the proportion of a mulatto's black blood.

8. WEDB to James Weldon Johnson (JWJ), April 15, 1924; JWJ to WEDB, April 17, 1924, WEDB Papers, Mass. Johnson told Du Bois that only White's expenses were fully paid by the national office; others financed their travel with speaking.

9. MWO, Foreword, and "James Weldon Johnson," in *Portraits in Color,* vii–viii, 1–17.

10. MWO, "W. E. Burghardt Du Bois," in *Portraits in Color,* 78–91.

11. MWO, "Reminiscences," *Baltimore Afro-American,* February 18, 1933, 24.

12. Henry Moskowitz to WEDB, November 10, 1928; WEDB to Members of the Milholland Committee, January 16, 1928; Statement, "The Milholland Bust Fund," October 2, 1928, WEDB Papers, Mass. William B. Hixson, Jr., *Moorfield Storey and the Abolitionist Tradition* (New York: Oxford University Press, 1972), 187–90.

13. Thomas made charges against Johnson and Du Bois at the November 1928 board meeting. The board suggested he retract and apologize for "intemperate and abusive language." Instead, Thomas came back in December with more charges, leaked to the press. Board Minutes, November 12, December 10, 1928, NAACP Papers, LC.

14. Board Minutes, February 11, 1929; MWO to Charles Edward Russell, October 31, 1928, NAACP Papers, LC. MWO to WEDB, March 5, 1929, WEDB Papers, Mass. MWO to Oswald Garrison Villard (OGV), January 5, 1929, OGV Papers, bMS Am 1323 (2921), Houghton Library, Harvard University (Harvard). MWO to ABS, March 5, 1929, ABS Papers, LC.

15. "20th Annual Report of the NAACP . . . ," 1930, OGV Papers, Harvard. "20 Year History of Negro in U. S. Reflected in NAACP, Says Founder," June 27, 1929, Moorfield Storey Papers, LC.

16. Board Minutes, January 7, April 18, May 13, October 14, October 28, November 11, 1929, NAACP Papers, LC. MWO to OGV, January 30, 1928; "20th Annual Report of the NAACP . . . ," 1930, OGV Papers, Harvard. MWO to ABS, June 28, 1929; JES to ABS, April 19, 1929, ABS Papers, LC. MWO to JWJ, April 23, 1929, JWJ Collection, Yale Collection of American Literature, Beinecke Rare Book and Manuscript Library, Yale University (Yale).

17. "20th Annual Report of the NAACP . . . ," 60–61; OGV to MWO, December 16, 1929, OGV Papers, Harvard. Board Minutes, December 9, 1929; MWO to Richard Storey, December 17, 1929, NAACP Papers, LC.

18. MWO to Walter White (WW) [January 5]; Daisy Lampkin, February 21; Richetta Randolph (RR) to WW, January 14, all 1930; Board Minutes January 6, 1930, NAACP Papers, LC. MWO to WEDB, January 3 [1930], WEDB Papers, Mass. MWO to JES, January 20 [1930], JES Papers, Rare Books & Manuscripts Division, Astor, Lenox & Tilden Foundations, New York Public Library (NYPL).

19. Board Minutes, October 13, December 8, December 29, 1930; MWO to William Pickens, April 25, 1930; MWO to Dan Kelley, August 29, 1930, NAACP Papers, LC. "Statement from Mr. Bagnall and Mr. Pickens . . . ," September 30, 1930; Isadore Martin to ABS, October 4, 1930; JES to NAACP, December 24, 1930, ABS Papers, LC.

Ovington thought the Parker nomination battle "taught the South that they cannot insult the colored voter with impunity." When Parker was rejected she observed: "Walter White has been carrying the work for a year . . . and has done remarkably well. He put over the Judge Parker fight." Kenneth W. Goings's book *"The NAACP Comes of Age: The Defeat of Judge John J. Parker"* (Bloomington: Indiana University Press, 1990), is one of several monographs on specific NAACP cases.

20. WEDB to JES, December 18, 1930, ABS Papers, LC. WEDB to JES, December 18; JES to WEDB, December 18; MWO to WEDB, December 20;

WEDB to MWO, December 24, all 1930; WEDB Papers, Mass. MWO to Daisy Lampkin, December 19, 1930, NAACP Papers, LC.

21. Program, 22nd Annual Mass Meeting," January 4, 1931, JES Papers, NYPL. Board Minutes, January 5, February 9, March 9, April 13, 1931, NAACP Papers, LC. Minutes of the Committee on Administration, January 12, 19, 26, February 2, 24, 1931; WW to MWO, JES, ABS, WEDB, Isadore Martin, January 6, 1931; WW to WEDB, March 6, 1931, ABS Papers, LC.

22. Dan T. Carter, *Scottsboro: A Tragedy of the American South* (Baton Rouge: Louisiana State University Press, 1969; reprint, New York: Oxford University Press, 1971), 3–10.

23. An example of this assumption is in James E. Goodman's 1990 Princeton University dissertation, "Stories of Scottsboro." In his chapter "Walter White and the NAACP" (77–87), Goodman assumes all controversy in the organization is from challenge on economic issues, with White and Du Bois on the same side. The dissertation was published in New York by Pantheon Books, 1994.

24. Carter, *Scottsboro*, 5–6. Board Minutes, April 13, 1931, NAACP Papers, LC.

25. Board Minutes, May 11, 1931, NAACP Papers, LC. WP to WEDB, April 4, 1931 [May 4]; WP to ABS, May 4, 6, 1931; MWO to WP, April 30, 1931; WP to MWO, May 5, 1931; WW to "Bob and Herbert," May 3, 1931, ABS Papers, LC. WP to MWO, May 2, 3, 1931, JES Papers, NYPL. Carter, *Scottsboro*, 61.

26. MWO to WEDB, May 13, 1931; WEDB to MWO, May 20, 1931, WEDB Papers, Mass.

27. Three legal files on Scottsboro, 1931, 1932, 1933–1937. ABS Papers, LC. See also Dan Carter, Randolph Boehm, and Martin Schipper, eds., *Guide to the Papers of the NAACP, Part 6: The Scottsboro Case, 1931–1950* (Frederick, Md., 1986). James Goodman's "Stories of Scottsboro" tells the story from the perspectives of various participants, including the defendants; white Alabamians; the two women, Price and Bates; the Communist Party; an ACLU volunteer and journalist, Hollace Ransdall; Walter White and the NAACP; liberal white southerners; middle-class southern blacks; northern white intellectuals; parents; defense attorney Samuel Liebowitz, and Judge Horton.

28. MWO, *The Walls Came Tumbling Down* (New York: Harcourt, Brace and Company, 1947), 231–36. MWO, "Reminiscences," *Baltimore Afro-American*, October 22, 1932, 24. Carter, *Scottsboro*, 103; 192–239, passim. Richard Cortner, *A Mob Intent on Death: The NAACP and the Arkansas Riot Cases* (Middletown, Conn.: Wesleyan University Press, 1988), 192, 194. MWO, "Diary of Trip . . . ," MWO Papers, WSU.

29. MWO to JES, December 15 [1931]; [JES] to MWO [December 16, 17, or 18, 1931] (draft); MWO to JES December 19, 1931, JES Papers, NYPL.

30. WW to WEDB, November 12, 1931; WEDB to WW, November 13, 1931; WW to JES, November 17, 1931; WEDB to JES, December 8, 1931; WEDB to ABS, December 8 and 15, 1931; ABS to WEDB, December 16, 1931, ABS Papers, LC. WEDB to Charles Edward Russell, December 15, 1931; WEDB to MWO, December 15, 1931 (with MWO note); Charles Edward Russell to WEDB, December 17, 1931, WEDB papers, Mass.

31. WEDB to Charles Edward Russell, December 15, 1931, WEDB Papers, Mass.

32. "To the Board of Directors" [December 1931]; [WP], "found with December, 1931"; Robert Bagnall to WEDB, December 22, 1931; RR to WEDB et. al., December 22, 1931; Robert Bagnall to WEDB, "found with December, 1931 material" [December 22, 1931]; WP to WW, December 22, 1931; JES to WEDB, December 29, 1931; WEDB to JES, December 31, 1931, WEDB Papers, Mass. Board Minutes, December 21, 1931, NAACP Papers, LC; John Haynes Holmes to JES, January 8, 1932, Charles Flint Kellogg notes, Kellogg Papers, WSU. MWO to RR, December 22, 1931; RR to MWO, December 22, 1931; WP to RR, December 22, 1931, RR Papers, Brooklyn Historical Library; Herbert Seligmann to MWO, December 24, 1931, MWO Papers, WSU.

CHAPTER 10

1. Mary White Ovington (MWO) to Addie Hunton, October 6, 19, Moorfield Storey, October 7, 13, December 6, 14, "Mr. Spingarn" [Joel Spingarn—JES], December 23, 26 all 1920, MWO office diaries, 1920–21, Board Minutes, October 10, 1921, NAACP Papers, Library of Congress (LC). MWO to James Weldon Johnson (JWJ), April 9, 1920, JWJ to MWO, September 21, 1920, JWJ Collection, Yale Collection of American Literature, Beinecke Rare Book and Manuscript Library, Yale University (Yale). JWJ to Arthur Spingarn (ABS), January 13, February 7, 8, 1921, ABS Papers, LC; JWJ, "Report of the Secretary to the Anti-Lynching Committee," January 21, 1921, Moorfield Storey Papers, LC; MWO to Conference of Executives, January 27, 1921; MWO to ABS, February 8, 1921, ABS Papers, LC. MWO to "Mother," February 12, 1921, MWO Papers, Archives of Labor and Urban Affairs, Wayne State University (WSU).

2. MWO to "Mother," February 16, 21, 28, March 12, 1921, MWO Papers, WSU; MWO, *The Walls Came Tumbling Down* (New York: Harcourt, Brace and Company, 1947), 221–22; MWO to ABS, April 2 [1921], ABS Papers, LC.

3. A. Lincoln Harris to MWO, February 22, 1928; Georgia D. Johnson to MWO, February 27, 1928; MWO to Georgia Douglas Johnson; Sue Hill; V. R. Anderson, all March 5, 1928; MWO to Richetta Randolph, May 11; Laipat Rei, August 30; John Lathrop, October 18; Marguerite Tucker, November 28,

all 1928, NAACP Papers, LC. MWO, "Reminiscences" *Baltimore Afro-American*, February 4, 1933, 24. *The Walls*, 214–19, 223–24. MWO to Grace Johnson, June 29, 1928, JWJ Papers, Yale.

4. MWO to Mary McDowell, June 4; James Gutmann, October 5; Robert Abbott, October 6; Mrs. W. T. Holmes, November 16; Edgar Webster, December 6; H. A. Hunt, December 21, 1926; Janie Porter Barrett, January 4; Maggie Walker, February 1, July 12, 1927; Janie Porter Barrett to Richetta Randolph, September 20, 1926; Maggie Walker to MWO, January 25, March 21, 22, 1927, Margaret Tyler to MWO, December 3, 1926, NAACP Papers, LC. E. E. Just to MWO, June 28, 1927, MWO account books, MWO Papers, WSU. JWJ to MWO, March 12 [1926]; W. E. B. Du Bois (WEDB) to MWO, November 9, 1926, WEDB Papers, University of Massachusetts (Mass.) MWO, "Revisiting the South: Changes in Twenty-One Years," *Crisis*, vol. 34 (April 1927), 42–43, 60–61; "A Woman Who Answered Prayer: Charlotte R. Thorn and the Calhoun School," *Woman Citizen* (March 1927), 18–19, 48–49.

5. Merle Curti to MWO, May 29, 1929, MWO Papers, WSU; Smith College Bulletin, 1927–1932. Merle Curti to author, July 27, 1991.

6. The Washington, D.C., schools considered using *Portraits in Color* as a text. MWO to Will Alexander, February 28, 1928; MWO to Bernice F. Davies, August 30, 1929; Garnet Wilkinson to MWO, October 3, 1928, NAACP Papers, LC.

7. MWO, *The Walls*, 222–23; "Reminiscences," *Baltimore Afro-American*, February 4, 1933, 24.

8. Walter White (WW) to ABS, June 21, 1932; MWO to ABS, April 18, 1933, ABS Papers, LC. MWO to WW, April 6, 1932, NAACP Papers, LC.

9. Board Minutes, March 14, 1933; MWO to William Pickens (WP), March 28, 1932 [September 5, 1933], NAACP Papers, LC. MWO to JES, March 24, 1933, JES Papers, Rare Books and Manuscripts Division, New York Public Library, Astor, Lenox and Tilden Foundations (NYPL).

10. MWO to WW, April [12], 16, 1932; MWO to WP, May 11, 1932; MWO to Lillian Alexander, December 5, 1932, NAACP Papers, LC. MWO account books, MWO Papers, WSU. The Feminist Press published the newspaper articles in 1995 as *Black and White Sat Down Together: The Reminiscences of an NAACP Founder.*

11. MWO, "Diary of trip beginning March 4, 1933," MWO Papers, WSU. Except where indicated, narration of the 1933 trip will be based on this source.

12. MWO, "Visits to Branches," MWO Papers, WSU.

13. MWO to WW, March 24, 1933; Fannie Granton, May 2, both 1933; MWO to [WP?] fragment, [1934], NAACP Papers, LC.

14. MWO to ABS, April 21, 1933, ABS Papers, LC. MWO to Fannie Granton, June 20, May 2; Mrs. F. A. Sumner, May 2; Frances Bartholomew, May 29, all 1933, NAACP Papers, LC.

15. She did a trial run in Philadelphia and Cheyney State Teacher's College, with speeches "at all conceivable times" on "sociology, war, and interracial matters, not to mention NAACP." Board Minutes, NAACP, January 8, 1934; WP to MWO, August [12] [November]; MWO to WP, August 10 [September 5]; WW, September 12; Daisy Lampkin, November 1, 6; RR, November 7; Montgomery Gregory, November 6; Leslie Pinckney Hill, November 13; Mary McLeod Bethune, November 27, all 1933, NAACP Papers, LC.

16. MWO, "The Year of Jubilee," *Crisis* 41 (January 1934), 7–8. As she rushed to the elevator to begin her southern trip, Roy Wilkins said he was publishing the 1909 Call with Ovington's and Villard's names. Frantically she wrote from Washington, D.C.: "What you are doing is frightful for me. Everyone will think that I wanted the credit." She suggested removing her name and leaving Villard's: "This Call, like the one twenty-five years ago, was written by Oswald Garrison Villard, but it is signed (in spirit?) by the thirteen officers, and the 376 presidents of the Branches that operate all over this United States." MWO to Roy Wilkins (RW), n.d. [February 1934], RW Papers, LC. Ovington also published "The New Year and the New Year Campaign" in the *Crisis* (February 1934), 39.

17. MWO to WP, February 12, 1934; [MWO], speech, June, 1934, NAACP Papers, LC.

18. MWO to ABS, April 18, 1933, ABS Papers, LC. MWO, "Students Eager for Interracial Forums," *Crisis* 41 (June 1934), 181.

19. MWO to William Rosenwald, January 15; WP, February 7, 12, 14, March 2; Frank Turner, February 12, 21, March 2; RR, February 12; Miss Black, March 3; WW February 14, 15; Miss Thorpe, February 13; RW, February 19, March 6, 1934; NAACP Papers, LC. MWO, "Report to the Board by Miss Ovington re: Southern Trip," April 9, 1934, "Visits to Branches," MWO Papers, WSU. MWO to JWJ [March 5, 1934], JWJ Collection, Yale. MWO to Charlotte Hawkins Brown, March 19, 1934, Charlotte Hawkins Brown Papers, Schlesinger Library, Radcliffe.

20. MWO to ABS, March 9 [1934], ABS Papers, LC.

21. MWO, "Report to Board . . . ," MWO Papers, WSU. Board Minutes, April 10, May 14, 1934; MWO to WP, March 23 [1934], NAACP Papers, LC. MWO to ABS, March 2, 9, 20, 25, 1934; [?] to WW, April 28, 1934, ABS Papers, LC.

22. Board Minutes, July 19, 1934, NAACP Papers, LC.

23. MWO to ABS, July 22, 1934, ABS Papers, LC. Ovington joked with Wilkins: "It's a very different world from Minnesota and I don't know that I want you to handle the publicity at Oklahoma. You might forget to say 'sir' to a white reporter and while martyrdom may help the cause, we haven't enough workers to lose any!" MWO to RW, March 6, 1934, NAACP Papers, LC.

24. Oswald Garrison Villard (OGV) to MWO, July 26, 1934, MWO Papers, WSU. MWO to OGV, July 22, 1934, OGV Papers, bMS Am 1323 (2921), Houghton Library, Harvard University (Harvard).

25. Board Minutes, April 8, 1935, NAACP Papers, LC.

26. MWO, Memo April 9, 1935; MWO to RR, WW, both April 11, 1935, NAACP Papers, LC.

27. A. C. Roker and H. A. Berry to MWO, April 8; MWO to Herbert Lehman, April 29; telegrams, letters to MWO, April 10 ; MWO to Jane Addams, April 29; MWO to WW, May 24, all 1935, NAACP Papers, LC. To MWO from Ira W. Jayne, April 8; Ellen Winsor, April 28; Charles Edward Russell, April 10; John Haynes Holmes, April 5; Butler Wilson, April 6; Anna McClintock, April 11; press release: "Miss Ovington Expresses Appreciation . . . ," April 8, all 1935, MWO Papers, WSU.

28. MWO to RR, August 14, September 23, October 4, 8, 1935, NAACP Papers, LC. MWO account books, MWO Papers, WSU.

29. MWO to WP, November 18; "Memorandum from Miss Ovington" to JES, ABS, Louis Wright, WW, RW, Charles Houston, Miss Jackson [November 14]; MWO to RR, November 14, all 1935, NAACP Papers, LC.

30. Board Minutes, November 25, December 9, 16, 1935, NAACP Papers, LC. In accord with Ovington's November 18 memo, among the program goals was "Raising as early in 1936 as possible a Legal Defense Fund." Jack Greenberg, *Crusaders in the Courts: How a Dedicated Band of Lawyers Fought for the Civil Rights Revolution* (Basic Books: New York, 1994), xvii, 5, 19–20. Greenberg mentions Ovington only in a quote from Du Bois about NAACP founding (she was a "spiritual descendant . . . of the Abolitionists"), and among the original seven directors of the Defense Fund. She was the only woman in that group.

31. MWO to OGV, March 25, [n.d.] 1935, OGV Papers, Harvard.

CHAPTER 11

1. Mary White Ovington (MWO) to Grace Johnson [June 1938], James Weldon Johnson (JWJ) Collection, Yale Collection of American Literature, Beinecke Rare Book and Manuscript Library, Yale University (Yale). *Berkshire Courier,* June 23, 30, 1938, Great Barrington, Mass.

2. Interviews with May (Mrs. John) Dellea, Alford, Mass., July 4, 1989, Elizabeth Kingsbury Friedmann, Foxboro, Mass., October 16, 1990. *Berkshire Courier,* August 16, 1928, September 9, 1937, Great Barrington, Mass. MWO to Grace Johnson, June 28, 1938, JWJ Collection, Yale. Letter to author from Donald S. Harrington, Community Church of New York, April 10, 1993.

3. MWO to Grace Johnson, August 13, October 20, 1938; January 18, March 21, 1939, JWJ Collection, Yale.

4. MWO to Grace Johnson, January 18, March 21, 1939, JWJ Collection, Yale. Dr. Edmund Devol, to Whom It May Concern, June 14, 1939, MWO Papers, Archives of Labor and Urban Affairs, Wayne State University (WSU). MWO to Walter White (WW), July 4, 1939, NAACP Papers, Library of Congress (LC).

5. MWO to WW, July 4, 1939; WW to MWO, July 6, 25, 1939, NAACP Papers, LC. Register of Deeds, Southern Berkshire County, Great Barrington, Mass., June 24, 1941. Interviews with May (Mrs. John) Dellea; Catherine Dellea Smith; Laura Keeney Tucker, July 4–6, 1989. For books left at Riverbank, as well as for visits and encouragement, the author is fondly indebted to Gloria and Milton Matthews, the present owners.

6. MWO to Arthur Spingarn (ABS), November 28, 1940, ABS Papers, LC.

7. MWO to Roy Wilkins (RW), March 3, 1942; MWO to WW, May 9, 1942, NAACP Papers, LC. MWO to ABS, March 6, 1942; MWO to WW, April 14, 1942, ABS Papers, LC.

8. MWO to RW, July 14, 22, 1942, NAACP Papers, LC.

9. L. D. Reddick, the paid investigator for the report, was Johnson's student at Fisk. JWJ to MWO, April 29, 1939, JWJ Collection, Yale.

10. MWO, "Report of Miss Ovington on Textbook Investigation by Mr. Reddick," April 11, 1938; ABS to MWO, April 8, 1938, JWJ Collection, Yale.

11. MWO to WW, July 27, 1946, NAACP Papers, LC.

12. MWO to Richetta Randolph (RR), May 20, June 23, 1941, January 28, February 2, June 15, October 1943; MWO to RW, July 22, 1942, NAACP Papers, LC. Ray Stannard Baker to MWO, May 3, 1943, MWO Papers, WSU. MWO to Grace Johnson, January 13, 1944, JWJ Papers, Yale.

13. MWO to WW, August 27, 1943; MWO to RW, August 29, 1943, NAACP Papers, LC.

14. MWO to Arna Bontemps, October 5; Thomas Elsa Jones, October 6; RW, November 24; Lucille Black, December 15, 1943, NAACP Papers, LC. MWO to Grace Johnson, January 13, 1944, JWJ Papers, Yale. MWO to ABS, November 24, 1943, ABS Papers, LC.

15. MWO to RW, November 24, 1943, January 6, 1944; RR, December 8, 1943, January 17, March 11, 1944; Lucille Black, December 15, 1943; RR to MWO, January 17, 1944, NAACP Papers, LC. MWO to ABS, December 16, 1942, ABS Papers, LC. MWO to Oswald Garrison Villard (OGV), November 30, 1942, RR, "Response to Presentation," January 4, 1943, OGV Papers, bMS Am 1323 (2921), Houghton Library, Harvard University (Harvard).

16. MWO to RR, February 9, April [?]; RR to MWO, March 14; RW to MWO, March 21; MWO to RW, March 23, all 1944, NAACP Papers, LC. Esther Jones to Mrs. [Charles] Ovington, June 1, 1944, MWO Papers, WSU. MWO to ABS, March 23, 27, April 1, 7 [1944]; MWO to RR, April 13, 1944,

ABS Papers, Moorland-Spingarn Research Center, Howard University (Moorland). MWO to [Grace Johnson], [Spring, 1944], JWJ Collection, Yale.

17. MWO to ABS, May 3, May 4 [1944], ABS Papers, Moorland.

18. Mrs. Bowman to WW, June 5; ABS to Mrs. Bowman, June 13; WW to MWO, August 4; MWO to ABS, WW, RW and Louis Wright, NAACP and RR, October 17, November 1 [with note from Randolph]; MWO to WW, November 15; Edward Dudley to Judge Herbert T. Delaney, all 1944, NAACP Papers, LC. MWO, account books, 1944, MWO Papers, WSU. Mrs. Elizabeth Ovington to William Pickens (WP), October 8, 1944; MWO to WP [December 1944; December 1945], WP Papers, Manuscripts, Archives and Rare Books Division, Schomburg Center for Research in Black Culture, New York Public Library, Astor, Lenox and Tilden Foundations (NYPL).

19. MWO to Grace [Johnson], January [1945]; August 8 [1946], JWJ Collection, Yale. Dr. Alvan L. Barach to MWO, March 23, 1945; WW, July 13, 1945, MWO Papers, WSU. MWO to ABS, March 26; WW, July 23, both 1945, ABS Papers, LC. MWO to RW, January 30; Miss Maxwell, September 20; WW, September 25, all 1945; Board Minutes January 2, April 9, June 11, 1945, NAACP Papers, LC. MWO to ABS, May 4, 1945, ABS Papers, Moorland.

20. MWO to WW, July 23, WW to ABS, July 31, WW to MWO, July 19, 31, all 1945, ABS Papers, LC. MWO to WW, July 13, 1945, MWO Papers, WSU. RW to RR, January 2, June 29, 1945; RR to RW, August 1, 1945, in RW Papers, LC. MWO to RW, April 25; RR to WW, April 26; WW to RW, July 5; MWO to WW, September 25; Board Minutes, September 10, October 8, 1945, NAACP Papers, LC. MWO to ABS, June 29, 1945, ABS Papers, Moorland. MWO to RR, July 9, 15, September 18, 1945, RR Collection, Brooklyn Historical Library.

21. WW to RW, October 27, 1948; RW to WW, August 14, November 23, 1945; WW to W. E. B. Du Bois (WEDB), September 21, 1945; WEDB to WW, January 4, 1946; RW to Carolyn D. Moore, n.d.; Emergency Committee for W. E. B. Du Bois and the NAACP . . .; Suggested Draft of a Reply to DuBois statement . . . , October 11, 1948, RW Papers, LC. Board Minutes February 13, July 7, October 8, 1945; September 13, 1948, NAACP Papers, LC. WW to [Lillian A. Alexander], November 29, 1945; "NAACP Ousts DuBois, Founder," *New York Post*, September 14, 1948; WW to WEDB, October 5, 1948, ABS Papers, LC. WEDB to OGV, April 3, 1945, OGV Papers, bMS Am 1323 (946), Harvard. For the story from Du Bois's point of view, see Shirley Graham Du Bois, *His Day Is Marching On: A Memoir of W. E. B. Du Bois*. (Philadelphia and New York: J. B. Lippincott Company, 1971). Founder Oswald Garrison Villard also had problems with the NAACP in 1946, when he was not reelected as a vice president. See Board Minutes, March 11, 1946, NAACP Papers, LC.

22. MWO to WEDB, April, June 22, August 2, 1945; May 10, 1946, WEDB Papers, University of Massachusetts (Mass.). MWO, *The Walls Came Tumbling Down* (New York: Harcourt, Brace and Company, 1947), 299.

23. Philadelphia Fellowship Commission, "America's Other Voice," May 6, 1945, in "Within Our Gates" Series, by John Scheuer; Henry Winfield Wheeler, "The Spider's Web," *St. Louis American*, July 18, 1946.

24. Eighth graders, Howard Kennedy School to MWO, May 24, 1946; J. Goodal to [NAACP], [1947], MWO Papers, WSU.

25. Beth Torrey to MWO, December 23, 1945; Arthur Croley to MWO, March 6, 1946; Mrs. Maxwell to MWO, [June 1946], November 10, 1947; Rosemary [Ferrar] to MWO, August 21, 1946, MWO Papers, WSU.

26. MWO to WW, February 25, July 26, 1946; MWO to ABS, October 16, 1946, NAACP Papers, LC. MWO to Carrie Overton, September 16, 1946 [1947]; [Carrie Overton], "File, Ovington Biography," ms fragment, n.d., MWO Papers, WSU. MWO to Grace [Johnson], August 8 [1946], August 20, 1946, JWJ Collection, Yale.

27. MWO from Robert Giroux, December 19; Arna Bontemps, December 30; RW, December 26; MWO, Card and Gift List, 1946; Louise Callin to MWO, December 18 [1947], MWO Papers, WSU. MWO to WW, December 24, 1946, April 11, 1947; MWO to RW, December 24, 1946; Board Minutes, January 6, 1947, NAACP Papers, LC.

28. MWO, manuscript, 1947; John Haynes Holmes (JHH) to MWO, December 31, 1945; Ida Pruitt to MWO, January 9, 1946, Edward Weyer, Jr. to MWO, February 7, 1946; Claude Pepper to MWO, n.d.; MWO, account books, "The Poor Are Fed First," MWO Papers, WSU. MWO to JHH, n.d., JHH Papers, LC.

29. MWO to WW, November 26, 1946, April 11, 1947; Board Minutes, 1946, 1947, 1948, NAACP Papers, LC. Betty [Kingsbury] to MWO, January 18 [1946]; [Carrie Overton] to Mr. Newsom, March 15, 1947; MWO to Mr. Newsom, June 5, July 12, 22, 1947; John Newsom to MWO, June 6, August 7, 1947; Rita Cuddihy to MWO, August 19, 1947; WW, "Introduction to *The Walls Came Tumbling Down*," MWO Papers, WSU. MWO to OGV, July 11, 1947, OGV Papers, Harvard.

30. John Newsom to MWO, October 28, 1947; "Excerpts from Letters Concerning 'Walls . . . ,'" November 7, 1947; Day Kincaid to MWO, January 7, 1948; Geraldine Morris to MWO, December 17, 1947, MWO Papers, WSU. OGV to MWO, September 24, 1947, OGV Papers, Harvard.

31. MWO, account book; Betty [Kingsbury] to Aunt May, January 18 [1947], Ned [Merritt] to Aunt May, n.d., Louise [Callin] to Aunt May, February 14 [1947], Nick [Kingsbury] to MWO, December 31, 1946; Florence Barlow to MWO, September 10, October 4, 14, November 19, 1947, MWO Pa-

pers, WSU. The affairs of Georgia Ovington in Paris are recorded in dozens of letters between various parties.

32. MWO to Mr. Newsom, October 24, 1947, MWO Papers, WSU. MWO to OGV, September 25 [1947]; October 24, 1947, OGV Papers, Harvard. C. C. Burlingame to JHH, January 28, February 11, 1948; MWO to JHH, January 31 [1948], April 8 [1948], JHH Papers, LC. MWO to RR, December 14, 1948, RR Papers, Brooklyn.

33. MWO to RR, December 14, 1948; May 5, December 20, 1949; April 1950; Helen Kingsbury to RR, June 6, 1950; RR to Charles Flint Kellogg, July 6, 1969, RR Papers, Brooklyn.

34. The January 1950 examination was by Dr. George F. H. Bowas, in Auburndale. Court Records, Middlesex County, Massachusetts; Certificate of Death, City of Newton.

35. RW to NAACP Board, July 16, 1951, JHH Papers, LC. Board Minutes, September 10, 1951, NAACP Papers, LC. "Mary White Ovington, Founder of NAACP, Dead," July 28, 1951, 5, WP, Letter, August 18, 1951, 4, *Baltimore Afro-American.* "Ovington, Mary White," Obituary; *New York Herald Tribune,* July 17, 1951, 16; *New York Times,* July 16, 1951, 21. "Why We Print This Story," *Baltimore Afro-American,* August 18, 1951.

Bibliography

WORKS BY MARY WHITE OVINGTON

BOOKS

The Awakening. (Play). 1923. Reprint, Freeport, N.Y.: Books for Libraries Press, 1972.

Black and White Sat Down Together: The Reminiscences of an NAACP Founder. Reprint of "Reminiscences," *Baltimore Afro-American,* 1932–33. New York: Feminist Press, 1995. Edited by Ralph Luker, Afterword by Carolyn Wedin.

Half a Man: The Status of the Negro in New York. New York: Longmans Green, 1911. Foreword by Franz Boas. Reprint, with an introduction by Charles Flint Kellogg, preface by Roy Wilkins. Schocken Books and Negro Universities Press, both 1969, and Hill and Wang, 1970.
> "Attitude of a Negro Bricklayer on Union Policies." Reprint, Eric Foner, ed. *The Black Worker, vol. IV.*

Hazel. With illustrations by Harry Roseland. New York: Crisis Publishing Company, 1913.

Phillis Wheatley: A Play. New York: Schulte Press, 1932.

Portraits in Color. New York: Viking Press, 1927.

The Shadow. New York: Harcourt, Brace and Howe, 1920. Reprint, Freeport, N.Y.: Books for Libraries Press, 1972. Serialized in England in *Outward Bound* (1921) and in Ireland in *Irish Christian Advocate* (1924).

The Upward Path: A Reader for Colored Children. Edited with Myron Pritchard. New York: Harcourt, Brace and Howe, Inc., 1920.

The Walls Came Tumbling Down. New York: Harcourt, Brace and Company, 1947. Reprint, Arno Press, 1969, Introduction by Rayford Logan; Schocken Books, 1970, Introduction by Charles Flint Kellogg. A portion was reprinted as "Early Years of the NAACP" in Larry Cuban, ed. *The Negro in America.* Glenview, Ill.: Scott Foresman and Company, 1964, 89–93.

Zeke: A Schoolboy at Tolliver. New York: Harcourt, Brace, 1931.

ARTICLES, PAMPHLETS, POETRY
(Unsigned work that is likely by Ovington
is indicated with [MWO] before the entry)

"The Acting Chairman's Western Trip." *The [NAACP] Branch Bulletin*, September 1918, 41–42.

[MWO]. "Address by Booker T. Washington. . . ." *New York Evening Post*, August 30, 1906, 12.

"Algiers: In the Land Where the Sons of the Desert are the Children of France." Place of publication unknown. In MWO Papers, Wayne State University.

"Anti-Lynching Conference of the NAACP." *Survey*, vol. 42, May 17, 1919, 292.

"Atlanta: A City Nursing Dead Ideals." *Colored American*, July, 1905, 389.

"Atlanta Riots." *Outlook*, vol. 84, November 17, 1906, 684.

"The Atlanta Situation: Many Negroes Moving from the City. . . ." *New York Evening Post*, December 26, 1906, 5.

"The Beginnings of the NAACP." *Crisis*, June 1926, 76–77.

"Bogalusa." *Liberator*, January 1920, 31–33.

"By the Playground" (poem). *Outlook*, vol. 77, July 16, 1904, 648.

"A Christmas Happening" (story). *Crisis*, December 1923, 60.

"Closing the Little Black Schoolhouse." *Survey*, vol. 24, May 28, 1910, 343–45.

"The Colored Woman in Domestic Service in New York City." *Household Research Bulletin*, May 1905. Copy in MWO Papers, Wayne State University, 3 pp.

[MWO]. "Commercial Growth of the Negro. . . ." *New York Evening Post*, August 30, 1906, 12.

"Compelled to Dance With Negro, She Says." *Crisis*, February 1911, 30.

"Conference on Negro Advancement." *Survey*, vol. 30, June 7, 1913, 322.

"A Day of Praise in the South's First of the Year Meeting in Alabama." *New York Evening Post*, January 26, 1907, 2.

"Democracy and Humanity." *Forum*, February 1925, 274–75.

"Dudley and His Mule." *Crisis*, June 1932, 189, 203–4.

[MWO]. Frances Gardiner Davenport (editorial). *Nation*, November 30, 1927, 589.

"Franklin and the Negro," in J. Henry Smythe, Jr., *The Amazing Ben Franklin*. New York: Frederick A. Stokes Co., 1929, 230–33.

"Fresh Air Work Among Colored Children in New York." *Charities and the Commons*, vol. 17, October 13, 1906, 115–17.

"Gretchen Talks to Her Doll" (poem). *Four Lights*, April 21, 1917, n.p. Clipping in MWO Papers, Wayne State University.

"The Gunpowder of Race Antagonism." *American City*, vol. 21, September 1919, 248–51.

"The Harvard Annex." *Packer Alumnae*, Winter 1892.

"How the National Association for the Advancement of Colored People Began." New York: NAACP, 1914 (pamphlet). Also published in *Crisis*, August 1914, 184–88.

"Is Mob Violence the Texas Solution of the Race Problem?" *Independent*, September 6, 1919, 320. Reprinted as a pamphlet, New York, 1919.

"The Jeanes Fund." *Survey*, vol. 23, January 29, 1910, 590.

"John White Chadwick: In Memory" (poem). *Unity*, March 2, 1905. In MWO Papers, Wayne State University.

"Letter." *Crisis*, November 1926, 31.

"Letter to the Editor." *Messenger*, July 1918, 114–15.

"A Life of Service." *Colored American*, November 1906, 12.

"Mary Dunlop Maclean." *Crisis*. August 1912, 6.

"Mary Phagan Speaks" (poem). *New Republic*. August 28, 1915, 101.

"Master of His Fate." *Crisis*, February 1917, 164–65.

"Miss Mary White Ovington's Address Before the Brooklyn Ethical Culture Association." *Brooklyn Eagle*, December 20, 1897, 12.

"A Mount Discovery Musing" (poem). *Elizabethtown Post*, April 22, 1909, n.p.

"The National Association for the Advancement of Colored People." *Journal of Negro History*, vol. 9, April 1924, 107–16.

"Nativity" (poem). *Crisis*, December 1911, 76.

"The Negro and the New York Tenement." *The Voice of the Negro*, February 1906, 101–7.

"Negro Art." *Crisis*, July 1921, 104.

"Negro Banks and Banking. . . ." *New York Evening Post*, September 4, 1906, 12.

"Negro Energy and Thrift. . . ." *New York Evening Post*, September 3, 1906, 4.

"The Negro Home in New York." *Charities*, October 7, 1905, 25–30.

"The Negro in America: Today and Tomorrow." *Survey*, vol. 28, May 18, 1912, 318–20.

"The Negro in Art: A Symposium." *Crisis*, March 1926, 219–20.

"The Negro in Business." *New York Evening Post*, August 31, 1906, 7.

"The Negro in the Trades Unions in New York." *Annals of the American Academy of Political and Social Science*, May 1906, 551–58.

[MWO]. "Negroes in Conference: Workers for Self-Betterment at Tuskegee." *New York Evening Post*, February 20, 1907, 7.

"Negroes on Firmer Ground: Increased Attendance and Enthusiasm at this Year's Niagara Movement Conference in Boston. . . . " *New York Evening Post*, September 3, 1907, 7.

"The Negro's Position: His Comparative Helplessness in the South." *New York Evening Post*, September 7, 1906, 3.

"The Neighborship Association." *Pratt Institute Monthly*, April 1894, 1897, 1898; "Neighborship," November 1896.

"A New Reformation" (letter). *Nation*, October 12, 1940, 347–48.

"The New Year and the New Year Campaign." *Crisis*, February 1934, 39.

"The Niagara Movement: First Annual Convention at Harper's Ferry. . . ." *New York Evening Post*, August 17, 1906, 5.

[MWO and Mary Dunlop Maclean, eds.]. "Notes on Lynching in the United States, Compiled from The Crisis by The National Association for the Advancement of Colored People." 15-page pamphlet; NAACP, 1912. Can be seen in Arthur Spingarn Papers, Library of Congress.

"On Christmas Eve" (poem). *New York Evening Post*, December 24, 1914, n.p.

"On the New-time Negro." *Century*, vol. 83, January 1912, 470–71.

Pamphlet on the Black Codes, Ku Klux Klan, and "other points raised" by *Birth of a Nation*, 1915.

"The Penny Paper." *Outlook*, vol. 76, January 30, 1904, 280–83.

"Protection." *Crisis*, July 1912, 144.

"Quitting" (editorial). *Crisis*, October 1917, 307.

"Race Feeling as an Asset." *New York Evening Post*, September 8, 1906, 5.

[MWO]. "The Races Congress." *Crisis*, September 1911, 200–9.

"Reconstruction and the Negro." *Crisis*, February 1919, 169–73. (Reprinted as an NAACP leaflet).

"Reminiscences." *Baltimore Afro-American*, weekly from September 17, 1932 to February 18, 1933. Reprinted August 4, 1951–January 12, 1952. Reprinted in 1995 by the Feminist Press as *Black and White Sat Down Together.*

"Report of the Head Worker of the Neighborship Settlement." *Report of the Pratt Institute Neighborship Association, for the Year 1895–96.* Brooklyn: Press of George Mayer, 1896, 17–32.

"Revisiting the South: Changes in Twenty-One Years." *Crisis*, April 1927, 42–43, 60–61.

"Revolution" (poem). *Independent*, vol. 75, July 3, 1913, 20.

"Russian Liberals Want More War?" (letter to the editor). *New Republic*, January 27, 1917, 355.

"Segregation." *Crisis*, January 1915, 142–45.

"The Settlement in America." *Colored American Magazine*, June 1905, 331–35.

"Slaves' Reminiscences of Slavery." *Independent*, vol. 68, May 26, 1910, 1131–36.

"Socialism and the Feminist Movement." *New Review*, vol. 2, March 1914, 143–47.

"Some Publications Regarding the American Negro." *Library Journal*. March 1907, n.p.

"Son of a Carpenter." *Christian Register* (Partial copy in MWO Papers, Wayne State University).

[MWO]. "The South's White Problem." *New York Evening Post*, January 29, 1907, 7.

"The Spirit of John Brown: Exhibited at Convention. . . ." *New York Evening Post*, August 20, 1906, 8.

[MWO]. "The Spirit of John Brown: Still Beckoning. . . ." *New York Evening Post*, August 18, 1906, 8.

"The Status of the Negro in the United States." *New Review*, September 1913, 744–49. Reprinted in Philip Foner, ed. *The Black Worker*, vol. 5, 510–11.

"Students Eager for Interracial Forums." *Crisis*, June 1934, 181.

"The Sunny South and Poverty." *New Review*. March 15, 1913, 325–29.

"Ten Years of the NAACP, 1909–1919" (pamphlet). NAACP, 1919.

"Three Games." *The Brownies' Book*. May 1921, 135–36.

"To the Branches: Greeting." *Crisis*, May 1922, 22.

"The Treasurer Says." *Crisis*, February 1940, 57.

"The Treasurer Talks to the Branches." *Crisis*, April 1936, 116–19.

"Two Men of Negro Blood." *Crisis*, June 1931, 197–98.

"The United States in Porto [*sic*] Rico." *New Republic*, vol. 7, July 8 and 15, 1916, 244–46; 271–73.

"A Visit to the National Office." *Crisis*, May 1936, 144, 150.

"The Warm Dogma." *New Review*, December 1914, 691–93.

"The White Brute." *The Masses*, vol. 6, October–November 1915, 17–18. Reprinted by the NAACP as leaflet, 1915. Also in *The Walls Came Tumbling Down*, and *Black and White Sat Down Together*.

["William English Walling"]. *William English Walling: A Symposium*. New York: Stackpole Sons, 1938, 80–81.

"A Woman Who Answered Prayer: Charlotte R. Thorn and the Calhoun School." *Woman Citizen*, March 1927, 18–19, 48–49.

"A Word for the New Year" (editorial). *Crisis*, January 1924, pp. 103–4.

[MWO]. "Work of Negro Farmers: Experiences Related at the Tuskegee Conference." *New York Evening Post*, February 28, 1907, 14.

[MWO]. "Workers at Tuskegee: Vagrancy Discussed at the Southern Institution." *New York Evening Post*, February 26, 1907, 14.

"Working Girls' Clubs." *Northeastern*, July 1906. Copy in MWO Papers, Wayne State University.

"The Year of Jubilee." *Crisis*, January 1934, 7–8.

SELECTED BOOK REVIEWS

American Journal of Sociology. Review of *The Negro in the New World* by Sir Harry H. Johnston. Volume 17. September 1911, 270.

The Bookman. "The Negro's Gifts," Review of Alain Locke, *The New Negro*. March 1926, 98–99.

The Freeman. Review of *Finding A Way Out*, by Robert Moton. August 4, 1920, 500–1.

Herbert Seligmann, *The Negro Faces America*. August 25, 1920, 573–74.

The Survey. "Two Books on American Race Problems" (Ray Stannard Baker, *Following the Color Line,* and Alfred Holt Stone, *Studies in the American Race Problem*). June 5, 1909, 348–52.

"The Basis of Ascendancy" (Edgar Gardner Murphy's book by that title). November 6, 1909, 169–70.

W. D. Weatherford, *Present Forces in Negro Progress;* R. R. Wright, Jr., *The Negro in Pennsylvania;* George Edmund Haynes, *The Negro at Work in New York City.* January 25, 1913, 547–49.

William Holtzclaw, *The Black Man's Burden.* May 15, 1913.

Daniel Murray, ed. *Historical and Biographical Encyclopedia of the Colored Race.* 6 vols. June 14, 1913, 373.

Addresses on the Race Problem Delivered at the Southern Sociological Congress, 1913. January 31, 1914, 531.

L. H. Hammond, *In Black and White.* May 16, 1914, 201.

Maurice S. Evans, *Black and White in Southern States.* February 26, 1916, 644.

B. F. Riley, *The Life and Times of Booker T. Washington and Emmett Scott,* and Lyman Beecher Stowe, *Booker T. Washington—Builder of a Civilization.* January 13, 1917, 438.

Benjamin Brawley, *Your Negro Neighbor,* and Kelly Miller, *An Appeal to Conscience.* September 21, 1918, 699–700.

Ulrich Phillips, *American Negro Slavery.* September 28, 1918, 718.

Winfield Collins, *The Truth about Lynching and the Negro in the South.* March 8, 1919, 843.

Ovington's syndicated "Book Chat" column reviewed over 150 additional books, including the following:

Fiction such as Jessie Fauset, *There Is Confusion* and *Plum Bun;* Walter White, *Fire in the Flint* and *Flight;* Rene Maran, *Batouala;* Zona Gale, *Peace in Friendship Village;* E. M. Forster, *A Passage to India;* Jean Toomer, *Cane;* Carl Van Vechten, *Nigger Heaven;* Eric Walrond, *Tropic Death;* Nella Larsen, *Passing;* W. E. B. Du Bois, *Dark Princess;* Charles Chesnutt, *The Conjure Woman;* Rudolph Fisher, *The Walls of Jericho;* and Ambrose Gonzales, *The Black Border, Gullah Stories of the Carolina Coast.*

Poetry such as Claude McKay, *Harlem Shadows* and *Color;* Countee Cullen, *Copper Sun;* Langston Hughes, *The Weary Blues* and *Fine Clothes to the Jew;* James Weldon Johnson, *God's Trombones* and *The Book of American Negro Spirituals;* Georgia Douglas Johnson, *Bronze* and *An Autumn Love Cycle;* and Leslie Pinckney Hill, *The Wings of Oppression.*

Drama such as Paul Green, *The Lonesome Road;* Angelina Grimke, *Rachel;* Alain Locke and Montgomery Gregory, *Plays of Negro Life;*

DuBose Heyward, *Porgy;* and Eugene O'Neill, *All God's Chillun Got Wings.*

Dozens of books of history, political science, and sociology of the United States, Africa, and the Caribbean, some with an emphasis on race relations, such as Charles Wesley, *Negro Labor in the United States;* Carter Woodson, *The History of the Negro Church;* Frederick Detweiler, *The Negro Press in the United States;* Peter Neilson, *The Black Man's Place in Africa;* Sarah Mullin, *The South Africans;* and Blair Niles, *Black Haiti;* and some of more general interest, such as James Harvey Robinson, *The Mind in the Making,* and Hendrik Van Loon, *The Story of Mankind.*

UNPUBLISHED TYPESCRIPTS IN THE MWO PAPERS AT WAYNE STATE UNIVERSITY

Prospectus for the first part of the 175-page "The Cycle of a Race," and two chapters, 20 pp., Box 7, Folder 12. A further 11 pp. in Box 12, Folder 16, seems to be notes for a chapter on Negro literature and the image of the Negro in American writing.

> "Georgia, Invisible Empire State," 15-page typescript on antilynching from 1920s. Box 6, Folder 39.
> "The Poor are Fed First," 2-page typescript on the Russian Revolution. Box 6, Folder 38.

STORIES

"Alias Vera Fortune." 7 pp., a passing story, Box 6, Folder 15.

"Christmas Peace." 13 pp., Box 6, Folder 36.

Early draft of an untitled women's liberation story, from the teens. 10 pp., Box 6, Folder 30.

"Her Mysterious Journey." 20 pp., Box 7, Folder 1.

"The Nodding Head." 11 pp., Box 7, Folder 2. This is marked "Returned in Summer 1923 by Woman's Home Companion, McClure's, Colliers."

"One Fight More." 17 pp., a World War I story, Box 7, Folder 3, marked "Old material, refused once or twice and gave up thinking no one would print it whether they liked it or not."

"To Each His Fear." 4 pp., note says "this was published as a snap shot story; have been told it could be worked into a movie," Box 7, Folder 13.

Untitled, 3 pp., a story of a handicapped child, Box 6, Folder 16.

"A Wealth of Fancy." 29 pp., about a poor child from Hell's Kitchen who spends summers with a country family and tells them stories about her wealth in the city, Box 6, Folders 1 and 2.

"What Zeke Found," 7 pp., Box 7, Folder 14.

"Zillah," 25 pp., a passing story based on a real person, Box 7, Folder 18.

PLAYS AND OTHER WRITINGS

"The Spode Cup," 21 pp., Box 7, Folders 10 and 11.

Scenario for *The Shadow*, 6 pp. Box 2, Folder 20. Correspondence in relation to her attempt to market this includes Geraldine Deardorff, Assistant Story Editor, Selznick Studio to MWO March 4, 1947. "Mr. Selznick has asked me to thank you for your letter of February 18, and to reply to it for him. . . . We regret that it does not suit our production schedule at this time." Box 2, Folder 30.

The rousing good adventure story set in New England, "The Boy Detective" runs for 239 pp. in Box 6, Folders 17–28.

Incomplete fragments include 2 pp. of handwritten manuscript describing a natural setting and 3 pp. typescript of dialogue with an Irish brogue, Box 6, Folder 38.

3 pp. on Bridge, Box 6, Folder 38, and 3 typed pages, 12 handwritten, also on Bridge in Box 12, Folder 7; 3 pp. listing unusual words, organized by vowels and consonants, perhaps for crossword puzzles, Box 12, Folder 25; a one-page quiz on Kings, Box 12, Folder 7; 2 pp. of what appear to be notes for niece Betty Kingsbury's Ph.D. dissertation in ornithology at Cornell University, Box 12, Folder 25; 3 pp. of manuscript notes for an article on "The Horse and Buggy Doctor."

Dozens of pages of letters taken in dictation by Carrie Overton in a variation of Pitman shorthand that cannot be deciphered for the most part.

OTHER SOURCES

ARCHIVES

Atlanta University Center, Robert W. Woodruff Library. Papers of John and Lugenia Burns Hope (Microfilm Ed. by Alton Hornsby, Jr., Frederick, Md.: University Publications of America, 1984).

British Museum, London. Material on the First Universal Races Congress, University of London, 1911 ("List of Members . . ."; *Record of the Proceedings . . .*)

Brooklyn Historical Library. Papers of Richetta Randolph.

Chicago Historical Society. Claude Barnett Papers, The Associated Negro Press (Microfilm Ed. by August Meier and Elliott Rudwick. Frederick, Md.: University Publications of America. 1985).

Chicago, University of. Papers of Julius Rosenwald.
Columbia University. J. G. Phelps Stokes Papers; E. R. A. Seligman Papers; Lillian Wald Papers; Levi H. Wood Papers. Oral History Interviews with W. E. B. Du Bois; John Warren Davis; George Schuyler.
Federal Bureau of Investigation Files (obtained through Freedom of Information Act). Miscellaneous articles and reports.
Fisk University, Nashville, Tenn. Papers of President Thomas Elsa Jones.
Harvard University, Houghton Library. Oswald Garrison Villard Papers.
Howard University, Moorland-Spingarn Research Center. Papers of Marian Anderson; Archibald Grimke; Alain Locke; Arthur B. Spingarn; Joel E. Spingarn.
Library of Congress, Manuscript Division. NAACP Papers: Papers of Ray Stannard Baker; John Haynes Holmes; Arthur B. Spingarn; Moorfield Storey; Mary Church Terrell; Booker T. Washington; Roy Wilkins.
Massachusetts, University of. W. E. B. Du Bois Papers.
Middlesex County, Mass. Court Records, Newton.
Minnesota, University of, Social Welfare History Archives. Paul Kellogg; Albert J. Kennedy Papers. Settlement House Materials (Frances MacGregor Ingram speech at the 50th Anniversary of University Settlement, 1936).
National Archives, Record Group No. 257.
New York Public Library. Joel Elias Spingarn Papers, Rare Books and Manuscripts Division, Astor, Lenox and Tilden Foundations.
New York University, Tamiment Institute Library and Wagner Labor Archives. Greenwich House Papers; Papers of the Inter-Collegiate Socialist Society.
Radcliffe College Archives
Schlesinger Library (Arthur and Elizabeth Schlesinger Library on the History of Women in America), Radcliffe College. Charlotte Hawkins Brown; Leonora O'Reilly Papers.
Schomburg Center for Research in Black Culture, The New York Public Library. William Pickens Papers. Manuscripts, Archives and Rare Books Division, Astor, Lenox and Tilden Foundations.
Southern Berkshire County, Massachusetts. Court Records, Great Barrington.
Swarthmore College Peace Collection. Papers of Jane Addams.
Ticonderoga, New York. The New York State Historical Association of Cooperstown, New York. Papers of John Milholland.
Wayne State University, Archives of Labor and Urban Affairs. Mary White Ovington Papers; Charles Flint Kellogg Papers.
Wisconsin, State Historical Society of, Madison, Wisconsin. Papers of Anita McCormick Blaine, McCormick Collection; W. E. B. Du Bois Bibliog-

raphy by Paul Partington and correspondence between the two; Papers of William English Walling; Arthur I. Waskow Papers (verbatim, type-written transcripts of NAACP manuscript material later lost).

Yale University. James Weldon Johnson Collection, Yale Collection of American Literature, Beinecke Rare Book and Manuscript Library.

DISSERTATIONS AND THESES

Cryer, Daniel Walter. "Mary White Ovington and Oswald Garrison Villard: The Political Thought and Racial Attitudes of Two Founders of the NAACP, A Study in Contrasts," master's thesis, University of Minnesota, 1969.

———. "Mary White Ovington and the Rise of the NAACP." Ph.D. dissertation, University of Minnesota, 1977.

Goodman, James. "Stories of Scottsboro." Ph.D. dissertation, Princeton University, 1990.

INTERVIEWS AND CORRESPONDENCE

Curti, Merle
Dellea, Mary
Fishel, Les
Flaherty, Jim
Friedmann, Betty Kingsbury
Harrington, Donald S.
Joyce, Florence
Kingsbury, Theodore
Matthews, Gloria and Milton
Poplowski, Dorothy
Smith, Katherine Dellea
Tucker, Laura Keeney
Von der Heydt, Monaver Bechtold

PUBLISHED SOURCES

BOOKS AND PERIODICALS

Aitken, Roy, as told to Al Nelson. *The Birth of a Nation Story*. Middleburg, Va.: Denlinger, 1965.

The American Film Institute Catalog, 1911–1920. Berkeley: University of California Press, 1988.

Analytical Guide and Indexes to the Voice of the Negro, 1904–1907. Westport, Conn.: Greenwood Press, 1974.

Archer, Leonard. *Black Images in the American Theater: NAACP Protest Campaigns—Stage, Screen, Radio and Television.* Brooklyn: Pageant-Poseidon, Ltd., 1973.

Ashley, Anne. *William James Ashley: A Life.* London: P. S. King and Son, Ltd., 1932.

Ashley, William J. *The Christian Outlook: Being the Sermons of an Economist.* London: Longmans, Green and Company, 1925.

———. *Economic History of England (Introduction to English Economic History and Theory: The Middle Ages),* 1888.

Baker, Ray Stannard. *Following the Color Line: American Negro Citizenship in the Progressive Era.* New York: Harper, 1964; New York: Doubleday, Page, 1908. Introduction by Dewey W. Grantham, Jr.

Baltimore Afro-American. "Mary White Ovington, Founder of NAACP, Dead," July 28, 1951, 5; William Pickens, letter to editor, August 18, 1951; "Why We Print This Story," August 18, 1951.

Bannister, Robert C., Jr. *Ray Stannard Baker: The Mind and Thought of a Progressive.* New Haven: Yale University Press, 1966.

Beecher, Henry Ward. *Comforting Thoughts Spoken in Sermons, Addresses and Prayers.* New York: Brooklyn Historical Association, 1885.

Bergman, Peter, et al. *A Chronological History of the Negro in America.* New York: Harper and Row, 1969.

Berkshire Courier, June 23, 30, 1938.

Boas, Franz. Foreword to *Half a Man: The Status of the Negro in New York,* by Mary White Ovington. New York: Longmans Green, 1911.

Boston Herald. Articles, letters on *Birth of a Nation,* 1915 (in Arthur Spingarn Papers, Library of Congress).

Broderick, D. *Image of the Black in Children's Fiction.* New York: R. R. Bowker, 1973.

Brooklyn Eagle. "Neighborship Work: Miss Mary White Ovington's Address Before the Brooklyn Ethical Association," December 20, 1897; article on Packer Institute, May 13, 1954.

Brooklyn Life. Account of the wedding of Florence Ovington and Edward Barlow, vol. 1, June 14, 1880.

Bullock, Alan, and R. B. Woodings, eds. *20th Century Culture: A Biographical Companion.* New York: Harper and Row, 1938.

Carter, Dan, Randolph Boehm, and Martin Schipper, eds. *Guide to Papers of the NAACP, Part 6: The Scottsboro Case, 1931–1950.* Frederick, Md., 1986.

———. *Scottsboro: A Tragedy of the American South.* Baton Rouge: Louisiana State University Press, 1969; New York: Oxford University Press, 1971.

Carter, Everett. "Cultural History Written with Lightning." *American Quarterly* 12 (Fall 1960): 347–57.

Charities. Special issue, October 7, 1905.

Connolly, Harold. *A Ghetto Grows in Brooklyn*. New York: New York University Press, 1977.

Cortner, Richard C. *A Mob Intent on Death: The NAACP and the Arkansas Riot Cases*. Middletown, Conn.: Wesleyan University Press, 1988.

Crisis. Cover and editorial [W. E. B. Du Bois]. vol. 1, no. 1. November 1910; "N.A.A.C.P." May 1911; January 1912 (postcard of a lynching sent to John Haynes Holmes); summary of annual conference, June 1912; William English Walling, "The Founding of the NAACP." vol. 36. July 1929, 104.

Davenport, Frances Isabel. *Salvaging of American Girlhood*. New York: Dutton, 1924.

Davis, Allen F. *Spearheads for Reform: The Social Settlements and the Progressive Movement*. New York: Oxford University Press, 1967.

Dictionary Catalog–Teachers College Library, Columbia University.

Dictionary of American Reformers.

Du Bois, Shirley Graham. *His Day Is Marching On: A Memoir of W. E. B. Du Bois*. Philadelphia and New York: J. B. Lippincott Company, 1971.

Du Bois, W. E. B. *The Autobiography of W. E. B. Du Bois*. New York: International Publishers, 1968.

———. "Close Ranks," July 1918, and "Returning Soldiers," May 1919, the *Crisis*. Reprinted in Walter Wilson, ed., *The Selected Writings of W. E. B. Du Bois*. New York: New American Library, 1970, 170–72.

———. "Credo." *Darkwater: Voices from Within the Veil*. New York: Schocken Books, 1969. Reprint of 1920 ed., 3–4.

———. "Litany of Atlanta." In *The Book of American Negro Poetry*. New York: Harcourt Brace and World, 1922, 1959, 90.

———. "National Committee on the Negro." *The Survey*. June 12, 1909, 407–9.

Duster, Alfreda M., ed. *Crusade for Justice: the Autobiography of Ida B. Wells*. Chicago: University of Chicago Press, 1970.

Filler, Louis. *A Dictionary of American Social Reform*. New York: Greenwood Press, 1963.

Fishel, Les, and Benjamin Quarles. *The Black American: A Documentary History*. Glenview, Ill.: Scott Foresman, 1967.

Flexner, Eleanor. *Century of Struggle: The Woman's Rights Movement in the United States*. New York: Atheneum, 1973.

Hackett, Francis. "Brotherly Love." *New Republic*. March 20, 1915, 185.

Heilbrun, Carolyn. *Writing a Woman's Life*. New York: W. W. Norton and Company, 1988.

Hemenway, Robert. *Zora Neale Hurston: A Literary Biography*. Urbana and Chicago: University of Illinois Press, 1977.

Hine, Darlene Clark, ed. *Black Women in America: An Historical Encyclopedia*. 2 vols. Brooklyn: Carlson Publishing, 1993.

Hixson, William B., Jr. *Moorfield Storey and the Abolitionist Tradition*. New York: Oxford University Press, 1972.

Holmes, John Haynes. *I Speak for Myself: the Autobiography*. New York: Harper and Brothers, 1959.

Hoogenboom, Olive. *The First Unitarian Church of Brooklyn: One Hundred Fifty Years: A History*. Brooklyn: First Unitarian Church, 1987.

Howells, Dorothy Elia. *A Century to Celebrate Radcliffe College, 1879–1979*. Cambridge, Mass.: Radcliffe College, 1978.

Huggins, Nathan Irvin. *Harlem Renaissance*. New York: Oxford, 1971.

Hughes, Langston. *Fight for Freedom: The Story of the NAACP*. New York: W. W. Norton, 1962.

Humes, D. Joy. *Oswald Garrison Villard, Liberal of the 1920's*. Syracuse, N.Y.: Syracuse University Press, 1960.

Johnson, James Weldon. *Along This Way*. New York: Viking, 1933. Reprint, New York: Da Capo, 1973.

Jones, Byrd L. "A Quest for National Leadership: Institutionalization of Economics at Harvard." In *Breaking the Academic Mould: Economists and American Higher Learning in the Nineteenth Century*. Edited by William Barber. Middletown, Conn.: Wesleyan University Press, 1988.

Kellogg, Charles Flint. *NAACP: A History of the National Association for the Advancement of Colored People*. Baltimore, Md.: Johns Hopkins University Press, 1967.

Kornweibel, Theodore, Jr. "Federal Surveillance of Afro-Americans (1917–1925): The First World War, the Red Scare, and the Garvey Movement." Microfilm by University Publications of America, Inc.

Kusmer, Kenneth. *A Ghetto Takes Shape: Black Cleveland, 1870 1930*. Urbana: University of Illinois Press, 1976.

Lasch-Quinn, Elisabeth. *Black Neighbors: Race and the Limits of Reform in the American Settlement House Movement, 1890–1945*. Chapel Hill: University of North Carolina Press, 1993.

Lawson, John Howard. *Film: The Creative Process*. New York: Hill and Wang, 1964.

Lemons, J. Stanley. "Black Stereotypes as Reflected in Popular Culture, 1880–1920." *American Literature*, Spring 1977, 102–16.

Levy, Eugene. *James Weldon Johnson: Black Leader, Black Voice*. Chicago: University of Chicago Press, 1973.

Lewis, David Levering. *W. E. B. Du Bois: Biography of a Race: 1868–1919*. New York: Henry Holt, 1993.

Logan, Rayford. *The Betrayal of the Negro, From Rutherford Hayes to Woodrow Wilson* (originally *The Negro in American Life and Thought: The Nadir, 1877–1901*). Rev. ed. New York: Collier, 1965.

McKay, Claude. "If We Must Die." In *Blackamerican Literature*. Edited by Ruth Miller. Beverly Hills, Calif.: Glencoe Press, 1971, 334.

McPherson, James M. *The Abolitionist Legacy: From Reconstruction to the NAACP.* Princeton, N.J.: Princeton University Press, 1975.

———. "The Abolitionist Legacy: From Reconstruction to the NAACP." In *Toward a New Past: Dissenting Essays in American History.* Edited by Barton Bernstein. New York: Pantheon, 1968, 126–57.

Marable, Manning. *W. E. B. Du Bois: Black Radical Democrat.* Boston: Twayne Publishers, 1986.

Martin, Tony. *Literary Garveyism: Garvey, Black Arts and the Harlem Renaissance.* Dover, Md.: Majority Press, 1983.

Meier, August. *Negro Thought in America: 1880–1915: Racial Ideologies in the Age of Booker T. Washington.* Ann Arbor: University of Michigan Press, 1970.

———, and Elliott Rudwick. "The Rise of the Black Secretariat in the NAACP, 1909–1935." "Attorneys Black and White: A Case Study of Race Relations within the NAACP." In *Along the Color Line: Explorations in the Black Experience.* Urbana: University of Illinois Press, 1976, 114–19.

Monaco, James. *How to Read a Film.* New York: Oxford, 1977.

Moore, Mrs. James Lowell. "The Fayerweather House." Speech given January 24, 1939. *Cambridge Historical Society.* January 1939, 86–94.

New York Herald Tribune. "Ovington, Mary White" [obit.]. July 17, 1951, 16.

New York Journal. Review of *Birth of a Nation* by "Zit." March 15, 1915 (in Arthur Spingarn Papers, Library of Congress).

New York Sun. Review of *Birth of a Nation.* March 13, 1915 (in Arthur Spingarn Papers, Library of Congress).

New York *Times*, "Mr. Beecher on Trial," March 3 and 4, 1875; "Ovington Brothers Attached," August 21, 1896; "Ovington Brothers Assign," August 22, 1896; "Affairs of Ovington Brothers," August 26, 1896; "Business Troubles," September 10, 1896; "Booker T. Washington Honored," April 3, 1901; "Negroes Have an Inning at the Cooper Union . . . ," February 2, 1906; "Dinner Minus Color Line . . . ," April 28, 1908; "As An Admonition," April 29, 1908; "Conference to Aid Negroes," May 31, 1909, 3; "Whites and Blacks Confer as Equals," June 1, 1909, 2; "Prof. Boas Predicts Race Amalgamation. . . ." May 15, 1910, 2; "Won't Reopen Case of Ousted Teachers," January 17, 1918; "Mrs. Louise Ketcham Ovington" [obit.], April 5, 1927, 27; "Ovington's Leases Old Knabe Building," June 18, 1927; "Ovington's Moves to New Store on Opposite Side of Fifth Avenue," October 23, 1927, 22; "Ovington's Gives Lease for

436-5th Avenue," December 2, 1927, 42; "Charles K. Ovington Dies at Age of 73," January 10, 1930, 21; "Charles Ovington Will," February 2, 1930, 7; "Estate Appraised," April 21, 1931, 19; "Ovington, Mary White" [obit.], July 16, 1951, 21.

Nickerson, Marjorie. *A Long Way Forward: The First Hundred Years of the Packer Collegiate Institute.* Brooklyn: Packer Collegiate Institute, 1945.

"Notes on the Bellport Conference." *The Intercollegiate Socialist,* December–January, 1917–18.

Peiss, Kathy. *Cheap Amusements: Working Woman and Leisure in Turn-of-Century New York.* Philadelphia: Temple University Press, 1986.

"Persons with 50 P.C. Negro Blood 'Pass.'" *Baltimore Afro-American,* November 19, 1932, 1–2. (Summary of Caroline Bond Day, *A Study of Some Negro-White Families in the United States.* Cambridge, Mass.: Peabody Museum of Harvard University, 1932).

"Propaganda Among Negroes." In *Revolutionary Radicalism,* Report of the Joint Legislative Committee of the State of New York Investigating Seditious Activities, 4 vols., filed April 24, 1920, in the Senate of the State of New York, part 1, vol. 2, 1318–21, 1476–1520.

Record, Wilson. "Negro Intellectual Leadership in the National Association for the Advancement of Colored People: 1910–1940." *Phylon,* 17 (1956). 375–89.

Reviews of MWO, *Half a Man* in *American Journal of Sociology* (by S. Breckenridge) (November 1911); *American Library Association Booklist* (October 1911); *Annals of the American Academy of Political and Social Science* (November 1911); *Dial* (September 1, 1911); *Independent* (September 28, 1911); *Nation* (November 2, 1911); *Der Weltcourier* (August 1913); *Choice; Integrated Education; Kirkus Reviews; Library Journal; Manchester Union Leader* (1969).

Reviews of MWO, *The Shadow* in *Booklist* (June 1920); *Boston Transcript* (June 2, 1920); *Freeman* (October 6, 1920); *New York Evening Post* (May 1, 1920); *New York Times* (June 27, 1920).

Ross, Joyce. *J. E. Spingarn and the Rise of the NAACP.* New York: Atheneum, 1972.

Rouse, Jacqueline Anne. *Lugenia Burns Hope: Black Southern Reformer.* Athens: University of Georgia Press, 1989.

Rudwick, Elliott. *Race Riot at East St. Louis, July 2, 1917.* Carbondale: Southern Illinois University Press, 1964. Reprint, Cleveland: Meridian, 1966.

———. *W. E. B. Du Bois: Propagandist of the Negro Protest.* New York: Atheneum, 1969.

Russell, Charles Edward. *Bare Hands and Stone Walls: Some Reflections of a Side-Line Reformer.* New York: Charles Scribner's Sons, 1933.

The Second City of the World. New York: Republic Press, 1898.

Semonche, John E. *Ray Stannard Baker: A Quest for Democracy in Modern America, 1870–1918*. Chapel Hill: University of North Carolina Press, 1969.

Silva, Fred, ed. *Focus on the Birth of A Nation*. Englewood Cliffs, N.J.: Prentice-Hall, Inc., 1971.

Simkhovitch, Mary Kingsbury. *Here Is God's Plenty: Reflections on American Social Advance*. New York: Harper and Brothers, 1949.

———. *Neighborhood: My Story of Greenwich House*. New York: W. W. Norton, 1938.

Sims, Rudine. *Shadow and Substance: Afro-American Experience in Contemporary Children's Fiction*. Urbana, Ill.: National Council of Teachers of English, 1982.

Trattner, Walter, ed. *Biographical Dictionary of Social Welfare in America*. New York and Westport, Conn.: Greenwood Press, 1986.

Trolander, Judith. *Settlement Houses and the Great Depression*. Detroit: Wayne State University Press, 1975.

[Villard, Oswald Garrison]. Editorials. *New York Evening Post*, September 24 and 25, 1906; April 1, 1910.

Weiss, Nancy Joan. *The National Urban League, 1910–1940*. New York: Oxford University Press, 1974.

Wheeler, Henry Winfield. "The Spider's Web." *St. Louis American*, July 18, 1946.

White, Ronald. *Liberty and Justice for All: Racial Reform and the Social Gospel*. New York: Harper, Row, 1990.

White, Walter. "We Do Have White Friends." *Chicago Defender*, November 24, 1945.

Willensky, Elliot, and Norval White. *A Guide to New York City*.

Woloch, Nancy. *Women and the American Experience*. New York: Knopf, 1984.

Woods, Robert and Albert Kennedy. *Handbook of Settlements*. Russell Sage Foundation, 1911.

Zangrando, Robert. *The NAACP Crusade Against Lynching, 1909–1950*. Philadelphia: Temple University Press, 1980.

PAMPHLETS AND BROCHURES

In Brooklyn Public Library. Alice A. Chadwick, May 18, 1895; Brochure on Packer Centennial, 1945; Charles Pratt, "Morris Building Company: Astral Apartments, Greenpoint, New York," 1885.

"The Civic Club." 1921–22. In MWO Papers, Wayne State University.

Du Bois, W. E. B. "The Amenia Conference: An Historic Negro Gathering." Troutbeck Leaflets, Number Eight. Amenia, N.Y.: Troutbeck Press, 1925 (copy in Mary Church Terrell Papers, Library of Congress).

Healy, Margaret. "Neighborship Report." *First Report of the Pratt Institute Neighborship Association*. Brooklyn, 1895, 38–39.

"Lynching of Claude Neal." 8-page report of investigation and a 2-page brochure including photograph. NAACP, 1934.

"Opening Address of Mrs. Maud Wood Park: Chairman of the National League of Women Voters." Delivered at the Second Annual Convention, April 11–16, 1921.

Program. 22nd Annual Mass Meeting. NAACP, January 4, 1931.

Promotional Material for Troutbeck Executive retreat. Amenia, New York.

"The Schomburg Center for Research in Black Culture: The New York Public Library," n. d.

Smith College Bulletin, 1929 (Northampton, Mass.).

"20th Annual Report of the NAACP. . . For the Year 1929." 1930.

"Washington, D. C. Black History National Recreation Trail." Parks and History Association, 1988, 1989.

Wilkins, Roy. "Then and Now: NAACP 1909–1959." New York: NAACP.

Index